Allies and Obstacles

ALLISON C. CAREY, PAMELA BLOCK,
AND RICHARD K. SCOTCH

Allies and Obstacles

*Disability Activism and Parents
of Children with Disabilities*

TEMPLE UNIVERSITY PRESS
Philadelphia • Rome • Tokyo

TEMPLE UNIVERSITY PRESS
Philadelphia, Pennsylvania 19122
tupress.temple.edu

Library of Congress Cataloging-in-Publication Data

Names: Carey, Allison C., author. | Block, Pamela, author. |
Scotch, Richard K., 1951– author.
Title: Allies and obstacles : disability activism and parents of children with disabilities /
Allison C. Carey, Pamela Block, and Richard K. Scotch.
Description: Philadelphia : Temple University Press, 2020. | Includes bibliographical
references and index. | Summary: "This book explores the tensions between the
disability rights groups advocating on behalf of people with intellectual, cognitive, and
psychiatric disorders including autism and allied advocacy groups representing parents
with children in those communities. These groups diverge over issues like independence
and recovery, and in their cultural and political capital"—Provided by publisher.
Identifiers: LCCN 2019042677 (print) | LCCN 2019042678 (ebook) | ISBN 9781439916322
(cloth) | ISBN 9781439916339 (paperback) | ISBN 9781439916346 (pdf)
Subjects: LCSH: Parents of children with mental disabilities. | Parents of children with
disabilities. | Children with mental disabilities—Civil rights. | Children with mental
disabilities—Social conditions. | Pressure groups.
Classification: LCC HQ759.913 .C365 2020 (print) | LCC HQ759.913 (ebook) |
DDC 649/.15—dc23
LC record available at https://lccn.loc.gov/2019042677
LC ebook record available at https://lccn.loc.gov/2019042678

Printed in the United States of America

9 8 7 6 5 4 3 2 1

Contents

Acknowledgments

In many ways, this book is the product of decades of conversations and scholarship on disability activism as it emerges from, intersects with, and sometimes resists other forms of disability activism. Over this time, many people have contributed to the formulation of our ideas. We first acknowledge Ryan Mulligan, our editor at Temple University Press, the Temple University Press team, the peer reviewers, and colleagues who provided direct commentary on portions of the manuscript, especially Brian Grossman, Cheryl Narjarian Sousa, and Blyden Potts. A version of Chapter 6 was previously published as Allison C. Carey, Pamela Block, and Richard K. Scotch, "Sometimes Allies: Parent-Led Disability Organizations and Social Movements," *Disability Studies Quarterly* 39, no. 1 (2019), http://dsq-sds.org/article/view/6281/5183. We thank the *DSQ* editors and peer reviewers. We are deeply grateful for the time and perspectives given to us by the activists we interviewed and for all of the work they have contributed to transform the world and open opportunities for people with disabilities. We owe a debt of gratitude broadly to all the activists and scholars who push the boundaries of justice—in the streets, in classrooms, on the stage, at kitchen tables, online, and anywhere else. Each of us also has personal thanks to offer.

Allison

I am deeply thankful to my family and the Arc for giving me opportunities to engage with disability communities from an early age. My current interests were nurtured by my parents' ardent work to support all of their children in living fulfilling lives. While I was in graduate school and new to disability rights activism, the intrepid sociologist Steve Taylor was the first to explain to me the tensions that sometimes exist between parent activists and disabled activists and to challenge my assumptions of justice. After the release of my first book, Richard proposed collaborating on a book focusing on parent activism, and we are so fortunate that Pam joined us as well. It has been a joy to work with them. Friends and colleagues at Shippensburg University, the Society for Disability Studies, and the American Sociological Association supported and challenged this work through its many iterations in presentations. Nick Macy, a former student of Shippensburg University, assisted with interview transcription. I am indebted to the scholars and activists involved in various online collections, including the Disability Rights and Independent Living Movements collection at the University of California, Berkeley; Temple University's Visionary Voices; and Nicki Pombier Berger's collection Nothing About Us Without Us. Finally, I am deeply grateful to my husband and daughter for their continued love and support.

Pamela

I reiterate Allison's thanks to the Society for Disability Studies and the American Sociological Association and thank the Society for Applied Anthropology as well, for providing the opportunity for presentation, peer discussions, and review of early versions of most of the chapters in the book. The wonderful colleagues in these organizations provided thoughtful feedback, which I sincerely appreciate. I thank my Stony Brook University disability studies students and student volunteers who also listened to and read earlier versions of this book. Special thanks go to Elaine Cheung for assistance with formatting the references and other forms of research assistance with this project. My gratitude goes to the Anthropology Department at the University of Western Ontario. The department chair, A. Kim Clark; the faculty; and the students have welcomed me to my new academic home with open arms. I thank the people who agreed to be interviewed for the autism chapter and who shared their stories, especially Jeremy and Lisa. I am grateful to my family—my husband, Matthew Lebo, and children, Shoshana, Isaac, and Harrison Lebo—for their love and support. I am forever grateful to my mother, Barbara Kilcup, and my sister Hope Block, who are the reasons I undertook this project. I am thankful to my sister Karen, stepmother Dale, Aunt Marty, mother-in-law Fern, and the rest of the cousins, aunts, uncles, stepfamily, and in-laws who have provided so much loving care for Hope, Karen, and me since our mother and father passed away.

Richard

I thank my colleagues Allison Carey and Pam Block for their helpful and thoughtful encouragement and support throughout the creation of this book. I appreciate the assistance of my graduate and undergraduate students at the University of Texas at Dallas, who provided background research and help with editing, particularly Jingnan Bi, Brett Cease, Carla Ramazan, Rajadhar Reddy, Kara Sutton, and Yingyuan Zhang. As always, I am grateful to Jenny Keller and Grace Keller Scotch for all that they have given me and continue to share.

Allies and Obstacles

Introduction

When Peter Grant was born in the 1930s, his mother, Sophia, said that she knew at first sight he was "one of those," an infant with Down syndrome.[1] Stigma enveloped them. Sophia's friends stopped calling, the neighborhood children taunted Peter, and educators refused to accept him in public school. In response to her request for advice, doctors told her, "No, he can't learn. Medical science can do nothing for these children. The School Board will not be bothered with them in the public schools. He's happy. Give him a glass of milk and a cookie and let him sit on the chesterfield. Leave him alone."[2] Sophia Grant ignored this advice and instead dedicated herself to ensuring Peter's development through rigorous home schooling, untested therapies, and lots of prayer. Upon seeing her son develop both academically and socially, she wrote a memoir to encourage parents to "take courage" because these children could grow and enjoy life. Sophia reached out to other parents through her writing, yet nowhere in her memoir did she describe engaging in activism with other parents. While Sophia experienced isolation, other parents were beginning to unite and demand change, and their activism would alter the landscape of American society.

American parental activism regarding disability policy took root in the 1930s and 1940s and blossomed in the 1950s and 1960s. Parents joined together to fight for services for their children, such as nursery schools, recreational programs, residential options, and educational opportunities. They sought to transform the way society thought about disability, dismantling the long-held negative stereotypes that people with disabilities were deviant, unproductive, and incapable of learning and instead illuminating the potential abilities and inherent value in each human life. Eventually, they framed their activism in terms of rights, including the rights of people with disabilities as well as their families to be included in, respected by, and supported by society.

Parent activism took many forms. For example, Elizabeth Boggs emerged as an early parent leader in activism related to intellectual disability working in the 1950s and 1960s with state, national, and international organizations to establish "a fair chance" for every child.[3] Boggs cofounded the Arc (a national organization for people with developmental and intellectual disabilities), served on President Kennedy's 1962 Panel on Mental Retardation, and coauthored the United Nations' Declaration of General and Special Rights of the Mentally Retarded.[4] While Boggs used formal organizations and official political channels to create change, other parents focus on local, grassroots organizing, like contemporary intersectional activist Kerima Çevik, who strives to address social justice issues for people with disabilities in minority communities.

Some parents raise awareness through their creative projects. Like Sophia Grant did back in the 1950s, parents like Ron Suskind, father of a son with autism, and Michael Schofield, father of a daughter with schizophrenia, follow a long legacy of parent authors who share their experiences in writing as a platform by which to create change. Blogging, hosting chat rooms, and sharing virtual resources are the strategies of choice for some parents, like Keith Jones and Emily Landeau, who participate in the Rooted in Rights web-based series "Parenting without Pity," in which parents with disabilities share parenting advice especially for nondisabled parents of children with disabilities. Some parents take to the courts, like Charlene Frey, who sued her school district and in 1999 won the right for her son, Garret, who uses a ventilator, to receive nursing services as needed at school to ensure his inclusion.[5] And still other parent activism unfolds behind the scenes as parents support their children in becoming empowered activists, such as Zona Roberts's support of her son Ed, who broke barriers to become the first student using an iron lung to attend the University of California at Berkeley and went on to become a key figure in disability activism.[6]

While these parents may use different styles of activism and address different concerns, they share a vision of their children as valued members of society. Parent and blogger Lisa Morguess explains, "The bottom line is that my kid is not expendable. He is a human being with as much value as any other kid, who deserves the same opportunities as any other kid. Do you think he has nothing to offer, that you and your kids have nothing to learn from a kid like Finn? If you do, you are dead wrong. There are lessons in humility, compassion, perseverance and tolerance that Finn can teach you. You just have to be open to learning."[7]

The achievements of parent activism highlight the ability of everyday Americans to create positive change in our society and fight inequality. Parents helped usher in laws protecting the right of all children to a free and appropriate public education, to be free from undue constraint and segregation, as well as laws to prohibit discrimination. In addition to legislation, parents helped build the infrastructure of disability services available today, often starting with local projects in which parents simply helped other parents by sharing in day care or hiring a teacher to work with children otherwise excluded from the school system.

However, focusing on the achievements of parents leaves part of the story of parental activism untold. Parent activists have a complicated relationship with disability activism and disabled activists.

As parents began organizing, so too did people with disabilities who were learning to harness their political power to demand rights and empowerment. In the early and mid-twentieth century, distinct disability communities formed organizations to pursue their causes, such as the National Committee for Mental Hygiene, the League of the Physically Handicapped, and the National Association of the Deaf. In 1940 Paul Strachan founded the American Federation of the Physically Handicapped, an early national-level, cross-disability organization that fought for the rights of people with disabilities. Following in the footsteps of the African American civil rights movement, disability activism flourished in the 1960s and 1970s: the Independent Living Movement built an infrastructure to help ensure people with disabilities would have full access to the community; institutional survivors worked to close the institutions and establish community supports; Disabled in Action and ADAPT protested discrimination and claimed rights; the Deaf President Now movement demanded that Gallaudet University hire a Deaf president; self-advocates with intellectual disabilities and with autism began asserting their voices on disability policy; AIDS activists coalesced to fight against stigma and for medical research and treatments; disabled artists explored and celebrated the disability experience within culture; and Disability Justice activists challenged the overlapping systems of oppression such as racism, poverty, and colonialism that fed into and off of ableism.[8] The list could continue, but for our purposes we simply wish to show the breadth, variation, and vibrancy of disability activism.

Often, activists worked on distinct issues with distinct populations, allying when mutually agreeable and creating in effect multiple disability movements. Divisions arose as white activists with physical disabilities took center stage, leaving some communities, such as people with mental health diagnoses, intellectual disabilities, and chronic health conditions, feeling marginalized. The voices, achievements, and needs of minorities with disabilities (e.g., racial and ethnic minorities, immigrants, and the lesbian, gay, bisexual, and transgender [LGBT] communities) too often went unrecognized.[9] Although fragmented and imperfect, these fluid and diverse coalitions of people with disabilities emerged as a powerful political force demanding freedom, equity, accommodations in the workplace, accessibility throughout social institutions, self-determination, and social justice.

As activists with disabilities fought to be recognized as authorities in disability policy, parents operated in the same political arenas and also asserted their role as authority figures. Parents, though, tended to wield greater political and economic capital to influence disability policy, and their relationship with disabled activists was thorny. Although parents always argue that they are fighting to improve the world for their child, the goals they espouse at times differ dramatically from those of disabled activists. Organizations led by disabled activists tend to embrace disability pride and culture, recognizing the value of diversity and the importance of providing people support in discovering their individual strengths and desired patterns of life. Some parent-led organizations, however, stress cure and maximal normalization, striving to erase rather than embrace disability. Disabled activists typically fight for the empowerment of people with disabilities. Parents, on the other hand, may perceive the need for continued input and control and therefore are more likely to pursue paternalistic approaches to care, such as guardianship, supervision, and imposed treatment. Disabled activists tend to prioritize the perspectives and rights of people with disabilities, but parents may offer a view that complicates individual empowerment by including the perspective, needs, and interests of family members and care providers. Thus, although parents often situate their activism within the field of disability rights, disabled activists perceive some parental activism as contributing to disability oppression rather than fighting against it. Some parents, on the other hand, criticize disabled activists for erasing the needs of the most significantly disabled and their family members in order to portray people with disabilities as fully capable of exercising rights.

Two examples illustrate these tensions. Elizabeth Boggs (mentioned earlier) is remembered as an iconic leader of the parents' movement; however, she placed her son, David, in a residential institution at the age of seven, and, despite the growing condemnation of institutions and increasing availability of community services, he resided in a large state facility until he passed away. Personally and politically, Boggs resisted the call to close institutions. Defending institutionalization, Boggs stated:

> The "community" surrounding David's "home" is the campus of the state school. It is an ergonomic community; that is, one which has

been planned to suit the inhabitants. Its swimming pool is designed so that anyone can stand up in any part of it. . . . There is a restaurant where no one stares at the sloppy eaters. Nobody there thinks that it is inappropriate for a thirty-two-year-old man to use a swing on the playground by choice; it is not considered dehumanizing to let a man act like a child if he wants to. David is not restricted by any such environmental taboos. From his point of view this community is more facilitative and more enhancing than the town half a mile down the road.[10]

Boggs's continued legitimization of institutions idealized the creation of separate spaces for people with disabilities, regardless of the disability community's demand for full access to the community. Multiple awards and centers are named after Boggs, but few disabled activists honor her in the same fashion.

Not merely an issue of the past, friction between parent and disabled activists also can be found in the contemporary news. In 2016 a Wisconsin teenager with spinal muscular atrophy, Jerika Bolen, told her mother that she wished to be removed from her ventilator and be allowed to die while in hospice care. Jerika experienced intense pain and used a ventilator for approximately twelve hours per day. After long discussions and joint counseling, her mother agreed to Jerika's wish. Her family and community threw Jerika a "prom," attended by more than one thousand people, to celebrate her life and say goodbye. News outlets praised the teen, her family, and the community that made her last days so memorable. Jerika's mother saw herself as respecting her daughter's decision to exercise her right to die. "After all she has been through, I owe this to her," her mother told reporters.[11]

Not Dead Yet, an anti-euthanasia organization led by disabled activists, contested the family's decision. It may seem odd that disability activists who fight vehemently for self-determination would oppose the right to die, but Not Dead Yet expresses grave concerns about the context in which choices about death are made and the role of family members and medical professionals in these choices. Diane Coleman, leader of Not Dead Yet, stated, "I worry that there's an attitude in the health care profession that really writes people off with disabilities. I worry that people like Jerika . . . are in the throes of that, and without adequate support."[12] Nondisabled teenagers who experience other forms of pain and suffering—abuse, emotional trauma, addiction, poverty—are not encouraged to act on their suicidal thoughts; rather, society strives to improve their lives. In contrast, society sees those with incurable disabilities as hopeless and their lives as worthless; when cure is not possible, people with disabilities are expected to want to die. By offering people with disabilities the right to die without providing the right to health care or to supports that enable meaningful participation in society, society creates an ableist context that increases the likely desire for death while also creating the illusion of "choice."[13]

Bolen was removed from her ventilator and passed away. Bolen's mother described herself as an activist: "I don't know how to stop fighting for her. That's all I've done since the day she was diagnosed when she was 8 months old."[14] In the last weeks of her daughter's life, though, she found herself embroiled in contestation with disabled activists unhappy with her open support of the choice of death for her teenage daughter. Not Dead Yet issued a statement of mourning: "Jerika Bolen deserved better quality health care and the same suicide prevention that a non-disabled teen would receive. We ask one last question: What might have happened if Jerika's request for a 'last dance' had been met with overwhelming public and media encouragement to live instead of a massive thumb on the scale in support of her death?"[15]

Disagreements between some parents and disabled activists extend into many areas such as the use of segregated/specialized versus inclusive settings, imposed treatment versus self-determination, the value of cure versus the need for access and supports, and mandated supervision versus access to privacy, to name a few. While we can compare parents and disabled activists broadly, it is crucial to remember that parents are divided among themselves, as are disabled activists. Some parents align more closely with organizations led by disabled activists, while others organize in parent-led groups with distinct agendas. Parents are also divided by race, class, and disability. Thus, to understand disability politics and policies today, we must understand the divisions that have characterized parent activism, how and why divisions developed, what divisions are central to disability politics, and how such divisions might be addressed to build stronger communities. Not only does the literature on parenting and activism largely ignore these macro questions, but so too does most of the literature on disability movements, which tends to focus on activism by people with disabilities.[16] Even when parent activism is discussed in histories of disability activism, its role is rarely theorized.

In *Allies and Obstacles: Disability Activism and Parents of Children with Disabilities*, we conduct a macro analysis of parent activism using a social movement perspective in order to reveal and analyze the complex historical and contemporary relationship of parents to disability activism. To do so, we develop four case studies, focusing on intellectual disability, mental illness, autism, and a broad range of physical disabilities.[17] Each case study explores the specific ways in which activism developed among parents and people with disabilities, the points of alliance, and the key points of contestation. The case studies then serve as the basis to analyze parent activism across disability groups and across time. By combining the use of historical case studies with cross-disability and cross-movement analysis over time, *Allies and Obstacles* offers a major shift in the literature on parent activism. Whereas much of the literature focuses on a social-psychological perspective or studies of single organizations or single issues, our broad comparative approach enables us to consider a range of questions regarding how parent activism is positioned within the field of disability activism and thereby develop new insights into disability activism, policy, and the family.

Situating Parent Activism in Scholarship

Families in Need: Insufficient Progress and New Hurdles

Across parent activism related to disability, the dominant message has been and continues to be the lack of adequate supports and the daunting obstacles that hinder the success of children with disabilities and their families, such as inadequate educational programming, cuts to social services, a dangerous lack of awareness by law enforcement and medical professionals, and social stigma.

Decades of activism have led to significant improvements, but some aspects of the parent experience have changed very little.[18] Education is now mandated for all children, but few schools offer high-quality inclusive programming for children with disabilities, and parents often have to fight for even basic accommodations. After their offspring reach the age of twenty-one, an age when many young adults are launching independent lives, families hit the "disability cliff"—a time when mandated public education and services end, and families are thrust into the world of waiting lists, competition for meager services, and endless negotiations with "dense bureaucracies" laden with extremely complex rules and regulations.[19] To secure these elusive services, families must expend significant time and resources in advocacy efforts, a process that advantages the most privileged families.[20] Even if services are secured, parents must remain ever vigilant against the threats of shifting laws and policies, budget cuts, agency viability, and staff turnover, while also continuing to manage the mundane aspects of the complex and fragmented service system. Moreover, even with the emergence of the disability service industry, households with children with disabilities still experience higher rates of poverty, unemployment, and social-psychological hardships such as increased stress and depression as compared to households without children with disabilities.[21]

Neither these problems nor their solutions lie in the workings of the family alone. In contrast with heartwarming images of home as a comforting oasis isolated from the pressures and politics of the external world, disability exposes the deep intertwining of the so-called private and public spheres. Families (the "private" sphere) must confront systems of medical expertise, educational and service bureaucracies, cultural expectations of normality and productivity, and political policies (the "public" sphere) that swirl around their families with a dizzying array of opportunities and challenges that shape their everyday lives and identities.

Medicalization and neoliberalism are perhaps the most important factors shaping both the modern pressures on the family to raise successful children and the lack of public supports by which to do so. In the late nineteenth and early twentieth centuries, mothers were increasingly expected to harness the power of science in raising their children, a trend referred to as scientific motherhood.[22] Medical professionals claimed expertise in child-rearing (e.g., Dr. Spock), and state systems like education and social welfare increasingly monitored and surveilled children and their families. Mothers became the liaisons between public and private, tasked with using the latest medical and scientific developments to ensure the optimal development of children and their success in life. Mother-blame also became rampant.[23] According to the experts, overprotective mothers raised emasculated and dependent males; "refrigerator mothers," women accused of failing to build emotional bonds with their children, created social pathology and withdrawal; and poor, deviant, and disabled mothers passed their defective genes to their children either genetically or as a product of poor socialization.[24] In other words, "bad" mothers created and perpetuated disability;[25] good mothers, on the other hand, strove to erase disability through a commitment to the regimes of science.[26]

While the expectation of compliance with professionals is long-standing, the complexity of the knowledge, therapies, medicines, and systems is uniquely modern.[27] Parents are expected to learn cognitive, biological, and psychological science and manage the array of medications and therapies and their consequences, manipulating and molding their children's bodies and minds in order to optimize neural and physical capacity.[28] And, in a perhaps ironic twist, the more mothers worked to perfect their children, the more energetically the medical and educational communities diagnosed children with disabilities, vastly expanding the range of behaviors and demeanors that warrant diagnosis.[29] Being too energetic, shy, anxious, perfectionistic, rebellious, or conforming all emerged as possible indicators of disability. Disability—understood as a biological reason for impending failure—lurked behind every corner.

Child optimization is not just a fantasy born of narcissistic parents; it is driven by a highly competitive, neoliberal society in which only a few succeed and the consequences of failure are tremendous. Neoliberal economics encourage laissez-faire capitalism, privatization, and decreased government spending on social programs, alongside an ethos of individualism. In this context, people with disabilities are denied social supports yet encouraged to enthusiastically locate and embrace their individual opportunities for success. People with disabilities are denied jobs, yet are encouraged to become entrepreneurs, in essence told to create their own employment opportunities while large employers are allowed to avoid hiring them.[30] They are encouraged to become managers of their own services, yet there are insufficient services and little assistance for people whose disabilities may limit their ability to self-manage an entire staff, multiple service providers, and a complex schedule and budget. This situation is called "freedom"—a freedom in which people with disabilities have the rights to live in the community, work, and manage their own services, although not the social support or economic resources to ensure their ability to do so.

Families are called on to teach their children these entrepreneurial ways, create opportunities for them to thrive, manage the numerous care transactions, and support the attainment of an "independent" life. In doing so, parents must become lay doctors, nurses, therapists, educators, service managers, and advocates, all while erasing their own labor to showcase their child's successful independence. Mothers in particular exist in a bizarre nexus between the unflinching demands of selflessness imposed on mothers and the neoliberal ethos of individualism, self-interest, and competition for which they are preparing their children.[31] Sociologist Dennis Hogan summed up the situation by arguing that the responsibilities given to families after deinstitutionalization without corresponding public supports is "incongruent with the policy of emancipation."[32] Sylvia Hewlett and Cornel West argue in their 1998 book, *The War against Parents*, that the American family in general has been abandoned; a commitment to "untrammeled individualism" combined with corporate greed has derailed social policies supporting the family and led to a largely punitive child welfare system that blames families rather than supports them.[33] Thus, families with children who are disabled face significant hurdles, with only a punitive child welfare system and a meager disability system to assist them.

This incongruence creates particular tensions between parents and disabled activists. In seeking to gain supports for their families, parents expose the intense labor and care demands—even the "burdens"—of raising a child with a disability. Their pleas are at times desperate, and their descriptions of their children and their homelife may purposefully be used to provoke fear and pity. Disabled activists have largely rejected the narrative of disability as "burden" because it devalues and stigmatizes people with disabilities; in seeking a broad cultural and political shift in power, people with disabilities demand to be acknowledged as rightful citizens regardless of their need for support. Autistic activist Kelly Mullen-McWilliams states, "Autistic people don't want to be called broken, and they're tired of non-autistic parent advocacy that demonizes 'autism' and wails for a 'cure.'"[34] The proliferation of parent stories focusing on the burden of disability and parents' focus on their own needs and interests undermine the ability of people with disabilities to showcase their abilities and demand rights. But when activists with disabilities reject parent narratives of hardship, they potentially erase the lived experience of many caregivers who lack adequate support and who themselves become disabled from the stress and physical demands of providing care. Parents and people with disabilities end up potentially pitted against each other as they deploy different strategies to access some version of the "good life" that seems promised to Americans yet denied to people with disabilities and their family members.

The neoliberal context of service provision perpetuates divisions among parents as well, including long-standing divisions by class and race. When freedom guarantees only opportunity with no regard for equality of access or resources, inequality thrives. Scholarship shows that one's class position matters a great deal as families navigate disability systems. In interactions with disability systems and professionals such as teachers, therapists, and service providers, parents with class privilege are far more likely to negotiate outcomes that better address the needs of their children and respect their family's views, as compared to families with less money, education, and cultural capital.[35] Families with higher socioeconomic status (SES) are also more likely to interact with systems that are geared toward cooperation with parents, whereas lower SES parents are more likely to interact with systems geared toward enforcing the compliance of parents. For example, schools in wealthier districts more quickly acknowledge parent demands, whereas schools in economically distressed areas shape individualized educational plan (IEP) meetings to minimize parental input.[36] Higher SES also may better enable families to foster a homelife with an effective rhythm, structure, and embedded services to address the dynamic needs they face.[37]

Because systems are increasingly privatized and individualized, a gain for one family is just that—for one family—not a foundation for group advancement. In fact, in an environment of scarce resources, a gain for one family may be viewed as detrimental to other families as the small pool of public funds and services gets depleted. Thus, the gains for parents with high socioeconomic status do not typically trickle down to or include other families, but instead channel finite resources toward the wealthy and away from the poor and working class. Thus, while wealthy families believe that they are just doing right by their children, less wealthy families may perceive the wealthy as hoarding disability services and funding.

Racial inequality intersects and acts independently of SES. Minorities are disproportionately poor in America and therefore experience SES-related disadvantages. They also face barriers specific to race. Service systems are dominated by white professionals and culture, which means that minority families may experience language barriers, discrimination, and distrust of professional systems, especially when these systems play a role in legal enforcement such as identifying illegal immigrants, reporting unsafe conditions for children, and reporting inappropriate use of state benefits.[38] In trying to challenge these systems and fight for the needs of their children, minority parents experience marginalization within advocacy groups. Parent groups led by white parents tend to function in ways that are financially, culturally, or linguistically inaccessible, such as disseminating information via conferences, requiring payment for membership, fundraising through gala events, and following formal meeting procedures that may be unfamiliar to people without a professional background.[39] They also may seek to erase race or class variation in an attempt to focus on disability, thereby discounting the intersectional nature of oppression.[40] For example, parent organizations may not prioritize issues important to poor or minority neighborhoods such as the disproportionate educational segregation of African American boys labeled with disabilities or the dangers posed by law enforcement officials to minority men with disabilities. These decisions affect not only the framing of issues but also which groups mobilize alongside each other and how bureaucracies will respond.

Parent Activism and Parent Movements

How do parents respond to disability, given these intense pressures? Parents respond in diverse and complex ways. Parent organizations arise at different times and have different foci. Some are more focused on rights and the provision of social services, while others are more enmeshed with the medical model. Some frequently ally with organizations led by disabled activists while others have openly antagonistic relationships with them. Some parent organizations are national in scope with significant budgets and a policy presence, while others are purposefully local and grassroots.

Parents themselves are often highly pragmatic in their activism, seeking supports that meet their needs, are assessed as valuable within their local contexts, and are pursued as politically practical rather than solely based on an overarching political or philosophical approach. For example, parents may express an ideological preference for inclusion yet choose a disability-specific school because the local inclusive option for education is seen as low quality. In her discussion of parents' approach to medicalization, sociologist

Laura Mauldin describes parents as "ambivalent," navigating the advantages and disadvantages of a medical-model approach to disability.[41] In the case of activist organizations, we instead describe parents as often *purposefully flexible* in their commitment to a higher political philosophy as they strive to meet direct and immediate individual needs. This does not mean that parents do not strive to shape the world in particular ways (e.g., building a more inclusive society, supporting medical "progress" to diminish disability), but that parent activism is often related to direct, pressing needs and their perceived best outcomes for their child and family. These perceived needs and outcomes for their own child take priority over ideological commitment, and parents move within and across organizations and services as useful to them. As discussed by sociologist Jennifer Reich, the culture of "individualist parenting" justifies and even valorizes prioritizing the best interests (as perceived by the parent) of one's own child ahead of communal interests.[42]

A parent interviewee called Gail described this practical approach as she discussed her affiliation with both self-advocacy and parent groups. Ideologically, Gail felt more aligned with self-advocates and their fight to have their voices heard above, or at least alongside, parent voices. Criticizing parent groups, she stated, "It's . . . always from the perspective of parents, of themselves as parents, and I don't hear or see people with disabilities in that—in there at all." Yet she affiliated with parent groups insofar as they offered specific tools and resources: "I spend a lot of time and energy pursuing the material resources that my son needs to be optimized to the extent that it's possible in the landscape of education and therapy . . . so I use parent groups as a site for navigating that."[43]

This pragmatic approach to activism to meet individual needs speaks in part to the culture of individualist parenting, and in part to the challenge of meeting even basic daily needs. Ideological consistency is challenging when one struggles to achieve basic safety and well-being for one's child and/or family. Gail's approach also speaks to the fragmentation of the parent experience and activism. Parents face bureaucratic systems, with categorical labeling, distinct services, and complex types of funding. To best address needs within certain systems, parent organizations typically focus on specific disabilities or disability categories (e.g., developmental disabilities, mental illnesses), and parents enter into activism specific to the particular system(s) with which they interact (e.g., education, vocational rehabilitation/employment, medical treatment, criminal justice) and/or the particular needs they experience (e.g., access to assistive technology, greater inclusion, a larger budget for services, safety). As the family's needs change, often their activism changes, shifting, for example, from activism related to education to work and residential opportunities.

Some parents do develop a wider lens for their activism beyond the work required to meet their own family's needs. Sociologist Larry Jones refers to the smaller groups of parents who serve as state and national opinion leaders as cosmopolitan parents. Yet he also notes the often wide ideological gap between them and parents with a more local approach, who lag conceptually behind and are primarily concerned with their own children and their own organization's services, viability, and growth.[44]

Insofar as parents organize into what we might call a "parents' movement," however diverse, fragmented, and pragmatic it is, two characteristics dominate. First, parents articulate a relational model with regard to the impact of disability and public responsibility toward people with disabilities and their families. The disability experience is shaped by and affects society, and societies must take responsibility for supporting people with disabilities and their families. Second, parents assert parental expertise and authority in making choices regarding their child's best interests and demand autonomy from state control, even when receiving services/supports from the state. Thus, at the same time that they demand society support people with disabilities and their families, they reject social mandates that limit their authority over their children.

Building a Relational Model for Support

For most parent activists, disability is not an individual experience; it is a relational phenomenon affecting individuals, families, and communities.[45] Not only do parents identify the problems experienced by their children (whether these be understood as caused by biological or social factors), but they also identify the associated problems experienced by themselves and other family members, such as intensive care demands, social exclusion, discrimination, and loss of income and opportunities. Parents see the needs and rights of their children as intimately interwoven with their own. Education, for example, is important for the child's well-being, but it is also important for the parent's well-being; the denial of education stunts development for the child and diminishes opportunities for the parent who is expected to provide round-the-clock care and an education. Individualistic models of rights are particularly misinformed when the state *expects* the family to provide care well beyond the age their offspring become adults and provides no alternatives for care. Thus, as parents demand individual rights for their children, they also argue that *parents* have rights.[46]

Moreover, disability affects the broader society, and the society shapes the disability experience. The appeal to communal responsibility can be driven by a negative portrayal of disability and its effects, such as when Autism Speaks asserts the need for public funding to eradicate the "epidemic" of autism that they see as devastating families and communities. From this perspective, so terrible are the consequences of the autism epidemic that society must invest public funds toward cure and eradication. But it can also be rooted in a more positive view of disability tied to the social model. The social model of disability argues that many of the negative consequences of disability—for example, poor performance in school, low employment rates, poverty, social isolation, and low self-esteem—are due to environmental barriers, including barriers that are architectural, political, or rooted in prejudice.[47] Therefore, the capacity of the individual and family is shaped by the physical and social environment, rather than resting solely in the individual. Improving the situation for people with disabilities requires social reform to address the wide range of social barriers experienced by them. This model also shifts the understanding of rights from individual to social/relational. Rather than seeing a right as an individual claim (e.g., I have a right to assemble with others as I wish; I have a right to an education), a right mandates relational obligations (e.g., I have a right to assemble with others, which means that public services and transportation must be made accessible, and those in charge of such services and transportation have an obligation to ensure accessibility so that I can assemble with others).

The social model created a revolutionary path forward in rights, allowing people with disabilities to simultaneously demand equality—to the same opportunities as other people—as well as equity—to *different* supports and the accessibility required for their equal participation. For instance, the Individuals with Disabilities Education Act mandates that children with disabilities, like all other children, receive a free public education *and* guarantees a right to an accommodated education appropriate to their educational needs. Using the social model, insufficient infrastructure and programming of schools causes educational failure, not the child's disability.

The social model also allows parents to highlight the barriers they face and to demand society address their concerns. This shift in focus, though, may be disconcerting for disabled activists. Moreover, parents tend to assume that the needs of people with disabilities and the needs of parents can be addressed in mutually beneficial ways. As noted, the right to an education benefits both the individual with a disability and the family. However, parents' interests, needs, or rights may deeply conflict with the interests, needs, or rights of the person with the disability. For example, when parents assert their "right" to refuse to provide care to adult offspring, people with disabilities may be forced into institutional care unless community residential options are adequate. When parents assert their right to make medical choices for their children, without any parameters related to human rights, children with disabilities may be sterilized, institutionalized, or subjected to treatments with adverse effects while searching for cure or normalization. When parents center their own needs and interests under the umbrella of disability rights with little regard for the potential conflicts of interest, people with disabilities are displaced and disempowered.

Parent Claims to Authority and Autonomy

Potential conflicts are further exacerbated by parents' claims to authority over their child (and adult offspring) and autonomy from the state. In many ways, parents' claims to authority and autonomy are the hallmarks of parent movements. Parents may engage in lots of forms of activism, but parents who prioritize claims to their own authority and autonomy are activists in a "parent movement."

As noted earlier, the medicalization of disability and of childhood undercut the perceived expertise and authority of mothers with regard to their children. Furthermore, in the American welfare system the state positions recipients of services and assistance as "dependents" who are subject to state control and surveillance.[48] Thus, the growth of institutions and the emergence of vast professionalized and publicly funded systems of care undercut the authority of parents to control and guide the lives of their children with disabilities. Institutionalization required that children with disabilities become wards of the state, stripping parents of their authority. Within institutions, residents experienced terrible neglect and violence, and parents often felt powerless to prevent this harm. Even for children who remain with their families, services create professional and state avenues into one's "private" home, and these services can quickly become coercive, particularly for families who may not meet the cultural expectations of white, middle-class professionals.[49] Parents and their offspring may have their homelife monitored, experience blame for perceived disabilities, and be expected—whether they wish it or not—to abide by certain medical/professional therapeutic regimes and cultural norms such as standards of cleanliness, routines, and particular forms of discipline.

Parents, though, resist the stigma of dependency and the associated social control, pointing to the devastating harm done to people with disabilities and their families as a result of public decision-making about disability and state control. White, middle-class parents of children with intellectual disabilities have been particularly successful at asserting their own status as "good citizens"—law-abiding, hardworking taxpayers—to position themselves, and by extension their offspring, as "deserving" of high-quality services delivered without stigma.[50] They fight for the right to be assumed to be a well-functioning family, to be allowed to pursue their values and interests, to maintain a parental right to be *the* voice of their child's best interests, and therefore to exercise authority over involvement in service systems including what services are used, how services are delivered, and what goals are pursued. In other words, *as parents fight for state support, they also fight for autonomy from state control.*

The delicate balance of autonomy from state control while receiving public support rests on the recognition of authority—who is in control? The Independent Living Movement argued that despite the receipt of services, people with disabilities should retain self-determination and control over their own lives. In doing so, people with disabilities challenged the liberal criteria of autonomy and rationality typically required to exercise rights and promoted an expansive view that values the potential of many people previously excluded to make decisions and exercise control over their lives with supports.[51] They also strive to position themselves as *the authority* on disability issues in the political realm.

Parents, though, often fight for the recognition of their authority to make decisions for their child and even adult offspring. A disabled activist and mother of a disabled child, Corbett OToole, argues that parental authority over services for disabled children should be incorporated directly into service systems: "In our system, parents should always be our children's primary Case Managers, and we should be trained and paid," thereby building the skills of parents and recognizing their authority in decision-making for their child. She continues, "Parent advocates often say, and I agree, that the parent is the only one person who sees and loves and believes in their child—their wholeness just the way they are right now."[52] The assertion of parent authority may explicitly challenge the tenets of the disability movements and their insistence on self-determination, particularly when claims to authority undermine the authority of adult offspring to direct their own lives. Just as parents may publicize the deficits of people with disabilities in order to secure services, they may showcase the deficiencies of adults with disabilities to independently exercise rights and self-manage in order to show the need for parental authority. For example, parents of adults with mental illnesses point to the ways in which mental illness and associated conditions such as homelessness and drug use diminish people's understandings of their own best interests. In an interview, a mother of a son with significant cognitive disabilities and self-injurious behaviors worried that her adult son would "die with his rights on," a phrase she used to refer to the protection of his self-determination rather than what she believed he actually needed to survive, including twenty-four-hour surveillance and a safe environment adapted to his needs.[53] Parents may conceptualize intervention and even guardianship as rights for those who are unable to recognize or pursue their best interests.[54] Indeed, for parents of adult offspring with significant disabilities, the very fact of their continued role as caregivers serves as proof that their offspring are not adequately independent for full self-determination.

Although the problem of authority is most evident in relation to adults with disabilities, it exists even for parents of minors. Disabled activists point out the challenges for children with disabilities as they are raised by nondisabled parents who may have deeply negative views about disability. In *Far from the Tree*, Andrew Solomon eloquently explains that in some families the children are so different from their parents (e.g., deaf children, LGBT+ children, autistic children) that the children, metaphorically and sometimes literally, speak a different language. Parents may struggle to learn, or even reject learning, this different language, expecting the child to conform to the family, not vice versa.[55] These children experience minority status within their own family and face similar prejudices.

Even without prejudice, substitute embodiment is challenging. Parents may assert that they speak for their offspring, and they may have good reason to do so; without parental intervention the interests of the person with a disability may be ignored. But in representing an offspring's identities and interests, parents may displace the subjective experience of those with disabilities and nullify their voices and abilities while emphasizing parents' own perspectives and needs. This process of substitute embodiment, or "embodiment by proxy," is not a simple process, even for the most loving or intimate of companions.[56] OToole, quoted above asserting parental authority, interestingly also criticizes nondisabled parents in relation to their disabled children. She notes how deeply problematic it is that nondisabled parents will often raise disabled children "isolated and kept away from disabled adults," in inaccessible environments where they neither learn the best skills to navigate the world with their disability nor develop pride in their disability identity and the history and politics of disability.[57] She states, "Instead, nearly all families put their energies into trying to get the disabled child to fit into a predetermined mold of inadequate and broken disabled person, one who will never quite succeed."[58] Thus, at the same time that OToole as a parent demands the power to control her child's destiny, she questions the record of nondisabled parents in raising proud and empowered disabled citizens. This quandary within OToole's writing is indicative of the dialectical tensions within the family; the family is both a site uniquely positioned to resist external oppression and a site fraught with internal power dynamics, where "multiple vectors of oppression coalesce."[59]

Fundamentally, the conferring of authority and autonomy to parents reinforces inequalities within the family that are supported by inequality outside of the family. Susan Moller Okin, in her classic work on gender in the family, explained that treating the family as if it were "private" and free from state regulation in effect masked the patriarchy that had long been actually supported by public social institutions including the law, religion, and economy.[60] Similarly, as a result of discrimination and the lack of affordable, accessible housing options with services, adults with disabilities may have few options other than residing at home. Inside the "private" sphere of the home, though, disability laws carry little weight; within the family one has little legal claim to the rights of accessibility, privacy, sexual expression, or freedom of assembly. Within the home, children and adults with disabilities may face intense surveillance and restrictions. This is not to say that all homes are oppressive; it is to say that homes *can be* oppressive and, without available community services, people with disabilities have no recourse or protection from this oppression.

Taken together, the central features of a parents' movement—a relational approach and a claim to parental autonomy and authority—constitute an ironic combination. The relational approach demands that the public accept responsibility for the needs and rights of people with disabilities and their families, while the claim to autonomy resists the imposition of collective mandates. This combination protects family members from state violence, but it also undercuts the attempts by disability activists to establish collective mandates to ensure deinstitutionalization, community accessibility, and liberty and rights.

Parent influence in the legislative process illustrates this tension as parents fight alongside disabled activists to establish collective mandates but also as a distinct group to preserve parent autonomy from such mandates. For example, parents fought both for and against deinstitutionalization. The compromise that emerged in the 1999 Supreme Court case of *Olmstead v. L.C.* declared unnecessary institutionalization to be a violation of the Americans with Disabilities Act yet also allowed for "necessary" institutionalization as determined by medical expertise and parent or guardian wishes. This compromise challenged institutionalization while also allowing for institutionalization to occur when seen as appropriate by medical professionals and parents. Similarly, the Individuals with Disabilities Education Act established a clear preference for integrated education but also gave teachers and parents flexibility in making decisions regarding appropriate placement, thereby legitimizing educational segregation.

Scholarship on other parent movements similarly documents the use of parent autonomy/authority to undercut collective mandates while at times reinforcing conservative values such as family/gender hierarchy and religion. In America, activists have wielded the banner of "family values" as a tool to resist state expansion of social programs, deny support to diverse family arrangements by denying them the status of "family," and challenge antidiscrimination efforts. Parents against mandatory vaccinations use the mantle of parent authority to resist mandates based on collective public health. Transnationally, activism based on the family can be used to reject collective political philosophies including socialism and the Western ideal of individualism.[61] Thus, we should not be surprised to see the prioritization of parental authority in disability activism and the prioritization of their child's interests as perceived by parents. These features can both enable resistance to state tendencies toward violence and dehumanization of people with disabilities and undercut collective mandates to ensure particular rights and outcomes such as accessibility, inclusion, and self-determination. Because of its protective power, simply removing parental authority exposes the most vulnerable people with disabilities and their family members to clear risks. A romanticized faith in parent authority, however, carries its own risks.

The Field of Disability Activism

When examining parent activism, scholarship has tended to focus on micro, social-psychological analysis, such as how parents perceive their activism, their pathway into activism, and the challenges they face in enacting change. The macro, social movement perspective we use directs analysis to other questions, such as how parent activism is positioned within a broader field of social movement organizations, with whom they ally and against whom they fight, what divisions exist across parent activists, and how parent activism is understood by other disability rights organizations.

A macro, social movement perspective reveals a field of social movement organizations dedicated in some way to influencing disability policy and encourages a relational analysis of the interaction among organizations such as the ways in which organizations coordinate collective action via mechanisms like resource sharing and boundary work, as well as the fragmentation and disconnections among organizations.[62] Using this perspective, we consider the ways in which parents support and contribute to activism alongside people with disabilities or the extent to which they operate a movement with distinct organizations, goals, and strategies. We examine the ways in which disabled activists and parents ally and when they go their separate ways or even compete with and oppose each other. This approach moves the analysis away from an analysis solely of parent perspectives or an analysis of the parent-offspring relationship to the relationship across social movement organizations.

Ideologically, at the heart of disability activism are grassroots organizations led by disabled activists, which vary in their foci including prioritizing protest, rights, social justice, and self-help. When we look at the players influencing disability policy, however, we see a wide range that also includes parent organizations, service providers, professional organizations, health-related organizations, and charities. Parents may see the advantages of alliance with organizations led by disabled activists, in particular when working on cross-disability rights legislation and legislation that confers funding for community services and supports. Parents may also choose, in addition to or instead of allying with disabled activists, to ally with service providers, professional organizations, health-related organizations, and charities, all of whom are powerful allies depending on the change desired.

As our analysis shows, parents tend to lend their power to certain organizations more than others. Parents are more likely to advocate for a single disability or a disability category like developmental disability or mental illness, fight for the provision of services and supports (rather than a full range of rights or broad social justice issues), and use legitimate channels toward achieving social change. They are also likely allies with a range of professional "experts," including organizations that have a medical/cure focus, which many disabled activists consider outside of and even antithetical to the disability rights movements.

Parents are also less likely to be found in organizations that demand control by people with disabilities, represent a broad disability alliance, or use disruptive techniques, like ADAPT or Disabled in Action, although these organizations are central to disability activism. As what sociologists refer to as a *new social movement*, disabled activists strive to transform the dominant culture and identity politics into one that values and includes people with disabilities as equal participants.[63] Parents enter into the terrain of disability activism with their own specific experiences and concerns, usually without much knowledge of or connection to organizations run by people with disabilities. Parents tend to connect with other parents, not to activists with disabilities. Even though parents often challenge the stigma that confronts their child and family, they may not see the relevance of disabled activists for their particular child or issue, particularly if their perspectives conflict.

Even if the rhetoric and goals of parents and disabled activists align, the presence and political power of parents in and of itself may still be problematic for activists with disabilities. Activists with disabilities assert the capabilities of people with disabilities and their own control over the political disability agenda. The very presence of parents may suggest incapacity. These tensions are exacerbated when parent organizations hold more power or symbolic sway at the political table than organizations run by people with disabilities. Parent organizations like the Arc and Autism Speaks are some of the most powerful players in disability policy, typically with larger budgets and staffs than self-advocacy organizations run by people with intellectual disabilities or autism. Organizations led by minorities with disabilities have an even harder time influencing national disability policy. Activists with disabilities typically want parents as allies, recognizing the crucial role parents play in the lives of their loved ones and in policy. However, they also want to *own* the issue and have allies follow their lead, a relationship that activists with disabilities have not always been able to establish or maintain.[64]

Parents, however, rarely feel like they occupy a position of power or privilege. In the face of massive bureaucracies, fiscal policies and laws, and a political system dominated by professionals and cost-cutting bureaucrats, parents struggle to have their voices heard. Opposition by people with disabilities may seem like one more threat, further undercutting their vulnerable position. The ideals of integration and empowerment espoused by disabled activists may feel like yet another demand placing pressures on an already tapped family. Thus, while parents and disabled activists often work in conjunction, alliance can be tense to say the least.

In navigating the complex political landscape, many parents' groups professionalize over time. The largest parent organizations have a tendency toward professionalization, hiring experts in grant writing, lobbying, and service delivery management, for example. Professionalization enabled some parent organizations, including the Arc, the National Down Syndrome Society, and United Cerebral Palsy (UCP), to move away from a purely parent agenda and to more openly embrace a disability rights agenda. Professionals sometimes proudly claim that they, more so than parents, can see the "big picture" rather than the needs of a specific child. Because they hold a big picture view and because they have interacted with so many families, they can also imagine more positive futures for specific children. Professionalization, though, can lead to other effects as well. The Arc and UCP run a vast infrastructure of services, with professionals focused on ensuring smooth and efficient management. The goals of service delivery management are very different than the goals of advocacy, and the demands of activists with disabilities may become a nuisance to be managed rather than a rallying cry for radical transformation. Professional fundraisers and grant writers also excel at utilizing effective strategies to increase cash flow, sometimes with little regard for the ethics of particular strategies; for example, the Jerry Lewis telethons profited from the creation of pity, and Autism Speaks campaigns profit from the creation of fear. Indeed, several organizations that began as local grassroots organizing have evolved into sizable enterprises with extensive staffs (largely paying people without disabilities) and budgets.

In line with the analysis by Hanna Rosqvist and her colleagues, parent organizations are more likely to present a "reformist" discourse that promotes rights yet retains the centrality of a deficit model to legitimatize parental power, whereas activists with disabilities are more likely to present a strident view that demands full membership, respect, the centrality of their perspective, and the recognition of their power.[65] Not surprisingly, alliance is most likely when disabled activists position themselves on more moderate ground, such as seeking services, access to treatment, and freedom from discrimination. Parents as a group are neither simply obstacles nor allies; from the perspective of disabled activists they are perhaps best framed as "suspicious" or "sometimes" allies, at times enthusiastically organizing alongside disabled activists, at times opposed, at times shifting positions or seeking a middle ground, and at times simply ignorant of or disinterested in them. Parents use this flexibility to address a range of issues they see as pressing, rather than focusing on rights, justice, and empowerment.

We also see a wide variation both within and across parent-led groups. As a brief comparison, parents of children with intellectual disabilities were among the parents to first organize on the state and national level to influence disability policy. The largest of the parent groups related to intellectual disabilities—the Arc—certainly has conflicts with organizations led by disability activists, but it is also among the most likely of parent organizations to build alliances with them. The Arc tends to draw on the social model, maintain a focus on rights, and support some degree of self-advocacy, all of which help foster alliance. VOR (formerly Voice of the Retarded), on the other hand, has almost no alliances with organizations led by people with disabilities, or even with the Arc, because of its singular focus on maintaining large-scale, disability-specific service settings, a political position counter to the demands of inclusion made by self-advocates. The most heated debates are found among autism organizations, an acrimony popularly referred to as the "Autism Wars." Autistic activists such as members of the Autistic Self Advocacy Network claim neurodiversity as a valuable trait to be supported and accommodated by society, whereas some parents, in particular leaders of the national group Autism Speaks, invest heavily in medical research to eradicate autism and fund public awareness campaigns that depict autism as a devastating epidemic. Through our cross-time, cross-organization analysis, we examine the broad variation across parent organizations and consider why organizations emerge in different decades and are more or less likely to ally with disabled activists.

Imagined Futures

Alison Kafer's work explores the relationship between imagined futures and present realities, arguing "it seems entirely possible that imagining different futures and temporalities might help us see, and do, the present differently."[66] She later states:

> To put it bluntly, I, *we*, need to imagine crip futures because disabled people are continually being written out of the future, rendered as a

sign of the future no one wants. This erasure is not mere metaphor. Disabled people—particularly those with developmental and psychiatric impairments, those who are poor, gender-deviant, and/or people of color, those who need atypical forms of assistance to survive—have faced sterilization, segregation, and institutionalization; denial of equitable education, health care and social services; violence and abuse; and the withholding of the rights of citizenship. . . . It is my loss, our loss, not to take care of, embrace, and desire all of us. We must begin to anticipate presents and to imagine futures that include all of us.[67]

Parents and disabled activists may understand the present differently and imagine different futures. Through interviews with those affected by institutionalization including residents, parents, siblings, and staff, Madeline Burghardt documents very different perceptions of institutionalization. Survivors of institutionalization describe the institution as "the worst place I ever lived," and said, "They locked us up. Nobody wanted us in society. That's what we felt." Some parents, on the other hand, believed that their child's significant disability required a level of care they were unable to provide, justifying institutionalization for the child's best welfare. They did not imagine that their children could function well in society.[68]

In our interviews, when asked if and why parent-led groups are less adamant in demanding rights and inclusion than self-advocacy groups, one former facilitator of a self-advocacy group stated:

The expectations that other people have of what people's future capabilities and opportunities and possibilities are are never [of] the same breadth and scope and beauty as the people have themselves. They can only see so far. There are some . . . who can grasp it immediately once they can see it, and those are people who can really get on board. But for many, they just don't have—they can't see their family member in a job, owning their own home; they can't see them getting married. . . . They just don't have that same vision.[69]

Some parents urge other parents to begin listening to activists with disabilities and embrace their vision of the future. In a blog post, Melissa Stoltz explains:

I get it. I do. Some of what is said makes it sound like parents aren't important at all. Some of it sounds like we've done irreparable damage. . . . But when someone comes at you with anger, fear, and sadness, I think it is the perfect time to stay silent, listen, and get humble. The disability community is asking for allies, but that can only happen if we fully examine what the parental role means in the context of disability. That examination can only happen if we listen and carefully consider what we are hearing, rather than insisting that the disability community is wrong about its own lived experiences, its own desires, and its own hopes for the future.[70]

Other parents, though, sharply disagree with the criticism that they lack imagination or fail to listen. "Imagination" for these parents has become a code word used by activists and professionals to demand hours and hours of parent labor inventing solutions where the state and policy have failed. The appeal to imagination, they argue, erases the material realities of severe disability and replaces it with an unfunded, unsupported aspiration in which even the most severely intellectually and mentally disabled people work paid jobs and live self-directed lives. Those who cannot attain the ideals of competitive employment and self-direction are abandoned, and they and their families are blamed for their failures.

These tensions are not esoteric matters of philosophy. They have influenced disability policy and continue to do so. Rights rhetoric has become so common in today's culture that the term "rights" is used to aspire to almost everything positive imaginable. Parents talk of a right to feel accepted, to be self-determined, to be protected, to have one's needs met, to have choices, to freedom, to integration, to access, to participate, to equality, to be accepted as disabled/different, to specific services and supports. While these all sound fabulous in the abstract, in the arena of politics and funding, visions and organizations compete with each other. For some parents, their view of rights is dominated by self-determination and accessibility. For others, the prioritization of individual rights, integration, and freedom seem like abstract concepts imposed from external organizations over families with few resources and options, actually serving as a neoliberal excuse to abandon their family members to dangerous situations without the structure or supports that they need to prosper or even survive.

Allies and Obstacles celebrates parental activism and problematizes it. For better or worse, our intimate family members have tremendous power to shape our lives, on both a micro and a macro level. In the realm of disability, this influence potentially extends throughout one's life. Parents operate within systems that feel tremendously constraining, yet their agency also must be recognized. They have contributed to building a vast system of services, driving market demand for therapies and treatments, raising awareness, demanding rights, and variously enforcing both segregation and integration. They are a political force to be reckoned with, and they have shaped history, policy, and the experience of disability.

Chapter Organization

In *Allies and Obstacles*, we first set out to document the historical growth and complexity of parent activism. To do this, in Part I we offer four case studies, each its own chapter, focusing on intellectual disability, mental illness, autism, and a broad range of physical disabilities. These chapters do not represent the entire range of parent activism; activism related to blindness and deafness is notably absent, as is activism related to chronic disease. Each history could be far more extensive. However, the case study approach has particular advantages. Each case study provides the opportunity to show the broad historical transformations and effects of parent activism, as well as to delve deeply into the ways in which activism grew in each community and developed a particular relationship to disability activism and self-advocacy. In this way, we document varied histories of parent activism, illuminate similarities across histories, and explore variation in timing, strategies, and core issues in each community.

The case studies begin with intellectual disability because parents of people with intellectual disabilities have been on the forefront of parent advocacy. Chapter 1 highlights the ways in which parents moved toward a social model of disability and a rights approach, eventually offering some support for self-advocacy. These features fostered alliance with disabled activists; however, the role of parent organizations in delivering services, their claims to parent authority, and a sense that they have tried to control and co-opt self-advocates have often put them at odds with self-advocates with intellectual and developmental disabilities. We then move to mental illness in Chapter 2. Like people with intellectual disabilities, people with diagnoses of mental illness experienced similar conditions of institutionalization and exclusion, but in this case parent activism emerged in a later era. This case explores the rise of activism among "psychiatric survivors" who criticize the psychiatric profession and its relationship to parent groups who often focus on treatment, recovery, and even involuntary hospitalization. The case study in Chapter 3 examines parent activism regarding autism. Historically, children with autism were often subsumed into the population of children with intellectual disabilities, and it was not until distinct treatments and approaches were developed for autism that parental advocacy also became sharply distinct. When it did emerge, parent groups like Autism Speaks presented a highly medicalized view of autism and pursued a politics of eradication, in sharp contrast with autistic self-advocates. In

Chapter 4, we turn to a range of organizations with parent involvement related to physical disabilities. Many of these emerged around the same time as parent organizations related to intellectual disability, and this chapter shows the trends toward professionalization and the impact of fundraising in particular on parent advocacy.

The case studies serve as the basis for Part II, which provides analytic chapters examining parent activism across disability groups. In these chapters, we rely on historical comparative methods, interviews, and content analysis of organizational and internet sources. In Chapter 5, we examine the timing of parent activism to address why parent-led movements emerged in particular times. In Chapter 6, we consider the relationship of parent-led organizations to organizations led by disabled activists, building a model of the factors influencing parent activism, taking into account the timing, content/goals, and alliance strategies of parent organizations. Chapter 7 looks at the strategies used by parents to affect disability policy. Chapters 8 and 9 move away from an organizational focus to focus more on parents' perspectives and experiences. We explore the complicated ways in which parents conceive of and use the language of rights, and then we use a life course perspective to explore how needs and interests transform as both children and parents age. Finally, we conclude with an overview of our arguments and a practical discussion of alliance. Although this book in some ways focuses on tensions and divisions, ultimately we hope that bringing these divisions to light and shedding light on the varied perspectives will open opportunities for insight and pathways toward collaboration.

A Note on Language

Language related to disability is always controversial, and we see varied language conventions in play within different activist communities. *Person-first language* tends to be common among professionals and parents broadly; it is also the language recommended by Self-Advocates Becoming Empowered, the national self-advocacy organization for people within the intellectual disability community. This linguistic convention places the person before a diagnostic label in order to respect the holism of a person and the diverse identities a person may have. In other words, people are not defined by their disabilities. *Disability-first language* is common in other circles, such as among activists with physical disabilities and autistic self-advocates. Disability-first language prioritizes the shared collective experience of disability and expresses the value of that experience. Typical terms within disability-first usage are "autistic person" and "disabled people."

Other linguistic controversies exist. Some activists who have experienced diagnosis and treatment by the psychiatric industries refer to themselves as psychiatric survivors, indicating the harm committed against them, not by the mental illness but by the psychopharmaceutical industries that promoted mass institutionalization, forced medicalization, and aversive therapies. Some have also reclaimed the term "mad," playing with the double entendre: they are a proud collective gathered under the social label of "mad," and they are angered by the invalidation of their personhood based on this label. The term "crip" represents another act of reclamation, as some people with physical disabilities embrace the powerful imagery of diverse embodiment laden in this term.[71] In contrast, self-advocates with intellectual disabilities have not reclaimed the word "retarded"; instead, they have launched a successful campaign: "Spread the word to end the word."

In navigating the complexities of disability language, we strive to use the language conventions preferred by disability activists within each group when discussing that population. We also vary our language, moving between person first and disability first. We do this in an effort to be respectful to the various valued communities relevant to this project and their views on language. Also, the authors' own backgrounds embed them within communities that espouse different language conventions. Allison is most deeply connected to the intellectual disability community, in which self-advocates expect person-first language, and Pam is part of the autism community, in which disability-first language is highly valued. While our approach may not please all communities, we hope readers will understand the deep respect we accord various activist communities.

I

Disability Activist Communities

1

Intellectual Disability
and Parent Activism

When her son, Marsel, was born in 1985 in an Eastern European country, Emina quickly realized that almost no services existed for people with disabilities. Marsel had brain damage, leading to multiple disabilities including intellectual disability, cerebral palsy, and seizures. He is also nonverbal. At the time, her government was transitioning from a communist to a socialist government, and the new administration for the first time allowed the formation of citizen groups distinct from the political party in power. Emina, a professor of English at a prestigious university, allied with the psychological director at the country's only special education school to create a parents' group. Recognizing the value of her work, the recently created Ministry of Social Welfare added a new department of disability services in 1992 and invited Emina to serve as its first director. In the next two years, Emina worked to close the institutions, reopen facilities with educational and transitional programs, introduce inclusive education into the K–12 curriculum, and fund a program for caregiver support and personal assistance.

Emina moved her family to the United States in 1995 to study social work and to increase access to services for her son. Although change was happening in her home country, the process would move too slowly to benefit her son. She joined a family support services council and began promoting inclusive programming. Marsel wanted to be a part of everything, and Emina wanted him to be fully accepted in the same places and ways that her second son experienced. She stated, "I could get services for my kid, but they didn't make that big of a difference if he was separate. I needed to create a world where he was accepted."[1]

Now a professor of social work, Emina focuses her work on assisting organizations and programs in re-envisioning their services toward inclusion and training professionals in the field to implement inclusive programs. She engages in the nitty-gritty political and organizational work to create the administrative, funding, and staffing structures needed for inclusion. She collaborated in the formation of her university's disability studies program, created several inclusive recreational opportunities, and researches ways to build the social capital of people with disabilities. She continues to work with her country of origin and the World Bank, guiding international disability policy.

She often faces resistance from local parents who believe that her focus on inclusion is misguided. She has been accused of being a foreigner who does not understand America, of being a privileged professor who is not in touch with the needs of everyday families, and of being an ideologue who imposes her views on others. She notes that many parents are skeptical of inclusion because they believe that their child will not benefit or will be abused or bullied in inclusive settings. Usually, though, once they participate in inclusive recreation or try an inclusive day program, they see the differences. She also faces resistance from professionals. Professionals often define "inclusion" as one's physical presence in the community. Emina counters that we must support interaction, participation, and friendships. For example, bowling in the community is not inclusive if her son arrives, bowls, and leaves, all with a group of people with disabilities and paid staff, and then proceeds to the next disability-specific activity. But she is pragmatic. If organizations are not prepared for inclusion, she works directly with them to train the staff, redesign protocols, alter assessments, and address funding concerns. She finds "real resistance" to inclusion, but over the years the conversations have started changing and minds are slowly opening to the value of inclusion.

Marsel is now thirty-four. He lives in a three-person group home with roommates and staff of his choice, attends two day programs, attends several inclusive recreational programs, and has a life independent of (but still intertwined with) his mother. Change is still slow, though. Despite her work, his day programs still tend to define inclusion as his physical presence in the community, rather than ensuring that he has a valued role and friends in the community, and his staff deprioritize supporting him in making friends beyond his disability-specific programming.

Emina's story offers an example of parents who have to build programs from scratch, as many American parents did in the 1950s and still do. It also highlights that many of the systems created by parents in the 1950s like sheltered workshops and day programs were cutting-edge in their day but today are increasingly criticized for imposing segregation and low expectations on people with disabilities. Transitioning these systems toward inclusive practices is an ongoing struggle that deeply divides parents, as many of them prefer disability-specific services and others desire inclusive services. Some parents suggest that their children, especially children with significant disabilities, need disability-specific services and cannot benefit from inclusion, but Marsel challenges this idea; he needs twenty-four-hour supervision and supports but lives in a small, person-centered house, exercises choice, and uses his waiver funding to control his life, with input from his support team.

In the mid-twentieth century in localities around America, parents of children with disabilities stepped out of the shadow of shame that enveloped them and embraced an increasingly fierce political stance that within a few decades reshaped the opportunities for people with intellectual disabilities in America. When we consider activism among parents of children with disabilities, parents of children with intellectual disabilities have been on the forefront in many ways. They were among the earliest to organize, and they have been remarkably successful in achieving vast social transformation. Banding together and utilizing a range of social change techniques, parents helped build a more inclusive world, not just for their own children but for other people with and without intellectual disabilities too. In doing so, parents and their largest organization, the Arc, have become a common ally of disability rights organizations led by disabled activists and helped position people with intellectual disabilities alongside all people with disabilities as deserving inclusion and access.

Despite the idea of a "parents' movement," the aspirations of parents have always been diverse. The parents' movement began as a grassroots movement that was diverse in its goals and organization. As the movement gained national power and sharpened its advocacy tools, the largest parent organization for people with intellectual disabilities—the Arc—focused its agenda on disability rights and inclusion. While enabling greater alliance with disability rights organizations, the focus on rights and inclusion marginalized parents with different values and needs. The Arc's role as a major service provider also blunted its capacity to demand inclusion as it continued to operate segregated, disability-specific programs like sheltered workshops and day programs. Parents today remain divided on many issues, most visibly regarding their position on integrated versus segregated supports. Many parents see a role for specialized and segregated settings in meeting the needs of their children and adult offspring, believing that such settings provide more sheltered, nurturing environments that cater to the special needs of their children. Other parents fight to increase opportunities for maximal integration in housing, work, education, and other opportunities. Parents therefore are often pitted against each other.

Self-advocates with intellectual disabilities entered the political fray in the 1970s and 1980s, forming their own national self-advocacy organization in 1990. Locally, self-advocacy organizations vary considerably from support groups to focusing on macro political transformation. On the national level, Self-Advocates Becoming Empowered (SABE) allies itself with activists with disabilities, asserts control over its own agenda, and stridently advocates for inclusion and self-determination. SABE criticizes many parent and professional organizations, even the more progressive ones, for their continued support of segregated services and their domination of disability policy without including people with intellectual disabilities. For self-advocates, the fact that the Arc both tries to advocate for people with disabilities *and* runs one of the largest network of nonprofit services in the country represents a conflict of interest, impeding the Arc's ability to criticize and defund its own systems even when those systems hinder the self-determination of people with intellectual disabilities.

The rich history of the parents' movement for intellectual disability could itself fill a book, and, fortunately, an increasing number of studies have begun documenting this history.[2] This chapter has a narrow set of goals: (1) to explain the emergence and framing of parent activism and (2) to explore the contemporary tensions among parents and between parents and activists with intellectual disabilities and the consequences of these tensions.

Considering Intellectual Disability

Before we begin discussing the history of activism related to intellectual disabilities, we must first clarify the term "intellectual disability." Intellectual disability, like each of the conditions in this book, is a contested label.[3]

In general, intellectual disability is a label associated with three key components: (1) an IQ significantly lower than average (typically defined as 70–75 and below), (2) combined with significant limitations in "adaptive behavior" reducing a person's ability to meet the cultural and social expectations given their age, (3) which originates before the age of eighteen.[4]

Societies have always had members who were considered to have lower intelligence, yet the labels, the bases on which the labels were given, and the response to the labels have varied tremendously through history. Each label—such as "slow," "backward," "idiot," "imbecile," "feebleminded," "special," "mentally retarded," "mentally challenged," and "intellectually disabled"[5]—carried its own set of assumptions and definitions. For example, in the eighteenth and early nineteenth centuries when America was an agricultural society with a low level of literacy, most people were not expected to demonstrate mastery in reading, writing, math, or science. "Idiocy"—the legal term at the time—typically referred only to those with a very significant disability, and people with milder forms of intellectual disability went mostly unnoticed.[6] In contrast, in the early 1900s America's elite felt anxious about the changing demographics and power dynamics related to industrialization, urbanization, and mass immigration. In this context, professionals generously applied the label "feeblemindedness" to a broad range of people deemed socially undesirable, including criminals, single mothers, poor people, and immigrants.[7]

We like to think that in our day and age medical diagnoses are objective and apolitical; however, the political maneuvering of disability labels is by no means an issue of the past. For example, in 2002, in the case *Atkins v. Virginia*, the Supreme Court prohibited the death penalty for people with "mental retardation" (the medical term most commonly used from 1950 to 1990) because it constituted cruel and unusual punishment. In response to this ruling, some states, including Florida and Texas, created stricter definitions to reduce the number of people who could claim this new protection.[8]

The Emergence of Parent Activism Related to Intellectual Disability

Although some form of "intellectual disability" has been acknowledged throughout American history, there was not collective, organized parent activism related to it for most of that time. Parent activism was encouraged by medicalization, blended with rising expectations, increasing resources, and new political opportunities, much of which was driven by the growing institutional system.

Early Barriers to Activism

Social movement scholars have long noted that oppression alone is not sufficient to lead to activism. For much of early American history, life was challenging for people with intellectual disabilities and their family members, yet there was little activism to rectify the situation.

In the late 1700s and early 1800s, when America was a young nation, social policy rarely identified disability as a significant concern unless it impeded one's livelihood or threatened the functioning of the community. Disease and disability were common, living conditions rough, and literacy rates low; in these conditions, community members expected a high prevalence of mental and physical disabilities, and families and communities provided support as feasible.[9] There was not yet a medical or a social service infrastructure that identified intellectual disability as a specific problem or offered specific professional solutions for it. Although the situation was not ideal, engaging in activism to improve the lot of people with intellectual disabilities specifically would not have made sense in this context.

By the mid-1800s, care was becoming increasingly specialized and medicalized, leading to the emergence of institutions specifically for people defined as "feebleminded" (as well as institutions for people labeled as "insane"). In part, the growth of these new facilities represented a hopeful perspective. Reformers like Samuel Gridley Howe believed that education and training could transform people marginalized by disability or other life circumstances into upright and productive citizens.[10] However, the politics of institutionalization became increasingly dominated by eugenics and the desire to segregate and control those deemed abnormal, dangerous, and unproductive. Feeblemindedness, according to eugenicists, led to criminality, sexual promiscuity, and poverty. As it was believed to be a hereditary condition, diagnosis implicated the entire family and lineage as "defective." Given these views, much of the growth of institutionalization had little to do with the provision of "care" and more to do with imposition of social control.[11]

Not surprisingly, given the cultural climate of the day, many parents felt a deep shame regarding disability in their family and chose to deny its existence. For some families this meant raising their child as "normally" as possible, in ways closely aligned with expectations of the day. For other families, it meant hiding the child or placing the child in the growing institutional system away from their families.[12] Professionals increasingly recommended early institutional placement, especially for children with Down syndrome, whose disability could be diagnosed at birth by its physical manifestations. Doctors told parents that families and communities lacked the skills to provide the necessary care whereas institutions would offer safe and nurturing environments. Good parents, according to most doctors, placed their child with intellectual disabilities in an institution.[13]

Despite the promises, institutional care was atrocious. Institutions grew, but funding did not keep pace. Before long, most public institutions were overcrowded, understaffed, and characterized by abuse and neglect rather than treatment and education. For example, as early as 1937 Pennsylvania Governor George H. Earle said he "found conditions [in public institutions] that were so lacking in humaneness as to be almost unbelievable in a great civilized Commonwealth."[14] Despite many promises of reform over the years, conditions worsened, fueled by overcrowding and limited resources.[15] New York's Willowbrook State School was designed for four thousand people, but by 1965 it held six thousand residents in conditions that led Senator Robert Kennedy to call it a "snake pit."[16] Most institutional residents never received educational or rehabilitative services, and their disabilities were made worse through neglect, isolation, and abuse. Families were made to feel ashamed for having a child with an intellectual disability, and they were faced with terrible choices: to forfeit their child to the institutional system in hopes of proper care or raise a stigmatized child at home with no supports.[17]

One might imagine that such terrible circumstances would prompt activism, but there was little macro-level activism before the 1940s. Parents were isolated, ashamed, and lacked a vision for some better alternative future. The institutional system explicitly encouraged and even forced parents to cut ties with their institutionalized offspring and forfeit their legal parenting rights. Parents had little power in their interaction with administrators, and they feared that any complaints would be met with retaliation by institutional staff. Retaliation might come in the form of the denial of already meager services to their child, the denial of "rewards" such as play time or a weekly shower, or abuse. A parent of an institutionalized child wrote in 1948, "Parents with this type of child are handicapped by the fact that there is no other way to care for them and if they state their belief that something is wrong with the manner in which an institution is managed, the child may not even get what attention he is receiving."[18] In addition, because most parents did not live in close proximity to the institution, and speaking openly about disability met with social disapproval, building social ties with other families was challenging at best. Many parents felt socially isolated and marginalized, even though thousands of other parents were experiencing similar heartbreak. Of her many trips to Willowbrook State School, a sibling recalls, "All these people who had so much pain in common, so much insight to share with each other, never talked to each other, because of the shame."[19]

Institutions also hindered collective activism among the residents. To consider why, it is useful to compare institutions for people with intellectual disabilities with the specialized schools for students with blindness or Deafness, which did foster disability activism. Specialized schools for Deaf or blind students typically taught students a valuable set of skills such as Braille and American Sign Language (ASL), and these skills enabled students to build a sense of shared community. In these collective communities, students recognized the vast and diverse abilities of people who shared their experience, and they had the opportunity (many for the first time) to collectively explore their capabilities and dreams. Moreover, these schools provided training for several years with the expectation of their students' return to the community and their engagement in society as productive citizens.[20] In contrast, institutions for people with intellectual disabilities functioned largely as custodial warehouses and rarely offered education or training. The residents often became more, rather than less, disabled, too often allowed to roam naked and sit for hours at a time with little to do. Without attention to basic hygiene, disease spread. Residents suffered abuse from other residents and from staff, and the institutional administration intensely restricted their movement and activities. Under these conditions, residents struggled for mere survival; they did not gain the requisite skills to engage in activism, the sense of collective pride that typically undergirds activism, or the hope of returning to the community. Thus, for people with intellectual disabilities and their families, the segregation imposed through institutionalization seemed unlikely to offer an effective catalyst for change.

Factors Promoting the Rise of Parent Activism

The growing institutional system, however, did sow the seeds for change in particular ways. Medicalization and related social policies increasingly identified particular people as "feebleminded" and treated them accordingly, creating a building block for a collective identity and eventually collective resistance. "Embodied social movements," in which the politics of the body are central, often arise in relationship to a medical diagnosis, treatment, and prevention policies that are contested by those diagnosed.[21] In other words, although much of the same oppression existed prior to the establishment of a medical diagnosis, "without a disease definition or an official diagnosis sufferers are left to make sense of their own illness experience," and therefore they have little basis for building a shared collective identity or collective resistance.[22]

Although institutions explicitly worked to isolate parents from each other, institutions also created a potential network of parents with something in common. When James Oakley set out to create a parent group in 1936, institutional administrators would not share names of the residents or their parents. He instead placed an ad in the Seattle paper seeking parents connected to the State Custodial School in Washington to discuss forms of collaboration. Thus, parents organized some of the first parent groups in the 1930s and 1940s as institution-specific collectives to address the needs of their children through fundraising, monitoring the institutions, and providing other forms of support for the institution.[23] These groups were hardly radical. Parents organized in a fashion similar to a parent-teacher association (PTA) to build cooperation between families and school professionals, to harness the resources (e.g., money, time, energy) of parents to improve the school and their children's lives, and to provide social support to each other. That said, they served as an important step in breaking down shame and building a valued collective identity.

Institutionalization also created a growing infrastructure of resources, policies, and professionals focused on intellectual disability and an associated set of promises of care or treatment.[24] The institutional system expanded rapidly through the early and mid-twentieth century and received significant and steadily increasing funding.[25] Public funding for special education and vocational rehabilitation also grew quickly.[26] In other words, disability, and intellectual disability specifically, became a significant budget line for state administrations. With that much money dedicated to intellectual disability, the goals, uses, and amounts of that money could be contested.

And contestation made sense to parents. For all the money being spent, institutions produced dismal outcomes. Professionals, institutional administrators, and the state promised parents that the institution would provide care, education, and friendships with similar peers. These promises raised the expectations of parents, but the system failed to deliver.[27] As summarized by a parent, "[Residents] come for help and care. What they get is custody."[28] In early America, parents did not feel entitled to any support just because their child had a disability. But now, after years of listening to professional advice extolling the importance of treatment, enduring separation from their children, dealing with signs of institutional abuse, and seeing millions of dollars being channeled into systems of professional "care," parents felt angered by the lack of quality services and the money wasted relative to the promises they had been given.

This sense of injustice affected not only parents with children in institutions but also parents who wanted access to education and treatment while keeping their children at home. Indeed, the first parents' group on record related to intellectual disability, the Council for Retarded Children in Cayuga County, Ohio, was not institution specific. Parents organized it to address the exclusion of children from public education. They began arguing that (1) the state and professionals had an obligation to deliver on their promises of education and treatment, (2) the money already dedicated to institutional care could be better spent on providing actual education, treatment, and productive work opportunities both in institutions and in the community, and (3) more funding was required to ensure that institutions and new community services fulfilled their stated mission. Thus, the growth of the institutional and professional system to address intellectual disability raised expectations and created a pot of dedicated money for service provision, yet the system failed to meet expectations, thereby sparking the motivation for activism.

As parents' activism grew, they were further advantaged by a series of political opportunities, beginning in the 1940s with World War II and President Roosevelt's New Deal.[29] President Roosevelt, who had a physical disability as a result of childhood polio, encouraged federal and state monetary commitments to programs such as vocational rehabilitation, access to assistive technology, and special education. Then in the 1960s, the Kennedy family rose to power, and they had a particular interest in intellectual disability. John's sister, Rosemary, had an intellectual disability, and he created federal opportunities for social change.[30] Parents cultivated additional political access. For example, the friendship between parent activist Arthur Trudeau and Rhode Island Congressman John E. Fogarty encouraged Fogarty to become an early champion of disability rights. Thus, parents enjoyed, and in part created, an exciting new era of political access and opportunity, and organized to seize it.

The burgeoning African American civil rights movement showcased the possibilities of social change, a range of techniques to pursue change, and the power of demanding rights. As we see in the next section, parents drew on the civil rights movement to create a new frame, a new way of understanding the problems and solutions related to intellectual disability, and to experiment with new strategies to enact change.[31] While parents rarely engaged in the direct protest strategies of the civil rights movement (e.g., marches, boycotts), they did begin to imagine new ways that professional expertise and resources could be harnessed to offer rights and opportunities instead of charity and segregation. They also saw the advantages of using the legal system as a tool to fight for justice. In the expansive service system that was emerging, parents wanted a place at the table in decision-making, and they wanted their children and their families to be respected and served well. Increasingly, they said they wanted "rights."

The Evolution of Parent Activism

Grassroots Activism and Meeting Families' Needs

Because of the conditions discussed above, in the 1940s, 1950s, and 1960s, parents began organizing to raise awareness, create basic services, and find fellowship and support.[32] According to historian Katherine Castles, by 1950 there were at least eighty-eight local parent groups in nineteen states, with a total of approximately 19,300 members. In 1950, the Arc[33] was founded, the first national organization of parents to advocate on behalf of people with intellectual disabilities. By 1960, it estimated its membership at 62,000 members, and now boasts its position as one of the largest nonprofit organizations in America.

Early local groups were often focused on meeting the basic needs of families who lacked access to any kinds of services or supports. Activist Eleanor Elkins described the earliest years of the Pennsylvania chapter of the Arc (PARC), "We tried to find out what each [family] needed the most and tried to work toward that."[34] Kate Fialkowski remembered that, at a time when many families were still ashamed of their children with intellectual disabilities, her mother encouraged the creation of supportive parent communities:

> I think that one of the most amazing things about our mother is that she helped people come out into the light of day, you know, . . . not fighting the system, not fighting anything, not going to court, none of that, just come outside, tell your neighbors what you need. Call me. Call each other, and so these parents' groups started forming where parents could support each other. Parents could go over and watch each other's kids so they could get out five minutes, have five minutes off or go to the grocery store and do something. But it was pretty—it was just really, really remarkable that there were whole families that were just trapped inside their house.[35]

Organizing offered parents a sense of solidarity and opportunities for collective problem solving. To meet their varied needs, parents used multiple strategies: building support systems; spreading awareness; creating local demonstration projects including the creation of schools, day care programs, recreational programs, and sheltered workshops; demanding inclusion in community programs; and ultimately engaging in a range of political activism such as lobbying and court action to demand change.[36] Schools, classes, and programs for children with intellectual disabilities began popping up throughout the country, often managed and staffed by parents. Parents were largely responsible for the grassroots growth of community services for this population.

One of the most pressing needs early on was to raise awareness and dispel common stereotypes regarding intellectual disabilities. Challenging the view of eugenicists and medical professionals, parents argued that their children were not defective or a threat to the nation. They were merely developing more slowly than other children, and could learn if given love, acceptance, education, and opportunity. Whereas the label "feebleminded" was associated with depravity, parents encouraged the use of a new term, "mental retardation," to reflect the idea that these children experienced slowed development (as opposed to a more fundamental and inferior variation of development that led to moral depravity). The term "special" also came into vogue to indicate the value and unique needs of these children.

Parents argued that, in many ways, their children were just like other children: gentle, lovable, innocent, and pure, with "a child's happy faculty of living in a world where play is a reality."[37] Yet their children were also unlike other children because they needed more, not less, of the same basic things that other children needed: more hours of education, more services from professionals, and more love and attention. The Arc's statement of rights at the time captures these ideals, stating that children with mental retardation have "in general all the needs of other children" yet are "exceptional, not because they differ from us all in having these needs, but because they have additional or exceptional needs over and above the needs common to the majority."[38]

Early parent activism relied on a medical model to some degree. They understood mental retardation as a disability that would be medically identified, that services would be based on diagnosis, and that the goal would be to move as close to "normality" as possible through the receipt of professional interventions. Research into diagnosis, prevention, and cure were identified by the Arc as key goals. However, the medical model was only a minor part of their new frame. In fact, parents sharply criticized the medical community for abandoning their children and offering little in the way of hope or treatment. Parents of children with Down syndrome were some of the first parents of children with disabilities to offer a strong and direct challenge to the medical community's role in child-rearing, most likely because they were confronted with medical prejudice immediately at the birth of their child and even in the 1960s received advice to institutionalize their child early in life.[39] For example, doctors told the parents of Nigel Hunt after his birth in 1947 that, regardless of how much effort they exerted, he would always be an "idiot."[40] Despite this prognosis, Nigel grew up able to read, write, travel, and make friends, serving as living proof of the error of medical prognosis. Twenty years later, his father, Douglas Hunt, assured parents "that the 'experts' are often wrong and that almost all defective children are capable of being taught a great deal more than people care to admit."[41] Similarly, in the 1940s doctors told Sophia Grant that her son would never learn or go to school.[42] Grant demonstrated, though, that through a rigorous routine of home education her son could learn basic math and reading, some French, and to play the piano. Grant's condemnation of the medical profession was explicit and harsh: "People do not know what to do, and yet they have the audacity to give such authoritative and final advice to the distracted mothers who come to them. . . . A word of comfort here, mothers. Don't let them get you down, for they have not the slightest idea what to do with these mentally retarded children. In fact, it is a waste of time to consult them."[43]

Since there was no medical cure for intellectual disability and the medical treatment that had been offered—institutions—had been disastrous, parents saw medical professionals as offering little other than low expectations. Increasingly, they turned to educational professionals and the social service system to provide a host of supports to encourage their child's development and participation. Thus, parent activism stressed *the social model of disability*, emphasizing that the denial of opportunities (not the disability) limited their children's chance to develop. Therefore, inclusion and services, not medical cure, were the best responses.[44] Parents challenged exclusion and prejudice against their children. In 1952, the Arc summed up its mission as the following: "To give every retarded individual the opportunity which is the birthright of every American—the opportunity to develop to his or her fullest capacity."[45] All children, including those with intellectual disabilities, deserved the right to participate in society.

The rhetoric of the Arc created an illusion of a more unified movement than what really existed. While the Arc blossomed, there were many varieties and strands of parent activism inside and outside of the Arc. The Arc's organizational structure provided considerable flexibility in the goals and activities of its local and state chapters. Some parents focused on improving or expanding institutional care, while others wanted to build community services. Among those in the community, some had children already in public schools and they sought to enhance education in the public schools or create additional services, while others were denied access to public education and had to create classes or schools to serve their children or fight to gain entry to public schools.[46] Some parents had adult offspring who needed jobs and supports outside of a school context. Some parents focused on specific conditions like Down syndrome, what was becoming known as autism, or the needs of people with severe or multiple disabilities, while others wanted to address children with disabilities more broadly. Many non-Arc groups existed as local support groups, to deliver services, and to address local goals.

Race and class also divided parents, evidenced by several city- and state-level histories. A 1968 study of the Providence, Rhode Island, chapter found the average Arc member to be a white, married female, although Providence was (and is) a diverse city.[47] David Goode's 1998 study of New York City's Association for the Help of Retarded Children similarly describes it as a largely white, middle-class organization, despite the diversity of New York City.[48] For Washington state, Jones reports that the minority membership of the Washington Arc was "miniscule," and there was limited interest in addressing issues of poverty or race.[49]

Unifying the Agenda and the Civil Rights Frame

In the 1950s and 1960s, the Arc treated the variation in goals and strategies among parents mostly as an acceptable diversity of interests and needs. As parent activism became more national in scope and politically successful, though, the Arc focused its agenda more clearly on rights and inclusion, allying with a cadre of lawyers and professional advocates to advance its agenda via lobbying and the courts. This focus led to greater unity of purpose but also to deeper fissures among those who differed in philosophies, goals, and resources.

The fight for education exemplified this shift. Initially, parents worked to create educational opportunities in their local communities in whatever ways seemed most efficient and effective for them. As activism grew, parents began dreaming of sweeping educational reform at the state and even national levels. The fight for education fit well with the emerging civil rights framework, arguing that children with intellectual disabilities had rights like all other children. In preparation for legal action, PARC passed "A Bill of Rights for Pennsylvania's Retarded Citizens" (1969), affirming that "every retarded person, no matter how handicapped he is, is first of all in possession of human, legal and social rights. As much as possible retarded persons, whether institutionalized or not, should be treated like other ordinary persons of their age are treated in the community."[50] Parents argued that equality did not simply entail the provision of the *same* opportunities to all people. Children with disabilities should have the same right to education, but they also needed *additional* services and supports appropriate to their needs. Equality had to take differences into account and provide necessary services and supports. Additional educational services were not charity; they too were a right.

In 1971, in *PARC v. Commonwealth of Pennsylvania*, parents achieved a monumental victory. The court mandated that all children with disabilities receive a free, public, appropriate education. The court endorsed the principle of the least restrictive environment, specifying that "placement in a regular public school class is preferable to placement in a special public school class and placement in a special public school class is preferable to placement in any other type of program of education and training."[51] Furthermore, it affirmed parents' right to due process in relation to educational decision and to participate in such decisions. The decision opened the doors to thousands of children who had been denied a public education. Other court cases quickly followed, and in 1975 Congress passed the Individuals with Disabilities Education Act (IDEA), originally titled the Education for All Handicapped Children Act, a milestone in the fight for civil rights for children with disabilities. By 1984, more than 90 percent of disabled children were receiving an education in integrated schools.[52]

Parents were jubilant at their victory, but it raised concerns for some parents. Parents of institutionalized children worried that expanded public education might lead to the defunding of institutions. Assurances were made to ease those tensions. For example, in Washington, parents encouraged the addition of a provision ensuring that no child could be removed from the juvenile court without guardian approval, thereby convincing parents that public education would not lead to deinstitutionalization.[53] On the national level, IDEA expressed a preference for integrated education but also conferred significant power to educators and parents to determine the most "appropriate" education, a loosely defined phrase that could include an integrated class, a disability-specific class, or a disability-specific school (among other options). Thus, children gained the right to an education, *and* parents gained a voice at the decision-making table and a significant degree of flexibility in defining the best education for their child.

Success in educational reform emboldened many parents to push harder for institutional reform and the reallocation of funds to community services. This battle more forcefully divided parents. Parents had long criticized the conditions of public institutions as well as the lack of available services both in institutions and in the community. At first the Arc did not advocate deinstitutionalization; in fact, some parents begged for an expansion of the institutional system. Parents believed that institutional overcrowding and poor staffing caused abuse and neglect, and these problems could be rectified through reforming and expanding the institutional system as well as expanding community services.[54] For example, in a 1952 letter to a governor, an activist parent begged for more institutional beds:

> A mentally retarded child is not a temporary problem—it is a lifetime problem. He must be given the opportunity to live in his own world, with friends of his own kind—not made to bear the abuse of normal children who never realize how cruel they can be—and also from society in general who never heard of the problem of mentally retarded children because nobody ever made any effort to help these children publicly as they have polio or cerebral palsy victims.[55]

As time passed, though, parents became increasingly frustrated with the institutional system, its continued neglect of its residents, and the state's singular reliance on it rather than on providing a continuum of services. Arc leaders came to see institutional preservation and community care *as competing*, rather than complementary, paths to meeting the needs of people with disabilities. A parent explained, "This pouring of public dollars into an archaic and deteriorating residential system in turn perpetuates the shortage of community services which, in turn, accentuates the urgency for the creation of additional residential services which are storing up an ever larger number of individuals since those ready to be returned to the community cannot be released because of the inadequacy of supportive community services. A vicious cycle indeed."[56]

Families came together to sue the state regarding institutional conditions. In *Halderman v. Pennhurst State School and Hospital* (1977), Judge Broderick found that Pennhurst "provides confinement and isolation, the antithesis of habilitation,"[57] and he became the first judge to mandate that all residents be moved into community placements, in effect ordering the closure of Pennhurst. In the same year, parents sued the state of New York in a historic class action suit, *New York State Arc v. Rockefeller,* regarding conditions at Willowbrook State School.[58] Willowbrook had become infamous as the largest public institution for people with intellectual disabilities, the site of unethical medical experimentation on residents,[59] and the subject of the 1972 national exposé by Geraldo Rivera, *Willowbrook: The Last Disgrace.* It took three years for the consent decree to be issued mandating community placement for residents and an additional twelve years before Willowbrook closed its doors.

In 1968 the Arc demanded immediate eradication of inhumane treatment and improvement in the quality of care in state institutions, and in 1971 President Nixon declared deinstitutionalization to be national policy, alongside a commitment to the building of community services. At the 1982 Arc National Convention, Arc delegates approved a resolution declaring the right of all persons to community-based services, regardless of the severity of their disability.[60] Parents had again played a major role in ensuring the rights of people with intellectual disabilities and preventing their segregation and abuse.

While some parents applauded the suits that led to institutional closure, other parents were horrified at this aggressive action against institutions and the public airing of the "dirty laundry" of the institutional system. Mandated closures intensified the division among parents. Many of the parents who had engaged in activism and even lawsuits, including the mother of the lead plaintiff in *Halderman v. Pennhurst*, desired reform, not closure. They feared closure would lead to the loss of services and the dissolution of long-standing relationships with institutional administrators. Parents were also outraged by the Arc's use of class-action suits, creating a legal class covering all residents regardless of the sentiments of the parents and thereby *usurping* parental authority. Parental authority is a central tenet of the parents' movement, and undercutting it was unforgivable to some parents given their experience of helplessness in dealing with institutional and medical systems. They wanted to be empowered and offered choices, not displaced by national organizations who claimed to speak for their children.

For the Arc, it became increasingly clear that it could not simultaneously advocate for all families *and* pursue a disability rights agenda framed in terms of community integration for all. The goal of parental authority undercut a rights agenda for people with disabilities that mandated community inclusion. One direction would have to be prioritized. The Arc opted to focus its national-level political agenda on pursuing rights, primarily defined as maximal opportunity for integration. This decision created internal and external tensions. Internally, the Arc's commitment to the rights agenda was undercut by its desire to maintain a base of parent support, its role as one of the largest service providers for people with intellectual disabilities with a vast infrastructure of segregated services, and its relatively decentralized organizational structure, which gave it little control over the local chapters, who deliver services.

Externally, the Arc faced growing competition both in advocacy and in service delivery. Parents unhappy with deinstitutionalization did not just remain silent; they organized in support of institutional and segregated or "specialized" facilities and in opposition to mandated community inclusion. Polly Spare, who would become president of Voice of the Retarded (VOR), a national group dedicated to maintaining facility-based residential and congregate care options, illustrates this path. Spare became a prominent parent activist while opposing the closure of Pennhurst. Her daughter, Sandra, was born in 1952. Sandra was nonverbal and required significant care throughout her lifetime. When Sandra was young, Spare worked with the local Arc to create local programs for people with disabilities. But even with help at home, advocacy skills, and growing community programming, Spare believed she could not provide a sufficient level of care and supervision to keep Sandra safe. When Sandra was ten, Spare placed her at Pennhurst. She was dismayed when Judge Broderick mandated Pennhurst's closure and fought the decision. Spare explained, "I preferred the institutional structure for those who were the most severely disabled because of their needs. We did not have doctors in the community who were familiar with all of this."[61] Spare argued that deinstitutionalization deprived her daughter of access to high-quality care at the site chosen by her family. Control over her daughter's care was wrested away from her and her husband and placed instead in the hands of advocates who sought to fund a system of community services regardless of one's desire for them. Although she did not win the fight to keep Pennhurst open, she did secure state funding for Sandra to live in a private facility, in effect moving her from one institution to another, more expensive institution. Spare emerged as a leader of VOR and a role model for those who would fight against deinstitutionalization in other states.

VOR was not the only organization to emerge or splinter off; the number of competing voices in the political marketplace grew substantially after

1970. Other service providers proliferated to meet unmet needs and reap the benefits of expanded funding opportunities. Local parent groups flourished, inspired by the success of the Arc but without being tied to its structure or particular political agenda. Additional national groups emerged to complement and compete with the Arc's national prominence in intellectual disability policy, research, and advocacy. For example, TASH is an important coalition of parents, professionals, and self-advocates founded in 1975 and dedicated to promoting the inclusion of people with significant disabilities, a population that was often overlooked in policy and service delivery. The National Down Syndrome Society was founded in 1979 to focus on specific issues that were not receiving sufficient attention. In particular, because of the physical manifestations of Down syndrome, children with this condition experienced especially harsh stigma. In the modern era of prenatal genetic testing, fetuses with Down syndrome become targets of eugenic eradication. Similarly, parents of children with autism also created organizations dedicated to the conditions and concerns they felt were specific to autism. And people with disabilities, and with intellectual disabilities in particular, organized and stridently demanded inclusion.

The Rise of Self-Advocacy

People with disabilities emerged as a key force in shaping disability law and policy in the late 1960s and their power grew through the 1970s and 1980s. The Independent Living Movement, ADAPT, the Disability Rights Education and Defense Fund, and the National Council on Disability, among other organizations, became potential allies in the fight to close institutions and gain rights, but they also questioned the paternalism and authority of parents, especially nondisabled parents, to speak for their disabled family members. As long as activism by people with disabilities was dominated by people with physical disabilities, though, the presence of parents of people with intellectual disabilities seemed legitimate; parents represented a group of people who could not represent themselves. The rise of self-advocacy by people with intellectual disabilities fundamentally challenged parents' role as a voice for the intellectual disability community.

Like the parents' movement, self-advocacy began as local groups formed in different states, and different countries, with little connection to each other.[62] In 1973, three staff members and two residents of Oregon's Fairview Hospital and Training Center attended a conference for people with "mental retardation" in British Columbia. They resolved to form their own organization, but they wanted theirs to be run *by* people with intellectual disabilities. Self-advocate Valerie Schaaf explained, "We wanted to let those in authority know we are just like them and would like to be treated in the same way.

How would you like it if someone did all your talking for you?"[63] In 1974, People First was created in Oregon. In Nebraska, Ray Loomis struggled to transition to community living after deinstitutionalization and he had a "brainstorm" to create a self-directing group to support people as they transitioned into the community.[64] His group, Project Two, quickly became a political force as former institutional residents publicly shared their experiences and worked to close Nebraska's institutions. At a public forum on institutions in 1977, after a parent offered support for the continued funding of institutions, Project Two members detailed their painful experiences in the institutions and their desire to be in the community. According to Paul Williams and Bonnie Shultz, "It was the first time that mentally handicapped people in Nebraska had spoken out for themselves and against institutionalization of people with handicaps. It may have also been the first time that county officials, businessmen and others really listened to what mentally handicapped people had to say. Speaking for themselves had become a reality."[65] At the end of the 1970s, Project Two was the only organization in Nebraska explicitly demanding the closure of institutions. In Pennsylvania, Luann Carter and support worker Mark Friedman organized a conference in 1982 that led to the formation of Speaking for Ourselves.[66] Former president Roland Johnson explained that its purpose was to "get people out of institutions. Make sure that people can get their rights. Stand up for the client; stand up for people's rights. Make sure that they get all that they can to better the system. And make sure [abuse] does not take place in other places—[community living arrangements] and group homes—because I been a victim to [sic] abuses in places."[67] The self-advocacy movement grew through the 1980s, and by 1986 at least twenty states had self-advocacy groups. In 1990 self-advocates founded the first national self-advocacy organization by people with intellectual disabilities, Self-Advocates Becoming Empowered (SABE).

Self-advocacy organizations vary, with some more focused on peer support and others on pursuing a political agenda. The organizations share a commitment to respect, inclusion, and empowerment of diverse people regardless of abilities and disabilities. SABE's mission is to "ensure that people with disabilities are treated as equals and that they are given the same decisions, choices, rights, responsibilities, and chances to speak up to empower themselves; opportunities to make new friends, and to learn from their mistakes."[68] SABE explicitly chose to align itself with disability rights organizations led by people with disabilities, not with the social service system, professionals, or parents. They created an organizational structure that ensured people with disabilities controlled its leadership.

Self-advocacy has played a significant role in the claiming of rights by and for people with intellectual disabilities, and it has had a complex

relationship with parents' organizations. Many parent and professional organizations have offered tremendous support to self-advocates, including
offering funding, staff facilitation, and space for self-advocacy groups, but
the relationship grows tense when disagreements emerge, such as over the
value of segregated services, guardianship, and political control.[69]

Points of Agreement

There are many points of agreement and collaboration among parent activists and self-advocates. The fight for improved quality and quantity of care
and supports is a defining feature of disability activism for almost anyone
involved. Parents and self-advocates point to continued deficits in education, including children who are isolated or in inappropriate programs
without assistive technology and appropriate supports. Access and expertise
are also insufficient in medical care.[70] Parents and self-advocates argue that
the limited quantity and quality of services and supports has a direct impact
on safety in institutional, family, and community settings. People with intellectual disabilities are particularly vulnerable to abuse, neglect, and harm
as a result of many factors such as physical and social isolation, social devaluation, ignorance, lack of appropriate supports, lack of options for affordable accessible housing and services, and disregard of their victimization by relevant professionals.

Self-advocates and parent activists also tend to agree that they face a
system in which the choices are nonexistent, too few, or terrible. Self-
advocate Liz Obermayer describes it this way:

> But I have a disability. . . . Nobody allows me to make choices. People
> tell me all the time what to wear, what to eat, what job to have and
> who are my friends. Is that fair? I say no. But I have a disability . . .
> people don't listen to me anyway. . . . why should I give my opinions?
> I fight so hard for somebody to listen . . . just want someone to lis-
> ten . . . and give a damn about what I want.[71]

Families similarly resent this lack of choice, although parents may focus on
their own set of choices, not choice by the person with a disability, as shown
in a statement by the Arc:

> No parent really chooses to put his or her child in an institution. It
> is only when no other options are presented that a family "chooses"
> to take this heart-wrenching step. And no persons with mental re-
> tardation "chose" to go to a state institution. Many of us were told to

forget we ever had a child with disabilities and to place them in an institution. Instead, we took our child home and raised him or her (typically with little or no public support or services), formed the Arc and got federal and state laws passed to educate our children in public schools.[72]

The fight against discrimination tends to be a shared cornerstone of disability activism. Discrimination can manifest itself in many ways, even threatening the right to exist. The National Down Syndrome Society (NDSS), for example, challenges the prejudice among medical and science professionals that leads prenatal testing of Down syndrome to be used toward eradication with no consideration of the value of a life with Down syndrome. In discussing prenatal testing with parents, doctors present Down syndrome as a defect, which must be discovered to give parents a "choice" about their pregnancy. In making this choice, parents are given little information about prognosis or the actual lives of people with Down syndrome. Of women who are informed that their fetuses carry the markers of Down syndrome, the vast majority abort.[73] NDSS does not wish to limit choices or access to abortion but rather to challenge the medical framing of this population as defective and the ways in which the testing process encourages selective abortion. Self-advocate Frank Stephens beautifully articulated this concern in official testimony:

> I am a man with Down syndrome and my life is worth living. . . . Some people say that prenatal screening will identify Down syndrome in the womb and those pregnancies will just be terminated. It's hard for me to sit here and say those words. I completely understand that the people pushing this particular "final solution" are saying that people like me should not exist. That view is deeply prejudiced by an outdated idea of life with Down syndrome. Seriously, I have a great life.[74]

Conflicts

Along with agreements, many conflicts remain between parent activists and self-advocates. Most notably, the feud over institutionalization continues and now has broadened to consider the level of segregation acceptable in a range of services, including schools, day programs, sheltered workshops, and group homes. Self-advocacy groups took an early and clear stance against institutions. In contrast, many parents supported institutions, and even those groups that advocated deinstitutionalization allowed it to proceed at a glacial pace. For example, People First of Tennessee was the first disability organization in Tennessee to demand all institutions be closed. It issued the following statement in 1994:

> We believe institutions are harmful and limit life choices. Institutions stop people from exercising their rights and leading a normal life. People with disabilities should have a choice to live where ever and with whomever they want. Any person regardless of disability should have the same opportunity to receive supports and services as anyone else. All services and supports should be in the community. Therefore, we believe all institutions should be closed and the people set free.[75]

Mark Friedman and Ruthie-Marie Beckwith, self-advocacy facilitators, recall, "This caused a stir in the disability community and branded People First as a radical organization with unrealistic viewpoints about deinstitutionalization."[76] Embracing this radical image, People First formed an alliance with the protest-oriented disability organization ADAPT and learned from them strategies of social resistance. As self-advocates increased pressure to close institutions, parents, professionals, and state officials escalated their attempts to silence self-advocates: officials excluded People First "rabble-rousers" from hearings, support workers refused to assist self-advocates in attending meetings, and parents dismissed self-advocacy as the mindless parroting of radicals without intellectual disabilities. Yet, despite these barriers, self-advocates' first-hand accounts of institutionalization proved essential to deinstitutionalization.

Debates about institutionalization have widened to include disability-specific, segregated services. Sheltered workshops, congregate day programs, and larger group homes were once seen as cutting-edge community services because they prevented institutionalization. Now self-advocates and some parents criticize the system of disability-specific, segregated services as creating a pervasive set of mini-institutions that perpetuate social and physical segregation into the modern day.[77] For SABE, freedom of choice requires inclusion in the community; segregation denies the fundamental rights to freedom and denies people with disabilities the same choices as other Americans. For SABE, institutions are any places where people with disabilities do not have choice or control over their lives. People with disabilities should have the full range of typical choices enjoyed by other people: choices of whom to date, when to go out, and where to live; however, this range of choices is impossible to attain in a large-scale, segregated facility.

Self-advocate Jawon explains that his organization seeks to close all institutions and institution-like services because people cannot be free when they are told when, where, and for how long they will proceed through their day: "It's like they're prisoners, but they're not prisoners; that's the sad part about it."[78] The "Integration Mandate," laid out in Title II of the Americans with Disabilities Act (ADA), legislates a preference for individuals with disabilities to live their lives alongside people without disabilities and with the same set of opportunities as people without disabilities. Sociologist and inclusion advocate Steve Taylor argued that the state has no obligation to fund segregated services, which undermine the integration mandate and deny people their civil rights. Instead the state should only channel public money into services that promote integration.[79]

Self-advocates and parents who fight for inclusive services and supports have much evidence to prove that people with intellectual disabilities, especially people with significant disabilities, tend to have superior outcomes in inclusive settings.[80] The community provides real-world opportunities to engage in valuable social roles, to interact with diverse people in diverse situations, and to make independent choices, all of which are essential for people with intellectual disabilities to enjoy meaningful and fulfilling lives. Integration also demands that expertise related to disability be embedded within the community and therefore decentralized. Segregated settings, on the other hand, tend to use asymmetrical systems of power, imposing an understanding of people with disabilities that focuses only on their diagnosis, needs, and deficits, and breeding low expectations. Simultaneously, segregated settings *remove* the imperative for community professionals to become experts in disability and legitimize their ignorance and discrimination, as if the "proper" place for people with disabilities is in disability-specific settings. Thus, they subvert the quality of community services by channeling resources out of the community and into segregation. Channeling resources into segregated services does not create a neutral "choice" between segregation and inclusion; it actively diminishes the likelihood and quality of inclusion and accessibility.

Although the decentralization and deprofessionalization of services enables community integration, these trends have not pleased all parents. Many parents are constantly frustrated by the ignorance, lack of expertise, and lack of opportunity in the community related to disability, and they turn to specialized centers, which can seem like an oasis in a desert of services. For example, VOR activist Sara defends her choice to place her son at a regional residential facility, stating, "When you have a Center, and I really believe this, the reason why it works so well is you have graduate level people roaming the halls, so if you as a direct care worker who has a high school education and learned on the job can't handle this behavior, or doesn't know what to do, you know the nurse walked in, the psychiatrist just walked in, the director walked in, speech therapist, physical therapist, whatever. . . . You're getting a graduate education without going to school because these people are there and therefore the resources are there to help you be more than you are."[81]

Education activist and parent Dori Fern describes the frustration that led her to seek a specialized, disability-specific school for her son: "Special ed is treated as one generalized mass of swept-under trash, at least in the N.Y.C. education system. I would rather fight the [Department of Education] every year to fund my kid's 'restrictive' private school education (and it is an epic fight for middle class families like ours) at a place where his learning needs (so-called 'disabilities') are supported, than have his confidence battered year after year in the public school system. Been there, done that."[82]

Even Gail, a parent known for promoting self-advocacy and inclusion, chose to place her son in a private specialized school because of the range of supports and services offered to him there and the school's loving acceptance of him as a person. Explaining her choice, she states that she wishes all schools could be like the disability-specific school her son attends: "I want the world to be like this [the school for children with disabilities]. I want to feel like we mean it when we say everyone is valued . . . not just tolerance of difference."[83] Rather than integrate her disabled son into schools without the resources to serve him, she wishes her nondisabled son and his friends could all be at schools with a full range of programs, services, and people. She admits that choosing a disability-specific school despite self-advocates' emphasis on inclusion led her into "a politics that I don't feel clear on."[84] Indeed, sociologist Valerie Leiter found that parents frequently use IDEA (the civil rights law that guarantees children with disabilities access to a free, appropriate public education) to fight for *segregated* educational programming, because they believe segregated educational placements offer a better education and experience than the integrated experience actually available to their child.[85]

Similar feuds rage over sheltered workshops.[86] Sheltered workshops are seen by SABE, many activists with physical disabilities, and some parents as perpetuating a system of segregated, underpaid work and legitimizing the discrimination of employers against people with disabilities. When asked his top priority as a self-advocate, Sam, one of the self-advocates we interviewed, stated, "Equal pay in sheltered workshops, no matter if they do part time or full time. The importance of equal pay for everyone."[87] Other parents, though, argue that their offspring cannot work at the pace and standards required of a typical workplace and do not have available opportunities for paid work. Therefore, sheltered workshops provide a valuable alternative that fosters a sense of independence, ability, and social belonging even if one cannot succeed at a job in a competitive marketplace. Large-scale congregate day programs, group homes, and recreational programs are marked by similar debates.

Another pressing issue is control and decision-making authority, on both the micro and macro levels. On the micro, family level, debates about the merits of guardianship are fierce. On one side are those who seek to promote self-determination and reduce and regulate the use of guardianship. Guardianship is meant to protect people, but it does so by removing the person's rights, which may leave the disabled person vulnerable to exploitation and abuse. The history of exploitation by guardians is extensive; people with intellectual disabilities have been deprived of their funds, forced to live in terrible situations, institutionalized against their will, and sterilized, all with no say in their own lives and almost no opportunity for redress. There are many who question whether rights restrictions and guardianship really protect people and whether parents can be trusted to act in the disabled person's best interests rather than their own.

A number of cases document that parents and their offspring do not necessarily share the same views or interests, making guardianship problematic. In 2013 Jenny Hatch made the news. Hatch, a woman with Down syndrome, lived with friends, had a romantic relationship, and volunteered in her community. After she was hit by a car, her parents decided to pursue guardianship because they felt she needed greater supervision for her own protection. They were awarded it and placed her, against her wishes, in a group home. Hatch, supported by the Arc of Virginia, took her parents to court. According to the Arc of Virginia's brief, "Extensive research has found that the vast majority of people with intellectual disabilities, including Down syndrome, can live successfully in their own homes and make their own choices." The brief argued that guardianship in this instance did not support her in independence but rather led to her placement in a "segregated group home, isolated from her job, her friends and her community."[88] The court agreed and removed her from guardianship. Given the paternalism common among parents, a reliance on guardianship can be worrisome indeed.

Instead of guardianship, self-advocates and some parents have engaged in efforts to enhance self-advocacy and systems of support rather than control. Self-advocate Mark, for example, attributes his success as a self-advocate in part to the important role played by his mother, who fostered his development as a self-advocate, traveled with him, assisted him in preparing speeches, and sometimes spoke with him, especially when they were addressing families. To spread public awareness of self-advocacy and the views of self-advocates, parent Nicki Pombier Berger conducted oral histories with self-advocates and posted videos and transcripts on a public website. On an organizational level, the Arc and other organizations often support self-advocacy groups, providing office space for meetings, funding for events, and leadership training opportunities. Organizations also work to modify guardianship laws to enhance opportunities for self-determination even for those under guardianship.

Despite the concerns related to guardianship and the desire for self-advocacy, though, some parents see guardianship as an essential *right* for people with intellectual disabilities. The Arc included the right to guardianship in its early blueprints developing its rights agenda. Michael Bérubé, a well-known author, disability studies scholar, and father of a son with Down syndrome, argues, "The idea that the interests of cognitively disabled adults should be expressed by the votes of guardians and surrogates seems unassailable to me, and an important means of combatting everyone and everything that would seek to deny people with cognitive disabilities the full status of political personhood."[89] Parents feel the need for guardianship to (1) protect their loved ones and (2) to resist the control that state agencies and professionals have over their loved one's life in the absence of formalized power by parents. In other words, some parents argue that the absence of guardianship does not enable self-determination; rather, it gives "the system" all the power and deprives the family of the ability to protect their loved one. "The system" has not served people with intellectual disabilities well in the past, and there's little reason to have faith in it now.

Issues of voice and decision-making power operate at a macro level as well. In national policy making, the political dominance of parent and professional groups, even if they support self-advocacy, poses significant problems for self-advocates and the goal of disability empowerment. Two main problems emerge. First, insofar as self-advocacy groups are funded and directed by the Arc or other organizations, self-advocates are constrained in their ability to criticize the system. Some Arc chapters have supported self-advocacy groups in establishing independent organizations, but others maintain self-advocacy groups as a subunit within the Arc. Of self-advocacy rooted within provider or professional organizations, self-advocacy facilitator Doug states in an interview, "It's very disempowering. Self-advocates are always looking to see what they are allowed to do. . . . There's a very profound difference between saying, 'This is your bank account; it's your name on it, and you need to decide, and I'll help you in the process' versus 'You have to come ask me.'"[90]

When there are conflicting interests and political positions, self-advocates perceive that parent and professional organizations protect their own interests, leaving self-advocates out in the cold. "Power," according to

Doug, "is the elephant in the room." Sheltered workshops, for example, have come under increasing criticism from self-advocacy organizations for offering dead-end, segregated work experiences that teach little and rarely lead to integrated employment. Doug explains, "The Arc can say, 'There shouldn't be any institutions,' but when it comes to sheltered workshops, the Arc runs sheltered workshops, and so what comes to the fore is power and money, and the Arc is not willing to give up their sheltered workshops. In these national debates, the Arc has far more power."[91] A facilitator from another state concurs, and explains that large advocacy organizations and service providers like the Arc do not sacrifice their funding or their seat at the table when self-advocates are excluded or people with disabilities are segregated. They build alliances with self-advocates when useful, but cannot be counted on to put the goals of self-advocates above their own interests in funding and power. But self-advocate Debbie Robinson emphasizes that self-advocates often take the lead in demanding inclusion. In deinstitutionalization, "There was no if, ands, buts about it and somebody had to take the lead and we did. We took the lead." She continues, "That was a big shift, um, back in those days cause we didn't have the power. . . . [S]elf-advocates never had, didn't even know what control was."[92] Now self-advocates have learned that their voices are essential to protect and demand their rights; they cannot count on others to do it for them.

The Legacies of Parent Activism

Parents have played a major role in securing a broad range of rights of people with intellectual disabilities, including challenging discrimination as it relates to institutionalization and the denial of rights and creating the legal and policy infrastructure for community-based services, including in education, work, residential supports, and leisure. Parents also challenged professional paradigms including addressing harmful language and approaches, protecting people from unethical research practices, fighting for a right to treatment and services, and building expertise in fields including medical and dental care, the criminal justice and legal system, education, and social services. Broadly, they helped usher in positive understandings of disability to end stigma and prejudice, and parents' groups have provided training and supports to parents and self-advocates to know and fight for their rights.

For those who imagine that macro political systems cannot be changed, parent activism in intellectual disability is a vivid display of the power of passionate, everyday Americans to create a better, more inclusive world. However, in many ways, the success of the parents' movement also created some of its most enduring problems. Much of the legislation created promotes a neoliberal service system in which parents and their offspring have an individual obligation to fight for individual rights (e.g., to educational accommodations, to community services) and to make individual choices as "consumers" regarding public and private dollars for education, treatment, transportation, and other "services." Thus, political public decisions are individualized and depoliticized. In this depoliticized marketplace, the Arc becomes positioned as one among many possible services providers, rather than a social movement, and parents often lack an awareness of its historical or contemporary political role.[93] To access rights, parents must navigate an incredibly complex set of rules and services structured within an unequal and obscure system to gain the best opportunities for their child. This breeds vast inequality. Indeed, the inequality inherent in the service system and in advocacy organizations is so stark that it makes the claim of fighting for "all children" dubious.

Moreover, parent activism built an expansive infrastructure of community supports, but many of these rely on models of segregated, congregate care, run by professionals without disabilities. In these systems, people with intellectual disabilities are primarily defined by their disability, positioned as dependent, and maintained in poverty with few choices in their life. Ironically, although the Arc positions itself as a rights organization, self-advocates criticize the service system it facilitates. The very power of the Arc, in contrast with self-advocacy organizations, may seem to diminish access to rights for people with intellectual disabilities.

As the Arc increasingly focused on the macro politics of inclusion and rights, which required sophisticated lobbying at the state and national levels, its ability to provide and draw on grassroots support from families diminished. There continues to be a proliferation of local, grassroots parents' organizations to address specific local needs and encourage local community-building. These local groups emerge with very different "flavors" depending on the local environment, culture, and needs. As "accidental activists"[94] typically with little knowledge of disability prior to the diagnosis of their own child, most parents working to get through their day do not have the macro politics of disability rights in their repertoire of knowledge and do not consider it central. When the Arc or disability groups step in to local areas to fight for rights, they can at times appear to local parents to be an outside agitator imposing a dogma, rather than an ally working for the fulfillment of rights. For example, to better establish integrated education, in the 1980s the Washington Arc decided to file a series of complaints against school districts with low rates of inclusive education. Larry Jones reports, "Since the Arc had no active members in many areas, the charges of being outsiders were hard to rebut. The accusation was most telling where there were competing organized parent groups which opposed the closure move."[95] The Arc, therefore, receives criticism from some parents as being too focused on inclusion and disregarding their interests, while also being criticized by other parents and self-advocates for not demanding disability rights strongly enough and for protecting the interests and authority of parents.

Conclusion

Parents of children with intellectual disabilities were in many ways trailblazers in the fight for disability rights. They were among the first parents to challenge medical authority, draw on a social model, and demand rights. Among parent organizations, they have also been among the strongest supporters of self-advocacy. However, their activism often focused, especially at the local level, on securing services and supports for their children, rather than embracing a full-fledged rights model that positioned people with intellectual disabilities as rights-bearing decision-makers. Parents created a system of services that, while progressive in its time, is now often considered deeply problematic. As parent-founded organizations, including the largest one, the Arc, built their national presence, they tried to unify their agenda around community integration, but their role as service provider and their commitment to parents' wishes muddied their ability to meet this ideal as they continued to offer segregated services and usurped the authority of self-advocates. Thus, self-advocates criticize parents' domination in disability policy and their slow efforts at reform. Meanwhile, other parents criticize the Arc's commitment to a model of rights rooted in community integration rather than parent authority.

2

Psychiatric Diagnosis, Disability,
and Parent Activism

Pete Earley, a professional journalist in the Washington, D.C., area, was the father of three children, the oldest of whom, Mike, was a college student in New York City. In his senior year, Mike began to experience troubling symptoms of mental confusion, disrupted sleep patterns, and odd behavior. Pete reached out to him and consulted with a psychiatrist that Mike reluctantly visited. Mike insisted that nothing fundamental was wrong and resisted seeking additional medical help.

Mike began to develop obsessive fantasies about a female friend and appeared to be experiencing a breakdown, but refused treatment. Pete tricked him into going to a hospital emergency department, where he was involuntarily administered an antipsychotic drug and then discharged. He returned to his parents' home. After several days Mike took the family car and crashed into a parked car. Police took him into custody and returned him to the hospital, where he stayed for a week and was given a diagnosis of bipolar disorder. After discharge, Mike reluctantly visited a psychiatrist but refused medication. After some time living with his mother, Mike resumed his life in New York, finished college, and started a job.

After several months, Mike's symptoms reemerged. In Pete's eyes, Mike was delusional and clearly in need of assistance. Pete brought him to another hospital; however, Mike would not consent to treatment or medication. The psychiatrist did not see Mike as a danger to himself or others and could not force Mike to receive treatment. Pete called the local police, but they also said they could not get involved unless Mike broke the law. After a series of confrontations at home, Mike began acting out in public and broke into a nearby house, where he broke a glass patio door and urinated on the carpet. The police arrested him. Pete was encouraged to claim to police officers that Mike had threatened him, which led to Mike's involuntary admittance to a psychiatric hospital instead of jail. The hospital, however, would not administer medication without Mike's consent. Mike faced two felony charges. After months of negotiations, the victimized homeowners reluctantly allowed Mike to plead guilty to misdemeanors and thereby avoid incarceration.

Pete's experiences with his son led him to turn his journalistic focus to the intersection of mental illness and the criminal justice system. Drawing on an in-depth case study of how people with mental illness fared in the courts and jail in Miami, Florida, Pete published a book on the topic with strong recommendation for reforms, including training law enforcement officers in how to respond to incidents involving people with apparent mental illnesses, diverting such individuals away from incarceration and into treatment, relaxing the civil rights protections that prevent involuntary treatment, and enhancing family input in decisions to compel the use of psychotropic medication.

Mike accepted treatment with a new psychiatrist, who prescribed medication with fewer negative side effects. Even with only the misdemeanor convictions, Mike experienced significant difficulty obtaining even a low-wage job. But he stayed on medication and again lived independently, eventually resolving to pursue a graduate degree.[1]

As shown in this chapter, parents often feel disempowered and unable to assist or control their offspring experiencing mental illness, and therefore may push for greater ability to impose treatment, medication, and surveillance. Their sense of urgency is heightened by the likely intervention of the punitive system of criminal justice. Activists with psychiatric disabilities, however, assert that involuntary commitment is a violation of basic civil rights, and that anti-discrimination measures and community supports to ensure access to health care, jobs, and safe housing are far better ways to improve their lives. From their perspective, institutionalization and loss of control adds to trauma and rarely resolves it.

Although both people with psychiatric diagnoses and people with intellectual disabilities experienced the harsh segregation of institutionalization, well-organized parent advocacy regarding mental illness emerged much later historically than parent advocacy regarding intellectual disabilities. Moreover, when parents did organize nationally regarding mental illness, they focused much of their effort on advancing medical treatment. In contrast, parents of people with intellectual disability emphasized the need to secure civil rights and community services. Parents' focus on treatment for mental illnesses, including involuntary treatment, resulted in many tensions with organizations led by people with psychiatric diagnoses. The medical and service systems, as well as pharmaceutical companies, further exacerbated those tensions by co-opting family members into pro-treatment advocacy, whereas advocates with psychiatric disabilities themselves remained more independent of and critical of medical systems. As a result, in the area of mental health, organizations led by parents have often worked independently of organizations led by activists with disabilities.

Considering Psychiatric Diagnosis

Psychiatric illness is a particularly contested condition compared to many other types of impairment. Mobility and communication impairments, as well as absent or ill-functioning body parts, are often considered to be self-evident, and their presence and implications for treatment and functioning are rarely subject to debate. Cognitive and intellectual impairments may be less visible, and may only be relevant in certain social and historical settings, but their existence is rarely in doubt. In contrast, psychiatric conditions may only be considered as actual disabilities when they persist over time and significantly interfere with social functioning. Even then, serious and persistent mental illnesses may be perceived as incidental, voluntary, or a failure of moral character rather than as legitimate impairments requiring treatment.

Moreover, the set of symptoms that constitute mental illness shifts, at times dramatically, by time and place. The identification of aberrant mental processing and perspectives and resulting behavior is intractably interwoven with a culture's norms and expectations.[2] Even modern medical/psychiatric definitions of mental illness rely heavily on cultural expectations. Definitions in the *Diagnostic and Statistical Manual of Mental Disorders* (DSM), the diagnostic reference work that represents consensus among psychiatric providers, for example, use vague and culturally contingent wording such as "inappropriate," "bizarre," "unexpected," and "maladaptive" in identifying mental illness. The result is that the same behavior may be seen as mental illness in one culture, but not in another. For example, Native Americans may expect mourning to involve visions of and communications with the deceased, and as such they do not interpret such visions as mental illness, whereas for many other Americans visions of ancestors serve as a signal of mental illness.[3] Thus, depending on culture, symptoms such as intense sadness, anxiety, excitability, confusion, or hallucinations may be perceived as dangerous, eccentric, or normal.

Over time and cultural space, there also have been significant differences between the responses to someone with a "mental illness" depending on whether their behavior was interpreted as sinful or evil, as a special or spiritual gift, or as a disease. Historically, people who today would be seen as mentally ill, particularly people with delirium, seizures, or fits, may have been charged with demonic possession or witchcraft, resulting in banishment, imprisonment, or death sentences.[4] Neglect of personal, communal, and spiritual responsibilities were also seen as leading to mental symptoms, requiring various, often religious, acts of piety, healing, cleansing, or discipline to reverse.[5] In ancient Greece, Hippocrates was among the first to reject the role of magic in health and instead look at natural causes of mental "illnesses." The resulting solutions, however, could be just as cruel, including bloodletting, freezing baths, and isolation in an effort to balance the fluids in the body.[6] Such disparate theories existed side by side throughout history.

Within Western culture, the rise of scientific medicine since the nineteenth century meant that physical illness, whether infectious, genetic, or degenerative, became subject to medical authority and treatment. The field of psychiatry made similar claims to medicalize mental illness, claiming jurisdiction over defining and responding to mental illness, defining individuals with psychiatric symptoms as ill and in need of medical intervention to cure or at least manage their disease. Various disciplines fought for authority over conditions perceived as mental disorders, but psychiatrists have largely been successful at securing dominance.

Even since medicalization, responses to mental illness have varied by historical era, from asylums that isolated and incapacitated those held in them, to violent and invasive medical procedures, to chemical and pharmaceutical interventions, to psychotherapy, to community-based treatments. The birth of psychiatry relied heavily on the residential mental hospital to secure and congregate patients for treatment and research, and eventually the repertoire of treatment included invasive psychosurgery, electroconvulsive therapy (ECT), powerful psychoactive medications, and a variety of drastic methods designed to combat illness through shocks to patients' systems.[7] The mass institutionalization of people with mental illness produced widespread neglect and abuse, while yielding little success in terms of cure. Indeed, the stress, violence, and isolation of the institution often fostered mental illness rather than cured it.[8]

Psychiatric authority and the harsh forms of treatment on which it relied were challenged in the twentieth century on several fronts by reformers within and outside of the profession. Proponents of psychoanalysis, influenced by the work of Sigmund Freud but by midcentury representing a range of approaches to understanding the human psyche, claimed the mantle of science for treatments based on conversation between analysts and patients. The community mental health movement also challenged the effectiveness of hospital-based interventions. The movement advocated for community mental health centers that would heal mental patients through engagement in community life, later aided by a host of increasingly effective medicines. Advocates for deinstitutionalization and civil liberties embraced the concept of due process championed by the African American civil rights movement. These legally focused activists characterized the forced commitment to mental hospitals as unlawful servitude, and called for requirements that would make it far more difficult to restrain, confine, and treat those with psychiatric diagnoses contrary to their stated will.

While a variety of political forces had supported the expansion of state hospitals as sources of employment and economic development for the largely rural communities in which they were typically located, these interests ultimately were overcome by the desire for state governments to control expenses in the more fiscally constrained era following the sustained post–World War II economic expansion. For those managing state governments, the call for expansion of community-based services legitimated the withdrawal of financial support from public institutions in favor of less expensive community alternatives that might qualify for federal subsidies.

Federal legislative activity cemented the move to community-based care.[9] President Kennedy signed the Mental Retardation Facilities and Community Mental Health Centers Act of 1963, diverting construction funding away from hospitals and into the creation of community service centers. The enactment of Social Security Disability Insurance in 1956, Medicaid and Medicare in 1965, and Supplemental Security Income in 1972 provided systemic funding streams for the treatment and material support of people with disabilities living in the community. Thus, the 1950s through the 1980s in America marked a fundamental shift in mental health care from the asylum to community-based care. Whereas institutions were known for widespread abuse, overmedication, and a failure to effectively support recovery and reintegration into society, community-based treatment promised to protect patient rights, embed treatment within community settings, and foster patient participation in the world.

Unfortunately, though, the hoped-for outcomes of community-based treatment were subverted by a lack of public investment, system fragmentation, and racial politics. Alongside civic and professional ideals, fiscal conservatism dominated the political reasons for closing institutions. Rather than having access to an expansive set of community-based resources to ensure their success, people with mental illness too often faced a paucity of even basic necessities such as counseling, housing, and income support. Government fiscal austerity in the 1980s sharply exacerbated homelessness, although political rhetoric blamed the release of the mentally ill from institutions, rather than social policies, for the growing crisis of homelessness.[10]

Fiscal austerity led to a disastrous lack of services. Children with psychiatric diagnoses have access to some education-related services provided by public schools under mandates of the federal Individuals with Disabilities Education Act (IDEA). Some states offer transitional services to those aging out of the public school systems, but even the most generous programs fail to address many important needs.[11] Mentally ill adults, however, have little guarantee of access to needed medical or support services, and often lack the financial resources and coping skills to manage on their own. Andrew Scull writes of the result of the massive and fairly abrupt discharge of mental patients from state hospitals into the community:

> Many psychiatric casualties have been thrust back into the arms of their families. Here, largely bereft of official support or subsidy, unpaid carers (mainly female) are left to cope as best they can. These burdens are massive, and ultimately, for many families, simply intolerable. . . . Families for the most part cannot or will not absorb all of the burdens the new policies impose, particularly over the long haul.[12]

Some individuals discharged from state facilities had access to support services from public or private agencies, but many people were left with the possibility of seeking support, including personal care, health insurance, and other forms of assistance, from their families. Alternatively, deinstitutionalized individuals entered life on the street and/or an alternative and potentially more dangerous form of incarceration within the criminal justice system.[13]

This inadequate service system is fragmented across many administrative systems that do not work effectively together. Common and vital services—such as vocational rehabilitation, housing supports, income supports, health care, education, and social rehabilitation—all may have different eligibility criteria and administrative agencies and lack mechanisms for cross-agency communication. Even for the most educated of consumers, the system is daunting. In addition to structural fragmentation, Kerry Dobransky documents "institutional fragmentation"; in other words, even within any given service or bureaucracy, competing logics—such as empowerment versus fiscal accountability—diminish the effectiveness of service.[14] In particular, the goal of consumer empowerment is undermined by the logic of accountability, billing based on narrow treatment standards laid out by Medicaid, and the clinical imperatives of expertise, hierarchies, and surveillance.

In the landscape of deinstitutionalization and the absence of effective systems of community care, the racial politics of mental illness shifted and incarceration in prisons became far more common. Historically, hospitals for the mentally ill primarily served whites.[15] Yet, in the 1950s and after, as African Americans protested to gain civil rights, public discourse on mental illness warned of the dangers of violent and unhinged African American men. Jonathon Metzl documents, for example, the shift in schizophrenia diagnosis from a focus on passive white women to "angry" black men.[16] The politics of fear, combined with a relentless War on Drugs, led to increasingly punitive responses to social deviance and a sharp rise in mass incarceration, particularly among men of color.[17] Currently, African American men constitute a disproportionate percentage of those incarcerated, the majority of people in prison are diagnosed with a mental health disorder, and the prison system is the largest provider of mental health services in our nation.

Without adequate community care and with the looming threat of incarceration for deviance, expectations for care fell heavily on families. Ron Honberg, national director of policy and legal affairs for the National Alliance on Mental Illness, states, "When everybody else goes home, the families are the ones that step up and provide care. . . . They are always there, when no one else is."[18] Despite the expectation of family care, the state offered families almost no financial, social, or even educational support to do so. Indeed, adults have rights to medical privacy and consent that prevent families from ensuring their family member receives treatment or social services. Given the high expectations for care combined with the neoliberal neglect of public funding and supports, it might not be surprising that a recent survey of mental health caregivers found that 74 percent reported stress related to caregiving, 52 percent reported that their health had been negatively affected, and 47 percent felt socially isolated.[19]

Finally, along with the shifting dynamics of mental illness, its increasing prevalence must be considered. Mental illness has transformed from a malady of a small percentage of the population to an expansive set of symptoms and conditions that 30 percent of the adult American population reported experiencing in a twelve-month period in the early 2000s.[20] About 18 percent of the American population seeks treatment for mental health or addiction problems every year. According to Allan Horowitz, "In the decade between 1985 to 1994 alone, the number of prescriptions for psychotropic medication soared from about 33 million to about 46 million. The brand names of medications such as Prozac have become as generic as 'kleenex' or 'xerox.'"[21]

This expansion especially affected children. In the early twentieth century, children were assumed to be largely free from the troubles of the adult mind, little research or specialization existed in child psychiatry, and children were rarely institutionalized in hospitals for mental illness. Whereas in 1910 only 0.2 percent of those admitted to institutions were under the age of fifteen, recent statistics suggest that approximately one in five children have a diagnosable mental illness.[22] Some of the most common diagnoses include attention deficit/hyperactivity disorder, mood disorders, conduct disorders, panic and generalized anxiety, eating disorders, and (most consequentially) schizophrenia.

The explanation for increasing prevalence can be debated—whether it signals actual decreases in coping and wellness, increasing attention to illnesses that were previously ignored, or an expansion of diagnosis and treatment primarily driven by medical industries for profit, or some combination of these (or some other reason). Without doubt, however, the increasing reliance on community services, the lack of such services, and the threat of incarceration, combined with increased identification of mental illness in children, created a context ripe for parent activism. Before discussing the rise of specific organizations, however, we must also add to the context a discussion of psychiatric patient movements that emerged related to institutionalization and deinstitutionalization.

Psychiatric Patient Movements

Whereas organized parent advocacy for intellectual disability emerged before self-advocacy, activism among people with mental health diagnoses emerged before parent advocacy for mental illness.

Former patients who were treated in state mental hospitals formed advocacy movements beginning in the early twentieth century to eliminate or radically change institutional care, and they gained a prominent role in the public policy debate about mental health in the 1970s. One early reformer was Clifford Beers, a former patient whose 1908 book *A Mind That Found Itself* (with an introduction by William James) detailed Beers's harsh treatment in a series of Connecticut mental institutions.[23] Beers convened a group including philosopher William James and prominent psychiatrist Adolph Meyers, who founded the National Committee for Mental Hygiene (NCMH), a national organization that helped develop national standards for mental health treatment and obtain increased public funding for mental health services. Although founded by Beers, NCMH and its successor organizations largely limited participation to psychiatrists and other mental health professionals, and did not involve people with mental illness themselves, for most of the twentieth century.[24]

In its early years, NCMH encouraged the creation of one hundred community-based child guidance clinics in 1910 and the development of a "mental hygiene" program for the American military during World War I. In 1946, NCMH was influential in the passage of the federal National Mental Health Act that created the National Institute of Mental Health. In 1950,

NCMH merged with several other organizations to become an umbrella organization (renamed Mental Health America in 2006). The organization played an important role in the nascent community mental health movement: in 1955, it was instrumental in the formation of a national Commission on Mental Illness and Mental Health whose 1961 report led to the 1963 enactment of the Community Mental Health Centers Act (CMHCA). CMHCA promoted deinstitutionalization by providing grants to states to build community mental health centers as an alternative to state institutions. In the early 1960s, the organization also opposed unpaid labor by institutionalized patients.[25] More recently, Mental Health America pursued a number of projects to improve public awareness and reduce stigma associated with psychiatric conditions, promote expanded mental health services, and protect people with mental illnesses from discrimination.

One of the earliest known groups comprised primarily of former mental patients was Recovery Incorporated, now known as Recovery International (RI). RI was established in 1937 in Chicago by the psychiatrist Abraham Low as a self-help peer-to-peer group promoting recovery from mental illness. Its original members were thirty-seven former patients of the University of Illinois at Chicago's Psychiatric Institute who had received insulin shock treatments while institutionalized. In later years the group separated from the university but retained its connection to Low, who offered group therapy to members, although RI chapters were led by former patients. Following Low's death in 1954, the organization became solely peer led, and its meetings had similarities to twelve-step programs. By 1960, more than half of RI members had no prior history of hospitalization. Family and friends were allowed to attend meetings but not to participate.

With the growth of state mental institutions and their ultimate decline, former mental patients served as a pool for the creation of advocacy activity. Influenced by the racial civil rights movement of the 1950s and 1960s, many former mental patients advocated for the right to self-determination and against involuntary commitment, and vigorously opposed harsh treatments such as electroconvulsive therapy (ECT) and antipsychotic medications. Judi Chamberlin, a psychiatric survivor who cofounded the National Empowerment Center, explained that her time in mental hospitals was "the worst period of my life. My struggle to overcome the effects of this experience was what led me to become involved in the ex-patients' movement."[26]

An intellectual basis was provided by anti-psychiatry works by such authors as R. D. Laing and Thomas Szasz. Groups of former patients challenged the legitimacy of psychiatry, psychiatrists, and particularly harsh and involuntary treatments, identifying themselves as survivors with deliberate parallels to the Holocaust and claiming "mad pride," similar to assertions made by Black Power activists and advocates from other oppressed and marginalized groups. They asserted that society should be changed to accommodate their different ways of living rather than changing them to fit into society. Focusing on discrimination, Chamberlin explains that the psychiatric survivor movement advocates that "all laws and practices which induce discrimination toward individuals who have been labeled 'mentally ill' need to be changed, so that psychiatric diagnosis has no more impact on a person's citizenship rights and responsibilities than does a diagnosis of diabetes or heart disease."[27] Local activist organizations were established across the United States, with names drawn from the protest discourse of the 1960s such as the Alliance for the Liberation of Mental Patients, the Insane Liberation Front, and Project Release. National networks of these organizations were established, featuring a newsletter, the *Madness Network News*, published from 1972 through 1986, and an annual Conference on Human Rights and Against Psychiatric Oppression that met from 1973 through 1986.[28]

Psychiatric survivors were joined in their efforts by radical psychotherapists dissatisfied with traditional hierarchical therapies. These professionals engaged in civil disobedience with former patients against psychiatric institutions, publishing their own journal, the *Radical Therapist*, from 1970 to 1972, that featured articles by both therapists and ex-patients. However, the two groups vied for dominance of the movement, and eventually the alliance failed.[29]

Other allies of the psychiatric survivors' movement were legal advocates who focused on the civil rights of patients, particularly the right to make decisions about treatment, including refusal.[30] In 1972, the Mental Health Law Project (later the Bazelon Center for Mental Health Law) was formed to advocate for civil and treatment rights of patients in institutions, and a National Association for Rights Protection and Advocacy (NARPA) followed. Former patients comprised one-third of the NARPA board, and partnership between patient and legal advocates has persisted to the present.

In 1985, the overall former patients' movement split into a more radical National Association of Mental Patients (later the National Association of Psychiatric Survivors) that took a stance of complete opposition to ECT, psychotropic drugs, and hospitalization, and the moderate National Mental Health Consumers' Association that favored more incremental changes in the mental health service system and "a greater willingness to work within the mainstream mental health system."[31] One topic of contention focused on the term used to characterize movement members, with more radical advocates preferring "psychiatric survivor" while moderates favored the term "consumer."[32] Another arena of contention was within the Community Support Program (CSP) established by the National Institute of Mental

Health in 1977 to promote the growth of community-based services. The CSP organized annual meetings of mental health consumers, the National Alternatives Conferences, intended to promote community services and networking among advocates, but these conferences became settings for conflicts between "survivors" and "consumers," both of whom opposed institutionalization and supported a focus on recovery but who differed significantly over the possibility of forced treatment.[33]

As well as opposing the system of mental hospitals, patient organizations favored an alternative self-help approach to mental illness, founding grassroots peer support groups run by consumers rather than by psychiatrists and other clinical professionals. They contended that participation in treatment should be entirely voluntary, and that service providers should only be involved in treatment under the direction of those receiving the services. These groups paralleled other self-help movements in women's health, HIV/AIDS, and particularly the independent living movement for people with nonpsychiatric disabilities.

In its early years, the anti-psychiatry movement was largely dismissed by psychiatrists and other mental health professionals, who did not believe that patient perspectives offered any insights into mental health services or policies. However, as the need for developing robust systems of community-based services became clear with increasing deinstitutionalization, those experiencing mental illness (if not their more outspoken activist organizations) came to be seen as valuable partners. In recent decades, individuals with histories of mental health treatment have become integrated into many systems of service delivery, planning, and research.[34] However, in many cases, "consumer" representation has come to mean the involvement of family members of psychiatric patients, with family members likely to outnumber and prevail over mental patients themselves when the two perspectives conflict.[35]

Tensions have persisted between former mental patients self-identifying as survivors and those (and their family members) representing themselves as mental health service consumers. This division may have been exacerbated by other differences between people taking these different perspectives. One account notes the class difference between survivors, who often lack financial resources or education, and consumers and family advocates, who more typically come from middle-class backgrounds that convey cultural capital useful in advocacy and political activity.[36]

Parent and Family Advocacy

Given that institutionalization inspired activism among some former patients with mental health diagnoses and parents of people with intellectual disabilities, why did advocacy among parents regarding mental illness emerge in a later historical era? The age and process of diagnosis for psychiatric disorders seem particularly relevant to explaining this phenomenon.

Social movement theory in sociology suggests that movement organizations are most likely to form when they can build on preexisting social organizations and networks.[37] African American civil rights groups grew out of African American churches and the historically black colleges throughout the southern and border states, and some early organizations within the disability rights movement were formed in the 1960s by people who knew each other in Veterans Administration rehabilitation facilities and summer programs for disabled children.[38] These social structures helped both to establish social networks and to foster a collective identity and shared sets of grievances vis-à-vis those programs and facilities. Similarly, parents of younger disabled children, such as the parents who formed the Arc and other advocacy organizations concerned with intellectual disabilities, got to know each other through association with the programs serving their children, including institutions.[39] The shared experience of institutionalization encouraged self-advocacy among some former mental health patients.

The development of a social movement among the parents of individuals diagnosed with mental illnesses, however, occurred in the late 1970s, later than activism among self-advocates and many parent groups. To some extent, this can be explained by the fact that many psychiatric conditions do not manifest themselves until adolescence or early adulthood. Diagnosis in early childhood may support the establishment of social networks among parents, whose children may receive services in public schools or other congregate settings. In contrast, there may be fewer naturally occurring relationships among parents of people who develop their conditions later. Parents with young children also focus their identity and social bonds on their children, and this connection may be less salient by the time offspring enter adulthood. Links among parents may also be hindered by the nature of some psychiatric disabilities, particularly when symptoms become more apparent as a form of antisocial behavior or withdrawal, further limiting the development of social networks. Moreover, when diagnosis occurs later in life, many offspring have established lives independent of their parents—socially, legally, and geographically—and they may have their own family and households; thus, parents have less connection to and responsibility for their adult offspring. Whereas parents of children with intellectual disabilities and autism often incorporate advocacy as a central part of their parent role and develop their skills across years, parents of adults with mental illness may not have needed to engage in advocacy until later in life, and at that time they may not still strongly adhere to their role as parent or have the necessary skills and knowledge for advocacy. Thus, the experience and understanding of institutionalization may be very different for families expected to institutionalize young children for whom they still see themselves as primarily responsible, compared with families whose adult offspring are struggling to maintain independence and adult roles.

Age of diagnosis also complicates parental advocacy because adults have independent rights. By the age of fourteen, children are granted certain rights to privacy by health care providers. Individuals who are legal adults may need to consent for diagnoses to occur, let alone treatment, and parents may have no legal access to information or participation in the processes of diagnosis and treatment. Lack of access may be further complicated by a perceived culpability of parents in mental health crises. In this day and age, few doctors blame parents for intellectual disability or autism, and most doctors respect those parents' intentions and expertise. In contrast, mental health professionals may look at parents with suspicion, associating mental illness with family trauma, neglect, or abuse. Further, patients may expressly deny their parents access to medical records.

The diagnosis process is also particularly complex and stigmatizing for people with mental illness, especially given the punitive societal response to mental illness. As a result of competing explanations of deviant behavior, the expression of symptoms may provoke official responses from school authorities, law enforcement, or other agents of social control that lead to removal from school settings or incarceration, but may or may not lead to psychiatric diagnosis or treatment. Minority adolescents, for example, are far more likely than white adolescents to be routed into the school-to-prison pipeline—given detentions, suspensions, and placement in alternative schools, rather than treatment for mental illness.[40] Thus, society's heavy reliance on social control agencies impedes diagnosis and thereby collective action based on a diagnosis.

Even when diagnosis occurs, it is frequently a complicated and stigmatizing process, coming about in indirect and complex ways, often in response to behavior viewed as deviant and as an outgrowth of labeling in diverse settings including secondary schools, law enforcement and juvenile facilities, and other social control agencies. Such settings may not have associated parental groups or promote collective parental participation. In some instances, those experiencing psychiatric symptoms may present themselves for treatment. In other cases, family members may seek care for their child. For many people, however, diagnosis may follow incidents in which their behavior comes under official scrutiny, which leads to detention and perhaps adjudication. An encounter with law enforcement may lead to diversion for mental health assessment that may in turn result in a finding of mental illness and referral for treatment. For others, criminal offenses lead to imprisonment, resulting in routine mental health and addiction screening, which in turn produces a mental illness diagnosis and referral for treatment during or after a period of incarceration. Many jurisdictions have developed protocols to screen offenders who appear to have some form of mental illness, with either subsequent diversion into psychiatric treatment or some form of special processing that takes psychiatric status into account. Therefore, while most diagnostic processes have important elements of social construction, conferring mental health diagnoses within the criminal justice system may have implications for the individual and the facility that go beyond medical appropriateness, and might include issues of adding (or reducing) cost, a desire to attach (or deny) culpability, administrative criteria, and even the availability of resources for managing inmates in alternative settings.

In any of these situations, the likelihood of parents or other family members developing connections to other families may be low. Such bonding may be doubly discouraged by the stigma associated with both criminal behavior and diagnoses of mental illness. Thus family members of individuals with mental health diagnoses typically do not form bonds with each other prior to official labeling of mental illness, and are unlikely to connect during periods of inpatient treatment. If they do form bonds, they may focus on criminal justice reform, not mental illness. Minority families in particular may prioritize the pressing need to protect their families and communities from social control by law enforcement that dominates their neighborhoods, and they may organize around issues such as Black Lives Matter, criminal justice reform, and the death penalty.

Nevertheless, parent advocacy has emerged. In contrast with inpatient services and imprisonment, many outpatient service providers promote the establishment of community ties, especially with family members, and support groups may be far more likely to form at this stage in the career of the patient, both for the patient and for family members. Support groups may begin with sharing feelings about coping with a loved one's behavior; the delivery of information about how to gain services, impairment-related insurance, or public benefits; or how to encourage the patient to continue using services. These experiences may ultimately lead to sharing grievances about system inadequacies, sharing strategies of advocating for family members, and ultimately to advocacy for increased budgets and policy improvements.

These stepping-stones to founding movement collectives may be encouraged by policies within many public and quasi-public bodies requiring or encouraging the participation of service "consumers" and their allies and advocates in policy making. Since the 1960s, community participation has become embedded into many community services,[41] including those in mental health, and many service systems organize formal advisory groups and forums for community input that bring together like-minded advocates. Despite the intent of encouraging broad participation by stakeholders, these settings may not be adequately accessible, some consumers may lack the capacity to participate, and others may resist engagement with systems of which they are suspicious. As a result, in many communities, "consumer" participation typically is undertaken not by those with diagnoses themselves but rather by their family members. The increasing rate of childhood diagnosis offers parents additional institutional routes into activism such as via individualized educational plan (IEP) meetings at school. Through these organized avenues, parents develop their social networks, develop advocacy skills, and take on the role of "representing" mental illness.

Emerging technologies further facilitated the growth of virtual communities based around social media, which may be particularly important resources for people dealing with shame and for people with little time or ability to leave the house to engage in their own self-care. In these communities, parents could begin sharing stories, information, and strategies for social change through electronic rather than face-to-face interaction.

The process of building collective activities can progress to the creation of formal organizations and, ultimately, to coalitions. Sometimes this occurs through a grassroots, bottom-up process, and in other situations, such as the creation of consumer or community advisory bodies, the process is more top-down. Mental health self-advocacy groups of "psychiatric survivors" and others rejecting the medical model of mental illness are most likely to create themselves through bottom-up steps, while parental bodies form via both directions.

Some support groups for individuals and families affected by mental illnesses are focused on mutual aid, information sharing, and peer support, while others include political advocacy in their agendas. Many such groups are small and local, while others are affiliated with larger networks. Some groups are led by or feature a prominent role for medical or other clinical professionals, while others emphasize peer support.

Parent and Family Organizations

According to the U.S. surgeon general's 1999 report on mental health, since the 1970s consumer and family organizations have played a "strong" role in making mental health policy. The report mentions "literally hundreds" of such grassroots groups.[42] At the time of the surgeon general's report, there were three principal national organizations of advocates for people with mental illness. The National Mental Health Association, later Mental Health America (MHA), has long played an important role, focusing primarily on the needs of children. While MHA was founded by providers rather than parents, many local affiliates have attracted family members to their advocacy activities, and include formal participation of family members.

Similarly, the National Federation of Families for Children's Mental Health (NFFCMH) has advocated for broadening services and greater family participation in decision-making about service delivery. NFFCMH was founded by a group of parent advocates who came together at a 1988 conference, "Families as Allies," sponsored by Portland State University and the National Institute for Disability and Rehabilitation Research (NIDRR), a federal agency. The stated goal of NFFCMH was "families and professionals working together," and the organization appears to have avoided an adversarial relationship with mental health providers, focusing instead on promoting "family-driven care" through curriculum development and training, public awareness, youth leadership development, and certification of "parent peer support providers" who offer support to other parents whose children experience mental illness. The organization received financial support from the Annie E. Casey Foundation in 1992 that allowed it to hire staff and open an office in Washington, D.C. Since then, it has held annual national conferences, promoted National Children's Mental Health Awareness Week, and partnered with several federal and state agencies. The organization currently has more than 120 local chapters in over forty states.

Among advocacy-oriented groups, however, the leading representative of families with adults who have diagnoses of mental illness is the National Alliance on Mental Illness (NAMI). Harriet Shetler and Beverly Young, two mothers of sons diagnosed with schizophrenia, founded NAMI in 1979 in Madison, Wisconsin, because of their dissatisfaction with the lack of available services and frustration at being blamed by professionals for their sons' mental illnesses.[43] The women invited other dissatisfied family members to a community meeting; over one hundred people showed up, and the first local affiliate of what was to become NAMI came into existence. In September of that year, 250 delegates representing eighty local groups from twenty-eight states gathered in Madison, Wisconsin, to form the National Alliance for the Mentally Ill.[44]

Within two years, nearly two hundred local NAMI affiliates had been organized, with several state-level networks in place and a national office in Washington, D.C. In less than a decade, NAMI included six hundred local and state affiliates in fifty states, with an estimated sixty thousand members, and a Washington national office with a staff of fifteen. Local NAMI affiliates were composed primarily of family members of people with mental illnesses, although those diagnosed are often members themselves, and service providers could join as well although not serve on affiliate governing boards.[45] Agnes Hatfield, one of the key NAMI organizers, noted the example of the Arc for family advocacy including the high level of commitment on the part of family advocates and its impact in creating social change.[46]

Given the paucity of services, NAMI fights for a range of community-based services, including housing, employment supports, and educational accommodation. The 1999 surgeon general's report on mental illness cited NAMI's formidable accomplishments and characterized the group as a "powerful voice for the expansion of community-based services."[47] NAMI's work, however, focuses on increasing the availability of and access to treatment and therapy. In the past, mental health professionals tended to blame parents for the mental illness of children, a legacy of psychoanalytic approaches to understanding mental conditions that characterized mental impairments such as schizophrenia to be the result of poor parenting skills, using terms such as the "schizophrenogenic mother." In contrast, the biomedical model rooting mental illness in chemical imbalances and neural disruptions alleviated parent-blame. In the 1980s, NAMI invested considerable time and energy to promote more biomedical research into the nature of mental illness.[48] While parents saw the medical model as reducing parental stigma, disability advocacy groups and in particular anti-psychiatry survivors largely rejected the medical model as pathologizing and individualizing mental illness and undercutting civil rights.

In support of the medical model, NAMI prioritizes the provision of information to parents that enables them to secure diagnosis and treatment. In "Learning to Help Your Child and Your Family," NAMI states, "Early intervention . . . is critical because mental health conditions often get worse without treatment. If you think you notice symptoms, schedule an appointment with a licensed psychiatrist or psychologist as soon as you can."[49] Resources are given regarding the warning signs of mental illness, treatment options, and professional organizations. NAMI has played a particularly crucial role in legislation to promote parity between health insurance coverage of physical and mental illnesses, in securing greater federal funding for mental health research and services, and in changes in the training of mental health professionals to reflect the perspective of mental health consumers.

While broadly supportive of the medical model, NAMI has challenged its traditional hierarchical model and instead insisted on what it calls a consumer perspective in the mental health system:

Educated by the programs of the self-help groups, families will learn to be more selective users of mental health services. They will ask more relevant questions about the nature of a service, the length and cost of treatment, and evidence of its efficacy. Practitioners will be required to explain their service in a clear, jargon-free language and to solicit family involvement. . . . Professionals who can work in true partnership with these more assertive families will be needed. Self-help groups form, in part, as a reaction against the power of professionals. . . . A sharp schism between stigmatizing professionals and the new family advocacy groups can be anticipated.[50]

Hatfield characterizes NAMI as expressing interests that are distinct from those of service providers.[51] NAMI advocates for individualized therapy driven by consumer needs and values, and members mentor peers to offer support. However, Hatfield does not recognize any distinction between the interests of family members of people with mental illnesses and the interests of those experiencing mental illnesses themselves. Indeed, family-driven, rather than consumer-driven, is perhaps a more accurate descriptor, as NAMI strives to ensure family representation in policy, family involvement in treatment, and services and supports for family members. NAMI has successfully sought family representation on state mental health planning boards.

NAMI also prioritizes the establishment of policies that support family participation in treatment. As noted, families often feel shut out of the treatment process. Creigh Deeds, whose son committed suicide, explained, "I never really understood the illness. . . . I was never given help."[52] Other parents state that medical professionals would not even give them broad information about mental illness. Chris Agnell, who also lost his adult son to suicide, describes that he was denied information and cut out of care planning.[53] To address this issue, parent organizations have worked to advance legislation that gives parents greater access to medical information and to increase access to involuntary and inpatient treatment. NAMI's director of policy and legal affairs, Ron Honberg, argues, "It just doesn't make sense to shut families out of the kind of basic information that they need to serve as caregivers."[54] The National Federation of Families for Children's Mental Health is even more explicit in its focus on family-driven care, prioritizing the valued role parents should have in directing care and services for their children.

Parent-led organizations strongly believe that parents and families "play a key role in supporting their children through both crisis and recovery."[55] Parents struggle to identify symptoms, locate services, and cope with behavioral symptoms at home. For children with mental illness to thrive in the home, the family must holistically be stable, functional, and well informed. Thus, a 2016 study of parents revealed a common belief among parents: "Build resilience in the family—you stand a better chance of helping the young person long term too."[56]

Most generally, parent-led organizations work to fight the stigma experienced by those who live with mental illness and the "courtesy stigma" experienced by their family members.[57] A parent described her encounter taking her child to see a professional: "I just felt something was wrong. I took her to see a counselor; I was so mad because the psychologist said I needed to learn to be a parent. I didn't think so."[58] There is a particular stigma against families with violent children. Some parents live in fear of their violent children, experience physical and mental abuse, or witness abuse by children with mental illness against other children in the house, yet are given almost no resources to deal with these situations and are blamed for them. Parents who resort to inpatient care feel vilified, yet many want more access to this option. In a compelling blog entry, parent Lisa Lambert argues that many parents remain silent, even when their children are violent, because of the stigma: "We need to be able to talk about our children and receive back compassion, understanding, and good advice. Until that happens, many of us will stay quiet."[59] According to author and parent Michael Schofield, stigma inhibits effective communication, access to treatment, and the hope for a full and meaningful life. "What they [children with mental illness] need is acceptance. What they need is for us to be telling them 'your illness does not define you.' We cannot go inside their minds and 'fix' them. But we can fix the world so they can live in it. Schizophrenia is not a death sentence. It is a disease that can and must be managed. But it is also just another part of the rich rainbow of humanity."[60]

Tensions between Organizations Led by Parents and Organizations Led by Activists with Disabilities

The family movement in mental health faced rejection by mental health professionals in its early years, but, by the late 1990s, families of mental patients had become an accepted stakeholder in community mental health service systems and policy-making networks. However, major differences in perspective continue between parents and disabled activists over forced treatment and involuntary commitment as well as the reliance on pharmaceutical interventions in mental health treatment, and these differences may not disappear as they reflect fundamental disagreements over goals and values in the experience of psychiatric conditions.

In her case study of the "consumer/survivor" movement, Tomes describes tensions between NAMI and groups of former mental patients over the legitimacy of parent perspectives in the movement.[61] According to Judith Gruber and Edison Trickett, "There is a fundamental paradox in the idea of people empowering people because the very institutional structure that puts one group in a position to empower others also works to undermine the act of empowerment."[62] The efforts of the medical and service system to empower consumers and family members tend to co-opt family members into a particular form of advocacy, whereas self-advocates have remained more independent of and critical of medical systems and therefore also of most parent advocacy.

Perhaps the most important conflict between NAMI and psychiatric survivor groups has been over the issue of involuntary treatment. This is acknowledged by a NAMI organizer, Agnes Hatfield, in her 1986–1987 article in the *International Journal of Mental Health*, in which she addresses what she calls the balance between rights and needs. She writes:

> One of the most troubling aspects of caring for the mentally ill is the inability of the family to insist on hospitalization even when the need for such treatment is abundantly clear to the family and the physicians. . . . patients have the right to make their own choices, but often cannot take responsibility for their decisions . . . and families feel bound by their moral values and love for their mentally ill members to do their best by them, despite the heavy odds against them.[63]

An early major figure in NAMI's leadership, psychiatrist E. Fuller Torrey, argued that deinstitutionalization has gone too far in separating people with mental illness from treatment, with the result that many people are harmed. Torrey is the executive director of the Stanley Medical Research Institute, a center for biomedical research on schizophrenia and bipolar disorders that collects postmortem brain tissues from people with those conditions. Torrey also founded the Treatment Advocacy Center, an organization active in lobbying for involuntary commitment that is credited with enactment of laws in 42 states as of 2005, including New York, California, and Florida, that enable outpatient commitment of psychiatric patients deemed to require medical supervision.[64] Torrey played an important advising role for NAMI in the 1980s and 1990s, campaigning for the group and donating proceeds from his book *Surviving Schizophrenia* to the organization. He was the keynote speaker for the 2002 NAMI national convention, and in 2005 Torrey received recognition for his financial and personal contributions to the group by being featured on its 25th Anniversary Celebratory Donor Wall. He has contended that the ability to force confinement and treatment on psychiatric patients should be reestablished, and he founded the Treatment Advocacy Center to strengthen outpatient and civil commitment by rewriting state laws to give greater discretion to the courts (in conjunction with family members and mental health professionals) to impose drug and other treatment for individuals with mental illness.

In April 2014, the Helping Families in Mental Health Crisis Act (H.R. 3717) was introduced in the House of Representatives by Rep. Tim Murphy (R-PA), a clinical psychologist, in response to the Sandy Hook school shooting by someone with apparent mental illness. The bill would give parents or caregivers access to adult patients' confidential medical records. NAMI and Torrey's Treatment Advocacy Center supported the bill, but the Bazelon Center and the Foundation for Excellence in Mental Health Care opposed it.[65]

Activists with mental health diagnoses and the Bazelon Center argue that the bill would strip privacy and self-determination from patients and encourage a resurgence of forced institutionalization, a practice that proved to be so harmful to so many people. The bill empowers families, who may be part of the problem, without the consent of the individual diagnosed. It also defines the conditions for involuntary treatment so broadly as to include homelessness, an inability to meet basic needs, and evidence that one would progress substantially with treatment. In essence, people could be involuntarily committed because of poverty or the refusal to accept treatment, even if they are not at risk of immediate harm to themselves or others, which seems to self-advocates like a blatant violation of civil rights. In response to a blog post explaining a parent's support of inpatient treatment, a fifteen-year-old former residential patient wrote, "Inpatient isn't always the best. It's hard in there. As a kid your're [sic] scared, you try to escape and you kinda do more stupid things because you're so scare and you don't wanna be there. I was in for a month and I have promised myself never to go back."[66] A thirty-three-year-old man who was committed at the age of thirteen responded to the same post: "The effects of these types of facilities is extreme. 20 years later and countless therapists and I still live with the emotional side effects on a regular basis. I struggle with trust, abandonment issues. I have almost no relationship with my mother (primarily because she committed me). . . . Committing your child to a place like this would be the worst parenting decision of your life. This action will forever change your child and your relationship with your child. You have other choices."[67] Another choice, for example, might include allying with people with psychiatric diagnoses to increase access to affordable housing, job and income insecurity, community-based health care, and safe neighborhoods.

Despite seemingly irreconcilable differences, Athena McLean reports some rapprochement and even collaboration between the survivor movement and consumer and family groups in recent years.[68] In 2006, the National Coalition of Mental Health Consumer/Survivors organization formed with representation from both sides of the divide among advocates, and that coalition and similar networks have worked to find a middle ground between total opposition to forced treatment and efforts to limit its scope.[69]

The middle ground can be hard to find, however. Even broad initiatives around stigma and awareness—initiatives that seem like points of agreement among parents and survivors—are criticized by survivors as too often reflecting the biomedical model and prioritizing treatment. Judi Chamberlin, the cofounder of the National Empowerment Center, notes, "A lot of what's called 'anti-stigma' work in mental health is controlled by people who are trying to medicalize it, and a lot of the money that's spent on what's called 'anti-stigma education' is really about getting people into treatment. . . . I don't even like the word 'stigma,' I prefer to talk about discrimination."[70] For survivors, self-empowerment and human rights must be front and center, and parent-professional groups rarely share this priority.

Other points of difference between NAMI and former patient perspectives have emerged since its founding. One ethical and political issue was the role of "consumer choice." McLean contends that NAMI has favored such choice within the private health care sphere, for individuals whose care is financed through private insurance, but has "ignored" the public mental health system where treatment has too often been limited to medication alone.[71] She writes, "NAMI supported consumerism only for those who valued the provider-consumer relationship and who had access to it. This kind of consumerism led to uneven empowerment based on class. In advocating biomedical treatment over community support, NAMI opposed services vital to help consumers of the public mental health treatment system with recovery beyond chemotherapeutic management."[72] NAMI also fails to address the broad social and economic inequity that leads to disproportionate mental health conditions among people in poverty and minorities. Similarly, NAMI takes a moderate stance on criminal justice concerns, advocating greater training of criminal justice professionals without a broader critique of the criminal justice system and incarceration as racialized, classist systems.

Another issue that turned into an embarrassing public controversy for NAMI has been its funding by large pharmaceutical companies. With its early emphasis on a medical model of mental illness, a natural alliance emerged between NAMI and the pharmaceutical industry in seeking expanded public funding for drug research. This relationship led critics to question the integrity of any discussion of medication-based treatments by NAMI. This partnership developed into a public controversy for NAMI in 1999 when *Mother Jones* magazine reported that pharmaceutical companies had donated $11.7 million from 1996 to 1999.[73] The largest donor company, Eli Lilly, "lent" a full-time executive to NAMI for help with strategic planning.

More recently, the *New York Times* reported on an investigation of NAMI and other nonprofits by Senator Charles Grassley (R-IA), who was concerned with hidden influence by big pharmaceutical companies on the American health care system.[74] The article reported that NAMI had acknowledged that more than two-thirds of its donations came from the pharmaceutical industry. The controversy resulted in the resignation of a NAMI board member, Dr. H. Richard Lamb. Despite assurances of change, it was believed that this pattern of funding had persisted since he joined the board in 2005 and that NAMI's dependence on the drug industry had made taking advocacy positions critical of the industry impossible.[75] Bioethicist Susannah Rose has contended that such conflict of interests, undisclosed until exposure by government investigation, undermine the trustworthiness of nonprofit advocacy organizations such as NAMI.[76]

While activists with psychiatric diagnoses do not tend to trust NAMI, the distrust flows the other direction as well. In part because NAMI's interests align with the biomedical and pharmaceutical industries, parents rarely see alliance with "mad activists" as a viable option. Indeed, to the extent that parents even recognize the existence of distinct organizations run by people with mental health diagnoses, they do not feel they can trust them, believing that self-advocates are quick to ignore the suffering of caregivers and to place blame on families. Schofield, for example, at the outset of his book, January First, explicitly criticizes self-advocates for increasing stigma against families and the difficulties they face. He explains that he created a closed online support group where he could receive advice and support "without fear of criticism, primarily from the anti-psychiatry movement, which, though it has many faces, basically denies that mental illness exists. They certainly cannot accept that it happens in children. Nevertheless, from my blog posts they concluded, based on what they believe, that I abused my daughter and that the true cause of Jani's condition rests in her parents and how she was raised."[77] For many parents, the stance of psychiatric survivors feels too radical as parents desperately search for effective therapies to alter what they see as a destructive and dangerous path for their family member and their broader family.

Conclusion

By some current estimates, 20 percent of children have a diagnosable mental illness, and mental illness seems increasingly common in adulthood as well. This shift in prevalence and demographics, combined with increasing pressure on families to provide care as a result of deinstitutionalization and lack of community support, the threat of incarceration, and increasing expectations of "consumer involvement" in community services, has drawn parents into advocacy. While involving a range of issues, their advocacy tends to support a biomedical model prioritizing access to treatment and family authority to intervene and even impose treatment. Over the years, parents have gained recognition as key stakeholders in mental health policy and within the service delivery system. Yet their positions often contrast with self-advocates who stress self-determination, community supports, and civil rights. Although these groups occasionally ally for certain measures, they represent fundamentally different worldviews about the distribution of power and the role of rights in modern society. Thus, the likelihood of consistent alliance is meager, whereas contentious politics are far more common.

3

Autistic Identity and Parent Activism

Jeremy was born in 2003, Lisa's first child. Concerns with language delay and regression led to evaluations, a diagnosis of speech delay, early intervention services, and eventually a diagnosis of autism before the age of twenty-four months. Jeremy used to get treatment from medical professionals affiliated with Defeat Autism Now, a cure-based approach treating autism and biomedical conditions believed to be associated with autism such as allergies and digestive issues.

Lisa is proud of getting her son enrolled in services within three weeks of the diagnosis, but she still has feelings of guilt for not figuring out that he was autistic and getting treatment sooner. His preschool program focused exclusively on applied behavior analysis (ABA) and mandated that parents refrain from using other treatments. Lisa was dissatisfied and learned from other parents that parents were secretly enrolling their children in additional therapies (such as speech and occupational therapy). The guilt of not doing enough for the children overtook the guilt of not following the rules of the service provider. Lisa and her husband made sure their son received speech therapy, physical therapy, and occupational therapy in addition to ABA.

Disagreeing with the organization's suggestion that Jeremy remain in the program another year, Lisa and her husband decided to restructure their lives to allow him to enter a different preschool with a special education itinerant teacher in addition to forty hours per week of home- and center-based services. The services included Medicaid-funded support staff who engaged in community activities and, as he got older, provision of assistive technology (cell phone and iPad), visits to the gym, community classes, and other therapeutic activities after school and on weekends, as well as the therapies he had already begun. Lisa's husband got a new job working the night shift, which allowed him to put Jeremy on the bus and take him to therapies after school and be home for providers until Lisa got home from her job.

Thanks to further advocacy, Jeremy again changed public school systems during middle school to be part of a newly formed local autism program, in which language acquisition and an alternative and augmentative communication (AAC) device, as well as sensory-based therapies, would be available. With support from family and amazing teachers and therapists, Jeremy now communicates using an AAC device, and he often uses typing to self-script his speech. When younger, Jeremy was completely nonverbal and was treated as if he was low functioning. He also had meltdowns (e.g., banging, yelling). Now he is a sixteen-year-old high school student, and his verbal communication is getting increasingly complex, as are his social skills. As his frustration with not being able to communicate diminished, so did his meltdowns. Jeremy communicates the most when he is doing what he loves, and what he loves the most is water—so when he is at the beach surfing or in his family pool, these are both happy times and times of fruitful communication. The family pool is brand new and alleviates stress, especially when swim lessons at an external pool are canceled. Jeremy has become extremely good at self-regulating, finding ways to comfort himself and often using words to do so.

Since Jeremy was a small child, Lisa's mantra, often repeated on social media, has been "progress every day." Lisa works with a group of high school students to organize a large fundraiser every year to fund quality-of-life programming for local autistic children. She is involved in parent advocacy, supporting other parents in school system negotiations and is active in several organizations including the Autism Community in Action (formerly Talk about Curing Autism), the Autism Society of America, and her local chapter of the Autism Society. Because Jeremy is only sixteen, he has many years left in high school, where he will remain until the age of twenty-one; however, Lisa and her husband are already working with the school on transition planning via vocational activities at school and skills acquisition in the community.

Lisa's story shows the variety of different approaches of "treatment" for autism, from biomedical approaches to ABA to education and the provision of communication supports, and the complexity of navigating these different approaches. To access a range of supports, Lisa and her husband engaged in intense advocacy and restructured their lives; they also benefited from social and human capital, like being able to move to a different school district and have a family pool. Lisa is white, has a master's degree, is deeply familiar with how school systems work, and has the means to live near some of the best school systems in the United States. Not every family is so privileged, especially families of color from impoverished areas. Less than twenty minutes away from where Lisa and Jeremy live is one of the lowest-ranking school systems in the country, where most of the students are minorities. A story of a family from this district would be a very different one.

While this is a story of intense commitment, it also highlights the pressure to "optimize" one's child, leading to hours and hours of therapies and treatments for young children. While intensive biomedical and ABA approaches are meant to enhance the skills of a child, autistic activists describe the potential trauma of these therapies, which seek to cure or erase the signs of autism, denying the value of autistic identities and forcing compliance to social norms. Though this family started out with the goal of "defeating" autism, they ultimately were not focused on erasing autistic traits or enforcing norms. They met and accepted Jeremy as he was, encouraging, supporting, and facilitating activities and interactions that brought him joy on his own terms, not based on some abstract concept of what constitutes "normal." Eventually Jeremy gained access to education and communication, but many other children remain subjected to treatment regimens focused more on erasing autism than on supporting the autistic individual.

There has always been variety in the way autistic people, their capacities, and their perceived limitations have been represented in biomedical, psychosocial, and cultural frameworks. In the early twentieth century, people who today would be diagnosed as autistic usually eluded that diagnosis; instead they were subsumed in populations of those with diagnoses of psychiatric or intellectual disability and subject to institutionalization as described in other chapters, were able to pass as odd or eccentric members of their communities, or in some cases were celebrated or marketed as savants. In the United States in the mid- to late twentieth century, autistic children and adults were often grouped together with children who had cerebral palsy and intellectual disability, under the broad umbrella of "developmental disability." The parents of children with these diagnoses banded together through national organizations such as the Arc and United Cerebral Palsy (UCP) to lobby successfully for the passage of legislation and the funding of educational and therapeutic supports for autistic children, as long as the autistic person was formally diagnosed before the age of twenty-one. Biomedical conceptualizations, though, have been the dominant framing of autism within autism-specific organizations since the mid-twentieth century.

In this chapter, we examine the evolution of autism parent advocacy organizations, which are often centered on biomedical diagnosis, treatment, and cure, and their relationship to emergent autistic citizenship movements, which are centered on the ideas of neurodivergence, neurodiversity, and autistic pride.[1] While some points of alliance have occurred, the relationship between the largest parent group—Autism Speaks—and autistic self-advocates is quite adversarial, marked by distrust and discord.

Considering Autism

Autism has been theorized, understood, and clinically and socially represented in different ways by professionals, family members, and autistics themselves. The paradigms under study in this chapter include the following:

- Biomedical interventions, such as psychiatric, psychoanalytic, genetic, and behavioral therapies/interventions, environmental toxins/allergen strategies, sensory integration, and so on (from the 1940s to the present)
- Parent advocacy for community-based education, behavioral therapies, and medical treatment (from the 1980s to the present)
- Autistic citizenship and self-advocacy movements centered on neurodiversity and pride (late twentieth and early twenty-first centuries)

These disparate paradigms have interacted with each other and shifted over time, emerging in distinct historical periods and then mutually supporting, coexisting separately, or coming into direct conflict in different ways at different times, in different places.

Compared to intellectual and mental disabilities, autism as characterized today was identified quite recently. The term was created in 1911 by Eugen Bleuler as a subcategory of another diagnosis he invented: schizophrenia.[2] In 1943 Leo Kanner and in the 1930s and 1940s Hans Asperger separately but in very parallel ways identified characteristics that we recognize today as autism.[3] The classic characteristics of autism included differences in communication, behaviors, and social interaction. It was not seen as a condition that could be cured or even treated, though psychoanalysis was popular and remains popular to this day in countries such as France and Brazil.[4] The definition of autism has changed over the years from a narrow list of traits to a spectrum of characteristics that may vary in frequency and intensity. Even in recent years significant changes to the definition of autism have taken place. In the 1994 fourth edition of the *Diagnostic and Statistical Manual of Mental Disorders* (*DSM-IV*), autism was characterized by four distinct diagnoses: autistic disorder, Asperger's disorder, childhood disintegrative disorder, and pervasive developmental disorder, not otherwise specified. In the 2013 *DSM-V*, these four categories are united under the single category of autism spectrum disorder.

Like the previous *DSM* (and pre-*DSM*) diagnostic criteria, the *DSM-V* definition is couched in deficit-based language so typical in the description of autism in scientific and lay contexts. Diagnostic criteria include, for example, *deficits* in social-emotional reciprocity, such as *abnormal* social approach and *failure of normal* back-and-forth conversation; *restricted, repetitive* patterns of behavior, interests, or activities such as *inflexible adherence* to routines, or *ritualized patterns* of verbal or nonverbal behavior. These symptoms must be present in the early developmental period and cause *clinically significant impairment* in social, occupational, or other important areas of current function, and these *disturbances* must not be better explained by intellectual disability or global developmental delay.

Consider the words and phrases italicized above: deficit, abnormal, failure, restricted and repetitive, inflexible, ritualized, impairment, and disturbances. Once a child receives this diagnosis, these are likely some of the first words parents hear or read. While the diagnosis is the gateway to needed services, the price seems very high. In the twenty-first century both parent advocates and autistic activists are trying to reframe the definition and conceptualization of autism to provide an understanding of the strengths and differences rather than just focusing on the challenges outlined in the *DSM-V*.

The project to reframe the conceptualization of autism is not new; some of the earliest scholarship on autism recognized the potential capacities of autistic individuals. In the 1930s, when Asperger was defining what came to be known as Asperger syndrome, he outlined positive as well as negative characteristics. In Asperger's first public talk on this topic, on October 3, 1938, he discussed one of the boys in his program, stating that it was impossible to distinguish between the impairments and the talents and strengths that together formed "natural, necessary, interconnected aspects of one well-knit, harmonious personality. We can express it this way: this boy's difficulties—which particularly affect his relationships with himself and other people—are the price that he has to pay for his special gifts."[5] Asperger even suggested that the talents autistic people had for pattern recognition could make them valuable code-breakers. This strengths-based approach was far ahead of its time, and it is ahead of the current time in many contexts. Unfortunately the contributions of Asperger were buried by World War II and the revelation of his own collaboration with Nazi euthanasia programs,[6] and the focus of autism research moved to the United States, where a deficit approach was deeply embedded.

Though the theories and framing of the diagnosis have changed through time, the deficit model of autism remained constant from the 1940s into the twenty-first century. According to the deficit model, autism resides in the individual. However, as reflected in the 2015 special issue "Conceptualizing Autism around the Globe" in the journal *Culture, Medicine and Psychiatry*, autism is constructed through and within shifting discourses, forcing individuals and families to negotiate the cultural production of neurodiversity across *DSMs*, paradigms, historical epochs, and sites such as schools, medical practices, activist organizations, and online forums.[7] Moreover, these sites are negotiated and experienced differently in different cultural and regional contexts.[8] Various diagnostic and therapeutic approaches are helpful or hindering, empowering or disempowering for individuals and families,[9] and lead to varied acceptance of diagnosis, therapy, custodial care, and identity as neurodivergent.

Language

This chapter features disability-first language. "Autistic people," "disabled people," and "people with disability experience" are the preferred phrases of scholarly and activist autistic communities in the United States because they indicate that disability is a collective experience, not a unitary pathology located in the individual. Individuals are not separated from each other according to diagnoses but are united by shared social experience. Of course, this is a highly contested and ongoing debate. Different disability communities prefer different language. Some are passionately "people first." Some are passionately "disability first." Most autistic activists prefer to be called autistic people, not people with autism. But there are parent groups and professionals who have very different opinions. Indeed, language is a central manifestation of divisions in how one understands autism. Thus, one cannot even discuss the debates without entering into them.

Paradigms of Autism

Refrigerator Mothers and Psychoanalysis

Leo Kanner in 1943 first commented on the cold and unfeeling mothers of autistic children.[10] In the 1950s and 1960s, Bruno Bettelheim popularized the notion that they caused autism in their children. In his 1967 book *Empty Fortress*, Bettelheim compares the behavior of autistic children to concentration camp survivors in describing their lack of affect. Though it is commonly repeated that Bettelheim compared mothers to Nazi concentration camp guards, he never made this statement, though he certainly made comments about a lack of empathy of mothers who never desired children and who were unemotional about them. Thanks to the popularity of Bettelheim's thesis, parents of autistic children experienced guilt that they had somehow caused the condition.[11] In the documentary *Refrigerator Mothers*, mothers discuss their experiences with this theory: "What have we done that is so awful that would drive a child into such a regression? I was told I had not connected or bonded with the child because of inability to properly relate with the child."[12] Other mothers were told that they were psychotic, and that was why their children were damaged. The mothers express anguish while recounting these stories and explain how damaging it was for them to be counseled in this way. As one mother says, "You were on the judgment seat as a mother, and he was your judge, he was your prosecutor, he was your everything. He was going to send you to mother hell because you made this kid to be autistic."[13] Lorna Wing writes, "By the time parents come around to seeking expert help they are usually unhappy, bewildered, guilt-ridden and completely without confidence in their own child."[14]

Early diagnosis presented autism as a psychiatric condition that came with little hope of treatment. The only options offered were institutionalization and treatments such as dousing in cold water, shock, restraints and eventually medication. In many locations and historical periods from the 1950s to the present, psychoanalysis—an approach focused on generating individual self-knowledge—was also recommended, and in some cases used as the primary treatment for autism. In many parts of the world this approach is now largely discredited, but it remains staunchly advocated as a treatment strategy in other areas.[15] These options failed to provide effective treatment and instead offered only simple physical warehousing, physical or chemical restraint, or some hoped-for level of self-knowledge. Even when parents were not directly accused of hurting their own children, they often found the experience of interacting with psychiatric professionals extremely cold and impersonal. For example, Clara Claiborne Park, author of the first autism parent narrative in 1967, and her husband began to feel angry and resentful at the cold and inconsiderate way in which they were treated in a psychiatric clinic to which they brought their daughter for assessment.[16] She reports their "experience of depersonalisation, of utter helplessness in institutional hands, of reduction to the status of children to whom situations are mediated, not explained."[17]

By the mid-1960s Bettelheim's assertions were contested and counter-explanations were provided. One counter-explanation was most notably developed by psychologist Bernard Rimland,[18] who was himself the parent of an autistic child. Rimland's research supported the notion that autism was caused not by sociopsychological experiences such as how parents behaved with their children but by environmental toxins such as mercury, air pollution, vaccinations, food additives, and candida due to the overuse of antibiotics. Rimland also accepted the possibility of genetic causes, but he saw these as triggered by environmental contaminants. Although Bettelheim's "refrigerator mother" theory has been discredited, Rimland's assertions still filled many parents with guilt and fear that they had failed to properly protect their children. This biochemical approach has come to be widely accepted by parents to this day, even though many of these assertions have themselves been partially or fully discredited. For example, the belief that vaccinations were a cause for autism is based on fraudulent research by Andrew Wakefield,[19] yet many parents still put faith in this theory.

Rimland and his successors succeeded in part because they offered an alternative to the "refrigerator mother" theory. Instead Rimland's theories offered a regime of cleansing the child's body and environment of toxins—these included avoiding vaccination, gluten, lead, and many other substances. Parents were expected to be ever vigilant for potential toxins, and failure to follow recommendations would, of course, have dire consequences for the child. So, although they were not directly blamed as in earlier theories of autism, parents were indirectly to blame if they failed to adequately detoxify their child and their child's environment.

The Invention of Developmental Disability

In the 1960s and 1970s children were often given the diagnosis of mental retardation (later called intellectual disability) rather than autism.[20] The diagnosis of mental retardation shielded parents from theories focused on parent-blame and was seen as a more hopeful diagnosis. Thus, a generation of children grew up misdiagnosed, but potentially well supported within the systems of support for children with developmental disability (DD) and mental retardation. At the time there were no effective treatments for autism, but, in part because of parent activism, there was a significant growth in educational, service, and therapeutic opportunities for children with mental retardation via organizations like the Arc and UCP. Starting in the 1970s, parents of children with DD (including autism, mental retardation, and cerebral palsy) advocated for therapies to address their children's sensory, communication, and other challenges. They educated themselves (maybe became DD researchers themselves) and raised money to support the research of health professionals whose approaches they found promising. One mother in *Refrigerator Mothers* describes her experience as a peer advocate:

> I became an activist because I wanted to help set the record straight. I wanted to help my child. It doesn't get better for your own child if

it doesn't get better for everybody. And nobody knows these children better than the parents who live with them twenty-four hours a day. So I always tell the parents, when they would call information and referral, "Nobody knows that child better than you. Don't let anybody tell you you don't."

While the diagnosis of mental retardation offered more access to resources, services, and opportunities for collaboration with other parents, it also meant generations of parents with autistic children never understood (or did not come to understand until much later) that their children were autistic. In addition to those folded into the movement around mental retardation, other children who might in the twenty-first century be considered autistic escaped diagnosis altogether or, if anything, were identified via secondary conditions such as psychiatric diagnoses (depression, obsessive compulsive disorder, etc.), although some of this group did receive diagnoses of autism as adults. Yet those children who did receive an autism diagnosis, usually those with very visible and pronounced classic characteristics including difficulties in communication and self-care, were considered unresponsive to therapy. Sometimes parents were encouraged to institutionalize these supposedly hopeless cases.

In the 1970s, the concept "developmental disability" gained political legitimacy. Parents of autistic children worked with parents of children with other developmental diagnoses, such as cerebral palsy and mental retardation, to pass the 1975 Developmental Disabilities Assistance and Bill of Rights Act (DD Act), which outlined the rights to education, treatment, and services for children with developmental disabilities.[21] The DD Act also established a legal definition of "developmental disability" that involved significant challenges across a set number of social, educational, and physical realms, manifested before the age of twenty-one. This could be any disability a person was born with or acquired before the age of twenty-one, but it usually referred to mental retardation, cerebral palsy, and autism. "Developmental disability" was a policy invention formalized through legislation that created an effective mechanism to ensure a pipeline of funding for children for diagnosis, education, and supports to transition to adulthood. What happened to children once they turned twenty-two is another story, as most adults with DD experienced a devastating loss of services once their school years ended.

While this legislation was supposed to ensure that children with a diagnosis of autism received the same kinds of services and funding as children with mental retardation, the perception that autistic children were untreatable limited their opportunities at first, even after passage of the DD Act.[22] It was only when the diagnosis of autism began to expand to include a wider range of characteristics that the range of services and treatments also expanded and became more lucrative. Correspondingly, a greater number of children with autism and their families began to access these services and treatments.

From Syndrome to Spectrum

On the basis of research by cognitive psychologists in the 1970s, professionals began to characterize autism as a spectrum of developmental disabilities with neurocognitive and social origins. Even today there is debate among professionals internationally as to whether autism is an "affective disorder" that includes psychotic and relational challenges or a neurological condition that includes challenges in social interaction, communication, and imagination, along with what has been described as "rigid and repetitive" patterns of behavior.[23] One prominent theorist from this era, whose work remains influential in the twenty-first century, was Simon Baron-Cohen. Baron-Cohen, Alan Leslie, and Uta Frith claimed that autistic people lacked a theory of mind.[24] In other words, autistic people were theorized to have a specific form of cognitive impairment preventing them from being able to understand and interpret the emotions, perceptions, and beliefs of other people, leading to social impairment. This theory is still popularly known and believed decades later, though it has been widely critiqued and discredited in many circles.[25] Ironically, Claiborne Park, a mother and the author of one of the first autism parent narratives, describes the psychiatrists she interacted with as unemotional and distant: "Their failure was one of imagination. For all their silent attention they were not able to imagine the thoughts and feelings of my husband and me."[26]

Researchers in the 1980s strengthened the trend to characterize autism as a spectrum, with the understanding that autism included a broad range of characteristics with differing levels of involvement.[27] Specific treatment strategies, such as applied behavior analysis (ABA),[28] Floor Time,[29] Sensory Integration Therapy,[30] and TEACCH,[31] were identified for autism. With the growth of treatment options, parents began to advocate for such treatments to be available in their local school systems as part of an accommodated education. In the 1980s and 1990s, as more children began receiving the diagnosis of autism and as more treatments were identified, the perceptions related to diagnoses shifted. Whereas a diagnosis of mental retardation or intellectual disability had been a pathway to services, now the diagnosis of autism was perceived by some parents to offer more hope for treatment and cure. Indeed, many parents of autistic children are careful to emphasize how intelligent their children are—sometimes calling them "twice exceptional" (indicating autism but also high intelligence).

One of the most commonly accepted treatments was, and continues to be, ABA. This treatment, developed by Ole Ivar Lovaas originally to change effeminate behavior in boys, was designed to teach autistic children how to communicate and behave in socially acceptable ways.[32] This is an intensive method, often involving twenty to forty hours per week of therapy for years, and so it is very expensive. However, the technique was strongly recommended by clinical professionals, and parents advocated successfully to have this therapy available to their children. Both parents and professionals believed fervently in the results[33] and passionately advocated (and still advocate) for ABA, as it is widely thought to be effective. Though it is only one of many therapeutic alternatives, it is certainly one of the most popular, and it is routinely recommended by doctors, psychologists, and educators. A parent explained that the parents she knew who refused ABA never saw the same level of functioning in their children that her son now enjoyed (excelling in a postsecondary vocational school), and she credited ABA.[34]

However, ABA as a methodology lacks rigor; there is no single technique performed in a uniform way. Rather there are a wide variety of practices with many regional and professional variations but all referred to as ABA.[35] In the extreme, ABA involves physical force to coerce autistic children into the desired behaviors, and some children have been seriously injured or killed as a result,[36] but many approaches to ABA do not involve physical force. Unless parents are well informed on the subject, they would not necessarily be aware of the variations in the practice of ABA or the potential stress or harm ABA might cause their children. For critics of ABA, parents and professionals act as agents of damage and trauma to their children by submitting them to extreme aversive therapies with the goal of enforcing conformity and compliance. One parent blog presents critiques of ABA including quotes from individuals with a variety of experiences and perspectives. For example, one person stated, "ABA is nothing more than child abuse. If these same techniques were used against a normal child, all HELL would be raised." A teacher said, "As a teacher, I have been horrified by things that were done to children in my classrooms in the name of ABA. It came across as incredibly disrespectful of the human being in question." And a third respondent stated, "There is also a high price that autistic children can pay when ABA is practiced in such a way that compliance itself is a goal—abuse, physical/sexual/emotional."[37]

Conversations about ABA are heated in professional and activist settings as well. In a meeting of the Neurodiversity Caucus held at the 2015 annual meeting of the Society for Disability Studies, a clinician of social work, Dr. Katherine Levinstein, describing herself as both the parent of autistic children and autistic herself, told a heartrending tale of submitting her son to ABA, leading to injury and ultimately death. She condemned

ABA in the strongest possible terms, and the autistic people in the room cheered. Family members were more reserved. A few audience members bravely asked questions such as what behavioral approaches the speaker would recommend (none), and at least one parent seemed almost in tears trying to grasp this concept. One or two people left the room. Elizabeth Grace, who identifies as autistic and was facilitating the meeting, said to the group, "When people get mugged, it's not their fault they lost their wallet." She was reminding the autistic audience that parents may be bullied by health professionals and that we should have some understanding that parents made choices under duress and with limited knowledge.

Twenty-First Century: The Autism Crisis and the Autism Industry

By the end of the twentieth century, a new approach to autism emerged with an emphasis on autism as an epidemic and on research to prevent and cure autism. Programs such as Autism Speaks and Defeat Autism Now! (DAN!) came to prominence, generating tremendous amounts of money for research into biomedical determinants of autism. Suddenly, puzzle pieces— the emblem of the organization Autism Speaks—appeared everywhere. Such organizations were sharply divergent from organizations such as UCP and the Arc that focused more clearly on education and social services. As legacies of Rimland's biochemical and environmental approach to autism, they were focused on cure and biomedical interventions. Not only was the philosophy different, but so was the nature of parent involvement, as the founders were wealthy, highly connected, and savvy in corporate strategies. Thus, although created by family members, Autism Speaks was never a grassroots group in the same way many other parent organizations have been.

Autism Speaks was founded in 2005 by Bob and Suzanne Wright, grandparents of a child with autism. They were not just any grandparents: Bob Wright served as president and CEO of NBC Broadcasting (1986–2001) and as chairman and CEO from 2001 to 2007 while also vice-chairman of NBC's parent company, General Electric. The Wrights successfully raised millions of dollars, including a $25 million donation from the founder of Home Depot, billionaire Bernie Marcus, to launch Autism Speaks.[38] They organized mergers with other autism organizations, including Autism Coalition for Research and Education in 2005, National Alliance for Autism Research in 2006, and Cure Autism Now in 2007, to centralize and unify autism advocacy.[39] According to its mission statement, Autism Speaks "is dedicated to promoting solutions, across the spectrum and throughout the lifespan, for the needs of individuals with autism and their families through advocacy and support; increasing understanding and acceptance of people with autism spectrum disorder; and advancing research into causes and better interventions."[40] Across these goals, they have been particularly focused on and successful in increasing investments in research. In its first nine years, Autism Speaks invested a half billion dollars focusing on science and research, and it successfully lobbied Congress to invest billions in autism research. It convened the top medical and genetic experts in the field, including collaborating with Google in 2014 to sequence a database of autism genomes. And it successfully lobbied the United Nations to place autism on the global health agenda.[41] Autism Speaks has also been a strong proponent of ABA.

Autism Speaks operates with a corporate model and excels at self-promotion and the generation of revenue. Its puzzle pieces are everywhere and have come to be synonymous with autism in the public view—puzzle pieces are often used to promote events, organizations, and activities that are not formally affiliated with Autism Speaks, but simply relate to autism. Despite the group's marketing success, it has been sharply criticized by activists for its lack of representation of the views of autistic adults and for not having autistic adults involved in the organization itself. Although Autism Speaks now has autistic community members on its board of directors, it will be a long and perhaps impossible process to make amends for a problematic history and to gain the trust of most autistic activists.

The Defeat Autism Now (DAN!) movement grew out of the Autism Research Institute founded by Bernard Rimland. The institute and DAN! were dedicated to understanding the medical causes and treatments of autism, which they see as related to an immune response to external toxins and foods. Dr. Mark Hyman's blogs, which were shared by parent bloggers, provide an example of saving a child from the "biochemical train wreck" within him.

> He had very high level of antibodies to gluten. He was allergic not only to wheat, but to dairy, eggs, yeast, and soy—about 28 foods in total. He also had a leaky gut, and his gut was very inflamed. Sam was deficient in zinc, magnesium, and manganese, vitamins A, B12, and D, and omega-3 fats. Like many children with autism, he had trouble making energy in his cells, or mitochondria.
>
> His amino acids—necessary for normal brain function and detoxification—were depleted. And his blood showed high levels of aluminum and lead, while his hair showed very high levels of antimony and arsenic, signs of a very toxic little boy.[42]

This was only the beginning of the bodily deficiencies and problems said to face this boy. The doctor described a regimen of dietary restrictions and supplements to address the "biochemical and physiological rubble" within the boy's system and bring about his "recovery." Within two months the boy was starting to talk, after ten months he had "lost" his autism diagnosis, and after two years he was on every level "normal."[43] Parent blogger and nutritionist Ashley Steinbrinck restates the story Hyman tells on his blog but adds specific instructions for parents on what they can do to detoxify their children by using special supplements and avoiding fluoride and vaccinations. She outlines dietary changes needed—foods to avoid and include (e.g., lots of fiber)—as well as recommendations for exercise (sweat detoxifies), massage, and relaxation exercises.[44] Recently DAN! has rebranded itself as an approach called the MAPS (Medical Academy of Pediatric Special Needs) and TACA (an acronym that once meant Talk about Curing Autism but is currently listed on the TACA website as the Autism Community in Action). These more neutral approaches focus on treating biomedical conditions that often exist alongside autism such as allergies and digestive issues rather than a focus on "curing" autism.

Though some of the central premises of DAN! and other such programs have been successfully disproven, most notably the idea that autism is caused by vaccinations, parents and some professionals sometimes still cling to such explanations and treatments like body cleansing. Steinbrinck ends her blog post in this frame of mind:

> Just remember, a time ago—the medical community also claimed there to be no connection between cigarettes and lung cancer. Although very different topics, the vaccination/autism controversy has many similarities. I just hope I live to see the same outcome for vaccinations as we did for cigarettes.

Parent rejection of science is tied to a long and often valiant disregard of medical recommendations, such as institutionalization and shock therapy. Warned by health professionals and other parents that they only have a "small window" to reach the "trapped" child,[45] yet untethered from science and distrustful of experts, parents are left to using their gut feelings to decide what to try and judging its impact.[46]

According to communication scholars Emily Yochim and Vesta Silva, celebrity Jenny McCarthy played a central role in promoting the discourse that parents must take medicine into their own hands because doctors and the medical and pharmaceutical professions were failing them: "Rather than engaging researchers in new ways of thinking about ASDs [autism spectrum disorders], drawing on experience and evidence, McCarthy challenges women to be ever more responsible for making impossible, individualized choices about their children's health."[47] Sousa recognizes this as a way of enshrining the success of privileged white, upper-middle-class mothers who have the ability and time to be the kind of "good" mothers defined by their era.[48] Though similar messages are passed on by African American celebrities such as Toni Braxton,[49] mothers who do not come from this privileged place, without the money or time to meet these ideals, are set up for failure.[50] This message that children can recover from autism if their parents make the right choices generates persistent and tantalizing narratives. The website of the Autism Community in Action collects stories of children who, with their parents' help, have recovered from or overcome autism.[51] These are written mostly by parents, but some contributions are from people identifying themselves as formerly autistic and have titles such as "Tears of Joy," "Music to Our Ears," "Child Blossoms with Family behind Him," "How Kelsi Found Her Voice," and "Devoted Grafton Mother Pushes Back the Veil of Autism." With a deep history of substantiated distrust of biomedicine, some African American autism support groups disseminate information that autism in African American communities was caused by vaccinations as a form of racial genocide.

Other groups advocated for large sums of money dedicated to research into genetic explanations with the goals of both preventing and treating autism (e.g., Simon Foundation partnership with Cold Spring Harbor). These genetic explanations were in direct conflict with DAN! and similar movements. Within genetic frames, families were understood as potentially having multiple members, including possibly the parents themselves, with autistic characteristics, though too mild perhaps to require diagnosis.[52] Some parents found genetic explanations comforting, a way for parents to find connections and similarities between themselves and their children. Parents might even joke about their own presumed "autistic" behaviors that they shared with their children (intense enjoyment of a particular hobby, or a need for organization and structure, for example).[53] Some parents indeed found that they were themselves autistic. A small subset of autistic individuals even professed that autism was a kind of genetic superiority—the next and higher step of human evolution—and saw themselves as superior to neurotypicals.[54] Others, though, grew concerned about the possible eugenic implications of targeting genetic indicators. Genetic indicators of Down syndrome have been used extensively for prenatal diagnosis, leading to high rates of selective abortion. Might this somehow happen in the case of autism as well? Cloe Silverman states, "Advocates' efforts to define an 'autistic culture' and 'autistic voices' remind us that genetic identities are only as fixed as the meanings attached to them."[55] Silverman also discusses examples of professionals who associate parents' potential autistic tendencies with their "perseverating" on certain non-evidence-based treatments.[56]

New and often controversial treatments exploded onto the scene, including brain surgeries, bleach purges, and treatments to take lead out of a child's blood.[57] Many of these claimed to cure autism. Parents faced enormous pressure—if they did not try everything (and everything came with a hefty price tag), then they were failing as a parent and dooming their child to a horrible existence.[58] Media images like the 2007 ad campaign from the New York University (NYU) Child Study Center encouraged these fears. The campaign asserted that autism was a kidnapper who would destroy children and marriages: "We have your son, we will make sure he will not be able to care for himself or interact socially for as long as he lives. This is only the beginning. Autism." Another ad warned, in handwritten capital letters, "We have your son. We are destroying his ability for social interaction and driving him into a life of complete isolation. It's up to you now. Asperger Syndrome." The ads emphasized the view (completely contrary to genetic explanations, which emphasize similarity) that autistic children are "changelings" entirely unlike family members who do not have the diagnosis. Of course, NYU treatments were the solution.[59] Similar threatening discourse emerged from groups like Autism Speaks, such as in its 2009 film *I Am Autism*, written to bring awareness of the "global autism epidemic."[60]

The NYU ads and the broader rhetoric of fear present a powerful and blunt example of the pressures on parents of autistic children to comply with professional treatment regimens or face terrifying consequences. Clearly in this narrative, failure to treat leads to disaster and this disaster is the parent's fault for not seeking treatment.[61] This discourse stands in sharp contrast to the campaigns publicized by groups like the Arc, which try to assert the value of all humans, regardless of differences, and the positive impact of social supports.

This brings us to the beginning of the third decade of the twenty-first century, when parents whose children have been diagnosed with autism face tremendous pressure to choose from varying and contradictory approaches and are under threat of "losing" their children if they choose incorrectly. Autism interventionists push parents to try everything to "defeat" or "cure" their children's autism.[62] What if the gluten they feed their children is causing their autism? What if they are denying their integral sensory needs? What if they are overprotecting them? What if they are not protecting them enough? If anything, the guilt experienced by parents of autistic children is stronger in this century than in the earlier decades of the refrigerator mothers. Bernice Olivas writes, "In one instance I read that my sons' diagnosis will send me spiraling into the same grief patterns as a parent who has lost a child. I am supposed to be angry, depressed, try to negotiate with God and the universe, until finally I accept my new reality. I read reports that say autism will be the dingo that eats my marriage and my money."[63]

Demands placed on parents are at their highest, while perceptions of their competence, which has been questioned since the very beginning, even to the point of assuming that autism was caused by the parents' incompetence as parents (and really as humans), are at their lowest ebb. Even with the waning of the earlier "refrigerator mother" theories, parents' opinions were still considered questionable across many contexts of autism discourse, whether involving discussions of therapies, environmental toxins, or genetic predispositions. Parents are commonly dismissed by researchers and professionals as "hysterical" and reactive, certainly not objective. Even established researchers who also happen to be parents of autistic children, or autistic themselves, are often accused of lacking objectivity. This becomes a tactic for researchers to discredit each other—under the assumption that parents or autistic people are inherently biased and unreliable.

Others, especially parents themselves, valorize the perspectives and observations of parents as the "real" experts on their children's health and well-being. In some of these discourses, parents know best and must reclaim their children from corrupt science and medical establishments. They reject evidence-based medical knowledge in favor of instinct: "Mothers must be hyper-vigilant, fully tuned into their children's minds and bodies, capable of researching medical debates, and in touch with God and their own parenting instincts."[64] Yet other approaches may be more complex and selective—rejecting some evidence-based options (such as vaccination) and embracing others (such as ABA). When "evidence-based" interventions have contradictory data (e.g., researchers say ABA works, but autistic people say it is traumatizing and damaging), it can be very difficult for parents to know whom to believe.

Media may depict parents as desperate people willing to try anything, no matter how questionable, or else uncaring people unwilling to try hard enough. In contrast, Cloe Silverman states that parents should be recognized as having "ethical agency." She writes, "It seems clear that they represent one community that has already thought long and hard about the ethics of treatment, the desirability of normalization, the difficulty of balancing respect, protection and care."[65] They face tremendous pressures to intervene, yet they also make choices about the way they will understand and address their own child's experience.

Autistic Activists Respond

Beginning in the 1990s, the first generation of autistic children educated in the 1970s and 1980s came of age and began to participate in conversations about autism, joined by some people first diagnosed as adults. They shared their experiences with various treatments and engaged in passionate debates with researchers, parents, and each other. Also, many parents of autistic children realized, in the process of evaluating their children, that they were also autistic. Many chose to publicly embrace this identity. We moved from an era primarily dominated by the concept of autism embedded in the deficit and medical model to an era with complex intermixtures of identity politics—where parents advocated for the services and supports their children deserved as citizens, and then those children grew up to advocate for themselves—and biopolitics still dominated by medical discourses.

Autistic activist circles had been forming since the late twentieth century and felt particularly energized by the 2007 NYU advertising campaign.[66] They also mounted protests when autism organizations presumed to "speak" for or represent the "voice" of autism[67] and organized an annual national day of mourning (March 5) to draw attention to the high number of autistic children and adults who have been killed in hate crimes, sometimes by their own parents.[68] Autistic activists have developed techniques of social media protest as well as in-person protests organized regionally. Recently they have begun to work with the disability rights, direct-action organization ADAPT to protest the use of shock devices for behavior modification.[69]

Also emerging in the late twentieth and early twenty-first centuries are virtual and embodied groups of autistic youth and adults. According to the Autistic Self Advocacy Network (ASAN) website, groups of autistic activists organized in the 1990s as part of the disability rights movement in the United States, ASAN was formed in 2006, and these groups of activists met for conferences such as AUTCOM and AUTREAT.[70] Some of these individuals became national and international leaders, appointed to government positions at state and national levels. This has also allowed the development of shared thinking and identity formation across diverse regional, national, and even international contexts. What does it mean to be an autistic woman, an autistic of color? To be neuroqueer? Concepts such as neurodiversity, neurodivergence, and neuroqueer originated in online blogs and scholarly publications.[71] These concepts attempt to create a cross-disability umbrella of understanding and acceptance that moves beyond autistic to cross-disability alliance and identity.[72] According to Steve Silberman:

> Neurodiversity advocates propose that instead of viewing this gift as an error of nature—a puzzle to be solved and eliminated with techniques like prenatal testing and selective abortion—society should regard it as a valuable part of humanity's genetic legacy while ameliorating the aspects of autism that can be profoundly disabling without adequate forms of support. They suggest that, instead of investing millions of dollars a year to uncover the causes of autism in the future, we should be helping autistic people and their families

live happier, healthier, more productive, and more secure lives in the present.[73]

Many of the treatments represented above have been critiqued by autistic activists who are part of ASAN, or the wider diverse worlds of autistic and nonautistic researchers and bloggers. ASAN and other autistic activist, scholarly, and artistic communities provide an alternative to traditionally pathologizing formulations of autism. Even the *DSM* diagnosis criteria, discussed earlier, have been reframed on the ASAN website to use less pejorative language. Though many autistic people selectively choose to use various benevolent and noncoercive approaches and therapies (e.g., gluten-free diet; occupational, physical, and psychotherapy), there is strong protest against therapies that lack a strong evidence base, especially when they are potentially harmful (bleach cleansing, chelation, ABA). Autistic activists strongly challenged the continued refusal to vaccinate after the research base for this was discovered to be fraudulent. Organizations that were founded to advocate against vaccinations (and in some cases continue to do so) were rejected by autistic activists as invalid sources of autism research or information. This is especially true in the case of organizations that had token or no representation from autistic activists or researchers.

Many autistic activists assert that the experience of ABA and other aversive therapies have caused post-traumatic stress disorder (PTSD) and worse.[74] Max Sparrow writes movingly about the conflicting perspectives of autistic adults who describe ABA as abusive and parents who see ABA as a means to help their children. She asks parents to consider the consequences of imposing hours of therapeutic work on small children, enforcing normalcy, and training children to be submissive to authority. She describes herself as "one Autistic adult, one person coping with therapy-induced PTSD, one person exhausted by the all-out war I see every day between people like me and people who love people like me, one person who wants to see a better world for everyone (but, I admit, especially for Autistic people)."[75]

Differing conceptions of functional ability provide an example where parent perspectives (or as autistic activists call them, paaarent perspectives) and autistic activist perspectives often come into conflict. Paaarents do not listen to autistic people, do not respect their children, may post pejorative things about them online where their children might find and read them someday, and are full of self-aggrandizement about their "struggle" with the "burdens" of raising an autistic child. Amy Lutz, for example, is seen as a paaarent. She states that the neurodiversity movement may actually be harming so-called low functioning autistic children and adults. By "low functioning," she means children who have what she calls "the trifecta of autism, intellectual disability and dangerous behaviors" (it is her description of these in relation to her child that renders her a paaarent to autistic self-advocates). She claims that ugly realities of "low functioning" autistics are erased from neurodiversity narratives, and their needs may become marginalized as, with changes in defining autism, they are now a much smaller percentage of the total population of autistic individuals.[76] On the contrary, others feel that resources are generally focused on children and adults with high need of continual support, while adults who can pass as nonautistic for periods of time may not be getting the supports they need and may crash and burn as a result.[77] Many who choose to emphasize spectrums and function labels may dismiss "high functioning" individuals as either cured or never really autistic in the first place.[78] There seems to be no room in these functional status debates for the possibility that people may vary in their abilities to function from moment to moment, day to day, and that even so-called high functioning individuals may have moments when they have trouble communicating, whereas "low functioning" individuals may have moments of crystal clarity.

Communication differences are central to the diagnostic criteria for autism, but self-advocates reframe these differences from the pathologizing clinical deficits to value-neutral or positive ways of understanding not just supposed deficits in communication but also potential strengths of autistic communication. Autistic communication is multisensory and multidimensional. It may involve language and speech, or it may not. Stimming, gestures, and other body language can be seen as forms of autistic communication, as can the forms of online discussion and interaction that autistic individuals have participated in since the birth of the internet. In fact, they might be credited with developing and expanding different forms, modes, and etiquette of online communication. Similarly, autistic communication has developed new techniques for people to interact in conferences and other public spaces. In disability and autistic conferences, it has become the norm to use communication access badges that allow people to visibly project if they are open to interacting with everyone (green symbol), open to interacting only with people they know (yellow symbol), or not open to interacting with anyone (red symbol). Such badges and symbols may vary in terms of complexity or meaning across contexts.[79]

Though we have been emphasizing the conflicts between parents, researchers, and autistic activists, it is important to note that some researchers and parents (some of whom are also autistic) work in close alliance with autistic activists. For instance, Kerima Çevik, Bernice Olivas, Morton Gernsbacher, and Rachel Robertson are parents and researchers who strongly express alliance with an autistic-pride approach in their writings.[80] Çevik, a parent activist who has a son who is a nonspeaking autistic, was recently diagnosed with autism herself. She draws attention to the need to identify multiple forms of intersecting inequality and build inclusive, safe, and equal communities through grassroots activism. Gernsbacher's research focuses on alternatives to deficit-based approaches. Robertson considers how motherhood can be shaped by a respect for neurodiversity as a culture. Olivas seeks an alternative to traditional autism narratives of tragedy and pain. Additionally, Olga Solomon's work considers the issue of presuming competence or incompetence of autistic people, which is also discussed in the earlier works of Douglas Biklen and Jamie Burke, as well as Christopher Kliewer and colleagues.[81] Solomon's analysis reveals disturbing truths about how communication and sociality are bound within relations of power that can provide opportunities for agency or suppress it. Ariel Cascio notes something similar in her discussion of rigidity. She discusses how the concept is often used by professionals as a descriptive autistic trait, even while those same professionals lack flexibility in the way they approach autism.[82] If we expect to see rigidity, is that all we see? And who are really the rigid ones?

Autistic activists fear that when parents focus on curing autism they actually may be shaming autistic children and adults into the closet. Autistic children and adults are pressured by parents and clinicians to pretend to behave "normally." In *Loud Hands: Autistic People Speaking*, a product of the Loud Hands Project, autistic activists talk about stimming and other autistic behaviors as positive and adaptive, not something negative to extinguish,[83] and *Typed Words, Loud Voices* focuses on communication strategies used by autistic people in addition to or instead of speaking.[84] These alternative forms of behavior and communication provide revolutionary alternatives to traditional biomedical narratives regarding autistic behavior and communication. They also open the field to consider unique behavior and communication as unique autistic cultural expressions and products. Melanie Yergeau describes this in her video blog "I Stim, Therefore I Am." She reflects on her five-year-old self and states, "Five year old body, there is grace. How you move is grace. Oddness and rigidity are grace. You lumber and you lumber. You are a head attached to a body, and the body is grace. Stiff and stimmy, stiff and stimmy, stiff and stimmy is grace."[85]

Autistic worlds, communities, and cultural expressions are emergent—they are emerging over time and also gathering critical mass. These are worlds with parents and without parents. These are worlds where autistic people become parents and their children may also be autistic. In contrast to "Deaf Culture" for and by Deaf people, which has seemingly had centuries to emerge, "Autistic Culture" is just coalescing.[86] A camp described by psychologist Elizabeth Fein is one example of that emergence.[87] It is a mostly parentless space, though sometimes parents participate in minor roles, or stories related to parent-child relationships become part of the narrative.

For many of the youth, this is their first experience at constructing alternative narratives about themselves apart from their parents and families. Fantasy worlds, such as the one created in the camp Fein studied, rewrite and expand social possibilities. They allow youths to slay their dragons and develop skills that can be generalized—but on their terms—in a way that values and even valorizes autistic traits, autistic community, and "autistic culture." Clarice Rios and Barbara Costa Andrade's discussion of how autism has been defined and redefined in Brazilian policy is another example of the emergent nature of autistic worlds.[88] Brazilian social movements for psychiatric liberation were initiated by professionals, not psychiatric survivors, and services for autistic children were advocated for by parents. Mad Pride and Autistic Pride are new concepts in Brazil, and for these to join together in solidarity with movements for disability access and social equality is a very recent, emergent shift in autistic world building.[89]

Within these autistic worlds are tensions and outright fractures between autistic people, parents, clinical professionals, and researchers—as there is no consensus about *anything* related to diagnosis and treatment. Parents may take their children for brain surgery, stem cell treatments, or lead removal treatments. Maybe autism is of genetic origin or maybe caused by vaccinations or some interaction between genes and environment. An evidence base is optional, but there are extensive literatures in favor of or against behavioral, diet, sensory, visual, or educational treatments. Some of the information is helpful, and some of it is terribly harmful, but it is all never-ending. The tensions emerging between parent groups and autistic self-advocacy groups are painful to see. Sometimes, as in the case of ABA, the adult children describe their experience with some evidence-based treatments that parents cling to as inappropriate, stressful, and even harmful or abusive.[90]

How can we get beyond these fractures? There are now educational rights for children, but the next step is to support the path of those children as they emerge into adulthood. What do *they* want for their future? Can we see a world where professionals, researchers, clinicians, parents are supporting autistic children and autistic adults in the ways they want to be supported? Where the singularities and the commonalities are both respected? There is evidence that parents are finding pathways through which to navigate these fractures with humor and grace. Olivas writes, "I'm not grieving; I don't feel irreversibly changed. I have no desire to put my son in a hyperbaric chamber and oxygenate him until he comes out normal."[91] Olivas is seeking autism discourses that are not about tragedy or pathology, and so is Maria Mombille, interviewed in the documentary *Refrigerator Mothers*.[92] In describing autistic people, Mombille states, "And they are whole! They are whole people. They just have a different culture, a different way of communicating, a different language. To us it might not make any sense, but logic they do have. Parents can receive them, learn their language, bridge the gap."[93] Cascio finds similar elements of autism pride or neurodiversity discourse in moms' groups in which moms are pursuing therapies (e.g., ABA and cure-based biomedical approaches) that contradict the neurodiversity agenda: "Parents navigate a variety of approaches and ideologies in treatment-seeking behaviors, often pulling from approaches that have been discursively positioned as incompatible."[94] Somehow the different discourses, even though contradictory, come to coexist, and parents may also move through stages of trying an approach, then moving on to other approaches, and ultimately creating hybrid approaches.

Conclusion

The experience of parenting autistic children has been pathologized from the very first conceptualization of autism.[95] It seems when one distorted representation is finally put to rest, another rises to take its place, and parents can be heroes to some and villains to others based on the staggering number of choices they need to make when navigating the numerous treatment, therapy, and life choices. Yet parents are trying to navigate pathways through these extremes to find alternative narratives of hope and accomplishment for themselves and their children, though how parents define these may vary radically. In concluding this chapter, let us consider the consequences of narratives that do not offer hope, as Olivas clearly outlines the toll in human lives when she writes about how some parents have chosen to take their autistic children's lives and sometimes their own as well:

> It's through the lens of such horror stories that we can most clearly see the impact of allowing the typical autism essay to direct and control the public identity of autism. A mother of a six month baby was so terrified of the specter of autism she chose to kill her child. Why? I believe that part of that answer is because the narrative of autism she heard in her public spaces painted a picture of hopelessness. The typical autism essay was part of the reason she believed that death was better than life with autism. Yet voice after voice of autistic adults tells us that life as an autistic can be beautiful, productive, and joyful. Would that young mother have hesitated to kill her child if the discourse of autism around her reinforced a more realistic, diverse, and rich picture of autism identity?[96]

In addition to providing alternative narratives of hope, we need to focus on rendering invisible experiences visible. Most autism narratives depict the lives of privileged, educated white people.[97] The idea of autistic people from ethnic and racial minority groups is so outlandish to some that one mother discussed the experience of doctors refusing to even give her clearly autistic child the diagnosis:

> We did not fit the mold. We did not fit the classic mold for autism. Which is white upper-middle-class, very, very bright. It was really not a negotiable issue. According to my doctors, my son could not be autistic. I was not white, and it was assumed I was not educated; therefore he was labeled emotionally disturbed. Here your child has a disability that you recognize, and they say no, you can't be that. You can't even be a refrigerator mother. The irony of it all.[98]

While going back in time to diagnose people as autistic retroactively is a tricky business, the historic and modern erasures of autistic black people from the discourses on autism are so egregious that reclaiming historical narratives becomes an important contribution to rendering black autistic lives visible.[99] Çevik provides historical and contemporary examples of African American autistic people, including eighteenth-century slave Thomas Fuller, who could solve complex math problems in his head; nineteenth-century musical prodigy Tom Wiggins, who lived in slavery, like many on the freak show circuit, long after abolition; Eugene Hoskins, who was written about in the early twentieth century because of his ability to calculate dates and his love of trains and train schedules; late twentieth-century musical savant Noel Patterson; and artist Stephen Wiltshire.[100] Çevik's blogs and the interviews with people like Dorothy Groomer and Maria Mombille in *Refrigerator Mothers* barely begin to scratch the surface of our need to make visible the erased narratives of autistic people of color and their families in the United States.[101]

Discourses about autism and autistic people have changed dramatically over the twentieth and twenty-first centuries, and relationships between parents and children and their lives together (or apart) have been influenced by these discourses. The pressure to treat and even cure autism clashes with the neurodiversity movement's desire to validate autism as a valued way of being in the world. In addition to understanding the changes that have come over time, it is important to consider how these discourses differentially affected people from different racial, ethnic, religious, and regional backgrounds, not to mention gender and sexuality, further exacerbating division and prioritizing some voices and some visions of autism over others.

4

Physical Disabilities and
Parent Activism

On January 29, 1939, Zona Roberts gave birth to her first child, Edward Verne Roberts, at the age of eighteen. Zona's husband, Verne, worked for the Southern Pacific Railroad, and the recently married couple lived in Burlingame, California, near Verne's parents. Ed was an active child, walking and talking early, and attended the local elementary school. Zona was a homemaker for several years, ultimately raising four children and volunteering for the PTA, and when Ed was twelve, she took a job as a census taker.

In 1953, following a baseball game, Ed came home ill and by the next morning had a fever and stiffness. After two days, Ed was hospitalized and subsequently became paralyzed. His paralysis included his neck and lungs, and he was diagnosed with polio and rushed into an iron lung to allow him to continue breathing. Ed was moved into a polio ward with other polio patients and stayed in the San Mateo hospital for nine months. Zona transferred Ed to Children's Hospital in San Francisco, which has a polio rehabilitation program that would keep him another nine months. She learned to drive so that she could visit him. When he completed the rehabilitation program, the Roberts family moved to a new house to better accommodate Ed's iron lung. Ed had become a quadriplegic, meaning his arms and legs were paralyzed, and he required mechanical assistance with breathing from the iron lung or a ventilator except for brief periods. Nevertheless, Ed was able to resume high school, first through study at home and then, in his senior, year attending classes at the school once a week.

Ed was ready to graduate in 1959 at the age of twenty, but the school counselor sought to have him remain in high school for another year. Zona lobbied the school principal, Ed's teachers, and the superintendent of schools until Ed was allowed to graduate. He moved on to the local community college, with Zona helping with transportation and writing out class assignments dictated by Ed. After two years, with Zona's assistance, Ed transferred to the University of California at Berkeley to study political science in 1962. The California Department of Rehabilitation reluctantly provided him with financial assistance, and the university required him to live in the campus student health center. Joined by other students with disabilities, collectively known as the Rolling Quads, Ed helped create a self-help group that became established as the Physically Disabled Students Program. Ed went on to play a key role in promoting independent living in Berkeley and around the nation.

While Ed was attending Berkeley, his father, Verne, was diagnosed with lung cancer, and he died in 1964, when the cancer metastasized. Supported by Social Security survivors insurance, Zona followed Ed's path to the College of San Mateo and then to UC Berkeley in 1967, graduating in 1969 and earning a teaching certificate the following year. Zona went on to work in the Physically Disabled Students Program while earning her master's degree in social work, and when the initial director left, she was offered the program director position. Zona later worked at CIL, establishing a counseling department. Her work at CIL came to include a focus on working with the parents of CIL's disabled participants, building on her experiences with Ed to help other parents accept and support their children's independence. In 1982, Zona left CIL to establish a private practice as a family disability counselor. She and Ed shared a house until his death and collaborated on many projects related to disability rights and independent living.

Ed Roberts, who died in 1995, was one of the key founders of the disability rights and independent living movements, served as California commissioner of rehabilitation, won a MacArthur "genius" award in 1984, and was the founding president of the World Institute on Disability. Zona Roberts was not only a crucial supporter of her son's independence and career but also an important figure in the disability community in the Bay Area and beyond.

Their story illustrates how parents and children can influence one another in promoting independence and rights for people with disabilities and working for institutional change.[1] Although few disability organizations in the 1950s were led by people with disabilities, Zona worked toward Ed's self-determination, supporting him in advancing his own work as an activist.

In the mid-twentieth century, as the Arc was forming, so too were several organizations of parents of children with physical disabilities such as cerebral palsy. For the first half of the twentieth century, most children with disabilities were denied access to public education, and many parents of children with serious impairments were encouraged to place their children in residential institutions.[2] However, in the period after World War II, parents increasingly chose to keep their children with impairments in their own homes. A corollary to this different approach was to seek expanded public support for supportive community-based services for disabled children. While many parents focused largely on the needs of their own children, a number of new or revitalized parent organizations were established to seek broader changes. Judith Sealander reports that by the early 1970s, over three thousand organized parent groups demanded access to schools for their children with disabilities.[3] Many of these groups, though, focused more on medical treatment, cure, and fundraising for medical research and treatment, creating large-scale fundraising campaigns that eventually became highly controversial among disabled activists.

While this activism emerged in the same historical era as the Arc, our discussion of it is placed last among the case studies for several reasons. These organizations either began as or became professionalized, some quicker than others, yet they rely on parents for support, and, therefore, they raise the issue of what constitutes "parent" activism. Activism related to physical disability is also fragmented across impairments. This chapter covers only a few of the largest and most influential groups, selected because of their size and social influence. For reasons of space, we do not address parent organizations focused on visual or hearing disabilities or chronic illness, which have important histories of their own, several of which have been addressed previously by other authors.[4]

In line with the other chapters, however, this history offers a window into the general trends shaping parent activism and its relationship with activism by people with disabilities. To discuss tensions with disabled activists, we focus on fundraising campaigns, and in particular the telethon, as emblematic of issues such as paternalism, the medical model, and the willingness to use pity to raise funds.

The Historical Context for Parent Activism

The post–World War II era in the United States was a transformative period in American history, a time of growing affluence, suburbanization, a celebration of traditional family roles and values, a growing commitment to universal public education and to scientific medicine, and a new sense of promise for and commitment to people with physical disabilities.

Following the hardships of the war and the Great Depression that preceded it in the 1930s, the post–World War II era was an era of rising American national prosperity. Unlike the aftermath of previous conflicts, which typically led to heightened unemployment, men departing from military service in the late 1940s and 1950s were largely absorbed in the rapidly expanding American industrial economy, whose goods were in demand in the recovering worldwide economy. The United States emerged from the war as the dominant power in terms of military presence, geopolitical influence, and the global economy. The United States replaced the global reach of the disintegrating European colonial empires in Asia, Latin America, and Africa, and engaged with the Soviet Union and its allies in a Cold War that included a series of regional conflicts. Domestically, the political aftermath of the New Deal and World War II was a rapprochement between management and labor, in which collective bargaining became institutionalized, and New Deal social insurance programs such as the Social Security system were preserved and strengthened.

In an era of increasing prosperity and advancement, education became central to the building of the American middle class. Improvement in public education (and many other public issues of the era) became framed in the rhetoric of America's Cold War competition with the Soviet Union. The Soviet launch of the Sputnik satellite particularly provoked a public outcry to upgrade American education. Both the general public and policy makers perceived improvements to public education as critical to national advancement and economic progress. The Supreme Court affirmed this perspective in its landmark *Brown v. Board of Education* decision, holding that effective participation in education was necessary for citizenship in the emerging economy.[5] The extension of a right to education from African American children to children with disabilities was neither immediate nor obvious; both groups of children benefited from and contributed to an overall movement toward procedural justice, a trend that also led the courts to identify rights to treatment and to refuse treatment for those involuntarily restricted.

The GI Bill promoted college attendance for returning military members; federal housing programs placed home ownership within reach for veterans, even for families with modest means; and federal and other public investment in the construction of new highways increased mobility, allowing families to reside further away from places of employment. Increasingly, those Americans who could left central cities for the suburbs, and the society became more family-focused and child-centered.[6] It must be emphasized that these developments were largely limited to white Americans; people of color faced a host of legal, social, and cultural barriers to upward mobility.

Despite increases in women's participation in the paid workforce during World War II, the return of male military service members into the domestic economy was marked by a cultural imperative for women, at least for middle-class white women, to give up paid employment outside of the home and embrace child-rearing and homemaking in rapidly growing suburban communities.[7] Popular media emphatically celebrated domesticity and insisted that the essence of feminine identity and value was to manage their homes and nurture their children. This child-centered focus, in which raising children and maintaining their families was considered the hallmark of womanhood and a necessary and valued art form for women, may have helped encourage a shift in parental responses to children with serious impairments. In previous decades, the prevailing medical and societal judgment mandated that children with physical or mental differences should be removed from their homes and communities and moved into isolated residential facilities.

The rise of parental activism was also fueled by the growth of grassroots social movements developing in response to other issues of exclusion. In the black civil rights movement, African Americans pushed for their children's inclusion in public education through lawsuits, protests, and civil disobedience. While protests and advocacy have always been part of American political life, the rising expectations for social and economic advancement of the postwar era promoted a belief that educational attainment should be open to all Americans, including children with disabilities.

While expectations regarding gender and race were changing, so too were ideas about physical disability. World War II led to a tremendous influx of disabled veterans returning home, and vocational rehabilitation gained prominence as a mechanism to return them to productivity. President Franklin D. Roosevelt's public persona downplayed his disability, yet he expressed support of a range of therapeutic services.[8] He stated, "No overseas casualty [should] be discharged from the armed forces until he has received the maximum benefit of hospitalization and convalescent facilities, which must include physical and psychological rehabilitation, vocational guidance, prevocational training, and resocialization."[9] Roosevelt's faith in rehabilitation further led him to found the Warm Springs Institute for Rehabilitation.

Over the next thirty years, federally funded vocational rehabilitation expanded considerably, as did the eligible populations. The focus on education and rehabilitation represented a particular model of disability integration and uplift based on increasing human capital, which, in turn, would restore patients into productive citizens. Disabled activists, however, promoted a different view. While appreciative of the availability of rehabilitation, disabled activists demanded that low employment rates be addressed as a problem of discrimination against people with disabilities. The League of the Physically Handicapped formed in 1935 to protest discrimination by the Public Works Administration, and the American Federation of the Physically Handicapped, founded in 1940, demanded that disability policy focus on discrimination and achieving the right to work. Federal policy instead continued to rely heavily on the medical model and the promise of rehabilitation.[10]

In this context, parents of children with physical and other disabilities increasingly were motivated to redefine the appropriate response to children who were born with or acquired impairments, and they placed their hopes both in education and in medical treatment and rehabilitation. While children born with serious impairments had previously been hidden away in remote and largely invisible residential facilities to live apart from their families and communities, parents, particularly but not exclusively from the white middle class, increasingly tried to maintain their disabled children within their households. To care for their children at home typically required forms of support beyond the household, and so parent activists called for expanded community supports to assist their children medically, educationally, and socially in ways that allowed them to stay at home with their families and to participate more broadly in their communities. While not explicitly addressed in the popular culture of 1940s and 1950s, children with disabilities may have been viewed differently within the newly child-centered American suburban culture, and thus there may have been greater interest in accommodating them in their families, homes, and communities.

Many of the leaders for these parents' groups originally came from the emerging suburban, usually white middle-class communities of that era. Parents of color, parents with lower socioeconomic status, and members of other marginalized groups often encountered particular problems with obtaining even basic medical support for their children with disabilities, as a result of racism, segregation, lack of financial resources, and less access to medical insurance. Moreover, excluded families often lacked the social and cultural capital to support collective action on behalf of their children. When parents belonging to marginalized groups did undertake political action, in many cases they framed their demands for basic health and human services in terms of civil rights, rather than as disability activism per se. Leaders in disability activism also failed to build alliances with the black community. The Black Panthers, for example, fought to improve access to health care in minority communities, demanding health care as a universal right for all Americans, yet only recently have disability scholars understood this legacy within a disability rights framework.[11]

One parent motivated to advocate for her child was Ilse Heumann, who at the age of twelve immigrated from Germany to live in Brooklyn, New York. Ilse's daughter Judith (Judy) contracted polio in 1949, at the age of eighteen months. When she reached school age, Judith was consigned to home instruction as the result of inaccessible schools that could not accommodate her disability and use of a wheelchair. However, Ilse became an active proponent for her daughter's access to education and other services, and as the result of her advocacy Judith was admitted to public school, although at first to a segregated "special" program. Ilse worked with other parents of children with polio and other disabling conditions who were relegated to segregated facilities or excluded altogether from public schools. Such relationships provided parents like Ilse with social support, shared information, and advocacy strategies, although in many cases they did not lead to the formation of formal activist organizations.

When Ilse found out that Judy was going to have to go onto home instruction for high school because there were no accessible high schools, she organized with other parents to force the New York City Board of Education to make some high schools accessible in each of the city's boroughs. Ilse's advocacy proved to be effective; Judy became the first child from her segregated classes at PS 219 to transfer from the segregated disability program into Sheepshead Bay High School, a newly constructed high school in Brooklyn, from which she ultimately graduated and attended Long Island University. Judith Heumann rose to prominence as one of the leaders of the disability rights movement, helping found Disabled in Action (New York) and serving in leadership positions in the Berkeley Center for Independent Living, the World Institute of Disability, the U.S. Department of Education, the World Bank, and the U.S. Department of State.[12]

Another activist parent outside of an organized group was Zona Roberts. Zona's son Ed contracted polio in 1953, at the age of fourteen, and was hospitalized for two years, often relying on an iron lung to breathe. Zona pressured the local high school to allow Ed to complete his high school education, and she encouraged him to attend college. Despite the barriers to success for a post-polio, ventilator-using quadriplegic, Ed graduated from UC Berkeley, helped form the Rolling Quads disability activist group, co-founded the Berkeley Center for Independent Living and the World Institute of Disability, served as commissioner of rehabilitation for the State of California, and won a MacArthur Foundation "genius" award.[13] In contrast with parent activism described in the preceding chapters, parent activism related to physical disabilities often fostered the maturation of their children into activists themselves, shaping confident leaders who would demand disability rights and lead disability organizations.

While the major focus of this book is on the parents of children with intellectual, developmental, and psychiatric impairments, parents of children with physical disabilities, particularly those with significant and complex medical conditions, also played an important role in changing the disability landscape. They created models for grassroots organizing, information sharing, and mutual support. They also advocated for increased public investment in research to treat and prevent disabling conditions, and for building public awareness about disabled conditions.

Parent-led groups were typically formed by parents of disabled children whose initial motivation was seeking assistance for their own children and building support networks for themselves. However, over time, some of the parents shifted their focus to more broadly promoting the status of other children who shared these disabilities. Alfred Katz, who conducted interviews with parent participants in United Cerebral Palsy (UCP) and the Muscular Dystrophy Association (MDA), writes:

> Among the active members of these groups, participation is particularly meaningful because the ideological convictions or "values" arise in the first place out of painful personal problems. Along with the individual desire for assistance with these problems grows the conviction of the possibility of achieving help through the organized instrumentality of the parent group. . . .
>
> There is developed a sense of working together with others on a common problem; a problem which becomes in the mind of these participants the particular property of the parent group. In the organization pride and sense of identity thus engendered, additional elements of a personally therapeutic nature to parents is experienced and reinforce the motivations for participation.[14]

However, as parent-led organizations succeeded in raising funds for research and expanded services, the entities evolved into established public charities and nonprofit organizations, and increasingly turned to professional managers to administer their growing operations. This change reflected an overall shift among advocacy groups in the United States at the end of the twentieth century from broadly participatory membership organizations to professionally led advocacy groups centered in Washington, D.C., and other governmental centers.[15] Parents continued to play key roles in the public face of the groups and in grassroots fundraising, yet they were less involved in many organizational activities. This shift in participation may have removed some of the concerns of parents from the priorities of the organizations. One potential arena for parent concerns was their relationship with medical and rehabilitation professionals.

Parents and Experts

One key issue that parent-led organizations have had to manage is their relationship with medical and rehabilitation professionals. Up through the early postwar era, many physicians' prejudices and lack of knowledge about disabling conditions led to endorsement of children's institutionalization. In the postwar era, parents increasingly rejected such counsel and sought to identify alternative, better-informed physicians who were supportive of keeping children with disabilities at home, to be cared for by their families. Groups such as UCP recruited medical experts supportive of this approach to be advisers. Such physicians were valuable allies who provided medical legitimacy to the parent groups and assisted them in directing funds they had raised to promising lines of biomedical research. Some organizations founded by or strongly identified with parents worked in partnership with medical scientists, and others focused almost exclusively on fundraising to support medical initiatives. Other parent-led disability organizations rejected the authority of medical experts altogether. By the 1960s, families promoting better circumstances for their children identified with the nascent self-help movement, an outgrowth of the second wave of feminism. These groups sought information, education, and services. However, many parent groups were slow to focus on the issues of inclusion and independence for adults with disabilities, which eventually placed some of the organizations in conflict with the groups representing disabled adults themselves.

One of the first (and best) analyses of the social situation of parents of children with disabilities was provided by John Gliedman and William Roth in their 1980 book, *The Unexpected Minority: Handicapped Children in America*.[16] In the book, Gliedman and Roth acknowledge the dependence of parents on the medical services provided by professionals to their children but encourage parents to play an executive role in managing their children's live and professional care. They write:

> We believe that the parent-professional relationship in handicap should be in accord with the traditions of civil society. Instead of professional dominance, there should be parental coordination, and not just by the affluent and well-educated parent who comes from the same cultural milieu as the professional. Parents should oversee and orchestrate the service that professionals provide their children. Parents of all races and social classes should be able to pick and choose among different experts, obtain outside opinions when dissatisfied with the services or advice provided by a professional, and constantly evaluate the professional's performance in terms of the overall needs of the growing child.[17]

According to Gliedman and Roth, the best way for parents to achieve this managerial role is to join with their peers: "It is essential that parents of handicapped children organize themselves into self-help groups. These can provide the parent with access to alternate information about services in the community, consultations with outside professionals, and moral support."[18] Perhaps the most significant and largest of parent-initiated groups in the United States has been the organization founded as the United Cerebral Palsy Association, which ultimately took the name UCP.

UCP

Cerebral palsy (CP) is "a disorder of movement, muscle tone or posture that is caused by damage that occurs to the immature, developing brain, most often before birth."[19] Diagnosis usually occurs in early childhood, and is associated with atypical reflexes and/or posture, involuntary movements, and unsteady walking. People with CP may have difficulty swallowing, focusing their eyes, walking, and with muscle stiffness. They may also have additional diagnoses such as intellectual disabilities, epilepsy, blindness, and deafness.[20]

At the time of UCP's founding after World War II, public school administrators routinely excluded children with cerebral palsy, and physicians and dentists refused to accept them as patients.[21] In many cases, physicians misdiagnosed CP as a form of intellectual disability (then known as mental retardation) and recommended that children with CP be institutionalized in "state schools," large residential facilities with few services, educational or developmental, available.

Parents of these children in New York State and other areas within the United States found each other and formed networks of mutual support that in some cases led to political advocacy. In January 1946, a group of parents met in New York City to discuss their experiences raising children with CP. Leonard and Isabelle W. Goldenson's daughter Genise (nicknamed Cookie) had CP, and the Goldensons became active advocates.[22] Along with Jack and Ethel Hausman, the Goldensons placed an ad in the *New York Herald Tribune* recruiting parents of children with CP who were frustrated with the lack of local services available to their children. There were hundreds of responses to the ad.[23] In September of that year these parents founded the Cerebral Palsy Society of New York City to support one another and seek better access to services for their children.

Other parent groups formed around New York State, and by June 1946 they had formed the New York State Association for Cerebral Palsy.[24] Goldenson, who was the board chair for the American Broadcasting Companies, spoke to a gathering of parents at the Astor Hotel in New York City, calling for the establishment of a national organization to bring together local parents' groups. The National Foundation for Cerebral Palsy was chartered on August 12, 1949.[25]

Alfred Katz wrote of the formation of several local parent groups in the New York area in the years after World War II. These groups of parents of children with cerebral palsy initially formed to share information and offer mutual support, founding an Information Center to collect and disseminate information about available treatment facilities and community resources for children and adults with cerebral palsy.[26]

The network of parent groups ultimately coalesced into a foundation with the broader goals of promoting CP-focused medical services and research, expanding community and social services, and raising funds to support both. Services supported by UCP in the early 1950s included outpatient and inpatient health care services, educational programs, vocational services, home care, summer camps and recreational services, and transportation. To support these services and organizational administration, UCP obtained growing financial contributions, with a budget of nearly $600,000 by 1953 that continued to grow through the 1950s.[27] Ultimately, Leonard Goldenson's economic position and leadership of a major television network meant that he was able to draw on his relationships with celebrities, such as the comedian Bob Hope, prominent physicians such as Dr. Sidney Farber, and philanthropists such as Julius Rosenwald, to raise funds and visibility for the cause of CP. The medium of television was a particularly powerful tool to raise awareness, increase public support, and appeal for contributions.

One effective strategy employed by UCP to reach the public was the telethon, a special televised appeal for funds featuring celebrities and disabled children who typically were portrayed as tragically affected by their disabling condition. Comedian Milton Berle hosted the first UCP telethon, a two-and-a-half-hour program aired in 1950. Later that year, a fifteen-hour telethon called Celebrity Parade was broadcast in Chicago. UCP went on to produce local telethons in Cincinnati, Philadelphia, San Francisco, and New York. Other charitable groups focused on disabilities affecting children followed suit.

Realizing the limitations of soliciting charitable donations, though, Goldenson and his associates, along with citizen volunteers from voluntary organizations concerned with multiple sclerosis, lobbied Congress to fund biomedical research into neurological disorders and establish the National Institute of Neurological Diseases and Stroke within the National Institutes of Health.[28] According to a history of neurological research at the National Institutes of Health:

> Citizen groups, representing research and care in multiple sclerosis, cerebral palsy, muscular dystrophy, epilepsy, and blindness, pushed for the establishment and funding of institutes relating to the par-

ticular disease with which they were concerned. . . . It was not until the late 1940s and early 1950s that these voluntary health organizations . . . became powerful enough to influence legislators.[29]

In addition to promoting governmental research programs, UCP directly supported prevention research through its own grants to biomedical researchers and helped support the development of a rubella vaccination in the 1950s. Through its Research and Education Foundation, established in 1955, UCP also worked to raise public awareness about cerebral palsy and solicit donations through public relations campaigns. Paul Longmore writes that UCP "aimed to dispel superstitious folklore about 'spastics' and end abusive institutionalization."[30]

Another factor in presenting UCP and issues facing children with CP to the American public was the 1952 publication of a memoir, *Karen*, by Marie Killilea, whose daughter Karen had CP.[31] Killilea was a white, middle-class, suburban New York housewife. The memoir told the story of a child brought up in a home in which her disability required many accommodations but was fully accepted by her family. The book portrays numerous struggles with the medical issues associated with a serious impairment but also the encounters with social stigma and the actions and strategies taken by Karen and her family to gain acceptance of her impairment and inclusion in community life.

Karen was born prematurely in 1940, with a birth weight of under two pounds. Their pediatrician told the Killileas that her diagnosis of CP meant that she was unlikely to "have any mentality" and would never be able to sit up, use her hands, or walk.[32] Consulting a neurologist, the Killileas were encouraged to "take your child to an institution and leave her and forget you ever had her."[33] Nevertheless, as she developed in subsequent years, Karen learned to sit up, attained limited mobility, and appeared to have above average intelligence. The Killileas consulted with more than two dozen physicians, many of whom expressed low expectations for their daughter. One spoke favorably to them of a society where children with conditions like Karen's were left on a mountaintop to die of exposure. Eventually, they found one out-of-town physician who offered hopeful advice and worked with them to develop a physical training program to improve Karen's fitness and mobility.

In Killilea's lively and heartfelt account, she speaks of the frustration she and her husband experienced in their search for positive help in managing Karen's condition and their desire to reach out to other parents of "CPs" who might benefit from sharing their experiences. They placed an advertisement in the newspaper in their suburban New York community, offering assistance to families whose children have cerebral palsy, and received coverage from their local radio station. The primary purpose for this outreach was to create a mutual support network for parents.

The Killileas obtained a list from their local health department of families with exposure to encephalitis, which was considered to be a potential precursor for CP, and Marie Killilea sent letters to several hundred families. When a family with a child with the diagnosis was identified, they were sent a questionnaire to collect further information. Eventually, they compiled a list of fifty-eight cases, with disturbing results:

> The average number of doctors consulted by each parent was fourteen. But the whole file was alarming: an oft-reiterated report of incorrect diagnosis, faulty prognosis, children growing up confined to bed, ninety-nine out of a hundred receiving no treatment or education, an appreciable number improperly confined to mental institutions because they could not be taken care of at home, others hidden in attics. One child was found kept in a box in the cellar of his home. Children and parents doomed by society—because it didn't know, care or accept. Here was no question of blame, but rather an urgent need to deliver parents and their children, and the public at large, from the dark womb of ignorance. But how?[34]

Killilea contacted a local group of parents of children with CP in Rochester, New York, and received a reply from its organizer, Ralph Amdursky, who had brought parents together with the help of a local radio commentator. A public meeting was held in the New York City suburb of White Plains, and 117 people attended. The meeting led to an article in the New York *Sun*, which in turn led to parent inquiries from around the region. In describing the process of organizing parent groups, Killilea writes, "We came to recognize C.P. as a social problem, and, like all social problems, we felt it should be the concern of each and every member of the community."[35]

Killilea's sequel to *Karen*, titled *With Love from Karen*, was published in 1963 and brings the narrative of Karen and her family up to Karen's teenage years.[36] While Killilea's political activism appears to have been largely eclipsed by her developing career as an author, by sharing the account of Karen's development, including setbacks and achievements, she may have helped reframe the experience of CP from a tragic and essentially negative experience to a story that paralleled the development of any child, thereby humanizing the experience of children with CP and their families. However, the story told by CP advocates was to take a much darker turn with their adoption of the telethon as a fundraising and public awareness strategy, as discussed later in the chapter.

Through the 1960s, UCP continued to play an important role in advocating for children with cerebral palsy and other disabling conditions (including intellectual and developmental disabilities), providing services, and addressing more general barriers facing people with disabilities. By 1964, UCP had grown to include more than 324 local affiliates, although there appear to be fewer at present.[37] There was considerable variation among local affiliates in their activities and priorities, with some chapters stressing direct service provision and others emphasizing advocacy, information, and referral. UCP's programs and services became a vast system of social services, including physical and occupational therapy, adaptive technology, early childhood intervention, training for employment and independent living, and community education. Nationally, UCP now claims to serve over 176,000 individuals every day.[38]

As with the Arc, as UCP grew it had to address tensions between its medical focus and fundraising techniques versus advocacy for disability rights and inclusion. Over time, UCP became less focused on medical research and services and more directly focused on issues of rights and services that support community integration. In its early years, UCP limited its political activities to the support of biomedical research and the promotion of special education and respite care, mainly through expert testimony and grassroots campaigns. In 1969, for example, UCP funded research that led to the development of a rubella (German measles) vaccine. Also in 1969, though, UCP more clearly aligned with other organizations focused on "developmental disabilities." The Arc, UCP, and other organizations agreed on the political advantages of incorporating several disabilities under one umbrella, worked to create a definition of "developmental disability" to unify groups, and advocated its formalization as a political category via the Developmental Disabilities Act of 1975, which defined developmental disabilities "to include mental retardation, cerebral palsy, epilepsy, and other neurological conditions closely related to mental retardation which originate prior to age 18 and constitute a substantial handicap."[39] UCP straddled the divide between the world of developmental disabilities like intellectual disability and autism and the world of physical disabilities like muscular dystrophy and polio. The Arc, as seen in Chapter 1, increasingly stressed the social model of disability, the provision of rights, and service provision, rather than the medical model, and the partnership between the Arc and UCP propelled and fortified both in this direction.

UCP created a Washington-based newsletter, *Word from Washington*, to inform affiliates about events in the capital. The newsletter became an important source of information on legislative and administrative developments of the Rehabilitation Act of 1973 and the Education for All

Handicapped Children Act of 1975. Later in the 1970s, UCP reversed its policy against legal advocacy, and established a Legal Advocacy Committee. Further, the association assumed a leadership role in political mobilization, forming coalitions with other disability-focused groups, including the Arc and other groups focused on intellectual and developmental disabilities, to promote expanded disability benefits, services, access, and civil rights for people with disabilities. UCP was an early member of the American Coalition of Citizens with Disabilities, led by disabled activists, which coordinated national efforts to implement Section 504 of the Rehabilitation Act in the 1970s and subsequent disability rights measures. In the 1980s, UCP was a key member of the Consortium for Citizens with Disabilities, which lobbied for passage of the Americans with Disabilities Act, and was active in support of Supplemental Security Income benefits for children with disabilities.[40] Thus, considering the range of parent-professional organizations, UCP became a relatively reliable ally of disabled activists, with a range of interests related to developmental and physical disability. Summing up their valued role in history, Natalie Jean writes, "UCP has been a leading advocate of expanding access for people with disabilities in education, employment, housing, and telecommunications."[41]

Muscular Dystrophy Association

Although not known primarily as a parent-led organization, the Muscular Dystrophy Association (MDA) has an origin similar to that of UCP, and at around the same time and location, New York City in the immediate aftermath of World War II. Muscular dystrophy (MD) is a group of diseases that cause progressive weakness and loss of muscle mass when abnormal genes interfere with the production of proteins needed to form healthy muscle. Symptoms of the most common form of MD begin in childhood, mostly in boys. Other types don't surface until adulthood.[42]

In 1950, six mothers of children with MD met at a clinic at New York City Hospital where their children were receiving treatment.[43] The mothers had experienced difficulty in obtaining information about the disease and available services, and they joined together to systematically share what they learned. The mothers organized a meeting in April of that year, reaching out through personal ads in several local newspapers. About sixty individuals attended this meeting, including other parents, relatives, and friends as well as some adults living with MD. The group formed an organization, incorporated in June 1950, with chapters in several boroughs of New York City. The organization's purpose was to promote research on MD among physicians, and efforts were undertaken to recruit members and raise funds. While its origins were similar to UCP's, MDA was less of a grassroots mutual assistance organization and more explicitly focused on fundraising for biomedical research.

Paul Cohen, a New York business leader with MD, is credited by MDA as its founder. The organization formed a Medical Advisory Board, and early in its history awarded a $1,500 research grant to Dr. Ade T. Milhorat. Within a year, activities expanded into the promotion of public policies that would support MD research and treatment, and professional staff were hired to run the organization and expand it to other states. In 1951 entertainers Dean Martin and Jerry Lewis concluded their television program with an appeal for donations to support MD research. The following month, Martin and Lewis repeated their appeal for funds in a network radio program. By 1956, MDA organized its first telethon, hosted by Martin and Lewis in New York's Carnegie Hall. The MDA telethon became an annual television special hosted by Lewis and dedicated to fundraising for "Jerry's Kids."[44]

Early financial sponsors of MDA included the Masonic civic group Tall Cedars of Lebanon of North America, the National Association of Letter Carriers (NALC), and the International Association of Fire Fighters (IAFF). Members of the NALC initiated a door-to-door solicitation for MDA. A group of Boston families with members who had MD approached a local fire station for assistance in fundraising, and this effort spread across Boston and ultimately nationwide, with fire fighters "passing the boot" to solicit donations, a practice that persists today.

MDA eventually offered a range of support services to children and families affected by MD, but its primary goals were fundraising for medical research and related policy advocacy.[45] This meant that establishing relationships with service providers was not a priority, while hiring staff for raising funds was stressed. Tensions developed between rank-and-file parents and the paid staff over organizational priorities, the role of the paid staff, and control over the group's rapidly increasing budget.[46] The emphasis by professional staff on fundraising and promoting biomedical research largely prevailed; by 1953, MDA had raised $3.5 million and had sponsored several medical conferences. Expansion was also a priority, and within a year of the founding of the first local chapter, forty chapters in eighteen states had been established, with numerous additional chapters in place by the end of 1952 and a total of seventy-eight chapters nationwide by late 1953.[47]

In subsequent years, MDA combined its controversial fundraising telethons with financial support for biomedical research on neuromuscular diseases, public education campaigns, and a variety of service programs supporting children and adults affected by these conditions. It operates a network of over 150 care centers and affiliates around the United States that connect research and clinical trials with providers and patients. MDA supports a Neuromuscular Observational Research Data Hub that aggregates clinical data for a variety of neuromuscular diseases to support research efforts, and offers educational conferences and events aimed at families and clinicians. Services offered include financial assistance for purchase of assistive devices, support groups, and summer camps and recreational programs for children.[48]

Easterseals

Although it is not an organization of parents, Easterseals (ES) has been a prominent advocate for children with physical disabilities for nearly a century in partnership with parents and their organizations, and it offers a model of a national disability-focused organization working with state and local affiliates to promote community-based disability services. ES is clearly an organization "for" rather than "of" people with disabilities, and while its activities have included many volunteers whose families have been affected by disability, its leadership has not deliberately incorporated people with disabilities or their parents.

In 1919 Edgar F. "Daddy" Allen founded a precursor group, the Ohio Society for Crippled Children, with the goal of expanding services for children with disabilities outside of residential hospitals and other facilities.[49] Daddy Allen, owner of a local business in Elyria, Ohio, had lost his eighteen-year-old son in a streetcar collision in 1907, and he dedicated his life to establishing a hospital in Elyria to improve access to medical services. Three years later, "Daddy" encountered Jimmy, a child with infantile paralysis (polio), at the hospital, and Allen became committed to expanding services to "crippled" children.[50] Working closely with local civic groups, primarily affiliated with the Rotary Club, Allen lobbied the Ohio legislature for what came to be called the "Ohio Plan," a system of local care facilities established in 1920. The facilities were funded jointly by state appropriations and local charitable donations (primarily from local Rotary Clubs).[51]

Similar organizations were quickly established in other states, including Michigan, New York, and Illinois, and in 1921 the state groups established the National Society for Crippled Children (NSCC). NSCC continued to grow in subsequent years, with twenty-three state affiliates by 1929, but during the depression of the 1930s, grassroots fundraising for the group became more challenging.[52] In 1934, NSCC began to sell decorative seals during the Easter season to raise funds and to promote awareness of the group. The seals, designed by a cartoonist from the *Cleveland Plain Dealer* newspaper, featured a child on crutches in front of a large white cross. Sale of the seals at Easter proved to be so successful that "Easter Seals" became a brand for the organization. The name was officially adopted in 1967, and NSCC became the National Easter Seal Society for Crippled Children and Adults, shortened in 1979 to the National Easter Seal Society.

In the later part of the twentieth century, ES was perhaps best known for its fundraising telethons, starting in 1971 and continuing for decades with celebrity hosts and featuring appeals that stressed the tragic nature of disability and the need for research on prevention. In addition to funding local medical and rehabilitation services for "crippled" children, Easterseals became an active participant in legislative advocacy for public funding for such services, supporting inclusion of Title V as part of the Social Security Act of 1935, which allocated federal funds to states for "services for locating crippled children and for providing medical, surgical, corrective and other services and care, and facilities for diagnosis, hospitalization and after care for children who are crippled or who are suffering from conditions that lead to crippling."[53] In subsequent years, Easterseals played the role of incubator for numerous voluntary organizations that offered services or conducted research on medical and social rehabilitation for people with disabilities, helping found the International Society for the Welfare of Cripples, which later became Rehabilitation International (1939); the International Association of Sheltered Workshops and Homebound Programs (1941); the American Academy for Cerebral Palsy (1947); the National Committee for Research in Neurological and Communicative Disorders (1950); and the Association of Rehabilitation Centers (1952), as well as the professional journal that ultimately became *Rehabilitation Literature* (1959).

While rooted firmly in the medical model of disability, and initially focused on promoting better access to medical services, Easterseals also has advocated effectively for the promotion of community supports and employment for people with disabilities, and by the 1970s was supporting efforts to remove architectural and attitudinal barriers and to expand access to mainstream public education and public transportation. In these efforts, Easterseals worked closely with parent organizations and disability rights advocates to promote more inclusive public policies and to expand funding for community-based support programs. For several decades, ES has been a major partner in advocacy coalitions promoting a variety of disability-related causes, including broader guarantees for the rights of people with disabilities as well as enhanced funding for public disability services. ES was active in lobbying for passage and implementation of the Individuals with Disabilities Education Act (IDEA), the Americans with Disabilities Act of 1990 (ADA), the Assistive Technology Act of 1998, the Ticket to Work and Work Incentives Improvement Act of 1999, the Achieving a Better Life Experience (ABLE) Act to help families of children with disabilities save without jeopardizing their eligibility for government benefits, and the Work-force Innovation and Opportunity Act that updated the public vocational rehabilitation system. ESS also has promoted more general legislation such as the Patient Protection and Affordable Care Act (Obamacare), which made health insurance more accessible to individuals with preexisting medical conditions; supports for caregivers in the Older Americans Act; and the State Children's Health Insurance Act (SCHIP) to expand insurance cover-age for children in low-income families.[54]

Tensions with Disabled Activists: The Telethons

Whereas self-advocacy among people with intellectual disabilities and au-tism is a relatively recent phenomenon, collective activism by people with physical disabilities has been part of disability politics since the 1930s, and their organizations have achieved prominence in disability politics. Parent and professional organizations for people with physical disabilities therefore operate in a very different political environment now, in which the ability and right of people with disabilities to speak for themselves are far better established. Organizations led by parents and professionals have found many points of collaboration with disabled activists, as already docu-mented, but collaboration has not always been easy. Here we use the issue of telethons, one of the most popular fundraising tools across the groups highlighted in this chapter, to point out several issues of contention includ-ing the use of the medical model, the reliance on images of pity to raise funds, and the overall power of organizations led by the nondisabled in disability politics.

Throughout American history, an active system of private charity has been represented as a sufficient alternative to government-provided benefits and services, although even charities with the widest reach are a weak sub-stitute for public funding. This was demonstrated in the Reagan era, when the administration justified cuts in public programs with the belief that the private sector would take up the slack, despite ample evidence that much of the so-called voluntary sector was highly dependent on governmental fund-ing streams.[55]

The late Paul Longmore describes how telethons were a distinctive cul-tural phenomenon in the 1950s through the 1970s, the era of early television in the United States.[56] Telethons built on the use of poster children in print media since the 1930s, displaying children as symbols of the impact of dis-eases that might be ameliorated through broadcast appeals for financial contributions. Telethons interspersed entertainment segments featuring celebrities with emotional appeals for contributions that presented people with chronic health conditions as pitiful, dependent, and hopeless. Within the American welfare state, while both biomedical research and services for people with chronic medical conditions were to some extent public responsibilities, the modest commitment of government funds led to efforts to supplement and enhance public funding with voluntary initiatives.

Although parent-led groups focused on physical disabilities were initially built at the grass roots around the goals of mutual support and information sharing, several of them grew into substantial fundraising organizations, with substantial professional staffs. And while parent groups in their early developmental stages concentrated on issues of inclusion and empowering families, with growth and financial success several turned to an emphasis on prevention. To highlight the need for prevention, instead of portraying the children as capable of full participation, they portrayed affected children in tragic terms that signaled the imperative of wiping out the disabling diseases. Longmore writes, "Stereotypes pictured children with disabilities as devastating burdens who made their families socially abnormal and shattered their parents' dreams."[57] Children with disabilities were often presented as helpless victims leading lives devastated by their conditions.[58] Telethons rarely portrayed the quality of life and achievements of adults with disabilities, or how inclusive practices and support services might be expanded to improve their opportunities and quality of life.

In addition to their negative imagery of impairments, the telethons supported a system of private charity that failed to address the broad array of public health concerns and discrimination experienced by people with disabilities and emphasized selective attention to those causes that most easily elicited public sympathy. They ignored structural issues, such as poverty, unemployment, racism, and the lack of accessible housing, to instead focus on the promise of cure. They focused on disabling conditions embodied by telegenic children in wheelchairs, ignoring mental illnesses, intellectual and developmental disabilities, other stigmatized conditions, and even adults with disabilities.

In the 1970s, activist groups of people with disabilities such as Disabled in Action and the American Coalition of Citizens with Disabilities mounted protests against the telethons and the flawed images of disability they promoted.[59] In the early 1990s, a new group, Jerry's Orphans, whose leaders were connected to the broader disability activist group ADAPT, challenged the telethons to remake themselves to promote a more positive view of impairment and of the lives of those with disabilities.[60] Fred Pelka quotes Mike Erwin, founder of Jerry's Orphans, as saying, "They give the public the idea that everything is taken care of, that there's no need to worry about discrimination or civil rights or social services, because 'those people' have 'their charities' to take care of them. We've never had a national conversation about who should be providing services, who should be funding research."[61]

Paul Longmore notes the divergence between the increasingly progressive stance of charitable organizations in their services and political activities versus the framing of disability found in their telethons and other fundraising appeals.[62] While telethons focused on raising funds for research that might eliminate disabling conditions and stressed the tragic incapacity of children living with various impairments, many other disability-focused charitable organizations generally supported and devoted resources for expanding community-based services, removing disabling barriers in the built environment, and promoting inclusive practices by public and private entities.

Supporting research and prevention is not intrinsically at odds with support for community-based services. Many medical charities support both, either within their organization or in partnership with others. However, different organizational cultures may emphasize one approach or the other in their operation, and each organization can have its own conception of the significance of having a disabling condition. Disability activists and purveyors of funding appeals typically have promoted drastically different views of disability and how it should be addressed, whether the essential problem is the impairment and its functional consequences or a disabling environment that does not adequately accommodate functioning. Chapter 3 similarly highlights this tension playing out between autistic activists and Autism Speaks. Nevertheless, parent advocates and activists with disabilities frequently have been able to join together in partnerships at the national and community levels to promote shared goals of inclusion and expanding support services for people living with disabilities. Moreover, the historical trend has been for most disability-focused organizations to support community inclusion in their mission if not in their core activities.

Telethons also raise issues of control over the narrative, politics, and money associated with disability, and the power of well-funded organizations, not led by people with disabilities, to dominate the public discourse and benefit from a pity discourse. Poet and performer Cheryl Marie Wade explains:

The biggest harm to me and to all disabled people with the telethon is that it's our primary image in the media. If it was one of a million images, we wouldn't be having this discussion. You know, they could have their little telethons as long as we are on there doing all the other kinds of things we do and all the other images of who we are. But I really resent that they present it as a charity. It is not a charity.

They are a megabucks corporation. No other definition would apply. Anything beyond that is just a lie.[63]

Wade is pointing out that the money raised largely funds able-bodied professionals and researchers, and provides very little return to people with disabilities in terms of either empowerment or ability to confront the real problems in their lives, such as discrimination and lack of access.

Yielding to changes in cultural tastes and to criticism led by the disability rights movement, and perhaps as well to the decline in broadcast television with the advent of the internet and social media, most telethons were abandoned by the mid-1990s. At the national level, funding partnerships with corporate sponsors were pursued. At the local level, various fundraising approaches were adopted that varied geographically. In some communities, parent-led organizations had become service providers, funded by client fees and by state subsidies. In others, traditional charitable events were undertaken, including gala dinners, golf tournaments, and fundraising runs or walks. In other localities, parent organizations became more narrowly focused on grassroots advocacy activities, sometimes in alliance with self-advocacy groups. Of course, these alternative fundraising techniques are also problematic. The gala, for instance, excludes people with lower incomes and relies on the beneficence of the wealthy, demanding the deflection and even erasure of the anger of victims of discrimination and exclusion.

Parent Organizations in the Twenty-First Century

Parent-founded organizations, largely run by professionals with parental membership, continue to wield influence on public policy and discourse, and that influence is likely to continue because they have the ability to generate resources, have acquired policy and communicative expertise, and have developed strategic alliances. On the policy level, the larger parent organizations focused on physical disabilities have worked effectively for decades in concert with national and local coalitions that include disability self-advocates to promote more inclusive and supportive government programs. (See Chapter 7, on strategies and policy.) The internet and social media have made it far easier for individual parents and local groups to gain access to information on medical conditions and to associate with other families through support networks, both of which were early goals for parent groups. These connections have reduced the social isolation that exacerbates the challenges associated with impairment. The availability of services for school-age children has been vastly improved by the legislative and legal victories of the movements for educational rights of disabled children, and that has led to rising expectations, which in turn may promote advocacy efforts.

However, barriers persist for many people with disabilities, and in particular gaining access to social assistance for adults with disabilities remains challenging in many localities. Gaining public support for inclusion of adults remains more challenging than has been the case for children, and the current political climate has promoted skepticism and moral questioning about the desirability and efficacy of public supports for those requiring assistance. This dilemma has been exemplified in the recent public debate in the United States over Medicaid and other public assistance programs, with popular support for community-based services in question and increasingly contingent on poorly conceived restrictions such as demands for extensive documentation and work requirements that risk limiting access to needed services.

In light of these social barriers, tensions between activists with physical disabilities and parent-professional organizations flare up, especially when parent-professional organizations prioritize the medical model, fundraise using strategies that play on pity, and assert political influence in contradiction to the desires of activists with disabilities. Nevertheless, many parents of individuals with physical disabilities have established social capital via support networks and political alliances, and the cultural capital of critical knowledge in negotiating complex bureaucratic systems, in their efforts to meet the needs of their family members. Whether their success will continue in decades to come will depend to some extent on their capacity to collaborate on an equal basis with the disabled activists whose struggles they share.

II

Cross-Disability Analysis

5

Timing

Factors Affecting the Emergence
of Parent-Led Organizations

While scholarship at times refers to "the" parents' movement, the case studies in Part I reveal great variation in the timing and goals of parent activism. When scholarship examines the timing of parent activism, it often takes a parent life course approach, such as Rosalyn Darling's classic work on activism as entrepreneurship, in which parents experience initial dissatisfaction, build relevant social networks to achieve change, challenge authority, and perhaps develop a deeply held activist role that resembles a career.[1] Other scholarship situates a particular parent movement in its historical context, such as work that explains the rise of parent activism related to intellectual disabilities in the mid-twentieth century. In contrast, we conduct an analysis across disability group, organization, and time to examine the factors that shape the historical timing of the emergence of parent activism across groups. In other words, why did parent activism arise in an earlier historical era for intellectual disability and cerebral palsy than for mental illness or autism? To conduct this analysis, we draw heavily from the case studies in Part I and add in other groups such as parents' groups related to blindness and deafness[2] as relevant to expanding and affirming our argument.

We argue that parent activism first emerges as a result of several factors including the historical construction and patterns of childhood diagnosis, the perception of relative deprivation, the emergence of resources, and the availability of relevant political opportunity structures including, among other things, interest in disability politics by prominent politicians and political activism by people with disabilities. More broadly speaking, childhood diagnosis potentially creates a form of cultural capital—a shared symbolic meaning—enabling parents to activate and claim other forms of capital such as financial resources and political influence. Early parent organizations transform the organizational and political context, creating new resources, political opportunities, and political constraints. This new context fosters the growth of later organizations, some of whom tap into the growing set of opportunities established by earlier groups and others of which resist the now-established political agenda and seek alternative goals and political agendas.

The Founding of National Parent Organizations

We begin by laying out the founding dates of various prominent, national, parent-led organizations. This list is not exhaustive; it focuses on intellectual disability, mental disability, autism, and cerebral palsy, and adds in several other parent groups as relevant and interesting given our theories.

Parent organizations related to intellectual disability and some forms of developmental physical disability such as cerebral palsy were among the earliest large, successful, national parent movements related to disability. United Cerebral Palsy (UCP) was founded in 1949, and the Arc, which focuses on intellectual and developmental disabilities, was founded in 1950. Although scholarship on "the parents' movement" in disability often focuses on this initial eruption of activity, many other national parent organizations emerged decades later. Related to mental illness, the National Alliance on Mental Illness (NAMI) was founded in 1979 and the National Federation of Families for Children's Mental Health (NFFCMH) in 1989. For deaf children, the American Society for Deaf Children (ASDC) was founded in 1967 and Hands and Voices (H&V) in 1997. The National Organization of Parents of Blind Children (NOPBC) was founded in 1983. Autism Speaks was not founded until 2005. In addition, we also see an emergence of other parent-led organizations related to intellectual disability including the National Down Syndrome Society (NDSS), founded in 1979, and VOR (formerly Voice of the Retarded), founded in 1983. See Table 5.1.

Parent Activism in the Mid-Twentieth Century

To examine the timing of these social movement organizations, we look first at the rise of the earliest organizations, including why they emerged in the mid-twentieth century and why national-level, organized parent activism did not emerge at this time for other diagnoses. We then look at later national organizations and consider the factors leading to their emergence,

TABLE 5.1. ORGANIZATIONS LED BY PARENTS

Organization	Founded	Mission
United Cerebral Palsy (UCP)	1949	Service delivery and rights advocacy for persons with CP and other development disabilities
The Arc	1950	Service delivery and rights advocacy for persons with intellectual disabilities
American Society for Deaf Children	1967	Advocacy for language-rich environments including American Sign Language (ASL)
National Alliance on Mental Illness (NAMI)	1979	Grassroots advocacy for people with mental illness
National Down Syndrome Society	1979	Advocacy for rights and well-being of persons with Down syndrome
VOR (formerly Voice of the Retarded)	1983	To challenge deinstitutionalization and fight for service options including large-scale facilities
National Organization of Parents of Blind Children (NOPBC)	1983	Division of National Federation of the Blind
National Federation of Families for Children's Mental Health	1989	Focuses on issues of children with mental health concerns and their families
Hands and Voices	1997	Provides resources for all families of deaf and hard-of-hearing children regardless of communication methodology
Autism Speaks	2005	Research and awareness related to autism

including the growth of resources and the political opportunities and constraints imposed as disability policy and funding structures took shape.

Required, but Insufficient, Factors: Oppression and Diagnosis

Oppression

When explaining the rise of activism, people often begin by explaining the various forms of oppression experienced by the group. Oppression, while central to most activism, is clearly insufficient as an explanation for when activism emerges. In the eighteenth, nineteenth, and early twentieth centuries, well before the rise of parent activism, people with disabilities faced many forms of exclusion and deprivation including poverty, unemployment, and social marginalization. These outcomes, though, were seen as rooted in personal and familial tragedy, *not* as a result of macro societal decisions within the realms of economics, politics, and culture to marginalize particular people. Later, in the early twentieth century, eugenics created an environment in which the oppression of people with disabilities became both more intense and more specific to disabilities, including mass institutionalization, compulsory sterilization, and immigration restrictions based on disability. Despite the intense oppression, parent activism still remained uncommon.

Diagnosis

Diagnosis is also necessary, but insufficient, to explain disability-related parent activism. Many people face hardship for myriad reasons. For an amorphous mass of people, there is little to unite them. Medical diagnosis may provide a form of cultural capital, undergirding a sense of shared experience and identity, and a set of interests regarding policies and resources for a specific population.[3] Indeed, without a diagnosis the activism studied in this book would not even be understood as "disability-related"; it instead would be framed in some other terms like education, civil rights, or criminal justice reform.

However, diagnosis paired with oppression is still not sufficient to produce activism. Legal definitions of intellectual disability and insanity existed when America formed as a new nation. Autism was first identified in 1911 and became a focus of research in the 1930s and 1940s. The importance of the diagnosis is not the diagnosis itself but its application to a group, including its prevalence and identification in children; the role it plays in mobilizing a set of resources, treatment, and policies targeting a specific group; and the ways it encourages a specific group identity with perceived interests and opportunities achievable through activism.

Factors Leading to Mid-Twentieth-Century Parent Mobilization: The Arc and UCP

In line with much work on social movements, we see that an *expansion of resources and political opportunities*, paired with a sense of *relative deprivation*, spur social movements far more quickly and successfully than absolute deprivation. In this case, the growing medical system of institutions and rehabilitation increased resources dedicated to disability, which parents then contested as a result of a growing sense of relative deprivation and political opportunities.

Resource Mobilization

The rapidly growing financial and professional capital related to the emerging infrastructure for disability services and treatment became a key focus of political contestation.[4] Through the early twentieth century, professional attention to and funding related to disabilities grew tremendously. For mental and intellectual disabilities, the increasing use of institutions centralized resources and expertise, supported the development of professional specialization in these diagnostic fields, and encouraged professional output in terms of research, interventions, and treatments.[5] The increasing creation, delivery, and funding of treatments generated the idea that the intellectual and mental disabilities could be addressed and improved, and opened the door for debate about how best to make such improvements, who should control access and delivery of treatments, how much funding should be allocated to treatments, and who should pay for the treatments (e.g., the state, insurance, the individual person). In particular, the growth of treatments and services *funded by the state* in public institutions encouraged debate concerning the use of public dollars. As institutional care grew, mental health became a significant portion of states' budgets.

State spending on education, special education, and vocational rehabilitation also grew. According to R. Rudy Higgins-Evenson, "During the first three decades of the twentieth century, trends toward centralized control over state mental health and educational systems raised spending on those items in almost every state, especially after 1920."[6] During the 1940s and 1950s, special education enjoyed a surge of support and public funding, and many states passed laws to mandate and support special education.[7] Public vocational rehabilitation programs, first created after World War I to aid disabled soldiers' return to work, also grew. In 1920, programs expanded to include nonveterans with physical disabilities; in 1943, they expanded again to include people with mental illness, intellectual disabilities, blindness, deafness, and other disabilities; and in 1954, amendments funneled still more funds into the politically popular programs.

Relative Deprivation

States promised that these professional and fiscal expansions would improve the treatment of people with disabilities, their access to independence, and their overall well-being. As documented in the case studies in Part I, however, institutions quickly dominated the landscape of disability services for people with intellectual and mental disabilities. As a result of both comorbidity and limitations in communication, people with cerebral palsy, autism, and even deafness were frequently placed in institutions as well. Institutions became overcrowded and under-resourced, ineffective at best and harmful at worst. Thus, the growing infrastructure created a narrative of positive expectations in which families thought that their family member would receive treatment, education, care, and even cure via a funded system of professional service delivery. Instead, it actually failed to provide sufficient care or cure, particularly for certain groups, and clearly created frustration and a sense of relative deprivation.[8] Furthermore this false expectation was paid for by the taxpayers, making these misguided claims a public issue rather than a reflection of poor consumer choice by individuals. As the failures of the institutional system were exposed by journalists, public backlash reinforced parents' suspicion that they had been mistreated. Meanwhile, community options were growing. Advances in psychopharmacology encouraged increasing community-based treatment, while special education and physical and vocational rehabilitation also grew by leaps and bounds, leading parents to wonder why their children were locked away in institutions or sitting at home without any services or treatment.

Political Opportunity Structure and Collective Identity

The political climate encouraged change as well.[9] After World War II, the national economy grew and provided a widespread sense of prosperity and optimism about the allocation of resources to America's poor and needy. Franklin Delano Roosevelt's New Deal and Four Freedoms promised Americans freedom from economic insecurity and political oppression. Rates of social activism overall grew as varied groups jockeyed to access and control these opportunities. The African American civil rights movement in particular provided key legal precedents, including the 1954 *Brown v. Board of Education* case desegregating schools, the frame of rights as a means to social justice, and examples of successful strategies such as use of the courts. Activism among disability groups, including those led by people with disabilities and those led by parents, particularly prospered as a result of FDR's personal interest in disability and his support for treatment and rehabilitation programs, followed by John Kennedy's familial connection to intellectual disability. The infusion of funding into community rehabilitation and education also meant that special educators and community therapists were well positioned and interested in assisting parents in challenging the dominance of institutional care and thereby expanding their own professional turf.

By joining organizations like UCP and the Arc, parents fostered a salient positive social identity for themselves, tied to a cause deeply related to their role as parent. Parents had once shied away from publicly admitting disability, but public revelations by celebrities like Dale Evans Rogers (wife and partner of Roy Rogers), Pearl Buck, and the Kennedy family opened the door for parents to tell their stories publicly without shame. They found the image of the misled parent and mistreated disabled child to be a symbolically powerful tool, especially given that parents did not have many other weapons by which to fight a massive state and professional system. Most important of all, perhaps, parents enjoyed the benefits of creating a sense of community with other parents, sharing resources, building grassroots services, and fostering a sense of belonging when they had for so long been socially marginalized. These new communities often began without a clear political agenda, for example focusing on social opportunities for their children and families, perhaps with limited and local political aims, such as starting a special education class. But as networks spread and interconnected, small local organizations became the base of a potentially powerful state and national constituency.

Thus, by the mid-twentieth century, we see a growing public disability infrastructure that provided a set of resources, paired with a sense of relative deprivation fostered by the mismatch between the promises of improvement and the reality of social isolation and despair. Utilizing their shared identity based on diagnosis, and harnessing the environment of political opportunity and their vast organizational network, parents' activism thrived.

Factors Explaining the Absence of National Parent-Led Organizations at Midcentury for Mental Illness, Deafness, Blindness, and Autism

Despite the factors discussed above, we do not see similar patterns in timing across national parent organizations. While there was activism related to mental illness, deafness, and blindness in the mid-twentieth century, there was little in the way of collective, national-level *parental* activism. For example, parents of children with autism may have been active in the Arc, but they had yet to organize separately under that diagnosis. To understand these absences, we must consider age, the historical timing of diagnosis, and the presence of activism by people with disabilities.

Age and Historical Timing of Diagnosis

Parent activism arose first among diagnoses identified primarily in children, including intellectual disability and cerebral palsy. Historically, "idiocy" and "feeblemindedness" were understood as lifelong conditions that emerged in childhood. As noted in a census report on the 1910 institutionalized population, "feeble-minded is, for the most part, congenital, and . . . admissions to institutions for this class of defectives usually takes place in the period of childhood or youth."[10] Indeed, 74.2 percent of institutional admissions in 1910 were youth nineteen years of age or younger; 25 percent were nine years of age or younger. In 1922, 76 percent of admissions were youth nineteen years of age or younger—the energetic application of the label "feebleminded" by eugenicists in the early twentieth century to a broad array of people defined as socially undesirable had led to increasing diagnosis and institutionalization, particularly for girls and young women seen as sexually deviant and for those regarded as chronic "problems" by social welfare or criminal justice systems.

Historically, diagnosis of cerebral palsy was even more concentrated among young children. Throughout its medical history, cerebral palsy has been associated with fetal and infant development, and the vast majority of diagnoses take place before age of five. Cerebral palsy involves brain damage, and, while estimates vary, approximately 50 percent of children with cerebral palsy have intellectual disabilities, and 20 percent are in the moderate or severe range. One in three children with cerebral palsy have significant mobility limitations, and one in four have identified deficits in verbal communication skills.[11] Historically, children with cerebral palsy were often assumed to have an intellectual disability, even if they did not, and speech disabilities limited their ability to challenge this assumption. Thus, it is not surprising that UCP and the Arc emerged at a similar time and as political allies. Although children with cerebral palsy and intellectual disabilities may have very different experiences in modern society, historically the diagnoses and treatment were often conflated.

In contrast, historically mental illness was seen as primarily an adult phenomenon. Through most of the nineteenth century children were assumed to be free from the troubles of the adult mind. In 1910, only 0.2 percent of inmates in mental institutions were under the age of fifteen, and 14 percent of those admitted were under the age of twenty-five.[12] In 1935, Leo Kanner published the first American text in the field, *Child Psychiatry.* It was not until the 1970s and 1980s that research and services for children with mental illness expanded rapidly.

Thus, in the 1940s and 1950s, intellectual disability and cerebral palsy were principally seen as *childhood disabilities* and therefore as the responsibility of families. Parents of children with these diagnoses experienced medicalization of their children and families at a time in their lives when their identities and efforts largely revolved around parenting. Early diagnosis meant that both the child and the parent were more likely to incorporate a response to labeling into their core identities and roles. Parents came to see themselves as the parent of a "disabled" child. On the other hand, when offspring received diagnoses later in life, the parental relationship is likely very different. While the job of parenting may never be done, by the time offspring reach their twenties, thirties, and forties, parents may perceive their relationship as a support system rather than as the bearer of a deep, moral responsibility for day-to-day care and well-being. The legal and social relationship is also different. Parents of minors are legally and socially responsible for their care, whereas adult offspring have gained legal status as adults, often have moved out, may have married and thereby established a new legal next-of-kin relationship, and thus parents exercise far less authority over their lives. Hence, the incorporation of activism into their core identity as parents and their success in activism are likely diminished because they have less ability to speak for their offspring and less control over the utilization of any system or service.

Interestingly, though, the age of diagnosis is not simply based on biology. Indeed, the age of diagnosis for mental illness is quickly changing. Children are now far more likely to receive a mental health diagnosis than they were in the early or mid-twentieth century, leading to greater involvement of parents in modern times. According to the Kids Mental Health Information Portal, recent statistics indicate that approximately one in five children (20 percent) has a diagnosable mental illness.[13] A study using data from 2001 to 2004 found a twelve-month prevalence rate for children ages eight to fifteen of 8.6 percent for attention deficit/hyperactivity disorder, 3.7 percent for mood disorders, 2.1 percent for conduct disorders, 0.7 percent for panic and generalized anxiety disorders, and 0.1 percent for eating disorders.[14] Scholars such as Linda Blum and Victoria Pitts-Taylor suggest that the increased rate of diagnosis of invisible mental disabilities is caused by the growing pressure on children and parents to meet high academic expectations in a supercharged, neoliberal, competitive society. Such an environment may cause issues such as anxiety and depression. It also encourages the use of labeling and medicalization to "help" children, especially white middle-class children, succeed in a high-pressure environment by lengthening attention, regulating mood, and leveraging resources including extended time and academic supports.[15] Regardless of the reason for the historical shift toward diagnosis of mental illness in children, we see its effect of parents becoming increasingly active.

Considering autism, it is understood as a condition that manifests in childhood, but its use as a diagnosis was limited historically. Although autism was first identified in 1911, it was not until 1967 that Barnard Rimland founded the Autism Research Institute and 1980 that autism was listed as a distinct medical diagnosis in the *Diagnostic and Statistical Manual of Mental Disorders (DSM)*. Rates of autism diagnosis have skyrocketed since the turn of the twenty-first century. Many parents of children who today would be seen to have autism were likely a part of movements related to intellectual or mental disabilities in the 1950s; as such, they were subsumed within movements that did not confer a specific identity or address the distinct needs of or solutions for people with autism. Indeed, disagreement over the nature and root cause of autism meant that families were not even consistently lumped in with one particular other group; some doctors and families considered it a mental health disability akin to schizophrenia while others framed it as a developmental disability akin to intellectual disability. It is not until after the establishment of autism as distinct from intellectual and mental disability, with specific treatments and programs, that we see the rise in diagnosis and of distinct national parent-led organizations advocating specific treatments, policies, and identity politics.

Activism among People with Disabilities

The presence of activism among adults with specific disabilities seems to reduce the likelihood that parents would create their own national organizations for those disabilities in the mid-twentieth century. For example, the early national organizations for blindness and Deafness were created by people with those disabilities, not parents.

Neither blindness nor deafness is primarily a childhood disability; both conditions are progressively more likely with age. According to the 2016 American Community Survey, 0.8 percent of children have visual disabilities, compared with 2.4 percent of adults, with the highest percentages among the oldest Americans.[16] Three in one thousand children are born with a serious or profound hearing loss, whereas three in ten adults sixty years of age or older have serious or profound hearing loss. That said, the numbers of children with these diagnoses were not negligible, and considerable attention was given to educating and treating both disabilities among children. The first school for the deaf was founded in 1815, funded by a parent of a deaf child, and Gallaudet University was founded in 1817. In 1829 the Perkins School for the Blind became the first American school for the blind, quickly followed by the New York Institute for the Blind and the Overbrook School for the Blind. For both deaf and blind children, residential schools became the preferred site of training and education. In contrast to institutions for people with intellectual and mental disabilities, these residential sites were far more likely to actually confer educational, vocational, and disability-related skills and to strive to return their students to the community upon graduation. While some students remained at or returned to the schools as adults to work, they did so of their own accord, not because they were forced to stay by parents or the state.[17] There were many heated debates, such as manual versus oral education for deaf students, but in general the quality of the education provided came much closer to meeting the promises of educators than was true of institutions for people with intellectual and mental disabilities.

The success of education and policy for blind and deaf children did not happen in a vacuum. Rather, deaf and blind adults became their own advocates and established national organizations to fight for equality. In 1880 Deaf activists founded the National Association of the Deaf, an organization led by the Deaf for the Deaf, created "to promote, protect, and preserve the civil, human, and linguistic rights of deaf and hard of hearing individuals in the United States of America." Members fought, for example, to defend the use of sign language, promote the hiring of Deaf educators, mandate access to civil service exams, and advocate the captioning of films. The National Federation of the Blind was founded in 1940 to serve as the "voice of the nation's blind," with the motto "Security, Equality, and Opportunity." Led for its first twenty years by constitutional law scholar and civil rights activist Dr. Jacobus tenBroek, the National Federation of the Blind fought to attain government pensions for the blind, access to civil service jobs, and minimum wage in sheltered workshops. Thus, children who were blind, deaf, or both did not have to rely solely on their parents to fight for their rights; adults with the same disabilities were actively engaged in political struggles on their behalf. Parents could ally with adult activists to fight for basic civil rights or focus their attention on local issues more specific to their own child, feeling relatively assured that adults with disabilities were engaged in politics. Similarly, the Muscular Dystrophy Association was created by a man with MD and led by professionals, and parents participated in that organization without creating their own. For mental illness, Clifford Beers, a former patient of a psychiatric hospital, founded Mental Health America in 1909. Beers also allied primarily with professionals to improve treatment and encourage community-based treatment options, rather than building a civil rights movement of people with psychiatric diagnoses. Although Mental Health America relied far less on parent involvement, parents did not form a national group of their own. In contrast, adults with intellectual disabilities were not politically organized until much later, and activists with disabilities focused little attention on confronting institutionalization and the broader marginalization of people with intellectual disabilities, leaving pressing needs for parents to confront.

Thus, parent-led national organizations did not emerge in the 1940s and 1950s for diagnoses that were not primarily childhood diagnoses (mental illness), for uncommon diagnoses (autism), or for which there was already activism led by adults with disabilities (blindness and deafness). Parents did not see themselves in that role, did not see the benefits or potential of organizing separately from the Arc or UCP, or did not feel compelled to fill the role of political activist given the presence of other national organizations led by people with disabilities.

Later Parent Activism: Expanding the Field

The Arc and UCP did not remain as the only large-scale, national parent organizations for long. Their success inspired many other parents to organize, and they established crucial building blocks for doing so. Some parents' groups fought to extend earlier successes to their own populations. The successes of organizations led by parents and by people with disabilities also led to oppositional organizing; in other words, the priorities of the leading organizations were not shared by all parents, and some organized to promote a different vision.

Building on Former Successes

The Arc and UCP, alongside disability rights organizations led by people with disabilities, created the groundwork for a vast expansion of parent activism. Many parents sought to capitalize on the growing disability infrastructure for their children. To discuss this expansion, we focus on four bases of expansion: supporting disability rights groups, building on legislative successes, creating or expanding service systems, and addressing specific issues and populations.

Parent Mobilization to Support Activism of People with Disabilities

Much of our discussion will focus on the ways in which the success of parent-led organizations encouraged the growth of other parent organizations. We start, though, by considering the work of activists with disabilities in reaching out to and grooming parents to support the disability rights movement. The National Federation of the Blind (NFB), founded in 1940, offers the best example of this outreach to parents. The NFB is a parent or umbrella organization to the National Organization of Parents of Blind Children (NOPBC), which has three thousand members. The NFB stridently fights for the equality of blind people, addressing issues of accessibility, access to technology and blind skills, and job discrimination. Parents, new to blindness, might think of it as a medical tragedy, but through the NFB they are introduced to a very different model. NOPBC materials explain, "We believe that the exact level of a child's eyesight should not restrict their choice of tools and techniques, and instead ask, 'Which are the skills and tools that will best enable this child to succeed?' . . . We further believe that blind people who are taught and who embrace effective non-visual skills, whatever their degree of eyesight, are capable of living a full and satisfying life."[18] The organization offers parents information and programming related to these nonvisual tools and to striving for their child's equality, as part of a larger organization run by and for blind people.

The American Society for Deaf Children (ASDF) is not a division of the National Association of the Deaf and claims no official connection; however, like the National Association of the Deaf, ASDF is led by Deaf activists and embraces issues such as the use of sign language as part of a "language-rich" environment, Deaf culture, respect for Deaf individuals, and access to

Deaf mentors. Many of its board members have ties to Deaf residential schools and colleges. Through ASDF resources, conferences, and magazine, Deaf activists expose parents and children to the social and political value of ASL, full access communication (ensuring that ASL is taught even to children who learn oral communication as well), and Deaf culture.

The National Black Disability Coalition is another example of an organization led by people with disabilities that explicitly welcomes families to join in their activism. We discuss this group in more depth in our later discussion of organizations that form to address issues and populations overlooked by dominant disability organizations.

In these organizations, then, we see activists with disabilities reaching out to parents in order to enlist them in the struggle for disability rights and to support parents in raising proud, empowered children with disabilities.

Building on Legislative Successes

Legislative successes of disability organizations help encourage and support greater activism. The passage of any given piece of legislation, rather than concluding a struggle, actually begins a long process of implementing the law, educating the public about the law, and protecting the law from being gutted, and thus requires a long-term commitment of activism after legislative success. For parents, the passage of the Individuals with Disabilities Education Act in 1975, for example, was a monumental achievement, ensuring all children with disabilities the right to a free and appropriate public education. With this right, children previously denied education had to be identified and enrolled in schools, services had to be delivered, parents had to be educated, and each individual battle over resources and placement had to be fought, school by school, district by district. This law inspired parents of children with autism and with mental illness to become more involved in translating it into improved access for their children, including fighting the schools for particular forms of treatments and accommodations within the schools. The 1975 Developmental Disabilities and Bill of Rights Act (DD Act) was another crucial piece of legislation that offered children diagnosed with autism funding and services similar to those for children diagnosed with intellectual disability. Prior to the DD Act, a diagnosis of autism left one largely without services, or treated within either the systems of mental illness or intellectual disability.

These successes also paved the way for future activists to imagine new legislative successes such as the 1990 Americans with Disabilities Act. As a recent example, the 2014 ABLE Act creates tax-free savings accounts for people with disabilities to ensure greater financial security. A host of older and newer disability organizations, including the Arc, Autism Speaks,

Easterseals, Muscular Dystrophy Association, National Down Syndrome Society, and United Spinal Association all lobbied in support of its passage.

Expanding the Disability Infrastructure

Alongside legislation, earlier successes helped created a massive infrastructure to support disability services as an alternative to institutionalization and exclusion. The Arc and UCP emerged as major service providers, offering a range of residential, vocational, and educational opportunities. The Independent Living Movement was in part formalized through government funding of a network of Independent Living Centers that provided resources and supports to people with disabilities, largely by people with disabilities, to live in the community. Other organizations arose to compete for service delivery dollars. Advocacy itself emerged as a viable revenue source as government, charitable, and corporate funding grew to support advocacy efforts. Grant funding now constitutes a significant portion of many advocacy organizations' budgets, and the source and focus of grant funding may influence the agenda of advocacy organizations.

The impact of increasing established funding opportunities for growth are nicely exemplified by the National Federation of Families for Children's Mental Health (NFFCMH). These parents were first brought together through a conference, Families as Allies, sponsored by the grant-funded Research and Training Center on Family Support at Portland State University. The federally funded Child and Adolescent Service Systems Program then gave parents the opportunity to present at conferences and national meetings related to childhood mental health and solidify their networks and mission. Established as an organization in 1989, NFFCMH secured a major grant from the Annie E. Casey Foundation to participate in the Urban Children's Mental Health Initiative; the grant allowed NFFCMH to fund an executive director and expand its policy mission. As the organization has grown, it has not only shaped the political agenda but also added new features to the disability advocacy and service infrastructure, such as National Children's Mental Health Awareness week and a program to certify Parent Support Providers.

Addressing Specific Issues Using the Rights Framework

Of course, one of the major reasons for the growth of new organizations is the identification of pressing unmet needs. For example, even though Down syndrome is a form of intellectual disability and thereby enveloped within the mission of the Arc, some parents felt that certain issues specific to Down syndrome were left largely unaddressed by the Arc, such as heightened stigma and the need to deliver information to parents quickly at or even before birth.

Down syndrome, because of its genetic markers and physical features, is more readily identified before or at birth and in casual interactions than many other forms of intellectual disability, and is therefore associated with a greater risk of prenatal abortion, being abandoned or given up for adoption at birth, and other forms of intense stigma. Thus, the National Down Syndrome Society emerged to fight for specific rights of this population.

Other parents have challenged the dominance of white, middle-class perspectives in large national organizations. The National Black Disability Coalition is led by minorities with disabilities, and they welcome families in pursuing their goals, including "to promote unity among Black people with disabilities, our families and our communities, to advance equity within the disability movement and our communities, and to foster opportunity for Black people with disabilities."[19] While the coalition uses common narratives of equality and opportunity, it recognizes that disability activism and its positive outcomes have not extended equally to the black community. Director Jane Dunhamn offers an example of the specific needs and marginalization of minority families:

> We received an inquiry from a support person assisting an African immigrant family. Their middle school child with developmental delays was found in school unconscious on the floor of the boys' bathroom with a belt around his neck. The child survived.
>
> The child was bullied because of his skin color, being a special education student and accused of being "gay." What we don't know: was the occurrence a suicide attempt or a lynching?
>
> The occurrence happened over a month ago. Today there still has been no public account of the incident by the school or family.
>
> What we know is the disability supports did not come to the aid of the family. It was a civil rights organization who came to the aid of the family. The supports have had a difficult time getting the family to understand the need to meet time lines.
>
> This story is not new. Too many Black families are unable to obtain justice for their disabled children. For most Black families to dedicate the time to the work for justice there is the real threat of interrupted employment who then find their delicate financial balance in jeopardy. How do we, the Black disability community, support each other when these injustices happen?[20]

Black parents who are discriminated against in their communities and in largely white disability activist communities may find the National Black Disability Coalition both welcoming and effective.

Although we focus on national organizations, many parents continue to desperately want basic social support and grassroots community connections and organizing. Thus, despite the existence of large national organizations, many parents form their own local initiatives to address their specific concerns, such as forming a play group, creating a safe space for parents to vent their frustrations and share information, or confronting local injustice. Intersectional activist Kerima Çevik argues that effective activism must have a heavy reliance on grassroots, local community organizing. Her son, a nonverbal young man of color with autism, relies on strong interpersonal relationships across the community to support his independence and protect his safety. Police training and legislation have failed to protect black men with disabilities, and instead communities must know if someone is in trouble and how to help them. She explains:

> I'm trying to build a grassroots understanding in people's minds that when someone who has a developmental disability or a psychiatric disability is in trouble, you don't call the police, unless that person is holding a weapon, truly holding a weapon—ok?—you don't call the police. There needs to be a whole different structure to this. There needs to be a wider circle of support for people with developmental disabilities. And it's not there and it's never been built. Disability is something outside of community responsibility. We as Americans tend to segregate these things, we tend to compartmentalize these things. We don't consider everyone who is a member of our community a part of a greater family, an extension of a greater community where everyone looks out for one another. That is one of the problems. There has to be something grassroots built so that people with psychiatric disabilities can support one another.[21]

For Çevik, national organizations have a valuable role, but they cannot perform this work; it is inherently local.

Oppositional Growth

While some activism built on the successes of previous activism to expand the rights framework and build the disability infrastructure, the established disability organizations also represented a set of constraints that some parents challenged (potentially via organizations that relied on the building blocks created by earlier organizations). As disability organizations increasingly cohered around and collaborated on a rights agenda, some parents challenged that agenda. One key point of opposition was integration and the community mandate. The Arc, UCP, and organizations led by disabled activists typically stressed integration and community-based services (although Deaf activists tend to promote Deaf educational and residential programs as a way to learn ASL and access Deaf culture). However, some parents found this focus misguided and narrow, shutting down parent choice rather than promoting it. VOR (formerly Voice of the Retarded) emerged explicitly to resist deinstitutionalization and to ensure the continued provision of large-scale, disability-specific services. Both NAMI and the National Federation of Families for Children's Mental Health are explicit about the need for guardianship and promote legislation to expand the use of involuntary institutional commitment, which they perceive as becoming too restricted through the process of deinstitutionalization. For these groups deinstitutionalization went too far, abandoning people without proper supports in the community.

Issues of cure are also a key point of departure. Earlier parent-led groups came to develop and rely heavily on the social model of disability to fight for rights and social supports and to criticize the idea that rights are contingent on cure or normalization (and that in the absence of cure or normalization people could be denied rights and institutionalized, sterilized, and so on). NAMI and Autism Speaks, though, tend to be much more focused on advancing biomedical research, treatment, recovery, and even cure, allying themselves more clearly with the medical profession than did earlier groups. Autism Speaks, for example, stressed the race for a cure for much of its organizational history; under some pressure from self-advocates, it has now adjusted its mission slightly, removing "cure" and instead seeking to "accelerate progress in science"[22] in identifying the causes, types, and treatments for autism.

Other organizations have rejected particular political stances as divisive and have tried to create nonpolitical parental organizations that offer resources and support for all parents. For example, the Deaf community has long stressed the importance of ASL. Some professional organizations like Auditory Verbal International, in contrast, advance an oralist agenda focused on improving people's ability to listen and speak orally, and discount the value of sign language. The feud over manual versus oral communication is long-standing and fierce, and is confusing and challenging for new parents, many of whom are hearing and unfamiliar with Deaf politics. Many parents pursue cochlear implants for their deaf children if feasible, and that choice instantly places them on the margins of the Deaf community. In 1997, parents formed Hands and Voices, a group that claims to be "nonbiased about communication methodologies"[23] and guided by the mission to overcome fractures related to communication strategies and provide parents with "the resources, networks, and information they need to improve communication access and educational outcomes for their children."[24]

Thus, although the disputes vary, newer organizations emerge not only to build on past successes and connect their specific population to the overall improvements in disability services and rights but also as a way to add alternative narratives and voices to those that became dominant in disability policy and thereby move disability policy and services in a different direction.

Conclusion

In summary, parent activism emerges at various times. Initially parent activism was spurred by a growth of resources and a sense of relative deprivation, in a context of growing political opportunities and collective consciousness, and delayed by an absence of diagnosis, childhood diagnosis, and the presence of activism led by people with disabilities. Early organizational successes influenced later organizations, providing a base for expanded activism as well as potential points of contestation.

6

Frames and Positions within the Field of Disability Activism

D isability activism, like other large social movements, is not unitary. It involves a field of organizations with different positions in relation to each other.[1] Some are cross-disability, others single disability. Some are international, others national, and others organized at the state or local level. Some limit themselves to legitimate channels of political influence, while others engage in civil disobedience and radical protest. They may variously focus on rights, social justice, self-help, awareness, and the arts. Some are led by people with disabilities, others by professionals, and others by parents. This diversity potentially creates competition and conflict but also potentially serves the movement to move forward on multiple fronts through productive alliance.

In this field, grassroots activism by people with disabilities constitutes the heart of the movement. Where and how do parent-led organizations fit in relation to organizations led by people with disabilities? In this chapter we look across parent organizations to consider how closely their organizational frames align with the key tenets of disability activism as led by people with disabilities. We then consider the extent to which frame alignment influences alliances between organizations led by parents and organizations led by disabled activists.

Research has shown that sharing a frame is a major factor in organizational alliance.[2] In any given social movement field, organizations may share an underlying frame that sets forth explanations and solutions to the "problem" at hand, or they may have fundamentally different understandings of the problem, its cause, and its solutions.[3] Organizations that share features of a frame therefore are likely to focus on similar problems and solutions and share common goals. Divergent frames breed competition regarding resources, control of the public discourse, and symbolic and organizational authority; however, organizations with divergent frames may nevertheless form strategic alliances based on specific shared goals and responses to outside threats.[4] For example, the Christian Right and disability activist organizations make "strange bedfellows," yet they came together in the 1980s to fight against euthanasia and the denial of medical treatment for infants with disabilities, and more recently to challenge abortion based on "genetic abnormality."[5] Although allied with the Right to protect fetuses and infants with disabilities, disabled activists who demand inclusion usually are at odds with the Right's focus on deregulation, the reduction of taxes, and the privatization of services and supports.

For "new social movements" that focus on creating social change in identity, lifestyle, and culture, rather than striving to achieve straightforward policy goals or address material inequality alone, issues of voice and symbolic ownership of an issue are pressing.[6] New social movements seek reliable allies who not only share a specific goal or broad frame but also display a commitment to the identity politics of the movement. This commitment entails respecting who "owns" the issue, placing the value of collaboration above one's own specific interests at times, and sharing a sense of grievance when an ally is wronged even if it does not immediately affect you.[7] This bridging work of allies shows that allies care about the issue, the *people* involved in the issue, and the *alliance* itself.

The capacity to build diverse and strategic alliances is central to the success of long-standing social movements, and, for disability activists, parents are an important ally, bringing to the fight a passionate interest, deep needs, symbolic authority and persuasive power, and economic and political resources. However, the political power of parents is also a potential threat to disability rights activists insofar as parents undermine and oppose disabled activists. To what degree then do parent-led organizations share a frame and ally with organizations led by disabled activists, or do their alliances come and go as partners of occasional convenience, or do they even act as oppositional forces?

Examining Frame Alignment and Alliance

Organizations led by activists with disabilities certainly differ, but to consider the alignment between parent organizations and organizations led by disabled activists, we identified common tenets that define organizations as being within disability movements led by people with disabilities. James Charlton argues that organizations within the disability rights movement share a focus on empowerment and human rights, independence and integration, and self-help and self-determination, summed up in the motto "Nothing About Us Without Us."[8] Paul Longmore suggests that disability rights activism shares the following features: the use of the social model to reform society, the use of the civil rights frame to demand the rights and means to participate in society, and the quest for individual and collective empowerment.[9] Drawing on these scholars and others, we identified three key tenets embraced by most organizations led by people with disabilities to be used for comparison with parent-led organizations:

- The prioritization of the social model rather than the medical model
- The goal of integration and equal access to the community's social institutions (e.g., work, worship, education) rather than exclusion, segregation, and disability-specific settings and programs
- The empowerment of people with disabilities rather than paternalism

By ideal type, these tenets should align such that organizations focused on the social model should also advocate integration and foster leadership among people with disabilities, while organizations focused on the medical model should also advocate disability-specific settings and paternalism.

We then consider the extent to which organizations that most closely align in framing across these tenets build alliance with organizations led by disabled activists. To examine alliance, we compare the policy positions and support of particular legislation of parent-led organizations with the positions advocated by organizations led by people with disabilities. To most efficiently consider the "position" of organizations led by disabled activists, we look to the organizations within the National Disability Leadership Alliance (NDLA), which describes itself as "a national cross-disability coalition that represents the authentic voice of people with disabilities" composed of fifteen national organizations run by people with disabilities with identifiable grassroots constituencies around the country.[10] NDLA includes ADAPT, the American Association of People with Disabilities, the American Council of the Blind, the Association of Programs for Rural Independent Living, the Autistic Self Advocacy Network, the Hearing Loss Association of America, Little People of America, the National Association of the Deaf, the National Coalition for Mental Health Recovery, the National Council on Independent Living, the National Federation of the Blind, the National Organization of Nurses with Disabilities, Not Dead Yet, Self

Advocates Becoming Empowered, and the United Spinal Association. While these are not the only organizations led by people with disabilities focused on disability issues, they represent a core set of organizations identified by activists with disabilities that have built a stable coalition on the basis of shared interests in the empowerment of people with disabilities and related goals.

This chapter relies on the historical case studies presented in Part I and also draws extensively on data collected from the organizations' websites, position statements, and policy activity to document their public position and alliances. As with Chapter 5, we focus on the organizations discussed in Part I but also bring in other national-level, parent-led organizations as useful for comparison, exploration of the model, and discussion.

To briefly summarize the key findings of this chapter, first, when we look at any single tenet, commitment within each parent-led organization is complex and fluid. In other words, organizations do not clearly subscribe to either the social *or* medical model but rather have some blend of reliance on the social and medical models. Similarly, parent organizations hold a complex and inconsistent stance toward integration versus segregation, and they engage in organizational practices that support limited empowerment while also imposing paternalism. Parent-led organizations rarely fully embraced one pole of a tenet to the exclusion of the other pole; rather, they tend to have a strategic mix to cater to different audiences and issues.

Although we expected the tenets to align (social model, integration, and empowerment versus medical model, segregation, and paternalism), this pattern was surprisingly inconsistent. Some organizations that relied heavily on the social model had nothing in their bylaws to mandate empowerment of people with disabilities and had few people with disabilities in positions of power. Across the tenets, although parent-led organizations are passionately driven to create change, they posit a vision at times misaligned with that of core organizations led by disabled activists. Thus, from the perspective of disabled activists—those for whom these tenets are fundamental to their mission and structure—parent organizations often fall short. They therefore may be viewed as "suspicious" in their commitment.

What impact does frame alignment have on alliance? Although parent organizations are inconsistent, some clearly exhibit greater frame alignment with organizations led by disabled activists, and these organizations are more likely to ally with them. Some even engage in "extra-issue bridge work," using their resources to support an organization or goal in support of disability activism even when it does not clearly benefit their specific population. They also, though, act independently and are willing to fight for their own constituencies' interests and power without the approval of disabled activists or their support.[11] In contrast, other parent organizations exhibit far greater frame misalignment, and despite their rhetoric and belief that they are fighting for the rights of their disabled children, they are more likely to pursue policy positions incongruent with those of disabled activists. These organizations occasionally form strategic alliances with disabled activists on specific issues, but are absent or even opposed to them on key legislative initiatives.

We turn now to a detailed exploration of the frames of parent-led organizations regarding each of the core tenets of disability activism: social versus medical model of disability, integration versus disability-specific settings, and empowerment versus paternalism. We then offer an in-depth consideration of the likelihood of alliance.

Framing and Parent-Led Organizations

Models of Disability: Social Model and Medical Model

No difference in perspective looms larger in disability activism than the tension between the medical and social models of disability. The medical model views disability as residing within the person and asserts the need for medical treatment and intervention to ameliorate and, if possible, cure or prevent disability. Doing so generally involves diagnosis—a process of identifying a person's deficiencies—and relying on medical professionals, including those who apply medical and quasi-medical technological supports and draw on medical culture and authority, to guide treatment. Thus, the presence of discourse about diagnosis and treatment and the presence of medical professionals in leadership are indicators of the medical model. The social model, in contrast, argues that the cause of disability lies in inaccessible and exclusionary environments that disadvantage people with particular bodies and minds. Therefore, it addresses disability by exploring, critiquing, and changing the environmental structures, including attitudes, processes, policy, and physical features. Fundamentally, the social model emphasizes the need to fight for social justice, including access to rights, equity, accommodations, and social supports, rather than medical intervention.[12] While disabled activists recognize the potential benefits of medical treatment, they also challenge its cultural and political dominance and seek greater attention to the social causes of and solutions to the problems experienced by people with disabilities.

Parents use a mix of strategies in pursuit of their and their children's interests, some congruent with the social model and others with the medical model.[13] We found that parent-led organizations tend to draw from both models, although focusing more on one than the other. We identified five configurations of the relationship between the social and medical models in the framings used by parent-led organizations.

Pure Social Model and Demedicalization

This frame focuses almost exclusively on the social model, prioritizing issues of rights and accessibility. In doing so, it demedicalizes disability, including deemphasizing the delivery of information on medical practice and treatment, biomedical research and policy, and collaboration with medical professionals. This frame also directly challenges the medical perspective and authority claims of medical professionals.

The National Organization of Parents of Blind Children (NOPBC) provides an example of an organization that primarily uses a social model and demedicalized frame. Its website offers very little medical information (e.g., information on diagnosis, biological causes of blindness, testing, treatments, clinical trials), no discussion or funding of medical research, and no legislative agenda items focusing on medical advancement. Rather than promote the medical paradigm, NOPBC lauds the expertise of the many blind activists who are part of its parent organization, National Federation of the Blind (NFB), stating that the NFB provides access to fifty thousand blind people to serve as mentors and role models with information about blindness.

NOPBC delivers information to parents on issues of equality and opportunity, such as education and employment, and on the "'skills and tools of blindness" (e.g., Braille, technology, training, empowerment), which are seen as "essential for the child's success both at home and at school" and best taught by blind people (not sighted professionals). It believes "that blind people who are taught and who embrace effective non-visual skills, whatever their degree of eyesight, are capable of living a full and satisfying life."[14] In other words, blind people need the opportunity to thrive as blind people, not contingent on cure.

NOPBC functions as a division of the NFB (one of the organizations in the National Disability Leadership Alliance), and the NFB website similarly rejects the medical model. It states, "You can live the life you want; blindness is not what holds you back. The National Federation of the Blind knows that blindness is not the characteristic that defines you or your future. Every day we raise the expectations of blind people, because low expectations create obstacles between blind people and our dreams."[15] Led by blind activists, the NFB says its mission is to integrate blind people into society as equals, and it focuses on issues of antidiscrimination and access, not medical intervention. Legislative priorities include issues such as access to technology and publications, employment, air travel equity, voting, and parental rights, with little attention to medical advancement.

Medicalized Support of the Social Model

Many people with disabilities and their family members focus on issues of social participation, opportunities, and rights (i.e., the social model) but *use* the medical system to claim rights and access funding and services that support participation, such as community habilitation, vocational rehabilitation, and personal assistance. These activists challenge medicalization but, simultaneously, realize their dependence on medical systems to fund services and supports for people with disabilities. This frame, then, advocates a limited medical model to support what is primarily a social model.

This "devil's bargain" has occurred with many achievements of the Disability Rights Movement, such as the Americans with Disabilities Act, which relies on diagnosis to claim rights.[16] Similarly, Section 504, one of the earliest civil rights accomplishments, is part of the 1973 Rehabilitation Act, using legislation guiding medical rehabilitation to secure antidiscrimination legislation.[17] The Individuals with Disabilities Education Act, which grants students with disability a free and appropriate public education, also relies heavily on diagnosis and evaluation by medical experts to legitimize claims for accommodations and supports.

United Cerebral Palsy (UCP) and the Arc both exhibit this approach. Each shows a clear commitment to the social model. Although most children with cerebral palsy receive some sort of medical treatment or therapy, medical treatment is not UCP's main priority. In keeping with the social model, UCP seeks to ensure that people with disabilities have the supports required to "live a life without limits," and its vision statement promotes a "life of inclusion for people with disabilities."[18] Its history page criticizes the role of medical professionals in institutionalizing and stigmatizing people with disabilities and explains that UCP's contemporary priority is to open doors to the community through supporting advancements in areas such as home ownership, health care reform, inclusive education, and competitive employment.[19]

Along with their adherence to the social model, UCP and the Arc also have a significant focus on the role of medicalized systems such as Medicaid in funding community-based supports and services. During the summer and fall of 2017, the Affordable Care Act and Medicaid were threatened by repeal efforts and budget cuts, and there was an outcry to protect Medicaid-funded services for people with disabilities. The right to live in the community directly hinges on programs funded through Medicaid.[20] As another example, UCP worked on the RAISE Family Caregivers Act, which directs the Department of Health and Human Services to develop a strategy to support caregivers providing services in the community. These foci are not principally about direct medical treatment per se, but rather about using the medical infrastructure to support community opportunities and access for people with disabilities.

Parent organizations are not alone in their willingness to use the medical infrastructure to advance an activist agenda. The most strident of disability activist organizations, such as ADAPT, work relentlessly to shift Medicaid funding to community-based long-term care (e.g., home health aides, personal assistance, funding for community transportation and programming) rather than institutional care. Even the largely demedicalized National Federation of the Blind supports the use of vocational rehabilitation, which relies on medical diagnosis and documentation, to gain access to community-based, competitive employment rather than low-wage work in sheltered workshops. Organizations operate within a broad political environment that ties disability rights and services to medical gatekeeping, and disability organizations have strategically used this association rather than solely pursuing a social model.

Health Care Equity

The medical model and social models are blended in a unique balance in the fight for health care equity. Challenging the medical model does not mean that one does not deserve access to high-quality health care on one's own terms. People with disabilities want and need health care; they just do not want treatments or cure imposed on them. Access to high-quality primary and specialized care, though, is limited for people with disabilities. Doctors may refuse to see patients with significant disabilities who may need extra time or supports to receive care, or they may choose not to accept Medicaid, further restricting access to health care for people with disabilities.[21] Other barriers to health care abound. It is, therefore, not surprising that many parent-led organizations, including the Arc, UCP, and the National Alliance on Mental Illness (NAMI), fight to ensure that people with intellectual, developmental, and mental disabilities are not disadvantaged in accessing routine and specialized care. The Arc position states, "The health care system must be aligned to principles of nondiscrimination, comprehensiveness, continuity, appropriateness, and equity. Both comprehensive public and private health insurance must provide for necessary health care without regard to the nature or severity of disability, pre-existing conditions, or other health status."[22]

For the Arc, health care equity is one of many equity issues. For NAMI, access to treatment as a fundamental right of people with mental illness is front and center in its platform. NAMI challenges structural biases built into the funding of health care that prioritize physical health and deprioritize mental health. It is at the forefront of fighting for "mental health parity," the idea that health care related to mental illness should be covered by insurance plans to the same extent as health care related to physical illness. NAMI notes that without parity, "mental health treatment is often covered at far lower levels in health insurance policies than physical illness, which means people do not get the care they need to experience recovery."[23] Organizations like ADAPT, the Arc, and UCP have fought to remove other structural biases in health care that disadvantage people with disabilities. For example, Medicaid's institutional bias prioritizes the payment of care provided in congregate, institutional settings, and many disability activist groups have fought to ensure that funding flows instead to community-based treatment and services.

Enhancing access to health care may also entail working with and training medical personnel to confront their biases. The National Down Syndrome Society (NDSS), for example, makes a particular effort to engage with medical professionals to improve outcomes for people with Down syndrome. Because of the visibility of the physical markers of Down syndrome prenatally and at birth, children with Down syndrome are particularly susceptible to early institutionalization, out-of-family placement in adoption services, abandonment, and abortion. Medical discourse and practice heighten these risks by defining Down syndrome as a birth "defect," promulgating testing for defects, neglecting to provide positive information about quality of life and community resources, and discounting the potential for a successful and meaningful life for people with Down syndrome.[24] In response, NDSS trains health care professionals to communicate the value of diverse lives to prospective and recent parents.

Outcomes for deaf children are also shaped heavily by interaction with medical professionals. The American Society for Deaf Children (ASDC) states that all D/deaf[25] children have a right to be valued and respected, to meet and socialize with other deaf children, and to achieve fluency in reading, writing, and, to their ability, speaking English; yet they recognize that professionals often fall short of advancing these ideals for deaf children. Thus, ASDC directly engages with medical, audiology, and educational professionals to enhance their capacity to appreciate the successes of D/deaf adults from all walks of life including people who use American Sign Language (ASL); to recognize the benefits of early language including early ASL; to connect parents with other parents and Deaf adults and children; and to provide information on schools and organizations related to Deafness. ASDC does not eschew medical intervention or technology but also argues that intervention and technology do not replace or diminish the need for Deaf culture and ASL.

Medicalization toward Mitigation and Social Inclusion

A fourth configuration is a pattern in which diagnosis and active medical intervention and treatment are seen as primary routes to greater social participation, inclusion, and status. This frame emphasizes the power of medical treatment and therapy to enhance normalization and decrease physically and socially problematic aspects of a condition, helping a person better function and be accepted in society.[26] Parent organizations using this frame advocate biomedical identification and treatment as a means toward mitigation, normalization, and social inclusion. Unlike the three prior frames, in this frame medical intervention is highly valued and prioritized, putting it more at odds with the agenda of core organizations led by disabled activists.

NAMI provides an example of an organization that values diagnosis and treatment as pathways to personal well-being and social inclusion. NAMI's mission statement reflects a broad array of goals toward "building better lives for the millions of Americans affected by mental illness, especially those with serious mental illness," including attention to treatment. NAMI "firmly believes that individuals with mental illness should have access to clinically appropriate medications, evidence-based services and treatment, including psychotherapy, that are provided in a person-centered approach,"[27] and access to a comprehensive array of treatment, services, and supports. For NAMI, increasing access to effective, evidence-based treatment helps remove the stigma of mental illness, whereas a refusal to acknowledge the value of treatment and medication is itself stigmatizing, subjecting people to a lifetime of suffering without recourse to the same kinds of supports readily given without stigma to people with physical conditions.

They highlight the importance of providing pathways to stigma-free treatment. For example, in a feature called "You Are Not Alone," NAMI members tell personal stories of mental illness. In one such story, "How Invalidating My Bipolar Disorder Invalidates Me," the author explains the many myths she must endure, such as "you don't need medication," "just think positive," "just calm down," and "you need to do yoga." Those unfamiliar with being bipolar, she writes, "have no idea how frustrating and exhausting the years of trial and error in medications and treatment can be. Still, I continue to seek treatment because the symptoms of not treating the illness were far worse. . . . For the first time in a long time, I am learning to deal with my feelings, emotions, and moods."[28] In another featured blog related to minority mental health, the blogger discusses the stereotype that one can "pray away" mental illness, and instead reassures people that treatment should be an acceptable way to live more active and successful lives.

Autism Speaks promotes the medical model even more strongly (as discussed more in the next section). Its website is structured to provide information on diagnosis and treatment, and Autism Speaks' targeted outcomes for the 2020s include "a better understanding of the causes and typology of ASD"; diagnosis "before the age of 2"; and "access to appropriate intervention, services, and resources immediately following diagnosis" and "throughout their lifetime."[29] The organization's priorities do not focus solely on a medical model. They include, for example, the goals of a better quality of life, providing transition planning for independent living, and providing lifelong supports. That said, the group's discourse clearly values the role of medical research and intervention as a means to increase quality of life and independence. In a statement on its "commitment to everyone on the autism spectrum," it states, "Many aspects of autism can be significantly debilitating, and that is why efforts to improve and deliver scientific breakthroughs are so important, with the goal of enabling those on the autism spectrum to be the best they can be—with autism."[30]

Mitigation focuses on long-term therapies, supports, and tools to enhance quality of life and inclusion, and many people with disabilities welcome access to these methods when they are useful and chosen. Yet therapies and medicalized supports also have the potential to feel coercive to people with disabilities for whom recovery is required to feel culturally valued or to access rights.[31] Cassandra Evans documents, for example, the ways that people with mental health disabilities are forced to meet "measurable outcomes" (e.g., attending support groups, medication compliance, displaying appropriate behavior) to obtain desired housing and services.[32] Thus, social service agencies may use the stages of "recovery" as a way to demand compliance and distribute privileges and basic liberties accordingly. Moreover, medical intervention may come to be seen as the only or the best path to inclusion and quality of life, a view that disabled activists explicitly critique.

Medicalization toward Cure and Prevention

The final frame related to the social and medical models prioritizes a medical understanding of the condition at hand and imagines a world that is best without the diseases that "plague" it. Rather than helping one live successfully *with* any given condition, the goal is instead to *remove* the condition. Insofar as this discourse challenges the medical community, it presents a call for more medical intervention—more research, treatment, drugs, and prevention. A cure and prevention approach assumes that a cure will reestablish a person's access to valued social roles; therefore one does not need to prioritize fighting for social supports, access, issues of social equity, or participation. Eradication is the fundamental goal. The unabashed, uncritical embrace of the medical model to eradicate disability is vehemently opposed by core organizations led by people with disabilities.

Parents of children with diseases, such as cancer and HIV, tend to have a strong commitment to cure and prevention. The American Childhood Cancer Organization, for example, is "determined to change [the fact that] childhood cancer is the number one disease killer of children."[33] Its website's "Facts" menu option offers resources on medical issues including childhood cancer statistics, diagnosis, types of childhood cancer, and information on clinical trials.[34] The group's advocacy includes promoting funding for new treatment of childhood cancer, providing educational resources for families, and helping "ensure that policymakers, researchers, and leaders in the healthcare community . . . have the tools they need to collect data and share as much information on childhood cancer as possible."[35] In this war on cancer, the medical community is clearly an ally, although not always an unproblematic one. The problem, however, is seen as the lack of medical and research attention to childhood cancer, and the solution is more medical research related to children and more access to treatment for children.

This model may seem appropriate for cancer, which is a potentially lethal, usually acute, illness from which many children experience remission and cure. The situation, though, is very different when this model is applied to disabilities that are lifelong, constitute integral aspects of one's being, and are seen by disabled activists as valued forms of human diversity.

Autism Speaks has drawn particular ire from disabled activists for its reliance on disease discourse in relation to autism and its focus on cure rather than supports and social justice. Autism Speaks describes autism as a disease, akin to cancer or AIDS. Indeed, the language of "epidemic" is commonly used to raise alarm and dollars for autism biomedical research.[36] Here the framing as illness provokes great anger in autistic activists because autism is typically considered a lifelong disability for which there is no cure, akin to developmental disabilities (e.g., intellectual disability, cerebral palsy), rather than an illness. For disabled activists, rights, supports, and services enhance quality of life for people with disabilities. Money and political capital poured into the hope of cure, they argue, has yielded little in the way of improved quality of life and instead increases stigma. Neurodiversity activists in the Autistic Self Advocacy Network, for example, challenge whether a cure is desirable, and instead posit autism as a part of human diversity, a different way to think, rather than a defect to be prevented.[37]

The 2009 Autism Speaks film *I Am Autism* offers a striking example of the problems of applying an illness perspective to disability. The film was written and produced by parents of children with autism to raise awareness of a "global autism epidemic."[38] This film presents autism as a *thing*—a disease—separate from one's child that invades and can be identified, attacked, and killed, a *thing* that vigilant parents can be victorious over and rescue their *real* children, their nonautistic children. As we can kill the cancer and recover our suffering children, we can kill the autism and recover the nonautistic child, or so the film suggests. But autism is a constitutive part of someone; it affects the way a person with autism thinks, interacts, and perceives. This statement is not meant to reduce people to their autism, but it is to say that people live with and grow as people with autism. Although Autism Speaks claims to fight against stigma, its representations of autism tend to be dark, frightening, and highly stigmatizing.

Because Autism Speaks frames autism as a disease, its home page links to a variety of stories from a biomedical model, including information on diagnosis and learning the signs of autism, a report on the health of people with autism, and news of a genome project. Its research priorities are overwhelmingly medical and focused on autism prevention: genome sequencing, global public health initiatives, the Autism treatment network, pre- and postdoctoral fellowships that bridge clinical and laboratory science, and the Preclinical Autism Consortium for Therapeutics to support clinical trials. The largest portion of its funding is invested in biomedical scientific research, much of it with the goal of eradicating autism. Its advocacy priorities list investment in research first, then legislation and services for adults to gain the support they need to live in the community as independently as possible.

In contrast, in modern materials the Arc and UCP almost never depict intellectual disability or CP as diseases that destroy children's and family's lives. That said, even organizations that focus much more on the social model still retain some aspects of the biomedical model used to pursue cure and prevention. Although NDSS recently changed its mission statement to brand itself as "the leading *human rights* organization for all individuals with Down syndrome," historically NDSS prioritized medical research including clinical trials and, more recently, initiatives like chromosome mapping and a National Institutes of Health registry of individuals with Down syndrome. Coming in line with the social model over time, however, its research priorities now focus more heavily on ensuring "that people with Down syndrome have the opportunity to enhance their quality of life, realize their life aspirations, and become valued members of welcoming communities."[39] The Arc also has a long history of promoting medical research, including research on fetal alcohol syndrome, specific chromosomal disorders, human genome mapping, and gene therapy. These now have a lesser role in the Arc's politics.

The tension between trying to value people with a disability and pursuing the eradication of disability is challenging.[40] Disabilities can be painful, limiting, and stigmatizing, and the opportunity for cure may be enticing. Yet the politics of cure and prevention positions the disability as inherently negative, something to be avoided, and a thing that causes suffering, and this position undercuts the value of people with that disability and their inclusion within the fabric of human diversity.[41] Over time, as they prioritized the fight for civil rights and inclusion, the Arc and NDSS diminished their biomedical focus. In contrast, Autism Speaks, a more recent organization, places the biomedical model front and center. In response to sharp criticism from the autistic activist community, it recently removed the word "cure" from its mission statement; however, Autism Speaks remains committed to an agenda that prefers a world without autism, thereby undercutting its ability to embrace neurodiverse people as valued and respected members of society.

Integration versus Disability-Specific Sites and Services

Except for the Deaf community's support of deaf schools, integration and accessibility of all spheres of social participation is a fundamental goal of most organizations led by activists with disabilities. Activists with disabilities demand access to all aspects of mainstream society, supports and services in the community rather than in institutional settings, and freedom from discriminatory practices that create exclusion. Disability studies scholars Sara Acevedo and Brent White push these boundaries even further with their notion of "radical inclusion." Inclusion as practiced typically centers the mythical "normal" child and builds inclusion around and in relation to normality. Radical inclusion centers the needs and embodiment of people with disabilities as a starting point and includes everyone else from there.[42]

Parents, though, vary in the degree to which they fight for integration in all aspects of life. In line with disabled activists, parents may demand access for their offspring to integrated schools, workplaces, leisure opportunities, and so on, but parents also often value disability-specific settings and services because they believe these settings are best configured to provide expertise, safety, and a sense of community among similar peers. In this category of integration versus disability-specific sites, we see three typical frames.

Integration

An integration agenda seeks the full and equal participation of people with disabilities in all of society's institutions, organizations, and valued social roles. The National Organization of Parents of Blind Children (NOPBC), for example, seeks to "create a climate of opportunity for blind children in home and society."[43] Its parent organization, the National Federation of the Blind, "believes in the capacity of the blind to be fully participating members of society, able to compete on equal terms with the sighted."[44] In the NOPBC's magazine, *Future Reflections*, a parent offers the following advice regarding education:

> Too often school officials and parents enter the IEP meeting believing that the student should be placed in an educational setting other than regular education. This is not appropriate. Each IEP team should begin with the assumption that the child will attend regular educational classes in the child's neighborhood school.[45]

Blind skills and technologies, as well as accommodations and accessibility, can be used to facilitate integration. Learning these skills, according to the NOPBC, does not require or justify long-term segregated education or segregation in other settings. The NFB further criticizes the use of sheltered workshops and instead advocates competitive employment opportunities.[46]

The Community Imperative, a philosophical and political statement demanding inclusion espoused by many disability organizations, including the Arc and UCP, offers another example of the value placed on integration. The Arc's position statement on inclusion reads: "All people benefit when persons with intellectual and/or developmental disabilities are included in community life. People with disabilities should be welcomed and included in all aspects of our society. This includes public activities, programs and settings, and private establishments which are open and accessible to members of the general public. People with disabilities should receive the supports they need to participate actively in community life without having to wait."[47] The Arc believes that the specific opportunities children with disabilities should have include the following: to live in a family home, to have access to needed supports, to enjoy typical childhood relationships and friendships, to learn in their neighborhood school in a general education classroom that contains peers without disabilities, to participate in the same activities as children without disabilities, to play with other children in community recreation, and to participate in religious observations and practices. They believe that adults with disabilities should have relationships of their choosing with individuals in the community who are not paid staff or family, live in a home where and with whom they choose, have access to needed supports, engage in meaningful work in an inclusive setting, participate in recreation and leisure available to the general public, and participate in religious observances and practices of their choosing.

The pursuit of inclusion envisions a community composed of diverse people with diverse needs, in which the community values all members and provides the avenues needed to support all members in meaningful participation. Anything less is discrimination. As mentioned, Acevedo and her colleagues push these boundaries even further with their notion of "radical inclusion," centering the needs and embodiment of people with disabilities as a starting point and including everyone else from there.

Least Restrictive Environment and Negotiated Access

Rather than full inclusion, the least restrictive environment (LRE) is a philosophy built into civil rights laws like the Individuals with Disabilities Education Act (IDEA) and into the service system for developmental and mental disabilities that states that people should have the maximal freedom possible given their capabilities and needs. This falls short of full inclusion, which is seen as an aspirational goal, which may not ever be reached. In principle, LRE demands full inclusion unless there are clear reasons to restrict it, but sociologist Steven Taylor noted that in practice it has been used liberally to legitimize segregation when deemed by experts and parents to be in a disabled person's best interests.[48]

A system based on LRE offers a continuum of services that vary in the levels of integration and freedom. For example, housing services might offer a continuum of residences and supports from independent living with personal assistance (full integration), to small group homes with some staff supervision and minor restrictions in the community, to group homes with significant supervision, greater restrictions, and less community interaction, to large-scale congregate facilities that are totalizing in nature such that agency rules dictate schedules and one has few contacts outside the disability service system. People with disabilities potentially move along the continuum based on professional assessments of their skills and successes at integration. For LRE advocates, the continuum offers a diverse range of appropriate supports and restrictions based on need. According to disabled activists, though, in practice this system too often presumes that restriction is acceptable, forces people to prove that they are worthy to be in the community, fails to teach people independent skills to advance them in the continuum, and determines placement based on open "slots" rather than a process that takes seriously why and when we should restrict liberty. The continuum therefore actually serves to justify segregation and undermines basic civil rights, treating rights as a therapeutic and administrative decision.

The Arc and UCP on the national level have moved increasingly toward advocating for full integration, but historically and still today retain strong elements of a continuum model in many of their local service delivery systems. On the one hand, both organizations have supported the Community Imperative and pushed for integration in education, work, and community services. On the other hand, many local Arcs and UCPs run disability-specific programs, including sheltered workshops, day programs, and agency-organized group homes. Placement in these settings often is determined by available "slots," funding streams, and professionally assessed skills, rather than a presumption of full inclusion and meaningful consumer choice. For self-advocates, these systems are particularly problematic when there is an encompassing system of large-scale, disability-specific settings, so that "consumers" move from one disability-specific setting to another, with little interaction with the community outside of the disability service sector and paid professionals, and with little control over these "services" and the content of them. In other words, people with disabilities live their lives within systems that offer little freedom or self-determination.

Shifting between the positions of full inclusion and LRE creates internal conflict within these organizations. The Arc's position on sheltered workshops and day programs offers a vivid example of internal conflict. Nationally, the Arc is moving away from sheltered workshops and toward support of competitive and integrated workplaces, and many state-level Arcs reflect national trends. For example, New York's Arc supported the move toward competitive employment, and several county-level Arcs began the process of transitioning their work programs to deliver integrated and competitive employment programs. In accordance with this agenda, the Rockland Arc, for example, began converting its sheltered recycling workshop into an employer for both disabled and nondisabled workers. Not all local Arcs, though, are convinced of the value or possibility of full integration. Putnam County Arc Executive Director Susan Limongello cautioned, "This upcoming transition will force many people into jobs that they may not want. Their current situation [including employment at a sheltered workshop] affords them real work and successful employment."[49] Hanns Meissner, executive director of the Rensselaer County Arc, stated that, if not for sheltered workshops and day programs, "they might otherwise be in nursing homes."[50] In other words, ending sheltered workshops might lead to negative, rather than positive, consequences if people cannot find or successfully fulfill the demands of competitive employment, and they may instead end up in even more restrictive and unfulfilling programs. Given a lack of confidence in both the ability of all people to hold competitive community-based employment and the willingness of employers to include and accommodate diverse employees, many parents fiercely defend sheltered workshops as an appropriate and valuable service to foster economic productivity and social participation. The value of inclusion is thereby challenged by local service providers and parents in order to deliver cost-effective and efficient services.

Disability-Specific Services and Settings

Some parent-led organizations operate within the LRE theoretical framework but focus their efforts on *ensuring* the provision of disability-specific settings. This approach is treated as a distinct frame, and there is a great deal of variability within this frame. In particular, some organizations advocate access to short-term disability-specific services in a disability-specific setting, while others advocate long-term disability-specific services and sites that tend to encompass the entirety of a person's lived experience (e.g., education, work, leisure, housing) over the life course. The former is far less controversial than the latter.

As noted earlier, the Deaf community stands apart in some ways from most grassroots disability activist organizations. The Deaf community sees itself as a linguistic and cultural minority and, as such, demands the means to transmit its culture and language via Deaf education provided by Deaf educators in Deaf schools.[51] In an information booklet for parents, the American Society for Deaf Children notes that "a center-based program brings a group of students with similar needs together in a centrally located school," with full access to ASL, accommodations, and involvement of Deaf adults. Hands and Voices, an organization of parents of Deaf and hard-of-hearing children, has no advocacy or policy branch, but it does offer resources including the National Association of the Deaf (NAD) statement critical of early educational inclusion: "Placement of all deaf and hard-of-hearing children in regular educational classrooms in accordance with an inclusion doctrine rooted in ideology is a blatant violation of the IDEA."[52] NAD has taken a strong stand against educational integration and instead promotes the use of Deaf schools, including residential placement. The value of Deaf education in a Deaf-specific school is tied to fostering Deaf skills and culture, taught by Deaf adults, to a community of Deaf children who build the skills needed to integrate in and across social arenas (e.g., employment, health care) facilitated by access to ASL interpreters. As this is a stance taken by the Deaf activist community to empower Deaf children and adults, it is seen as an acceptable choice by most disabled activists although it challenges the integration mandate.

Disabled activists have a much more antagonistic view toward parent-led organizations, such as VOR (A Voice of Reason; formerly Voice of the Retarded), that want to retain long-term, large-scale, disability-specific settings, including state-run residential facilities and sheltered workshops. Unlike schools, which are temporary, VOR fights to maintain long-term, comprehensive, disability-specific settings that encompass the life span and all spheres of life with little input from the person who is disabled.[53] This is directly opposed to a core value of organizations led by disabled activists.

VOR and other organizations that use this frame see value in concentrating professional expertise, centralizing services, offering a high level of supervision, and creating an environment they perceive to be safe. They argue, in light of LRE guidelines in federal law, that disability-specific settings are a required option and that disability-specific settings might be the most appropriate and least restrictive setting in which to serve particular people with disabilities. The VOR website, for example, provides a letter from VOR to Pennsylvania Governor Tom Wolf criticizing the planned closures of two large residential centers, explains why and how to oppose the Disability Integration Act (which is supported by many organizations led by disabled activists), and highlights the VOR report "Widespread Abuse, Neglect and Death in Small Settings Serving People with Intellectual Disabilities." The description of the report describes the "tragedies" that occur because of the "zest to move to a 'community for all' vision for people with developmental disabilities without adequately considering the ramifications of separating vulnerable people from specialized care and then doing away with a critical safety net (a/k/a deinstitutionalization)."[54] VOR activists share with disabled activists concerns over lack of safety in the community; however, VOR uses this concern to justify congregate care (with little attention to the abuses in congregate care) whereas activists with disabilities use this concern to demand more funding, training, and choice within the community.

VOR parents draw parallels between specialized care for people with intellectual disabilities and Deaf education (as well as retirement communities and other places where people with similar needs share services). The comparison falls flat for disabled activists, however. In contrast with Deaf education, few disability-specific skills are taught in large, congregate care for people with intellectual and developmental disabilities (ID/DD). For people with ID/DD, the key educational issues are the techniques, pace, and level of education, not the attainment of different skills such as ASL. Unlike Deaf schools, which employ significant numbers of deaf adults as teachers and administrators, agencies in the field of ID/DD rarely hire people with ID/DD in positions of power. In addition, there is no focus on the dissemination of a disability culture. Instead, the goal is either creating a lifelong space for people with disabilities who are perceived as unable to live in the community or maximizing normalization (attaining the greatest skills to fit within the typical culture). For disabled activists, integration, not segregation, is the most effective path to participation and acceptance. And, unlike Deaf education, disability-specific services for people with ID/DD might encompass residence, work, and recreation, throughout the life span, creating a totalizing experience that is separate from people without disabilities (except for employees and volunteers) and run by nondisabled professionals. Thus, support for a totalizing system of disability-specific sites for education, employment, leisure, residence, and other services for people with ID/DD is far more removed from the core of organizations led by disabled activists than support of Deaf education.

For organizations focusing on mental illness, the fight over integration is also very heated. Psychiatric survivors and mad activists argue that institutionalization is a violation of their basic civil and human rights, and people with mental illness benefit from treatment provided in the community. As a result of the passage of civil rights protections, it has become difficult to institutionalize people against their will for mental illness. In most states, evidence of harm to oneself or to others is the only legal basis for involuntary commitment. Many parents, though, specifically advocate to increase access to involuntary hospitalization and treatment. Under the current standard, people with mental illness might be homeless, unsafe, unable to take care of their basic needs, or in distress and without appropriate treatment, yet still be ineligible for involuntary commitment. Some parents and family members have fought to loosen the legal requirements for involuntary commitment and to create a procedure for mandated outpatient treatment for some people living in community settings. NAMI's executive director, Laurie Flynn, states, "Many families with a schizophrenic son or daughter have been extremely distressed because the commitment laws mean they have to wait for a crisis before they can get help, and they have to become legal adversaries" of their children in the process if their offspring refuse help.[55]

NAMI's official position states, "States should adopt broader, more flexible standards that would provide for involuntary commitment and/or court ordered treatment when an individual, due to mental illness[,] is gravely disabled, which means that the person is substantially unable, to provide for any of his or her basic needs, such as food, clothing, shelter, health or safety; or is likely to substantially deteriorate if not provided with timely treatment; or lacks capacity, which means that, as a result of the serious mental illness, the person is unable to fully understand—or lacks judgment to make an informed decision about—his or her need for treatment, care, or supervision."[56]

In the case of involuntary commitment and treatment, the issue of integration versus disability-specific services is not at all related to an empowered choice to participate in a disability community or disability culture. Rather, involuntary commitment imposes a disability-specific setting, asserts medical authority and imposes treatment on a person who resists such treatment, and restricts the person's right to resist. Many NAMI advocates see this treatment as essential for protecting the safety and well-being of people with mental illness, imposing care until the person can better engage in self-care. Indeed, for many family members, the right to integration is a ridiculous notion if their mentally ill loved one is homeless, off medications, and/or in danger. Integration under those circumstances hardly seems empowered. However, support for involuntary commitment and treatment using any measure other than harm is far removed from the vision of equal rights and participation espoused by the core of organizations led by disabled activists.

Power and Voice

A third major controversy related to framing and disability activism is the issue of power. Who speaks for people with disabilities and who makes what decisions in what settings? The position of organizations led by disabled activists is that decisions should be made to the greatest extent possible by people with disabilities. Parent organizations, as the very term suggests, place power in the hands of parents and/or professionals. This distances parent organizations from core organizations led by disabled activists. We identify three typical configurations of the relationship of power and voice revealed in the tenets of parent organizations.

Conferring Leadership on Activists with Disabilities
Although relatively rare in the scope of parent activism, some parents are members of organizations led by disabled activists. Among the organizations discussed in this chapter, the National Organization of Parents of Blind Children (NOPBC) best illustrates this model. NOPBC is a subunit of the National Federation of the Blind. Thus, parents are organized within and under a governing body controlled by people who are blind. The mission, funding, and policy decisions are all tied to the larger body. Parents are therefore positioned as allies to blind activists, rather than as competitors for authority, funding, and political power.

Using a different organizational model, the American Society for Deaf Children states that its board is "a group of dedicated parents and professionals" with no explicit reference to quotas of parents and deaf individuals in governance. That said, of the ten board members listed on the website with biographies (one board member had no biography), all (100 percent) were Deaf or hard of hearing, three identified as Deaf parents of Deaf children, and seven listed some affiliation with Gallaudet University. Thus, although positioned rhetorically as a group of parents and professionals, the board is a specific set of parents and professionals who are themselves Deaf and wish to educate and shape the experiences of children who are Deaf.

Parents have also joined or offered support to self-advocacy organization, either because they as parents might have disabilities or to support the self-advocacy of their offspring, or both. A blogger and the parent of a nonspeaking autistic youth of color, Kerima Çevick regularly critiques parent-led autism organizations and aligns with autistic activists and organizations to promote grassroots community-building and pay-it-forward activist models.[57] The parent of a son with Down syndrome, Nicki Pombier Berger supports self-advocacy by recording and disseminating the perspectives of self-advocates. Many self-advocates with intellectual and developmental disabilities speak about the positive role their parents have played in supporting their self-advocacy, including providing transportation, assisting in preparing and delivering speeches, and co-presenting. Zona Roberts, mother of disability rights leader Ed Roberts, offers another useful example of a mother who fought for her son's inclusion and, as he matured, supported his activism.[58] In this model, parent advocacy may be largely behind the scenes, supporting their family members and other self-advocates in taking the lead.

Parental Control with Inclusion of Self-Advocates and Professionals

The most common strategy of parent organizations is to build avenues of inclusion for self-advocates, while retaining considerable control themselves as parents. For example, NAMI's bylaws require that at least 75 percent of its board of directors be people with or who had a mental illness, *or* parents *or* relatives of a person with mental illness. They established a Peer Leadership Council of people who have or have had mental illness, and the chair of that council automatically sits on the board. Using the biographies listed on the NAMI website, of the five-member board leadership team, one person identified as a parent, two as family members, and one as a person with a mental illness diagnosis. Looking at the sixteen-person board (including officers), six identified as parents (38 percent), three as siblings (19 percent) (therefore, 56 percent identify as parents/family), and five as people with a mental illness diagnosis (31 percent).[59] Parents outweigh self-advocate control, but NAMI's board also has a sizable percentage of people with mental illness in leadership positions as well as a council to advance the interests of self-advocates. Among staff leadership positions (e.g., executive director, director of marketing) listed on the website, only one of thirteen staff members (8 percent) identified as a family member and no staff (0 percent) identified as people who have or have had mental illness. NAMI's programming priorities reflect a value on self-advocacy, including supporting the Peer Leadership Council, stressing person-centered participation in treatment and research, and providing tools for advocacy and involvement. That said, NAMI does little to draw attention to or ally with the psychiatric survivors' movement, or Mad activism, which is critical of psychiatric intervention.

The Arc bylaws require that a majority of the board of directors be parents or family members of people with ID/DD *or* people with ID/DD. The Arc also established a national self-advocates council and a siblings' council, among other councils, to serve in an advisory capacity. Of its board in fall 2017, four of the five national officers (80 percent) were parents. Of the entire board (including officers), sixteen of twenty-four board members (67 percent) listed could be clearly identified as parents, family members, or self-advocates. This included nine parents, four family members, and three self-advocates.[60] Here we see a dominance of parents and family members (54 percent), as compared to people with disabilities (13 percent). The Arc listed forty-seven staff members, forty-two of whom have bios listed on their webpage. Of these, three identified as parents, six as family members (21 percent parent/family), and one as a person with a disability although not clearly with an ID/DD diagnosis (2 percent). No self-advocates or people with ID/DD were identified among the staff (0 percent). Thus, in the day-to-day work of the organization, family members have some representation, while self-advocates and people with ID/DD diagnoses have little to none. The national bylaws require local chapters to meaningfully involve parents, family members, and people with ID/DD in leading and guiding the chapter but offer no specific percentage of the board or other specific guidelines for meeting this requirement. Thus, local chapters have more leeway in their board composition and likely have less involvement by self-advocates.

Looking at its programming, the Arc provides substantial support for self-advocacy, including supporting a self-advocacy council and an online forum for self-advocates. Many state and local chapters support self-advocacy efforts by providing funding, space, and supports, and by fostering recruitment. The Arc also works closely with Self-Advocates Becoming Empowered—the national self-advocacy group for people with ID/DD—and state-level self-advocacy groups. On the other hand, in 2017 the Arc website boasted being "the nation's leading advocacy organization for all people with ID/DD and their families," clearly asserting its power and prestige above that of Self-Advocates Becoming Empowered.[61]

Parental and Professional Control

Some parent-led organizations focus almost exclusively on parent/family leadership. VOR, for example, has a sixteen-member board, of whom fifteen (94 percent) are parents or siblings. One member is a caregiver, and none are self-advocates. There are no bylaws mandating any particular representation, although historically the board has always focused on family membership. VOR has almost no history of alliance with self-advocacy organizations, and it presents itself as the voice of people with ID/DD (or at least those who lack the skills to speak for themselves). Indeed, it openly criticizes SABE, arguing that self-advocates should represent themselves but not speak for all people with intellectual and developmental disabilities.

Autism Speaks lists a board of twenty-nine members, including twelve parents, two family members, and one self-advocate (an email with staff reported two self-advocates on the board); thus the board composition is 48 percent parent/family and 7 percent self-advocate (if we use the number reported in the email, 3 percent if we use website disclosure). The board is dominated by people with powerful positions in industry, including former CEOs and investment managers. Autism Speaks has no bylaw regarding representation of parents, family members, or self-advocates, and participation by self-advocates is a recent change likely resulting from criticism by autistic activists. Its website lists six staff leadership positions, and of these one (17 percent) is filled by a self-identified parent, and none (0 percent) by people who self-identify as autistic. Autism Speaks offers few resources for self-advocacy and no clear projects to foster or advance self-advocacy. As detailed in the next section, Autism Speaks also rarely seeks to ally with autistic self-advocates or organizations led by disabled activists, and instead prefers to connect with medical, psychiatric, and behavioral health professionals and the pharmaceutical industry to support its agenda of medical research and treatment.

Although historically a parent-led organization, UCP's current decision-making structure is dominated by professionals. UCP's website lists five officers and thirteen trustees. Of this eighteen-person board, five are parents or siblings (28 percent) and two are people with cerebral palsy (11 percent). In total, then, 39 percent of the board is composed of parents, family, and people with disabilities. The rest are people who offer professional expertise. UCP has no bylaws regarding representation on its board, and thus no requirement for family or self-advocate representation. Unlike VOR and Autism Speaks, though, UCP has a strong record of supporting self-advocacy and working with organizations led by activists with disabilities. Thus, it breaks the expected pattern that organizations with more emphasis on the social model and integration would also ensure leadership for people with disabilities.

Positionality and Alliance

As is evident from the above discussion, there is no simple, definitive typology of parent-led organizations. UCP emphasizes the social model and inclusion, yet it has no rule for self-advocate board representation and limited participation. American Society for Deaf Children has a high representation of Deaf people on its board and relies heavily on the social model, but it supports Deaf education delivered at schools specifically for the Deaf rather than at integrated schools.

That said, we see a tendency for support of the social model, integration, and power of self-advocates to cluster together in a parent-led organization and in effect to position such organizations closer to organizations led by disabled activists and orient them toward alliance. Still, the complex blending of frames and the retention of parental or professional control by parent organizations makes even these organizations "sometimes allies." On the other hand, reliance on the medical model, disability-specific settings, and parental or professional control also tend to cluster and in effect to position parent organizations further away from, and even in opposition to, organizations led by disabled activists and orient them more toward peripheral organizations like medical and human service industries. These organizations are less likely to form alliances. However, even when organizations do not agree in philosophy and oppose each other in some ways, they do at times engage in strategic alliances to support particular issues.

Because the National Organization of Parents of Blind Children exists as a subdivision of the National Federation of the Blind, the policy priorities are in sync. It "function[s] as an integral part of the National Federation of the Blind in its ongoing effort to achieve equality and opportunity for all blind persons."[62] Alliance is a direct outcome of the organizational structure.

In contrast, the Arc and UCP are independent organizations that are relatively consistent allies of grassroots disability organizations, but also pursue priorities less reflective of the disability rights or justice agenda and more geared toward achieving support for families and service providers. For example, the Disability Integration Act of 2017 (H.R. 2472) works to ensure the provision of long-term services and supports in the community, and this goal is a central priority of many organizations led by disabled activists. Alongside the Arc and UCP, supporters of this bill include disability activist organizations such as ADAPT, American Association of People with Disabilities, Autistic Self Advocacy Network, Little People of America, Disability Rights Education and Defense Fund, National Council on Independent Living, National Disability Rights Network, Not Dead Yet, and Self-Advocates Becoming Empowered. Parent-led organizations notably missing, for example, are Autism Speaks and VOR, who lack a focus on integration and strong ties with the disability community.

Reflecting a broader blend of alliances, the Steve Gleason Act of 2017 (S. 1132), which protects access to speech-generating devices through Medicare, is supported by the Arc and UCP, a range of organizations led by disabled activists (e.g., Autistic Self Advocacy Network, Disability Rights Oregon, National Disability Rights Network, Not Dead Yet), and professional and health organizations (Aging Life Care Association, Medicare Rights Center, Association of Assistive Technology). Again, we see Autism Speaks and VOR are notably absent.

Other priorities of the Arc and UCP, such as the Raise Family Caregiver Act (H.R. 3759, S. 1028), attract professional alliances more than do organizations led by disabled activists. This bill directs the Department of Health and Human Services to create a National Family Caregiving Strategy and Council to support family caregivers. The Paralyzed Veterans of America is listed among the supporters, but other organizations led by disabled activists are not. Instead, the list is composed primarily of health, aging, and professional organizations, such as Alzheimer's Association, American Academy of Family Physicians, Christopher and Dana Reeve Foundation, Family Caregiver Alliance, and National Council on Aging. Autism Speaks and Autism Society are both collaborators, but the Autistic Self Advocacy Network is not. The Arc and UCP are supporters, but Self-Advocates Becoming Empowered is not. Grassroots organizations led by disabled activists are not clearly opposed to the Raise Family Caregiver Act; rather, it is not their priority.

The Arc and UCP frequently collaborate with a set of professional organizations dedicated to issues related to intellectual and developmental disabilities. These organizations include the American Association on Intellectual and Developmental Disabilities, American Network of Community Options and Resources, and the National Association of Councils on Developmental Disabilities. In collaboration, they created the *Public Policy Agenda for the 115th Congress, 2017–2018*. SABE, representing self-advocates with intellectual and developmental disabilities, was not listed as part of this working group. This active collaboration across organizations without the involvement of SABE speaks to SABE's criticism of parent-led organizations. Thus, we can see for the Arc and UCP a tendency toward alliance with organizations led by disabled activists mixed with priorities that instead draw collaboration with professional and other parent groups.

When we look at NAMI's alliances, we see greater distance from the community of organizations led by disabled activists. Certainly there are shared policy issues, but NAMI's priorities are often not the priorities of disabled activists and vice versa. In the fall of 2017, the primary legislative priorities that NAMI promoted were two bills to promote mental health care reform: Helping Families in Mental Health Crisis Act of 2016 (H.R. 2646; see Chapter 2 for discussion of the 2014 bill, H.R. 3717) and Mental Health Reform Act of 2016 (S. 2680). Both pieces of legislation sought to increase access to mental health treatment in part through broadening the use of involuntary institutionalization and mandated treatment. To use H.R. 2646 as an example, it expands Medicaid reimbursement for inpatient care, gives families greater access to medical information, and allows and expands mandated treatment in the community. In her letter of support to Representatives Johnson and Murphy, cosponsors of the bill, NAMI executive director Mary Giliberti stated, "NAMI is pleased that HR 2646 includes a range of reforms that would improve our nation's failing public mental health system including efforts to focus on outcomes, break down barriers for consumers and families to access treatment, and expand the availability of evidence-based practices."[63] In the support of these legislative efforts, NAMI was joined by the Mental Illness Policy Organization and Mental Health America, leading professional associations related to mental illness.

In contrast, disabled activists, including the National Coalition for Mental Health Recovery (NCMHR) and the National Disability Leadership Alliance (NDLA), opposed both these bills. NCMHR's mission is to ensure that mental health consumers and survivors have a major voice in the development and implementation of mental health care policy. These groups object to the rights restrictions built into the law, as well as the control given to family members, who may be part of the mental health problem. Describing the bill, NDLA stated it would "silence our voices, reduce our choices, compromise our rights and restrict programs that protect our rights and safety. It would increase the use of involuntary outpatient commitment, coerced psychiatric treatment and hospitalization, heralding a return to the failed policies of the past."[64]

The framing of the law is also deeply problematic from a disability rights and justice perspective. In the database tracking all congressional bills, the summary of the bill reads: "Most Republicans argue that the main issue causing mass shootings is not guns but mental illness. HR2646, the Helping Families in Mental Health Crisis Act, is the main bill in this Congress tackling the issue of mental health."[65] This framing perpetuates the mythical connection between mental illness and gun violence, encourages stigma against people with mental illness, and promotes the notion that social control is necessary, albeit through mental health rather than imprisonment. NAMI accepts this problematic framing to build a strategic alliance with Republicans and increase the likely success of their goals. The social control perspective embedded in this law, however, is deeply antithetical to organizations led by disabled activists.

Autism Speaks' advocacy agenda has clear points of contention in relation to disabled activists, and they are positioned even further away from the disability rights and justice core. In listing their "legislative wins" in 2016, the top achievement is an increase in National Institute of Health funding to "accelerate biomedical innovations for people with autism." This act was broadly supported by a range of health, parent, and professional organizations such as the National Health Council, American Aging Association, ALS Association, American Foundation of the Blind, Association of University Centers on Disability, Easterseals, Mental Health America, National Alliance for Caregiving, National Down Syndrome Society, and the Spina Bifida Association. However, most of the organizations in the National Disability Leadership Alliance did not sign on.

Autism Speaks also builds alliances with the biomedical community by funding and encouraging biomedical research. For example, in 2012 Autism Speaks announced its partnership with an international consortium of scientists to support the development of new pharmacological approaches in treating autism.[66] Autism Speaks lauded successes in extending insurance coverage for applied behavioral analysis (ABA). Contrary to this position, though, the Autistic Self Advocacy Network states, "Until now, much advocacy for coverage of 'autism interventions' has focused on purely behavioral approaches, like Applied Behavioral Analysis (ABA). These interventions can be inappropriate or even harmful, and exclusive focus on coverage for behavioral interventions can result in limited access to evidence-based and emerging models that focus on improving relationships, communication skills, and development of skills that are meaningful to individuals' quality of life."[67] Autism Speaks' marketing decisions, which often present autism in a very negative light, also frequently put it at odds with the disability activist community. Autism Speaks' board showcases its strong relationships with the corporate world and a corporate perspective, with many board members in positions in marketing, investment, and the media at major corporations, and few members who represent social justice expertise. It has also been criticized for accepting donations from the pharmaceutical industry.[68]

Autism Speaks, though, does share a few priorities with disabled activists and with other parent organizations focused on developmental disabilities. For example, the ABLE Act (Achieving a Better Life Experience Act of 2014) created the opportunity for tax-free savings accounts to be used for disability-related expenses. This bill received widespread support from disability organizations including Autism Speaks. This fragility of this alliance, though, became evident when, late in the course of the development of the ABLE Act, politicians inserted a modification that allowed accounts only to people with disabilities manifested before the age of twenty-six. The exclusion of all disabilities that are not developmental in nature upset the disability community, and a broad coalition under the banner of the Consortium for Citizens with Disabilities signed a letter that opposed expansion of ABLE benefits for eligible individuals without addressing the age restriction that left many people with disabilities without access. The coalition included organizations such as the Arc, UCP, National Council on Independent Living, National Disability Rights Network, United Spinal Association, and Paralyzed Veterans of America. Neither Autism Speaks nor National Down Syndrome Society, two of the lead organizations in advocating the ABLE Act, signed the letter, forgoing their cross-disability alliance to ensure broader access to benefits for their specific constituencies.

Among the organizations studied, VOR is most consistently in a position of antagonism with disabled activists. While NAMI and even Autism Speaks at times find points of collaboration with disabled activists, VOR focuses on ensuring a "full range of quality residential options and services," including large-scale, specialized facilities, which disabled activists view as institutions and vehemently oppose.[69] Thus, they are not simply pursuing different priorities or sometimes at odds; they are almost always in direct opposition. For example, VOR's home page announces its opposition to a lawsuit filed by Disability Rights Ohio (DRO). The lawsuit, *Ball v. Kasich*, demands that Ohio prevent unnecessary institutionalization and do more to provide services in the community. VOR opposed this lawsuit, filed an amicus brief in opposition, and raised funds to finance its oppositional tactics.[70] Similarly, VOR opposed the Disability Integration Act, one of the most important legislative efforts of the disability community in 2019, arguing that it would move individuals "from their long-term homes into more isolated settings that provide fewer services, lower staffing ratios, and lower standards of care."[71]

VOR's focus on maintaining specialized facilities offers almost no opportunities for alliance with organizations led by disabled activists. In fact, the antagonism is so sharp that VOR is routinely ignored, excluded from participating even in shared interests like community safety standards, and mocked. The *Ragged Edge*, a magazine of the disability activist community, described VOR in its "The Gag" section as "a group of parents who once dumped their kids in institutions and today grease political wheels to keep them there." The magazine created a cut-out "puppet" of VOR founder Polly Spare saying things like "Frankly, my dear, they drooled. And in public! They were just . . . damp! All day long!"[72] VOR in turn disparages self-advocates as high-functioning activists who ignore the needs of the most significantly disabled. It instead allies primarily with unions and provider agencies that have a stake in the survival of specialized facilities rather than disabled activists.

In summary, we can imagine a field of disability activism situated around a core of organizations led by disabled activists as represented by grassroots self-advocacy organizations working toward equality and empowerment. Outside of the core, but often in alliance, are parent-led organizations like the Arc and UCP, which support self-determination and often advocate for rights and equity, but also serve the interests of parents, act as service providers reliant on bureaucratic models of management and disability-specific settings, and preserve political power for parents rather than people with disabilities. Further away from the core are organizations with a heavier focus on treatment such as NAMI, although they still have points of collaboration such as fighting stigma and increasing self-advocacy. Autism Speaks is well distanced from the core of disabled activists as a result of its highly medicalized view of autism, its support of treatment in professionally controlled spaces, and its relative lack of attention to issues of social rights, equity, and justice. VOR is furthest outside the field, considering itself a disability rights organization but viewed by grassroots disabled activists as completely antithetical to their mission.

Conclusion

This chapter illuminates several points. First, the very fact that parent-led organizations are parent-led tends to place them outside the core of disability rights and justice activism, subverting the ideal of empowerment and self-determination for people with disabilities. "New social movements" seek to upend traditional identity politics and gain cultural affirmation of the value of particular people.[73] Thus, in new social movements, it is imperative that marginalized people are seen as *owning* and *leading* their own movement. The political process itself is key to achieving the end. The very power of parents thereby potentially undermines disabled activists. This tension is exacerbated when parents present different frames and priorities than do disabled activists. The Arc, for example, reported net assets in 2016 of more than $16 million, far larger than most organizations led by disabled activists, thereby giving the Arc a political weight that is difficult for disabled activists to match.

Parents, however, rarely recognize this tension or their privileged position. Indeed, parents rarely feel powerful. In the face of massive bureaucracies, fiscal policies, laws, and professionals, parents struggle to have their voices heard, and opposition by people with disabilities may seem like one more threat, further undercutting their vulnerable position. Activists with disabilities, with their ideals of integration and empowerment, may feel to parents like yet another outsider placing pressure on an already tapped family, and yet another group that wants to invalidate their voice. Thus, while parents and disabled activists often work in concert, alliance can be tense to say the least.

Second, although parent-led organizations by their nature are at odds with disability activism as led by disabled activists, some organizations (at some times, for some issues) are much more involved and integrated into disability activism, and this is achieved by recognizing the value of the social model, embracing integration and equality, striving to support and empower self-advocates, and building consistent alliances with organizations led by disabled activists. Other organizations (at some times, and for some issues) are positioned much further away from the core of disabled activists, and indeed at times in opposition to them, especially insofar as they embrace a medical model, advocate for policies counter to integration and equality, deny self-advocates a voice, and build alliances with professionals and corporate interests rather than with disabled activists. In particular, parents may claim the symbolic authority of speaking for people with disabilities, presenting their own interests as the needs and rights of their children without recognizing potential conflicts of interests.[74] Tensions between parents and activists with disabilities are further exacerbated by the paternalistic and medical perspectives that at times permeate parent activism.[75] In doing so, parents cast the disabled child as the problem to be overcome, rather than the ableism, social exclusion, and cultural devaluation of disability that produce systemic inequality.[76]

Third, organizational complexities mean that internal frames and external alliances might shift frequently, yielding potential, yet suspicious and unreliable, alliance between parents and disabled activists. Parents may be less guided by a single philosophical stance than by the creative pursuit of a varied set of goals, through multiple strategies, that they deem appropriate for the best interests of their child and for their family.[77] As seen, the Arc both supports the Community Imperative and runs sheltered workshop and day programs at disability-specific sites. NAMI prioritizes the fight against stigma and discrimination, but also values the medical model (although with a focus on patient self-determination and involvement) of treatment and recovery. UCP draws on the social model of disability, yet has no guideline for board representation by self-advocates and includes few on their board. Each organization struggles with the ways in which it embraces disability activism and allies with organizations led by disabled activists while catering to its base of support, parents who ultimately want to retain control over treatment service options for their children—a desire that is deeply problematic from the perspective of disabled activists.

Finally, alliances themselves vary. New social movements seek reliable allies who not only share a specific goal or a broader frame around that goal but also display a commitment to the identity politics of the movement. This commitment entails respecting who "owns" the issue, placing the value of collaboration at times above one's own specific interests, and sharing a sense of grievance when an ally is wronged, even if it does not immediately affect you. The "bridging work" of alliance, then, shows that organizations care about the issue, the *people* involved in the issue, and the *alliance* itself.[78]

Strong partnerships can be built when disabled activists reach out to include parents and offer them avenues to gain knowledge of and access to disability activism. The model of the National Federation of the Blind may serve as useful in this regard, as it actively incorporates parents into its organizational structure. Parents too must come to appreciate the long-term value of the empowerment of people with disabilities in society. When the Arc and UCP refused to endorse a version of The ABLE Act that restricted eligibility, they exhibited a loyalty to people with disabilities outside of their specific focal populations, which builds trust.

Thus, we must build pathways toward interdependence, in which parents are supported by leaders in the disability community in enacting valued roles and disabled activists are supported by parents in the achievement of rights and justice. Moreover, as we strengthen the pathways for alliance, we must be mindful that disability activism led by disabled activists and by parents had been dominated by white activists with class privilege, especially on the national level, and that alliance building must consider ways to include the diversity of families and people with disabilities.[79] While we aim for alliance, we should also recognize that alliance is rarely without costs and sacrifices, and we must recognize these as well; parents, and specifically parents with class and race privilege, have their own interests and may not forgo their voice to strengthen the political position of activists with disabilities. Alliance may strengthen one's position with shared causes, but parents do not always share the perspective and interests of activists with disabilities and thus they will continue to exert an independent and politically influential voice, and to negotiate with disabled activists regarding the goals of disability policy and programs.

7

Social Movement Strategies
and Public Policy

I n addition to working on behalf of their own family members, parents of children with disabilities have in many cases worked collectively with other parents to seek changes in the status of children with disabilities more generally. They have tried to influence policies of local school districts and of various government agencies at the local, state, and federal levels.

In this chapter, we highlight some of the strategies of parent organizations in effecting social change. Parent organizations vary in which strategies they employ, but the key divisions rest more clearly on the framing and goal of the strategy than on the strategy itself. As an example, both the Arc and Autism Speaks engage in awareness campaigns, but they have very different messages about disability. That said, parent organizations do vary from organizations led by people with disabilities in one important strategy—the use of protest and civil disobedience. Parent organizations rely heavily on "legitimate" mechanisms of social change rather than protest or civil disobedience. In contrast to people with disabilities, parents tend to have greater access to legitimate channels of social reform, more to lose via illegal or dangerous protest, and less commitment to a radical re-envisioning of the world that demands the full rights and participation of people with disabilities. Thus, even when parents bring their resources to the fore as allies, they risk less danger, loss, and violence than do people with disabilities who may put their lives on the line as they fight injustice and exclusion.

From Individual Efforts to Collective Political Action

Parents of a child with a disability may experience barriers to collective action.[1] The stigma of disability may encourage parents to deny or hide their child's condition rather than seeking out others in similar situations. Further, disabling conditions are distributed across the general population, crossing class, ethnic, and geographic boundaries. Many parents of children with disabilities do not frequently interact with other such parents, and thus may not develop common identities or social ties with their peers. Families that include a disabled child may not live in the same neighborhood with other such families, or frequent the same establishments. Medical and educational gatekeepers have often communicated negative stereotypes about impairments that emphasize the inevitability of being excluded and left behind, which can discourage the development of a positive common identity and the potential for collective action to develop and promote common goals and mobilize activities to achieve them.

But these barriers can be overcome. Parents frequently seek out peers to gain information or mutual support, and such encounters may evolve into established networks that serve as a form of social capital and a basis for collective action. Early in the history of parent activism we see the simple strategy of placing an ad to identify other parents and bring them together. The case studies of parent activism for intellectual disabilities and cerebral palsy both include several stories involving parents who placed ads and tapped into a wellspring of need. Parents also meet via service systems, some of which deliberately promote interaction among the parents of the children being served and even draw on parents as sources of community or political support for their activities, and some of which may try to inhibit such organizing. As service providers, the Arc and UCP traditionally use their services not only to meet specific needs but also to raise broader awareness and build community among families, consumers, and parents. Service settings, like schools and day centers, offer parents the opportunity to meet each other and engage. As the mental health system shifted to community-based delivery, it explicitly sought consumer and parent involvement, bringing parents together.

Trends in information technology and the internet in particular have reduced the dependence of many families on making connections facilitated by specific physical programs or professionals. Families may now more easily link to others in similar circumstances, reducing their isolation. Organizational websites provide resources, announce events, and encourage engagement. Blogs, social media, and Listservs all provide parents with valuable ways to connect across distances and to share both publicly and privately. Parents with children with mental illness, for example, face particular shame and suspicion. At times they may want to speak publicly, but these parents also speak to the value of the anonymity found in the internet and member-restricted Listservs and chat rooms where they can share stories and information without the critical eye of the public or of disability advocates who may criticize their parenting and their perspective on disability.[2]

Federal laws and professional associations have also played a critical historical role in bringing children and adults with disabilities into community. The participation of parents in political activity has often begun with parents engaging with governmental agencies individually, on behalf of their own children. When parents have expectations for their children that are not met by local schools, health care providers, or community agencies, they may be unwilling to accept the lack of accommodations offered and work to enable their child's participation. Similarly, when parents seek to challenge or collaborate with professionals, they may use professional conferences and provider spaces as places to engage with other parents.

Public Awareness and Media Campaigns

Perhaps the most common or foundational mode of political activity undertaken by groups representing parents of children with disabilities has been the public awareness campaign. Sharon Barnartt and Richard Scotch write, "One of the most important tasks that social movements actively engage in is the production of meaning for participants, antagonists, and observers."[3] Collective action by movement participants and organizations can challenge existing meanings and create new ones through the social construction of collective consciousness, establishing and supporting new frames of interpretation that define social problems and propose solutions in ways that can mobilize support for social change.

Because of the stigma associated with disabling conditions, public discourse and popular culture in the United States have rarely given prominence to disability, with exceptions following America's military conflicts when veterans with disabilities have been publicly celebrated as embodiments of patriotism and sacrifice who were legitimate recipients of public support. Disability activists, including some parents, have sought to heighten awareness of disability within society and to reframe cultural concepts of disability, shifting them from a medical model associating impairment with incapacity and tragedy to a social model in which the removal of disabling barriers could promote independence and individuals who contribute to society. Barnartt and Scotch write, "The parents' movement mounted one of the first challenges to the status quo regarding disability. The parents were the first group to exhibit an 'oppositional consciousness' on a large scale and sustain it for a number of years."[4]

In the years after World War II, parents challenged the prevailing beliefs of medical professionals that children with impairments were best removed from their families and communities and isolated in segregated residential facilities such as state "schools" and "hospitals." Parents of children with intellectual disabilities promulgated accounts of their children as valued family and community members.[5] Parents such as Pearl Buck, John Frank, and Dale Evans Rogers published memoirs and personal stories about their children, describing their achievements and emphasizing their similarities to other children without disabilities. Parents employed a variety of media to shape public opinion about disability and the appropriate response to it, and recruited celebrities to help spread their messages. Parents also campaigned, first on behalf of their own children and then within the larger community, to question the exclusion of children with disabilities from public schools and public life.

Although groundbreaking in their time, these appeals had significant limitations. Parents' messages often emphasized their status as white, middle-class Americans, omitting parents who were poor and in communities of color.[6] And, while the appeals contributed to a cultural shift, they were insufficient alone to convince medical professionals and policy makers to change existing approaches that isolated disabled children.

Not all awareness campaigns, though, garner approval from activists with disabilities. Recent media reports of mass shootings focused attention on the perceived threats from individuals with mental illness. While there is no scientific evidence that individuals with psychiatric diagnoses are more likely to engage in violent activity than others, public fears have been raised about untreated mental illness, and policy makers have called for mass screenings, national registries, and mandatory treatment. The National Alliance for the Mentally Ill (NAMI), on the one hand, has tried to dispel these myths, but, on the other, has used the frenzy over gun violence to try to increase funding for prevention, mental health programs, and even involuntary hospitalization and medication.

A distinction might be made between public campaigns that rely on the medical model of disability and the social model.[7] As discussed, Autism Speaks and several other autism organizations have been sharply rebuked by disabled activists for presenting autism through the lens of the medical model, as an "epidemic" and a "threat" to children and families. Other parents' organizations disseminate information that is scientifically questionable and even harmful as they propound a range of dubious treatments and warn of the supposed risks of vaccination.

Campaigns that present disability as tragedy and people with disabilities as objects of pity often are associated with attempts to secure money, both in public appropriations and through private donations, for medical and rehabilitative research and services, as well as expanded eligibility for disability benefits. Such political initiatives frequently emphasize the incapacity associated with disability and the moral blamelessness of those who are unable to help themselves. Such political appeals, typified by the telethons of the 1950s and 1960s but also found in contemporary media commercial and video appeals, feature tales of woe about poster children (of all ages) whose lives will be ruined by their impairments unless help is found, particularly help in the form of a cure.

Political appeals of this sort have often been quite successful, and efforts have been made to medicalize a number of conditions to entitle those who have them to a flow of benefits and services for the "deserving" poor. For example, in response to advocacy by those affected by various illnesses, Congress has often appropriated more funds to biomedical research on those diseases and conditions than had been requested by the National Institutes of Health. Many public officials are reluctant to appear insensitive to appeals by those perceived as helpless and blameless. Through its mass marketing, Autism Speaks has raised vast sums and successfully lobbied for political apportionments for autism research. At issue in such political discourse is often the moral entitlement of those who are "afflicted," which is based on their impairment being a result of random victimization rather than their own choices and behavior. Disability rights groups led by activists with disabilities have been far less likely than parent-led groups to employ discourses based on the medical model or promoting tragedy or pity.

The politics of disability takes far different forms when advocates emphasize the social model of disability. Political issues are not simply about resources and moral entitlement, but may also include what social roles can appropriately be played by individuals with disabilities and how the state should support or restrict those roles. A campaign based on the social model of disability would focus on increasing access to participation and equity for people with disabilities in all spheres of life including education, employment, public services such as transportation, economic development, and civic life. By characterizing the social isolation and enforced dependency of people with disabilities as the result of social choices rather than as inevitable results of impairment, the social model suggests analogies between the social status of people with disabilities and other marginalized groups such as racial and ethnic minorities, women, or gays and lesbians. Within this political framework, disability politics can encompass disputes over civil rights.[8] Awareness campaigns therefore showcase the role of inaccessibility and discrimination in creating disadvantage, and seek social reform.

Creating and Delivering Services

Parents often find that if they want or need something, it is best to organize and deliver a solution themselves. This strategy retains parental control over quality and emphasizes parental expertise. Early in their histories, the Arc and UCP set forth to build model or demonstration projects to serve people with disabilities in the community. The Arc noted that ideally, once parents created these models, relevant community organizations and professionals would take them over. For example, parents might create an inclusive day care class, but ultimately some other agency would use the model to offer its own inclusive programming. Despite this goal, the Arc and UCP have emerged as major service providers, offering case management, respite, residential, vocational, leisure, and habilitation services. Indeed, on the local level, the Arc and UCP often function primarily as service providers, leaving the state- and national-level chapters to engage in political advocacy. In line with the social model, their services are not primarily medical; they focus on ensuring that people have the supports and services to live fulfilling lives in the community.

The Muscular Dystrophy Association (MDA, noted in Chapter 5 as a professional organization with significant support from parents) is an example of service provision in which the medical model dominates. MDA runs 150 MDA Care Centers, which "serve as the nexus for expert clinical care and medical research."[9] They offer diagnosis, treatment, and access to clinical trials for individuals living with MD, amyotrophic lateral sclerosis (ALS), and other neuromuscular diseases. MDA services also include some community supports, professional education, and summer camps.

NAMI, on the other hand, does not administer a vast array of services, and, in particular, it does not usurp the vital role, in its view, of mental health professionals; it does, however, encourage and administer peer-led programs offering education, skills training, and support to people with mental health conditions, family members, and community members. In doing so, it recognizes and develops the expertise of people who directly experience mental health conditions and enables them to become active participants in their own process of recovery. Other organizations, like Autism Speaks and VOR, do not prioritize the delivery of services, focusing instead on fundraising and political advocacy.

The role of service provision in disability activism is complex. Activists with disabilities recognize that people with disabilities may need a diverse and potentially extensive array of services to meaningfully participate in society, and creating the infrastructure, funding, and access to these services is central to disability activism.[10] It is not surprising then that some of the earliest disability activism focused heavily on service provision. The Independent Living Movement created a national network of centers offering resources, training, and supports to people with disabilities. In the Independent Living model, however, the service system is run *by* people with disabilities to empower people with disabilities. According to Ed Roberts, traditional service systems often created dependence, but the Independent Living model was designed to put people with disabilities in charge of their own lives and their services and supports. Independent Living Centers, though, rarely provided leadership opportunities or the services needed for people with intellectual or mental disabilities. These populations were mostly left to rely on services provided by parents and professionals.

Unlike the Independent Living Movement, services and supports as organized by parents largely place power in the hands of nondisabled staff and managers. Self-advocates have been critical of service providers, including those affiliated with parent organizations, for creating congregate settings guided by goals of efficiency rather than individualized support. And, as Arc leaders from the 1950s feared, when one becomes "the system," it is challenging to fight against it. That said, service provision is a key tool of advocacy, providing the services and supports people require for meaningful lives and increasing the resources that can be channeled into advocacy and other strategies of social change. Under pressure from disabled activists, social service delivery systems have moved toward increasingly integrated settings and individualized supports.

Lobbying and Policy Advocacy

In enacting widespread social change, parents have found lobbying to be a crucial activity. In the 1930s, parents of children with intellectual disabilities housed in state institutions founded groups that functioned primarily as support groups to augment resources provided by the facilities. These groups often initiated policy advocacy by seeking additional funding on behalf of the institutions, in some instances with "close ties" to professional associations whose goal was to enhance services provided by facilities that were all too often offering little more than custodial care.[11] Other advocacy groups representing children with conditions including cerebral palsy, deafness and hearing impairments, blindness, rheumatic heart disease, and orthopedic disabilities worked for the expansion of community-based services including an array of educational, vocational, and health services for children with disabilities,[12] for the transformation of residential facilities to ensure humane treatment and supportive services beyond minimal custodial supervision, and for national legislation to provide funds and promote services to children with disabilities as a national priority.[13]

Lobbying also plays an essential role in protecting prior legislative achievements. An example of effective lobbying geared toward protecting past successes occurred in the early 1980s, during the Reagan administration. Ronald Reagan had been elected on a conservative platform that included rolling back so-called unfunded federal mandates imposed during the 1970s and 1980s on state and local governments. One widely discussed example of such a mandate was the Education for All Handicapped Children Act of 1974, which later came to be known as the Individuals with Disabilities Education Act (IDEA).[14] The law required local public schools to provide a free and appropriate public education and related services to all children with handicapping conditions in the least restrictive educational environment possible. As discussed later in the chapter, the law was the result of parent-initiated lawsuits in response to the long-time exclusion of their children from public schools. When the law was passed, a commitment was made by Congress to pay half of the cost of services expanded as the result of the requirement. However, that commitment was never honored, and federal payments amounted to about one-tenth of the cost of special education services provided under IDEA, which led to widespread complaints by state and local officials about "heavy-handed" federal requirements that were not accompanied by funds to implement them.

Following an administration study of government regulations overseen by Vice President George H. W. Bush, the U.S. Department of Education proposed changes to the federal regulations implementing the special education law, changes that would have allowed greater flexibility to local districts, which in turn would have resulted in a far lower level of educational services available to children with disabilities in many districts.[15] However, the proposed regulations led to a firestorm of criticism from disability advocates, with a prominent role played by parent-led organizations.[16] Opponents included organizations of parents of disabled children, disability activists, special educator groups such as the Council for Exceptional Children, child advocates such as the Children's Defense Fund, and local and state educators. In eleven hearings held around the country to discuss the proposed regulations, parent representatives included both established national parent groups such as the ARC, NAMI, associations of parents of the blind and the deaf, and UCP; local coalitions of advocates from a variety of states including Oregon, Pennsylvania, Washington State, Louisiana, Virginia, California, and Tennessee; and several individual parents not affiliated with specific groups.[17] Parents stood out in their ability to draw on their families' personal experiences in being segregated or excluded from participation in public education. Parent testimony at the hearings communicated parents' "anger, fear, and frustration" at being excluded from the discussions leading to the development of the proposed regulations, an exclusion contrasted with heavy participation in the creation of the original regulations.[18] Following the conclusion of the hearings, the proposed regulations were withdrawn by the Reagan administration and never implemented.

Given recent threats to Medicaid and the Affordable Care Act, mothers of children with complex medical needs organized a new group focused on lobbying: Little Lobbyists. As the group describes, "A simple plan was formed: collect photos and stories of kids with complex medical needs from around the country and take them directly to their legislators. Deliver them in person with their own kids (and their ventilators, oxygen, wheelchairs, walkers, leg braces, feeding tubes, and more in tow) so lawmakers could see first-hand who needs the protection of the very laws and programs under threat."[19] These parents took their first trip to Capitol Hill in 2017, bringing personal stories directly to legislators in the hopes of protecting the rights and services of people with disabilities.

Large national-level parent organizations, including the Arc, UCP, NAMI, and Autism Speaks, participate in lobbying. The Arc and UCP focus their lobbying efforts on building the infrastructure for community supports and inclusion. NAMI lobbying activities are diverse, but the issues of mental health parity (i.e., creating an equally extensive, funded, and accessible system of mental health in comparison to physical health) and greater input in treatment by family members are foremost on its recent agenda. Autism Speaks prioritizes lobbying for research funding in the causes and amelioration of autism. For VOR, in its fight to preserve congregate care and institutions, lobbying is the primary tactic.

Lobbying does not come "naturally" for most parents. State capitals and Washington, D.C., are far away for many parents, and interacting with politicians may seem daunting. Thus, many organizations undertake extensive training for parents, and perhaps for self-advocates, to engage in lobbying. Parents are trained to deliver their stories effectively and to translate their needs into specific policy requests. Organizations, increasingly using social media, organize letter-writing and phone-in campaigns, specify days when visits to the capitol are facilitated and supported, and incorporate the voices of parents and self-advocates into lobbying material. The importance of lobbying has also pushed the professionalization of disability organizations, in order to amass and organize research, present policy briefs, and engage in the relationship-building required for effective lobbying.

Direct access to politicians is of course a key advantage in lobbying and has been fostered by many organizations. UCP and Autism Speaks were created by wealthy family members with access to extensive connections. Interestingly, UCP eschewed much political work until the 1970s, using its connections instead for fundraising. Autism Speaks has always been highly political, concentrating medical and professional expertise and modern corporate techniques to lobby for research funding in particular.

Lawsuits

Perhaps the most consequential strategy through which parent activism on behalf of children with disabilities has influenced public policy has been legal action. This strategy has been a centerpiece of the Arc's activism to influence national policy, and many parents across disability groups and individually use lawsuits to influence politics.

For the Arc, the lawsuit proved to be a forceful technique by which to demand rights. In the late 1960s and early 1970s, several federal lawsuits were filed by parent groups on behalf of their children with disabilities seeking their full access to public schools. Particularly active were the parents of children with intellectual disabilities who had been routinely excluded from public schools or relegated to largely custodial care in catch-all special education classes. Building on the concept affirmed in *Brown v. Board of Education* that equal access to public education was essential to participation, the Pennsylvania chapter of the Association of Retarded Children (now known as the Arc) sued the state of Pennsylvania to mandate the provision of public education to their children.[20]

One of the key figures in the case was a Philadelphia attorney, Dennis Haggerty. Haggerty's son, Dennis Jr., or Boomer, was diagnosed with a profound intellectual disability as a baby, and after years of difficulty obtaining services in the community, he became a resident of the Pennhurst State School and Hospital at the age of eight in 1967.[21] Haggerty Sr. joined the Delaware County ARC and became chair of their residential committee; in 1968 he was appointed by President Lyndon Johnson as a consultant to the President's Committee on Mental Retardation. After a series of frustrating visits with his son at the Pennhurst facility that revealed inadequate care, Haggerty pulled Boomer out at the age of nine and placed him in a private facility but continued to actively monitor conditions at Pennhurst. Another young Pennhurst resident, John Stark Williams, died in a fire at the facility, but his mother was not informed for a year and then was misled about the circumstances of his death. Haggerty urged the Pennsylvania ARC (PARC) to bring suit and in 1969 enlisted another attorney, Thomas Gilhool, a prominent practitioner of poverty law whose brother Bob was a Pennhurst resident, to file suit against the state.[22] In an oral history, Gilhool recalled that "the very greatest number of people sent to institutions were sent in their early teen years, usually to stay there for life. Why were they sent then? Because their families were alone. . . . And so, when their children started acting like teenagers—namely, getting considerably rambunctious and reaching out to take control of their world—the families were all alone in dealing with it."[23] Because many public schools would not accept children with intellectual disabilities, the only alternatives were the state institutions, but those institutions were essentially custodial and offered very few educational services.

In 1971, the U.S. District Court held that children with intellectual disabilities should receive "appropriate" education and training without regard to the cost of serving them. This finding was made on the basis of the Fourteenth Amendment to the U.S. Constitution, the equal protection clause. The court held that Pennsylvania had an obligation to place each child with an intellectual disability in a "free, public program of education and training appropriate to the child's capacity, within the context of a presumption that, among the alternative programs of education and training required by statute to be available, placement in a regular public school class is preferable to placement in any other type of program of education and training."[24] This ruling was to serve as the basis for national policy in a law passed by Congress four years later, the Education for All Handicapped Children Act of 1974, later renamed as the Individuals with Disabilities Education Act (IDEA).

Another key lawsuit filed by parent groups was *Halderman v. Pennhurst State School and Hospital.*[25] The case led to a ruling that institution-based services were inherently damaging to people with developmental disabilities, and culminated with the closure of Pennsylvania's Pennhurst State Hospital in 1986. The suit was filed in 1974 by the mother of Terri Lee Halderman, a Pennhurst resident, by parents of seven other residents, and by the Parents and Family Association of Pennhurst on behalf of two hundred additional families. The suit was subsequently joined by the U.S. Justice Department and by the Pennsylvania Association for Retarded Citizens, the litigant in the PARC case. The case made public the degrading and dangerous conditions and practices in the Pennhurst facility; in his ruling, federal district judge Raymond J. Broderick found that Pennhurst violated incarcerated residents' constitutional right to freedom from harm and to adequate treatment. While the legal basis for Broderick's ruling was made more complicated by subsequent decisions by appeals courts, according to Fred Pelka, the case "served as a model and impetus for similar deinstitutionalization litigation across the country. . . . Since Pennhurst, every major residential institution has seen its population drastically reduced; many have closed entirely, with the concomitant provision of community services."[26]

In the United States, parent groups have been very effective in securing court decisions that have established the rights of children with disabilities to public education and to decent treatment in institutional settings. Nevertheless, such advocacy may have limited results unless it is part of a wider political mobilization of people with disabilities on their own behalf, a process that requires both social solidarity and collective action. Moreover, lawsuits can also be used for other goals. VOR, for example, has participated in lawsuits to *prevent* deinstitutionalization and to prohibit the use of class-action suits, thereby using the legal system to hinder the Arc and disability activists in their goal of community integration.

Alliance-Building

As discussed in Chapter 6, alliance-building is also a way to effect change. On many issues in the decades since the development of a national disability rights movement led by people with disabilities, parent organizations have joined self-advocates as allies. Since the 1970s, groups representing parents of people with disabilities and organizations led by self-advocates have typically worked together to advance a variety of policy issues. One such issue has been the level of funding for disability services. There have been numerous attempts to reduce funding for programs that benefit people with disabilities during periods of fiscal austerity, such as under the Reagan administration in the 1980s and the more recent Tea Party era of the 2010s. Whenever fiscal conservatives in the executive or legislative branches of both federal and state government have attempted to cut funds for the provision of health or community-based disability support services, or to restrict access to benefits in programs such as Medicaid or Supplemental Security Income (SSI) through tightened eligibility criteria, parents and self-advocates have worked in coalitions to defend programs and their funding.

Another arena for collaboration has been to advance the rights of people with disabilities and to defend against subsequent attacks on the scope of these rights. In the 1970s, parent groups worked with organizations of people with disabilities to promote full implementation of Section 504 of the Rehabilitation Act and the Individuals with Disabilities Education Act. In the decades that followed, activists with disabilities and parent-led organizations worked together, often very closely, to support the passage of the landmark Americans with Disabilities Act (ADA) in 1990[27] and the Americans with Disabilities Amendments Act of 2008, in which Congress restored provisions of the original ADA that had been limited by federal court decisions.

However, there were some types of issues in which some parent-led groups and disability rights activists with disabilities were on opposite sides. One such issue was the status and role of custodial institutions. To oppose the extent of deinstitutionalization and preserve residential facilities, VOR has instead allied with unions and service providers, two powerful lobbies.

Medical professionals, health care systems, and even the pharmaceutical industry have also been key, and very well-funded, allies. NAMI has relied extensively on medical experts, such as E. Fuller Torrey, a psychiatrist, to support policies that strengthen the capacity of states to curtail the independence of adults with mental impairments.[28] Autism Speaks also relies heavily on medical experts to advance its agenda around the "epidemic" of autism.

Direct Action Protest

Direct action protest has been used extensively by disabled activists, particularly by groups like ADAPT and Disabled in Action. Histories of disability activism explain that direct action is a valuable technique for many reasons. For a population that is often disempowered, deemed incompetent, and barred from the practices of citizenship, active protest builds a sense of efficacy and collective self-identity crucial for mobilization, while also communicating to the world that disabled people have agency. Moreover, protest action like blocking inaccessible buses and crawling up the inaccessible Capitol steps captures media attention and creates a visual image of the exclusion and degradation faced by people with disabilities. Protests were a centerpiece of passing the Section 504 regulations to prohibit discrimination on the basis of disability and passing the ADA.

Parents, however, rarely engage in direct protest, and when they do it is almost always in legal forms. Parents tend to have access to legitimate channels for social change, using their economic and political capital and drawing on their symbolic capital specifically as "good" parents and citizens (an image that is challenged by civil disobedience). Marches and rallies are legal protest strategies that have become fairly commonplace and tame (with permits, traffic direction, and speakers), and we see what might be a trend toward increasing participation in these strategies. In 2017, when the Affordable Care Act and Medicaid funding were threatened by initiatives of the Trump administration, the Arc and other groups encouraged their members to attend marches and rallies to protect health care programs.

Parent involvement in civil disobedience, though, is very limited, and national parent groups rarely encourage or train parents to participate in civil disobedience, organize events of civil disobedience, or offer concerted support of such actions by disabled activists. Disabled activists participating in civil disobedience need support, such as people to bring food, administer medicines and care, serve as witnesses in police interactions, and organize signs. These are crucial roles that parents could serve, and some likely do individually, but not as organized members of a national parent-led group. The protesters also need "accomplices," able-bodied allies who are willing to risk violence and harm in the collective struggle for liberation. Grassroots activists criticize the "Ally Industrial Complex" by which people outside of a community build successful careers and prestige via taking the mantle of ally while exposing themselves to very few risks. An essay from the Indigenous Action organization states, "The risks of an ally who provides support or solidarity (usually on a temporary basis) in a fight are much different than that of an accomplice. When we fight back or forward, together, becoming complicit in a struggle towards liberation, we are accomplices." Rather than taking on the struggles and risks, "the self-proclaimed allies have no intention to abolish the entitlement that compelled them to impose their relationship upon those they claim to ally with."[29] To activists with disabilities, the alliance with parents may seem unbalanced and itself an act of domination.

Mobilizing Membership

Because this book focuses on national-level parent organizations, we wondered how national-level organizations, often heavily reliant on professional staff, mobilize parents "on the ground," so to speak. To what extent do parents participate at a grassroots level and in what ways? Membership surveys would be needed to best assess this question, but for our purposes we examined organizational websites to assess communication to the public about how parents and members could or should engage. These organizations focused grassroots mobilization heavily on fundraising, using parent support to pay for professional lobbying and research for macro social change. They also engaged parents in very directed ways to share stories and directly communicate with politicians. Marches and rallies were sometimes encouraged; protest was not.

UCP, which is the most professionalized of our focal organizations, has the most limited section encouraging members to get involved. While the organization is a service provider, lobbies, and engages in research, UCP's website encourages members only to donate, join the organization, learn more, and share on its blog site. Thus, while the organization participates in many strategies for social change, it does not prioritize building collective activism among parents, at least via its website.[30]

Autism Speaks focuses much of its mobilization on fundraising. Its "Get Involved" section has four headings, three of which involve money: fundraising, giving, and partnering. Its fundraising primarily promotes biomedical research into autism treatment and prevention, awareness campaigns, and lobbying. The fourth "Get Involved" heading, though, is advocacy, focused on the Advocacy Ambassador program, through which members learn legislative priorities and share their experiences with legislators, building direct relationships with legislators to educate and influence them.[31]

NAMI offers members several ways to get involved, but the avenues are still relatively limited. Donations, learning about mental health issues, and sharing one's story are key strategies communicated to members. NAMI members are also encouraged to take a pledge to end stigma (addressing their own behavior and influencing their communities in micro ways), to learn where politicians stand on particular issues and vote to support mental health causes, and to participate in trainings.[32]

The Arc offers the widest selection of routes to participate in activism. It offers on its home page a "Get Involved" section, which includes many of the typical strategies, like donating, becoming a member, sharing stories, and participating in the blog. The section's "Take Action" link, though, offers members quick and direct access to immediately see the Arc's legislative priorities and participate in the political process. The Arc requests stories on specific issues (e.g., the impact of Medicaid cuts, what community living offers). It also highlights a legislative initiative that changes regularly (e.g., Money Follows the Person funding), provides information on this priority, and encourages people to communicate with their legislators on the issue by providing contact information for legislators and an easy electronic way to communicate. By signing up for the Disability Advocacy Network, members receive additional information on priorities and campaigns. This additional information includes information on rallies and marches in relation to disability rights, services, and other issues.[33]

Again we see that parent organizations resist each categorization. Although the Arc and UCP are the most likely to rely on the social model (see Chapter 6), UCP offers few ways to get involved, whereas the Arc offers a more expansive list. Empowerment might be a more defining characteristic; organizations that rely most heavily on professionals may divert parent involvement into resources for their professional staff, whereas organizations that prioritize empowerment of family and self-advocates and are led by a higher proportion of parents and self-advocates may be more likely to foster a range of activities including direct lobbying and attendance at rallies and marches. Yet even this measure is not perfectly predictive: the Arc requires a majority of its board to be family or self-advocates, and NAMI requires 75 percent of its board to be family or self-advocates, yet the Arc seems to offer a greater range of opportunities for involvement than NAMI.

Conclusion

Since the inception of organized groups of parents of children with disabilities, the groups have utilized a variety of political activities to advocate for their children by influencing public policies and programs at the local, state, and national levels of American government. Parents have focused their efforts on media campaigns to change the culture, on building service systems to address needs, and on political advocacy to affect legislation and policy. They rely heavily on legitimate channels of social change, rarely venturing into protest or civil disobedience. Over time, national organizations professionalized, and their staff now channel grassroots parent participation in specific ways, particularly to donating money and directed political engagement via letter, telephone, and social media campaigns to share stories and opinions with legislators. While these organizations rely heavily on parent support, they do little to foster a collective sense of outrage across disability groups or the confrontational political strategies that are a central element of activism led by disabled activists.

Although parent organizations use many similar strategies, the goals for which they are used vary considerably. Any given strategy can be used to advance social services, fight discrimination, or advance a biomedical model of cure. Parents have sought to increase funding for disability services and biomedical and rehabilitation research, and to establish legal rights and procedural safeguards affecting their children's ability to live in a society free of barriers. However, in some cases, parents and their children have differing views of how best to balance protection from harm and the autonomy to live life as one chooses. How these opposing perspectives are resolved will depend on the political power to mobilize support and the ability to persuade policy makers and the public about the meaning of disability.

8

Narratives of Rights

The preceding chapters in Part II focus on an organizational level. In this chapter and the next, we move to focus more on the experiences and perspectives of parents. Whereas Chapter 6 examines the ways in which organizations frame disability activism, in this chapter we examine how parent activists frame their activism and in particular how they understand the idea of "disability rights." We first look at some of the broadest and most common uses of the term "rights" and then consider more controversial uses of the idea.

Parents may frame disability as a tragedy, a medical condition, a moral dilemma, or an issue of discrimination and rights, but what parent activists tend to agree on is the host of unmet needs they face. Need, rather than rights, is the common denominator across parent narratives. According to the Arc, "There are currently over 500,000 people with disabilities on waiting lists for home and community-based long term services and supports. The wait can be as long as 8–10 years in some states. This crisis results in unnecessary, unwanted, and costly institutional care; the desires of people with I/DD [intellectual and developmental disabilities] to live in and be a part of the community being denied; family members being forced to quit jobs or take on second jobs to help care for their loved one; and having to leave their loved ones unattended."[1] According to Mental Health America, in 2014 "56.5 percent of adults with a mental health illness received no treatment."[2] And according to a National Alliance on Mental Illness (NAMI) report, when they do receive treatment, they are faced with a system that is "currently regulated and funded in ways that often pressure front line staff to adhere to procedures, time frames and reporting requirements. Many staff have unrealistically high caseloads that do not leave room for the discretion and time needed to employ the art and science of healing."[3] An impersonal and demeaning system pushes people away from the support they need. As explained by a NAMI parent:

> My son's first [mental] break was when he was most open to the idea of engagement. He was scared and didn't know what was going on. He voluntarily went to see a psychiatrist, but the manner in which he was treated really closed the door at that opportune moment. The psychiatrist was proud of being the kind of doctor who tells it like it is. He told my son, "you have a mental illness and are going to be on medications for the rest of your life. They'll probably cause you to gain significant weight, and you probably won't be able to work in a regular job. If you don't take the medications, you are going to end up homeless, in jail or dead." My son's reaction was to reject that and to close the door on treatment.[4]

While the quality of care and supports in the community today is undoubtedly better than that available in the community or institutional settings in the 1970s, grave concerns remain. Direct care staff who work with people with disabilities in the community too often live in poverty. Service providers typically only require direct care staff to have a high school degree and perhaps a driver's license; many positions are part-time without benefits; and training is minimal and largely on-the-job. Not surprisingly, staff turnover is high. Trained social workers find that they can make more money working within the criminal justice or nursing home industry or doing administrative work rather than offering direct care to people with disabilities in the community. Trained medical professionals in the community may refuse to treat people with disabilities or people on Medicaid because it is time consuming, poses risks, and reimburses poorly.

Thus, many people with disabilities and their families do not have the level or quality of supports and services that they need to thrive in the community. Across disability groups, it should not be surprising that parent activism is centered on addressing the extensive unmet needs. Some of the most common areas are education, lifelong residential supports, work, and access to medical care and appropriate treatment. While the needs are clear, parents disagree on the appropriate way to address these unmet needs.

Education offers a vivid example, both of unmet needs and varied responses. In one example, the parents of a seven-year-old with Down syndrome sought an *inclusive* education for their son and eventually sued their school district to attain it. They described the following treatment: "In court, my heart broke as Liam's aide testified that he was once forced to stand outside in the rain because he wasn't welcome in class. She said that he was ultimately put in a trailer behind the school, away from credentialed teachers and isolated from his peers for the majority of the day."[5] Although they won their case, months later they still were in battle with the school district. According to Liam's parents, the school had not yet implemented accommodations or provided Liam with an aide. They wrote, "His rights are completely being ignored. This tactic is referred to as 'delay and deny.' It is a way to not give the child what they need and drain the family's financial resources so they eventually have to give up. . . . It's incredibly abusive."[6] The family resorted to an online petition and social media to raise awareness of their plight.

In a second example, an interviewee, Yvonne, uses the idea of rights to fight to maintain her son's enrollment at a large, *disability-specific school* that was slated to be closed in order to integrate children with disabilities into the public school. Yvonne described her son as a child with profound intellectual disabilities, frequent seizures, and medical complications, who is difficult to feed, throws up several times per day, and cries frequently. As a result of this combination of conditions and behaviors, she states, "he was like this time-bomb, going off all the time, and it was really difficult." Public school programs did not want to serve him, and even a school for orthopedically disabled children "didn't want him because he cried all the time and he obviously wasn't learning his ABCs." Yvonne found a center-based educational program with two hundred or more children in special education. Her son was placed in a classroom with children with multiple disabilities. "It was great because everything was there that they [students with disabilities] needed. They didn't need a nurse for instance to be constantly hovering over them, but there was always a nurse there, and occasionally something would happen where they really—they needed a nurse!" The state and disability activists wanted to close the center to increase educational integration, which from Yvonne's perspective would only move them back into the unwelcoming and ineffective settings they had left.[7]

Both of these parents faced a system that utterly failed to meet their child's needs despite the Individuals with Disabilities Education Act (IDEA). One fought for inclusion, and the other fought to maintain a specialized setting. Both used the language of rights to describe their activism. Parents tend to stress their child's needs and the ability to make choices, often among sadly unsatisfactory options, rather than an allegiance to a pure philosophical approach with regard to integration versus segregation or public versus private venue. As an interviewee, Erica, put it, "I feel that the services for people should supersede anybody's philosophy that people should be in a certain kind of place."[8] Another parent, Donna, stated, "You know, we should be talking about what people need and then be determining what's the best way for them to receive the services that they need, and that will also protect their rights."[9]

How do "rights" fit into the advocacy of parents, then? The rights frame offers several key benefits that are well recognized and used across parents: it focuses attention on issues of equity, recognizes people with disabilities as valued members of society, and provides legal mechanisms for creating and implementing change. Less commonly and in tension with some other uses, the language of rights is a tool to recognize the rights of the family and the right *to* family. Some families, though, criticize the way rights have been politically used, in their opinion, to subvert services and choices and to remove authority from the family. At times this criticism is used to advocate for greater integration and empowerment, while at other times it is used to advocate for disability-specific settings, protections, and family control and "choice."

The Power of Rights

Addressing Discrimination and Creating Equity and Access

Rather than positioning rights as a personal trouble, the rights frame calls attention to the disadvantages created by an unequal and prejudiced society that creates an inferior class of citizens. This use of "rights" is common and has been useful, both personally and politically, for families across various disability groups. Mental illness, for example, is highly stigmatized in our society, and parents have found it politically powerful to reorient discussion around issues of discrimination and stigma rather than personal tragedy or failed morality. Rick Warren began speaking out about discrimination against people with mental illness after his twenty-seven-year-old son committed suicide. "If I have diabetes, there is no stigma to that," explains Warren. He continues, "But if my brain doesn't work, why am I supposed to be ashamed of that? It's just another organ. People will readily admit to taking medicine for high blood pressure, but if I am taking medication for some kind of mental problem I'm having, I'm supposed to hide that."[10] This quotation from 2014 strongly echoes parents who stated back in 1951, "You would not deny schooling and playmates to a crippled child—should they be denied to my child because it is his *brain* rather than his limbs that is crippled?"[11] Thus, as articulated by the rights frame, the central problem is not the disability per se but rather the stigma and structures of exclusion that prevent children from accessing the supports they need.

The rights frame focuses attention on correcting society to ensure equity. For example, parents of children with ADHD described barriers to the right to education, such as punishment in response to disability-related behaviors: "It's discrimination when a teacher knows that your child has an IEP [individualized educational plan], has signed the IEP, and still requests that your child complete the work of his/her neurotypical peers—commenting about the lack of ability to get the work done. When a teacher knows that your child has a modification but chooses not to apply or enforce it, that's discrimination. . . . If your child is punished for having a disability, or for not being able to keep up when they are unable to do so, they are being discriminated against."[12]

Parents similarly look to rights to address inequities in work, such as pay below the minimum wage. Mississippi Representative Greg Harper (R), whose son has an intellectual disability, introduced legislation to end subminimum wages and require transition plans to move people with disabilities into jobs in the community at competitive wages alongside workers without disabilities. Harper stated, "Segregated, subminimum wage work is just an expression of low expectations that instills a false sense of incapacity in individuals who could become competitively employed with proper training and support."[13] For that reason, he supported a law to remove the exemption that allowed employers to pay people with disabilities less than minimum wage and thereby establish a right to fair pay.

Rights as a Broad Vision of Respect and Value

More than addressing discrimination specifically, rights provide a broad, empowering vision, in which people with disabilities are valued and respected as full members of a community. Parents across disability groups use rights as a language to communicate the value of their children. For example, Jaclyn Barney, coordinator of Parents for Inclusive Education, stated in court testimony, "In many respects, inclusive education is a civil rights issue as it allows students to be full members of their communities and, in turn, prepares them for real world experiences."[14] Specific academic outcomes are important of course, but the bigger issue may be the opportunity to be a part of society. Blogging on the Department of Education website, a parent wrote, "Inclusion is not about the grades or closing the gap, it's about belonging in society, it's about being part of a whole, it's about non segregation, it's about Brown vs. Board of Education. It's about civil rights. I find it crazy that someone would even try to take this right away from my child who has worked so hard to get what he's getting. It can be done, I don't care who argues with me on this subject, because I have proof that it can be done. And he's the first child to ever be included in our school district, so all of his teachers are green."[15]

People with disabilities have a broad right to *be* in the community and to be disabled in the community, because they are a part of the community. Describing an expansive view of her sibling's rights, an interviewee, Cindy, states, "My brother has the right to have a safe environment. He has the right to be out of his house and go places. He has the right to, if he chooses, to, well, throw a temper tantrum, too. He has the right to safety, he has a right to food, he has a right to housing, he has a right to proper care."[16] It's unclear if legally all of these rights are really enforceable, yet the claim itself asserts a broad view of what it might mean to build a world that recognizes and supports her brother as a valued member of society. In contrast with this view of broad inclusion, people with disabilities are too commonly excluded and even victimized in the community. Criticizing the justification of police brutality against people with disabilities on the basis of their "strange" behavior or disability-related noncompliance (e.g., not responding to a police order because of one's deafness or autism), parent David Perry explains that "being autistic in public isn't a crime."[17] For Perry, people with disabilities need to know that they can be who they are—including stimming, drooling, and making noises, for example—in the community without threat of lethal force used against them.[18]

Asserting Competence

Although parents vary considerably in their assessment of their family member's competence and the degree to which they advocate self-determination, rights are commonly used to assert competence, maximize independence, and challenge systems that deny liberty and self-determination—a necessary counterbalance to a system that long presumed the incompetence of people with disabilities. When Ryan King's parents were told by the Washington, D.C., social service system that King had to have a guardian for him to receive services, they were shocked. The need for services, they thought, should not a priori require that the recipient be declared incompetent. King and his parents decided to fight this archaic rule. King stated, "Everyone needs a little help sometimes. . . . But just because people need a little bit of help doesn't mean they can't be independent." His father agreed: "Everyone makes decisions—they make their own decisions—and Ryan is a whole person, and we want Ryan to be a whole person. If I force Ryan to do something or try to force him, I destroy his selfness."[19] His parents argued that their fight is not just about the availability of services in the present, but also about King's future; since King is under guardianship, when his parents die the state would step in, possibly appoint a stranger as guardian, and he would have no say over his life. This possible future was unacceptable to King and his parents.

Building self-advocacy is a crucial component to ensuring rights. Parents and parent organizations have individually and collectively supported self-advocacy in many ways. For example, one interviewee, Mark, attributed his success as a self-advocate in part to the important role played by his mother, who fostered his development as a self-advocate, traveled with him, assisted him in preparing speeches, and sometimes participated in events, especially when they were addressing families.[20] Younger parents, in particular, are encouraged to consider developing self-determination skills in their children. A parent of a teenager explained, "It is important the team hear from [my daughter] and respect her opinion. It also keeps them on better behavior when she is there, but most important I want her to learn to be her own advocate and recognize when school [is] not in compliance and how in her adult life she will need to use her advocacy skills on her own."[21] On an organizational level, the Arc, United Cerebral Palsy (UCP), and NAMI serve as examples of the varied ways to support self-advocacy groups through providing office space for meetings, funding events, offering leadership training opportunities, and creating organizational avenues to hold leadership.

However, as discussed later in the chapter, parents also subvert and qualify their support for self-determination by asserting parents' rights. Similarly, formal parent-led organizations undercut the power of self-advocacy even as they promote it (see Chapter 6).

Rights as a Path to Implementation

For some parents, the main appeal of rights is the effectiveness of rights as a path to implementing mandates that are defined in laws, especially for parents who are savvy about the law and how to use it. Thus, parent advocates stress the value of educating parents about their rights. Donna explains that schools and service providers will often try to avoid providing costly services, so prepared parents are a school's "worst nightmare."[22] In a lengthy story, Yvonne remembers her introduction to activism, when she called a friend to help her prepare for her first IEP meeting:

> What she said was, "You are not getting together for a little chat. There will probably be fifteen people in the room, and they all want you to do something, and you need to be aware of that," and she told me about getting records and reading the law and doing all of those things. And we went to that meeting, and there were at least a dozen people there, all around a table, and they had put kind of a stool at

the corner for—little stools for my husband and I to sit on, and they were going to tell us what they were planning to do with our kid. And it was just, you know, they read reports we had never seen before, and there were doctor's reports that we had never talked to the doctor about. All kinds of surprises. And so at that point, I decided the person I was going to listen to was [her friend], because she really knows what's going on. . . . She had two children with severe learning disabilities.[23]

Learning about the IDEA provided Yvonne and Donna a legal tool to protect their children and to demand participation in the educational process.

The establishment of laws and legal contestation regarding these laws potentially affects a broad group. Speaking about his family's recent court victory to ensure appropriate education for their son who has autism, the father stated, "We didn't want to pull him out of the school. We didn't want to take them to court. We didn't want to do any of this. But we were pushed into a corner and had to—to get what he was entitled to by law and what he needed."[24] Reacting to this court decision on a parent website, Amanda Morin, a parent of two children with IEPs, stated, "I'm thrilled, because I think it really empowers parents to feel confident when they go in the door [of an IEP meeting]."[25] Not everyone has the capital required to use the court system, but a single court decision potentially creates a ripple effect for many kids with disabilities; thus, the activism related to one child can potentially affect implementation for a large number of children.

Even without formal action, laws serve as an informal threat to compel action. When his daughter was denied services and treated poorly in a public business, Harold said he threatened the establishment with a lawsuit. "The ADA is great, because everyone's afraid of it. I wrote a letter threatening to sue, and the next week they treated [my daughter] like gold."[26] As discussed later in the chapter, though, both the use and threat of lawsuits are reliant on economic and social capital and therefore the power of the law often favors white, wealthy parents like Harold.

Rights for, of, and to Family

Although rights are typically conceived of as individual in nature, families have a long history of fighting for the rights of *families*. In doing so, they reflect the relational nature of rights—that one's rights are shaped by the access, opportunities, and rights of those around you. This position, though, can be complicated by internal, and often unrecognized, power dynamics within families.

Rights for Family

First, regarding rights *for* families, parents have long called attention to the need for services as a means to enhance both the well-being of the individual with a disability *and* the family more holistically. As stated by advocates for people with intellectual disabilities back in the 1950s, the state must recognize "that no child stands alone; that a child is part of a family and a community; that what happens to the family affects the child and certainly affects the family."[27]

Disability has a tremendous impact on the family, as does the provision of services, or lack thereof, and this impact *on the family* has long been used to justify services for the individual with a disability as well as for family members. A 2015 study of those providing care to a family member with a mental health issue identified significant negative consequences in terms of finances, health, and social participation.[28] A daughter caring for her mother with mental illness explained that she needs to earn an income sufficient to support her and her mother, attend college, and provide intensive care—an impossible set of demands. Without services for her mother, she would have to either quit school (reducing her chances of a well-paying career) or abandon her mother. She said, "I shouldn't be expected to quit school. It's my future."[29] The pursuit of the right to services is justified as a right of people with disabilities to enhance their well-being *as well as* a right of family members to be free of or assisted in meeting caregiving demands.

Similarly, a 2017 survey of thousands of caregivers of people with intellectual and developmental disabilities found that 35 percent had provided care for more than ten years. Ninety-five percent reported a negative impact on their work (e.g., 55 percent reported cutting hours, 32 percent giving up work, 17 percent retiring early, 33 percent turning down promotions), and 90 percent reported stress, including 48 percent who reported feeling extremely stressed. Twenty percent had a family member who had been waitlisted for the receipt of public services for over ten years.[30] Here again, this report on the negative impact *on family* is used to justify services and supports for people with disabilities. As Erica, a single mother of a daughter with medical and intellectual disabilities, explained, she could not find stable, suitable care for her daughter on the days off from school. "That got to be very, very frustrating because I just thought I couldn't survive like that. . . . It seemed like I eventually was going to have to not work and just be at home with her. And you can't—to me that would limit me."[31] Sue Swenson, executive director of the Arc from 2005 to 2007, argued that a model of individual rights is insufficient to ensure the rights of disabled individuals; it must be complemented with the assurance "that all families that include persons with disabilities can enjoy the support they need" to take care of their disabled family members and themselves.[32]

Rights of Family (i.e., Parents)

Second, regarding rights *of* family, families have fought not only for services and supports but also for the right of authority over decision-making in their families. Indeed, one of the core principles of parent activism is the idea that parents are the experts when it comes to their families, and their authority must be recognized (or at least their participation accepted and valued). One parent, Yvonne, explained that parents need input into the IEP process "because they're the experts on their child."[33] Jack stated, "Parents and guardians, their views should prevail, and usually they do know what's best for their child. I think by and large parents are capable, they are loving, and they are interested in what happens to their disabled child."[34]

Because they believe in their own authority, parents resist threats to it. They perceive these threats as coming from several sources, including the state (conceived of as laws, service systems paid for via public funds, schools), medical professionals, and disability advocacy organizations.

The state exerts a significant influence in the lives of families. Parent activism encouraged an expanded role of the state in families' lives; however, the expansion of the social service system and its infiltration into the family threatened parental authority.[35] Disability history shows that there are good reasons to be wary of state intervention in the family when disability is concerned. Eugenic and punitive state policies justified institutionalization, sterilization, and segregated education, harming many families, especially those characterized as single-parent, poor, nonwhite, and with disabled family members who were labeled "unfit." Institutions explicitly removed parental authority and transformed people with disabilities into wards of the state. In response, parents argued that families were "disabled" by the system and unable to effectively advocate for their child. In contemporary politics, parents still feel heavily and unfairly constrained by the state. Sara stated, "It's because someone else [the state] is paying for it; they've decided they can tell you what is best for you."[36] Yvonne explained, "Families . . . don't have a lot of power. The only power is when they can use the things that are in the rules and laws that give them a fighting chance to make sure that their kid is getting what they need. So the idea that parents are dictating what happens with their kid, I think, is really funny, because that rarely happens. You are always dealing with an agency; you're always dealing with people who may not like your kid or who don't want to spend the money or any of that."[37]

The state also is perceived by some parents as prioritizing the disabled person's right to self-determination, even when parents are the primary caregivers or will feel the consequences. This issue is discussed frequently among parents of adult offspring with mental illness. Laws that protect self-determination and privacy (e.g., the Health Insurance Portability and Accountability Act, HIPAA) are seen by many parents as major roadblocks to their effective advocacy for their children. For example, Chip Angell's son committed suicide after struggling with mental health issues, and Chip felt shut out of his son's health care, unable to inform the doctor of key information or to learn of his treatment plan. "Whenever we tried to get Chris into the hospital, we always ran into the fact that doctors wouldn't talk to us. Some doctors think they're protecting the privacy rights of the patient. Others simply use privacy as an excuse because they don't want to talk to someone with an idea contrary to their own, or because they can't be bothered to call someone back." He continued, "If we had been able to talk to the doctor, we could have told him that no matter how much this drug cost, we'd have paid for it."[38]

Deeply connected to and reinforced by the state, medical authority also represents a consistent threat to parents. As noted previously, parents of offspring with mental illness rely heavily on a medical system that often excludes them and devalues their expertise. Parents in other disability communities also feel their authority threatened by medical authority. For example, despite evidence of the positive effects of exposure to American Sign Language (ASL), many medical professionals advise against teaching it to deaf children, instead endorsing cochlear implants and oralism only.[39] And, despite efforts by parents to improve doctors' negative views of Down syndrome, medical professionals define Down syndrome as a "defect," identify it prenatally, and offer prospective parents very little—and mostly negative—information, in effect if not overtly encouraging high abortion rates of fetuses identified with Down syndrome. Thus, as documented in Chapter 6, several parent organizations explicitly work with the medical profession to deepen their appreciation of the value of their children.

The dominance of the medical mind-set in general can be deeply problematic for parents of children with significant disabilities. In her blog, parent Heather Kirnlanier spoke of how doctors too often metaphorically situate her daughter (who is diagnosed with Wolf-Hirschhorn syndrome) in a race that she is losing, and therapists push a therapeutic regime in which mothers are expected to act as full-time, in-home therapists. Challenging the medical perspective, Kirnlanier suggests "radical acceptance." She writes:

Somewhere after our first year with Fiona, the desire to change my kid died and got buried in that imaginary sand dune along with her nonexistent tip of chromosome four. The desire to catch her up in weight, the desire to keep her development as close as possible to her peers, the desire to make her into the standard-issue human, with its bipedal mobility and buh-buh B sounds. . . . It just . . . died. And I was freed into a deep acceptance for my daughter that felt bottomless. This did not mean that we didn't continue therapy. We did. Of course we did. But I no longer held onto desired outcomes with the same nervous, rigid tension of a clenched jaw. I gave my daughter opportunities to grow, yes, but I also trusted that her body would proceed in a manner we could always call, deeply and truly, *good*.[40]

After thinking deeply about the pursuit of normality, she came to realize that "living with a person who wants you to be fundamentally different than you are . . . is toxic. No matter the scenario."[41] The medical demand to intervene, at any cost—personally, financially, and physically—essentially overshadows the person's right to be who they are and the family's right to just be a family. Reclaiming these rights may entail rejection of the medical model.

A third set of external constraints on parental authority is activists with disabilities and the parents and professional advocacy groups promoting self-determination and inclusion. In other words, parents are divided, some siding with activists with disabilities and others opposing them, and opposing activists can be experienced as a threat to one's authority. Activists with disabilities demand that parents accept that inclusive situations are preferable to disability-specific settings, a belief that not all parents share. They also demand that the expertise of people with disabilities be acknowledged and their voice in policy prioritized. In both of the following quotations, family members speak of a coercive "they," a reference to the alliance between disability advocates and state policy makers who pursue inclusive policies. Sara explained:

> They're [disability advocates] saying . . . that Jason should be working around the non-handicapped. I don't think anybody is going to hire Jason, first of all, because he does hand-over-hand with envelopes and only when the person who is doing the other part is forceful and really pushes it, and for him to be paid ten dollars an hour, there's no company out there who would do it, other than for a token thing.[42]

Similarly, Cindy stated:

> They [disability advocates] wanna close the day habilitation services because we're making it too easy for the developmentally disabled to

not go find a job. Ooookaaayyy. So, you want my brother, who's not potty trained and has temper tantrums, to not have his day services and go get a job? Nobody's going to hire him; he's not going to have any place to go every day. His caregivers are gonna have to figure out what to do with him *every day*, to prevent him from having temper tantrums, because he won't stay in the house.[43]

To these family members, outsiders are removing valued choices, putting their view of the world ahead of parental decision-making. Yvonne clearly referenced advocacy organizations when she stated, "I have always believed in self-advocacy. I also think there are people like my sons who can't do that for themselves. . . . I don't like the anti-guardian push by advocacy organizations, which is just a way of pushing parents out of the way."[44] And Liz stated that, while she appreciates self-advocacy, activists with disabilities "should speak for themselves but not for all people with disabilities."[45] For these parents, parents' views should be prioritized over the views of other activists, at least for their own children.

To resist external threats to autonomy, the word "choice" plays a central role, especially in the narrative of parents who support disability-specific and congregate placements. When Yvonne described efforts to close the large, disability-specific school her son attended, she felt that external activists swooped in to remove options rather than provide them: "The emphasis shifted from everybody having an appropriate education or appropriate services as they got older to meet their unique needs, and it shifted to non-discrimination, and we can't have these kids in these [segregated] settings, and everybody should have a right to be in a regular classroom, and everybody should have a right to live in a certain way."[46] For her, the integration agenda pushed *one way* of doing things, in effect removing, rather than granting, the right to choose. Sara concurred: "There's this craziness approach, that it can't be congregate care. We do congregate for everything, from seniors with Alzheimer's to people in camp, college, you name it. Why not have economies of scale . . . rather than saying only four people in a group home, and you can't have an overnight nurse, you can't have a lot of things? . . . If you want to go to college, I'm not going to tell you you have to pick a school that's below a certain number in a small city, or a big. You pick it based on your needs and your wants and what works for you and your family."[47]

Furthermore, some parents argued that so-called inclusive choices are actually more restrictive. Cindy described her brother, Billy, who loves to walk and prefers to be outside in constant motion. At a large facility with grounds, he was allowed to move freely within the grounds: "You know, the fact that he could walk out of his cottage, go out on the back patio, or leave the back patio and wander the grounds." At his community-based group home, however, he is not allowed to leave the house unsupervised. "Now it's called 'wandering.' When he cannot go outside and walk, he throws temper tantrums and smears feces, which also get listed as 'behaviors.'"[48] Thus, in the congregate facility, where Billy had relative freedom of movement, he was considered to need only minimal supports (rated a 2 on the Supports Intensity Scale, SIS), but in the community his SIS rating increased to a 4. In other words, the inadequate staffing and lack of safe grounds produced a greater perception of disability and the imposition of surveillance and behavior modification to control his "wandering behavior." These family members are saying that rights as implemented through inclusion policies actually further restrict their loved ones and deny them opportunities that are more important to their happiness, such as freedom of movement and easy access to diverse activities.

What some parents frame as a reasonable "choice," though, other parents and disability activists frame as a denial of human rights. Family autonomy allows parents the freedom to resist external influences and make choices, but who protects the person with the disability from the family, especially given parents' penchant for advancing their own interests and promoting paternalism and normalization? Increasingly, parental authority and parents' claim to choice have been challenged, especially in relation to guardianship and choosing institutional settings for their offspring. Parents of deaf children, for example, have the legal authority to decide the communication strategy and treatment plan for their children. Some Deaf activists, though, argue that giving the parent an open choice of communication method for the child actually denies the basic human rights of that child. One's communication strategy "should be a child's choice, not a parent's. Is there really such a choice for the child? Because, typically a choice among parents and hearing professionals is metaphorically 99% oral. Is this truly a choice? The child is given virtually no choice. To give a child a true choice with the maximalized language acquisition in both languages (ASL and English) is to give him/her bilingualism. It's not only a child's choice, but also, more importantly, a child's human right to language regardless of the modality."[49] Thus, in this view, a child's right to full language should trump a parent's right to select language modality.

Other parent "choices," such as the use of applied behavior analysis (ABA), large-scale disability-specific settings, institutionalization, the denial of sexuality, and support of euthanasia, are similarly controversial and contested by disability activists as denying human and civil rights. As a few examples, parent-led Autism Speaks and the National Autism Association (but not the Autistic Self Advocacy Network, which is led by people with autism) fought for Kevin and Avonte's Law, which allows "voluntary" tracking of persons with diminished capacity, so that families and systems can better respond when people "wander" away from caregivers. Supporters, including some parents, argue that they have a right to track people with disabilities to ensure their safety and well-being and enhance the effective caregiving of parents.[50] Autistic activists, however, argue that tracking and surveillance invalidates their right to privacy and criminalizes autism.

Parents may even include institutionalization of their offspring as within their set of legitimate choices.[51] In her memoir, Fern Kupfer argued for expanded access to institutional placement for her son, who was still a minor and who had significant developmental delays and medical conditions: "It is their [advocates'] belief that the best place for every child is at home with his family. Even if that is true, it's not always the best place for the family. . . . In order for him to be in a less restrictive environment, everyone else has to be restricted."[52] Kupfer fought against the system's insistence that children reside with their family, and she eventually secured a residential placement for him. Psychiatric survivors and self-advocates with intellectual disabilities decry extended use of institutionalization as dehumanizing and ineffective, and they instead fight to enhance community-based treatment and services. They argue that the liberty of people with disabilities should not be sacrificed to meet the needs of people without disabilities.

A number of cases document that parents and their offspring do not necessarily share the same views or interests. In 2013 Jenny Hatch made the news. Hatch, a woman with Down syndrome, lived with friends, had a romantic relationship, and volunteered in her community. After she was hit by a car, her parents decided to pursue guardianship because they felt she needed greater supervision for her own protection. They were awarded it and placed her, against her wishes, in a group home. Hatch, supported by the Arc of Virginia, took her parents to court. According to the Arc of Virginia's brief, "Extensive research has found that the vast majority of people with intellectual disabilities, including Down syndrome, can live successfully in their own homes and make their own choices." The brief argued that guardianship in this instance did not support her in independence but rather led to her placement in a "segregated group home, isolated from her job, her friends and her community."[53] The court agreed and removed her from guardianship. Given the paternalism common among parents, a reliance on parental authority can be worrisome indeed.

Rights to Family

The preceding sections speak about the rights for and of families, but a third area, the right *to* family, should also be noted. The right to family was a centerpiece of the deinstitutionalization movement, demanding that all children have a right to live with their natural families and that all families have a right to receive the supports necessary to accomplish this. The United Nations Convention on the Rights of Children declared that all children, including disabled children, have a human right to live with their parents unless doing so is not in their best interests. Institutionalization, mass orphanages, and "Indian schools," which removed indigenous children from families to assimilate them into "American" culture, all posed a direct threat to this human right.

While the right to family may seem secure in the twenty-first century, the recent crackdown on immigration and the related policy separating children from their parents at the U.S. border has brought this issue back into the news. For example, in June 2018 headlines reported the removal of a child with Down syndrome from her mother, as well as the removal of a sixteen-year-old, Matheus da Silva Bastos, who has autism and severe epilepsy, from his grandmother upon their arrival at the border. All children need to be with their families; however, children with disabilities particularly need specific care and accommodations. In fact, many families immigrate specifically to secure medical care and social rights denied or unavailable to them in their home countries. The Hassan family was broken apart when father and son, both American citizens, traveled to California to seek treatment for the two-year-old's terminal degenerative brain condition, but his mother, a Yemeni national, was denied a visa.[54] For undocumented residents already in America, family life is also insecure. Irma and Oscar Sanchez were deported after following the advice of medical professionals in Texas that their infant, diagnosed with the rare condition pyloric stenosis, needed lifesaving care at a more specialized hospital in Corpus Christi. After their arrival at the Corpus Christi hospital, while they were waiting for their child's surgery, the couple was arrested.[55]

Although framed as a right of children, the right to family is vital for many adults with disabilities who continue to rely on their family throughout their lifetime. Dolores Gaspar Garcia, an American citizen, had few recourses to protect her older brother, who has Down syndrome and is not an American citizen, from deportation after a U.S. Immigration and Customs Enforcement (ICE) raid led to his arrest. Although he was thirty at the time of his arrest and detention, his forced removal from his family threatened his well-being both in the short term in the detention center and in the long term if deported to a country where he has no immediate family, no support system, and few skills to adapt to a new culture and language. Dolores started a petition to draw attention to his plight.[56]

America's extensive use of prisons and punitive child welfare system also threaten family integrity. People with disabilities are disproportionately represented in prison, and thereby removed from family and community supports. Because people who are poor and African American are also overrepresented among prisoners and because poor children and African American children disproportionately have disabilities, a disproportionate number of poor minority children with disabilities likely grow up without access to their parents as a result of unequal criminal justice policies. As discussed by Sylvia Ann Hewlett and Cornel West in their book *The War against Parents*, stingy and punitive social welfare policies also still rely heavily on family separation and dissolution.[57] Thus, while many white middle-class families feel their right to family is secure, punitive and racialized policies related to immigration, criminal justice, and social welfare pose considerable threats to nonwhite and poor families.

The Perceived Failures of Rights

Parents use rights to resist discrimination, demand respect, showcase the competence of their family member, enforce laws, support their own authority, and access choices. But parents also speak of the ways in which "rights" are used against them, as mentioned previously regarding the perceived threats of the inclusion ideology, antiguardianship and self-determination policies, and the growing power of activists with disabilities in shaping disability policy and options. Parents' concerns related to the rhetoric and implementation of rights also include the ways in which rights rhetoric demands compulsory productivity, masks neoliberalism and a disinvestment in disability services, and exposes people to unnecessary dangers.

Compulsory Productivity and the Fear
of Disinvestment in Disability

Politicians have too often justified the cost of rights to services, education, accessibility, and community for people with disabilities by promising to decrease their dependency and increase their productivity.[58] Iconic disability rights activist Marta Russell argued, "When George Bush signed the ADA in 1990, a bargain was struck. Disabled people's civil rights would be tolerated by the anti-government GOP, the party of business, as long as the ADA cost the federal government next to nothing and promised to get people off entitlements."[59] However, this utilitarian calculation does not add up for all people. For some people, providing a meaningful education and accessibility will cost more than their eventual productivity yields. The economic calculus behind the provision of rights may lead to divestment in services for people who may yield little to no economic return on public investment.

On the one hand, disability activists have maintained a steady commitment to those with the most significant disabilities. For example, as the commissioner of rehabilitation for California, Ed Roberts reprioritized funding to ensure that those with the most significant disabilities received services, rather than focusing attention only on those for whom a minor investment would ensure success. Roberts's vision was that all people, even those with the most significant disabilities, could work and exercise independent decision-making in their lives. On the other hand, politicians easily distort this vision into a rhetoric of compulsory productivity that sees value in people only insofar as they are able to eventually become productive, forcing people to be productive in a traditional capitalist economy or else abandoned to segregated services, social isolation, or family care.

We see this tension in modern debates regarding employment. Sheltered workshops are criticized for fostering segregation and poverty and denying people with disabilities the training and opportunities actually needed to enter the workforce. Activists with disabilities strive for a world in which all people have the accommodations and supports to contribute productively in a competitive, inclusive job placement, and therefore urge the closure of sheltered workshops and the creation of competitive employment at living wages. But some parents question the idea that all people can or should have to be productive and participate in capitalist competition. They fear that the idea that all people may become productive actually justifies the denial of *any* care for those who cannot be adequately productive for a competitive job. As we close segregated, congregate care, they ask: Are *all* people receiving a right to community or are the least able being left behind, abandoned now in isolated family homes, nursing homes, and prisons rather than institutions? Sociologist and parent Barbara Altman worries about the future of her son: "Sheltered workshops, which provided stimulating activities for Andy for years, are now being closed. This closing is best for most clients, but for some, like Andy, it means being relegated to day programs mostly populated by the elderly or, if there is no day program available, being placed in a nursing home. While I live, I won't let that happen."[60]

Thus the choice some parents perceive as *actually being made* is not between a world of segregation versus community integration but rather between segregation that is at least attentive to particular needs versus complete abandonment. Meaningful inclusion is not perceived as a likely option because it costs too much and requires too much support, and the state is unlikely to intensively invest in someone unlikely to yield returns. Disability activists counter that the solution is not to fall back on and legitimate segregation but rather to demand social investment in inclusion. Radical inclusion, for example, puts the participation of people with disabilities at the center and builds the inclusion of people without disabilities from that starting point.[61]

Rights as a Mask for Neoliberalism

Concerns regarding compulsory productivity and the abandonment of those with the most need directly relates to the connection between rights and neoliberalism. American rights tend to be "negative rights," which guarantee the freedom to be left unimpeded. The rights to free speech, to assemble, and to opportunity free of discrimination are all examples of negative rights. Negative rights come at little cost to the state other than ensuring people's freedom. "Positive rights," on the other hand, require that the state or others *actively provide* something or *invest* to ensure an outcome. The right to an education is a positive right; it requires the state to create, maintain, and implement a publicly funded system of education for all children. Disability activism has always demanded both kinds of rights, because the freedoms accorded via negative rights alone are not sufficient for the disability community to participate in society. Freedom and opportunity must be paired with investment in supports, services, accessibility, and accommodations to ensure the meaningful participation of people with disabilities.

Although people with disabilities require both negative and positive rights, neoliberalism promotes a view of freedom based on a laissez-faire economic system with little government regulation or public provision of services in favor of an open, private, capitalist marketplace. Thus, neoliberals tend to agree with disability rights activists that state-funded institutions, sheltered workshops, and public specialized schools for children with disabilities should all close, but they resist funding other community-based public services.[62] Rights become a political tool to mask fiscal conservativism, with little commitment to creating the material conditions necessary to practice freedom, make choices, and participate in society.

Christopher clearly articulates this economic calculation and how it affects his son, who requires twenty-four-hour care for complex medical conditions. His son resides in a large-scale center for people with disabilities. When asked if his son could be cared for in the community, Christopher said, "Oh, it's not impossible. The problem is, to do it properly, it's costly. . . . It's going to be enormously expensive. . . . They're [the state] not prepared to do so because they are trying to save money."[63]

Another parent, Erica, discusses the problem of rights when paired with a lack of investment in community services. Erica's daughter has frequent seizures and uses a feeding tube, and Erica argues that staff tend to be unreliable in attendance, have high turnover, and lack qualifications to administer medication and handle seizures, or to even recognize seizures. She states, "The staff aren't nurses, and they aren't trained appropriately. . . . What about at night if there's only one person on staff and three or four consumers. Somebody can have a seizure, and you can't wait for another staff member to get there [to handle the other consumers]."[64] For Erica, there is not a sufficient number of knowledgeable staff, or even just a sufficient number of staff, to deal with crisis situations that are bound to occur when you have individuals who routinely need significant medical intervention. Moreover, the system becomes privatized, putting the consumer or their family in charge of identifying and managing staff and services. Erica explains that although she is a single working mother, not only must she provide extensive care, but she must locate, manage, and monitor services. This would not be so daunting if she knew quality services and staff existed and that she could afford them, but no such assurances exist. She cannot afford services that meet her daughter's needs, so she must take time off from work to provide the services, which then makes paying for services all the more problematic. She feels trapped in an inadequate system that gives her the "right" to manage her daughter's care but does not provide the funding, time, resources, or services to actually do this successfully. Thus, the political wish that the delivery of rights will save money creates a dangerous demand for productivity and is related to a path toward divestment rather than investment.

Safety and Rights

Parents worry a lot about safety, and the relationship between safety and rights is complicated. Rights may protect someone's safety, but concerns about safety may also be used to deny rights to people with disabilities.

People with disabilities should have a right to be safe in their community, yet communities often fail them. For example, stories are abundant regarding abuse, neglect, and overmedication in group homes and other community-based services.[65] Cindy related a story about a friend's daughter who lived in a group home, "but because of her behaviors, they had her strung out on drugs just to keep her calm and quiet, you know?"[66] Harold decided against institutionalizing his daughter in the early 1970s and still feels a deep distrust of the system. As an aging caregiver in his eighties, he still believes that the care he provides, although now quite limited, is safer than relying on the state, because "who knows what you are going get. They don't care, and how would you know?"[67]

Lack of police training puts people with disabilities, especially minorities and people with mental and behavioral disabilities, at great risk when confronted by the police. Twenty-four-year-old Jamycheal Mitchell, an African American young man with schizophrenia, died in his jail cell while awaiting trial for shoplifting $5.05 worth of goods; Magdiel Sanchez, a thirty-five-year-old Deaf Latino man, died on his front porch when police called at his house and he did not follow their orders; and Connor Leibel, a white autistic teen, died after an altercation with the police. Connor was walking and "stimming," but the police officer thought he was on drugs, and he did not respond "appropriately" to police orders.[68]

Often parents and disability activists use a rights framework to address safety concerns, arguing that all people need to be included, respected, and given the right to the services and supports needed to live meaningfully in the community, not simply to be housed geographically in the community. Other parents, though, see the singular focus on rights as actually increasing the risk for people who cannot protect themselves. Sara explains, "It's an old saying, and it's not mine, you know, that Rob could die with his rights on, meaning that he could cross the street and get hit by a car, but he died with his rights on." As a person with pica (associated with compulsive ingestion of inedible objects) and self-harming behaviors, her son needs "lots of eyes" on him. "Staff can't go to the bathroom and leave him alone."[69] For him to be safe, he requires close supervision and a physical environment free of small objects. His mother worries that a focus on his self-determination undermines his access to a safe environment while the lack of resources denies him adequate staffing.

Family members of people with mental illness are especially likely to speak to the dilemma of rights and safety and worry that the rights to self-determination and privacy are prioritized over safety. One daughter, Destinee, spoke about her mother, who has mental illness (reversing the typical pattern of parent activism). She felt that she and her mother were trapped in a perpetual cycle of crisis-hospitalization-stabilization-decline-crisis. During brief hospitalizations, her mother would be placed on medications and stabilized. Back in the community, her mother lacked necessary supports and access to stable health care, affordable medications, and housing. She would go off her meds, become paranoid, stop eating, and spend recklessly, but her daughter could not legally intervene until there was proof that her mother was a threat to herself or others. For Destinee, the system protected *a* right (self-determination) but failed to ensure *the host of rights* (e.g., affordable housing, adequate community health care, personal assistance) that would ultimately protect her mother's quality of life and safety. Given the lack of these community supports, Destinee and other family members advocate greater access to guardianship and involuntary hospitalization, prioritizing (in their view) their family member's life and well-being over self-determination.[70]

Safety has been used not only to deny the right to reside in the community but also to deny access to a broad range of activities within the community. For example, safety is one of the key ideas used to deny people with disabilities access to romantic and sexual relationships. Rather than building competence regarding intimacy through sexual education and practical experience as happens for other children or teens, those with disabilities are often denied access to such knowledge and experiences.[71] Their resulting ignorance is then used as evidence that sexuality would be a danger to them. Participation in other areas is also denied by using safety as a reason. For example, when Miriam told her son's school administrators that he needed accommodations in gym for his complex medical disabilities, they "exempted" him from gym for his own safety.[72] Safety was used as a bureaucratic legitimation for isolation rather than for the provision of appropriate accommodations.

While safety should not justify exclusion, people also should not live in fundamentally unsafe environments. Without supervision (when needed), qualified caregivers, necessary supports, accessible buildings, medical care, and trained police, the community can pose numerous unnecessary dangers.

Justice-based approaches, emerging largely from marginalized communities, share a criticism of the ways in which rights rhetoric has served a neoliberal agenda while denying basic human rights such as affordable housing, food, and treatment. Unlike parents who often support segregated services, though, those using justice-based approaches advocate universal economic and social rights and broad social transformation attentive to the systems of racism and poverty that intertwine with disability oppression. They center the experience of marginalized populations and seek fundamental reforms such as redistributing or restructuring public education to minimize inequality, providing basic income supports to those in need, and providing universal health care.[73] They also tend to function at a grassroots community level, seeking ways to uplift and improve communities, respect people within their communities, and channel resources into those communities.

Competition for Resources

While there are clear philosophical differences among parents, there are also issues of money. As noted, neoliberalism decreases public investment and, in an environment of scarce resources, parents feel pitted against each other for these resources.

Rather than being individual decisions, each family's choices affect the choices available to other families. Moreover, because social privilege and resources affect access to choice, the exercise of choice by some privileged families may shape and constrain choices for other parents. For example, disabled activists argue that the maintenance of segregated services for people with disabilities pulls resources away from integrated options and thereby *reduces* their availability. This creates a vicious cycle of trying to solve the failings of community integration when resources are pulled away to support segregated settings. In assessing their options, parents may see a segregated option having more resources and "choose" that option, further perpetuating the system of segregation and supporting the argument that parents seem to "prefer" segregation. Parents who want their child included in the public school then face an under-resourced system, in part because of the choices made by other parents. It also creates a multiple-tiered system of service where those with resources can advocate for specialized services, but the public schools become sites where kids with disabilities, particularly those from families with fewer resources, are dumped and ignored. Thus, people who want inclusive settings have reason to blame other parents who choose segregated settings for the slow progress and lack of options.

Parents who want specialized settings in turn blame integrationist parents for gutting specialized services to pay for inclusive services. As money shifts away from institutional approaches, there is a cry from some parents to continue to support and expand "intentional communities," farmsteads, and village approaches that create disability-specific residential options for people with developmental disabilities. Well-known parent and disability studies scholar Michael Bérubé wrote in a 2018 op-ed piece, "Intentional communities hold great promise for families seeking to steer clear of the disability cliff. They bring together individuals with intellectual disabilities, and caretakers and assistants who are not disabled."[74] Neurodiversity activist Cal Montgomery countered, "It's understandable that Bérubé is looking for options that work for his family, and it's understandable that he is dissatisfied with group homes. However, it seems that his solution is misguided. Renegotiating the HCBS Final Rule [for Medicaid waivers to pay for home and community-based services] in the current political climate will inevitably result in a loss of real community-based settings."[75] Thus, the right to choose intentional communities pulls funding in a particular direction, thereby limiting other options.

Those who support institutions, intentional communities, and sheltered workshops see themselves losing out in the recent policy and financial shifts toward community settings. Jack adhered to this view, arguing that the closure of congregate settings was always about denying care to people, not providing it: "The hell of it is that there are tens of thousands of individuals in our state who are not given any services at all, yet ironically they [anti-institution lawsuits] attack institutions where the people get full services.

They haven't been successful getting people in the community services, so they come after us."[76] The institutions close, in his opinion, to access money to provide community services but not to provide better services for *his* child. Discussing that scarcity of money fosters division among parents, Cindy said parents used to fight together to provide a spectrum of options to meet all needs, but now they are told it is a zero-sum game: "You [policy makers] took the lion and the lamb, and you pitched them against each other, and you dangled the money and said that the money was the problem, and you had them at each other's throats for the money."[77]

Inequality

Parents often feel that resources are tight and that they are in competition to access their children's rights. The extent to which one receives disability rights depends heavily on active negotiation, and therefore one's socioeconomic status, race, and cultural capital are significant factors in determining receipt of rights and services. Parents recognize the significant role of their education and income, although they typically fail to problematize the ways in which their success may leave others behind. Rather, they imagine either that their success and activism is an individual phenomenon or that it helps all children.

Activists understand that their activism is enabled by human and social capital, such as being well educated, holding a prestigious job, having friends or connections that know the laws, being able to afford organizational dues and attendance at trainings and conferences, having time to dedicate to activism, living in a "nice" neighborhood with well-funded schools, and being able to move to a location with better education or services. For example, Jack noted that his specific career and income offered his family a resiliency that many other families did not have: "My career was as a lawyer. . . . Some families have broken apart because of having a disabled child, but in our case it has brought the two of us together and our children together more."[78] Knowledge is an important weapon, further supplemented by a display of one's willingness and ability to act on one's knowledge. It may not be coincidence that two of the interviewees who spoke about "threatening" organizations with lawsuits were men with significant incomes. Carmen Carley, an advocate for her son with autism and for other families seeking services, tells families, "Wear a fake diamond ring. Make them think you're ready to fight. Don't show them you're weak. Don't show them you're tired."[79]

On an organizational level too, we see a leadership structure influenced by socioeconomic status, but with leaders who maintain their faith in the ability of the organization to reach out to and help all people. Yvonne describes, "I think in a lot of advocacy organizations, the people running them are people who are well educated and usually from backgrounds where they have resources and money and that kind of thing. . . . But in [our organization] we talked to all kinds of people; we never assumed that somebody couldn't use the law to help their child. You know, that doesn't change if you're a different race." Even gender inequality was noted but not problematized. Yvonne noted, "Women tend to be more involved because—I don't know—it just works out that way, that women tend to be in charge of the children."[80] Erica, an African American single mother, criticized the way the system seems to assume that mothers stay at home and can support all sorts of educational and physical therapies, "as if I don't work or have other children."[81] Yet these activists did not see the organizations themselves as perpetuating inequality. Rather, the activist work of men, who often hold leadership positions, for example, was highly valued and presented as an indication of the broad, equalizing impact of disability on families.

Thus, while inequality was recognized, activists in large national organizations stressed the universal nature of disability. As explained by Sara, "One of the things about having a child with a handicap is that it's nonpartisan, it has nothing to do with your income, it's just all over the place. It can happen to rich, poor, white, black, you name it. You can have a child if you pick that straw instead of the other one, and for the grace of God, there goes everybody."[82] African American activists in national organizations similarly stressed commonalities.[83] Erica described her activism this way: "I'm speaking with all kinds of parents and trying to figure out where they fall and what their reasonings are, and ultimately what I want to do is have parents see the commonalities across what they want because I feel like there's been a lot of division and that parents are a lot more powerful when they act together, when the field isn't as fragmented and it isn't all about each side trying to conquer the other, because then they get more resources."[84] In describing the diversity of her organization, Becky stated, "Disability doesn't discriminate. In working with families, they come from all walks of life, and the only thing they do have in common is a family member with a disability. Certainly they need the means to get to meetings or have flexibility in their schedules, but the president is an older African American woman from the South with lower economic background, and it runs the gamut from her to a CEO in a northern big city."[85]

Thus, parents note inequalities but emphasize the commonality of the disability experience. In doing so, they fail to consider the serious ramifications of inequality and the way that they themselves may exacerbate it. Parents who engage in activism see themselves as helping all other families, but the benefits of activism largely go to those families with cultural capital to seek out and demand these benefits. Meetings and conferences are open to all, but this style of activism caters to middle-class families. The reliance on activism itself—the demand that parents learn the laws, negotiate with systems, fight for resources—advantage particular families. Emphasizing the universality of the disability experience largely ignores the effects of poverty, violence, and racism that contribute to disability and fails to create solutions attentive to these factors. Parents operate in a system that advantages families with a high socioeconomic status, and they also create activist organizations that privilege middle-class norms, yet they largely ignore the role of their own activism in preserving inequality.

As Amber Angell and Olga Solomon argue, ignoring race obscures not only differences in capital but also racism and discrimination. In their study of Latino "autism parents" (i.e., highly engaged, activist Latino parents of children with autism), they found that "Latino 'autism parents,' despite high-level expertise, may encounter vastly unequal treatment from administrators compared with White middle-class 'autism parents.'"[86] They argue that the narrative that minority families do not or cannot fight effectively fails to account for the active discrimination by school districts encountering minority families, even those with resources and expertise. To address discrimination, minority families may feel that they *must* deal with race and ethnicity alongside disability; however, such intersectional activism is rarely welcome in large, national organizations. Not surprisingly then, minority families may engage at local levels and in organizations that specifically organize around race and intersectional issues to better engage issues of disability, poverty, and racism, rather than relying on the largest parent-led organizations.

The Role of Disability

As we have seen, parents vary considerably in the ways that they use the idea of rights. Much of the use of rights talk cuts across disability groups. Parents from all disability groups use rights to fight discrimination, make claims based on available legislation, and protect their authority over their own families. There are no cut-and-dried patterns that suggest parents of children with one disability use the language of rights in fundamentally different ways than parents of children with a different disability. Disability is not the primary factor influencing one's understanding and use of rights.

That said, there are patterns tied to various factors. Parents of those with mental illness seem among the most likely to deprioritize rights as a way to claim competence of the person with a disability and instead to frame rights to justify their own parental involvement. This is likely because they more often feel shut out of the decision-making processes as compared with parents whose children grow up with disabilities.

We also see some pattern of aging parents and parents who describe their children as significantly disabled and unable to self-advocate as more likely to seek segregated, "protected" environments. Interestingly, though, there are and have historically been many parents who describe their offspring as having significant disabilities and who seek integration. Emina's son, Marsel, has a significant intellectual disability and requires extensive twenty-four-hour supports, yet she fought for him to be placed in a supported community house with roommates of his choice. He attends a day program, and she works directly with the administration and staff to create new strategies for meaningful community integration, such as volunteering and participating in community events and clubs. She explained, "People don't see how to do it; they don't have the training, so you have to push them, change the rules, give them strategies, and then talk to them again. It takes time."[87] Other parents create small businesses for their adult offspring, encourage integration at church, and demand inclusion generally. Thus, significant disability does not require segregation, but those who prefer segregated systems discuss their preference in terms of the severity of disability and their need or desire for expertise. Older parents remember fondly when parent organizations such as the Arc fought for "all" parents, to ensure a range of services, rather than "pushing" small, community-based, inclusive services, and thus root their activism in a long legacy of activism.

The fierce debate over inclusion and segregation seems to many parents to be a false dichotomy. Most parents accepted and sought out some combination of integration and segregation, determined by the quality of the options available to them. Even parents like Emina and Gail, who consider themselves fierce advocates for integration, placed their children in disability-specific programs because of a lack of feasible alternatives and the perceived high quality of the specific segregated program available to them. Other parents who are explicitly members of organizations that fight to retain disability-specific settings expected their churches, friends, and local businesses to welcome their children and used inclusive programs at various times, or even for other children in their household with disabilities. For many parents, adherence to strict ideology falls to the wayside in the face of pressing needs and actual choices. While for many individual parents the politics of integration versus segregation may seem needlessly polarizing, organizations are more likely to recognize the likely zero-sum politics in which funding to preserve disability-specific settings undercuts the growth and availability of inclusive opportunities and vice versa. While individual parents make a variety of choices among their local options, organizations operate with clearer political agendas that promote legislation, legal action, and funding.

Conclusion

Activists with disabilities and parents fight for "disability rights," and often they are speaking a similar language of antidiscrimination and access. As an abstract idea, rights are widely valued in America. Like freedom, independence, and happiness, a belief in the inalienable rights of individuals underlies the American collective consciousness, insofar as such a thing exists. An American pollster, John Zogby, goes as far as to argue that rights are *the* central defining feature of American culture.[88] Indeed, the idea of rights is so positively value-loaded that it can be layered on top of almost anything to make the position seem more appealing, more just, more "right." Thus, it is not surprising that parents with very different goals latch onto the idea of rights.

The conferring of rights and related state dollars, though, often comes with state oversight, surveillance, and measures of accountability that people with disabilities, their family members, or both find an unacceptable constraint on their autonomy. Once public dollars are allocated, it is unclear whether individual goals (e.g., freedom and autonomy) or state and public goals (e.g., equality, inclusion) should dominate. The imposition of public goals tied to the equality and liberty of people with disabilities leads some parents to experience "rights" as a constraining, rather than a liberating, force and thereby to resist these rights as infringements on their own parental authority and rights.[89]

Constraint and liberty are experienced in relation to one's social position. Disabled activists argue that constraints on parents are necessary for the liberty of people with disabilities. Parents, on the other hand, assert authority, often without recognizing potential conflicts of interests within the family. Some parents challenge the criteria of rationality and autonomy and fight for their offspring to have access to a full range of rights, but other parents rely heavily on and reinforce these same criteria to assert their own rights to make decisions for their children whom they portray as dependent and incompetent (including adult offspring). Disability rights as imagined by parents may empower people with disabilities, or it may empower parents to make decisions for their offspring.

9

Parents, Children, and Advocacy
across Life Transitions

D o parents' views on disability and their disabled children change over their life span? Memoirs and scholarship both indicate a developmental process by which parents' perceptions and insight, as well as their ability to advocate, change as they and their children age. The concept of fluidity as discussed by Sharon Barnartt provides a useful framework to consider that the idea of disability itself and the lived experiences of disability change over time, by setting and relationship, and by the task at hand.[1] The lives of parents are similarly fluid; parents age and may want or need to move, retire, or remarry. Because needs and interests change over time, advocacy is a lifelong endeavor. This fluidity of personal experience and roles stands in contrast to service systems that are fragmented, inflexible, and hinder transition from one life stage to another. "Transition" itself is often understood in social service settings as a once-in-a-lifetime event, occurring and being completed in the shift from school to adult life without further need for growth and new opportunities. Geographically, services and budgets do not easily transfer across state or even county lines, forcing parents and people with disabilities to choose between taking opportunities in another state or remaining proximate to where services and supports have been established.[2] Thus, despite the fluidity of people's lives, the service systems presume and enforce stagnation. This chapter reviews some of the key advocacy triggers and events across the life span for parents.

Initial Reactions

For most parents, disability diagnosis involves at least some amount of fear, guilt, grief, or anger. Parents soon experience disability stigma toward their child and family, and are propelled into navigating the complicated possibilities and decisions regarding how to approach disability and which interventions, if any, to adopt.[3] All new parents face a time of transition, but the experience may be much more jolting and emotional when the child is disabled, and parents may go through a period of adjustment as the child they dreamed of having recedes, giving way to an understanding of their actual child and his or her needs. If the child acquires disability later, while in childhood or as an adult, there is a related period of transitioning from the old life to the new one.[4]

Parents are rarely adept at advocacy in the midst of their child's diagnosis, but a number have later reflected on this experience to help improve other parents' advocacy. Some parent scholars study the parent experience of diagnosis to shed light on the stigma and barriers families and people with disabilities immediately face. Notable examples include Sara Green, who analyzes birth narratives, and Douglas Engelman, who examines the protracted and challenging experience of mental illness diagnosis.[5] Parent organizations such as the Arc, Autism Speaks, and the National Alliance on Mental Illness (NAMI) sponsor initiatives to improve the processes of identification, diagnosis, and prognosis. The National Down Syndrome Society pays particular attention to genetic counseling and prenatal diagnosis, working to ensure that medical professionals are able to provide well-balanced information to parents, rather than narrowly defining fetuses with Down syndrome as having a birth "defect."

Once embedded in the new world of disability, parents must navigate what it means for them and their families. An extensive literature documents the potential harmful impacts a disabled child can have on a family,[6] and some parent writings affirm the difficulty, stress, and even intolerable aspects of raising a child with a disability. Some memoirs from the twentieth century, such as those of John Frank, Fern Kupfer, and Michael Schofield, showcase the lack of services and intense family struggles.[7] Modern parent writings also at times give a window into that trauma of disability. Angela McClanahan describes intense family struggles in her account of coping with the onset of childhood mental illness and urges the provision of a host of better options, including residential care; Kim Stagliano strives to put a lighthearted spin on the many challenges of raising multiple children with autism; and other parents cry out for help, unable to manage the intense demands presented by complex medical illness, unmanageable mental illness, or significant disability.[8] While these perspectives may be honest and revealing of the parent's experience, self-advocates often criticize parent revelations as disrespectful of the children whose lives are being documented without their permission and who are being represented in ways that could be humiliating and hurtful.[9]

Other parents explicitly set out to offer parents a tale of hope and acceptance. A well-known essay by Emily Perl Kingsley from 1987 describes what it is like for a parent by using a metaphor in which one plans a trip to Italy and ends up in Holland instead. Kingsley enjoins that, though the pace of life and experiences are different, this new experience is still worthwhile and ultimately satisfying, just in a different way:

> The important thing is that they haven't taken you to a horrible, disgusting, filthy place, full of pestilence, famine and disease. It's just a different place. . . . It's a little slower-paced than Italy, less flashy than Italy. But after you've been there for a while and you catch your breath, you look around, and you begin to notice that Holland has windmills, Holland has tulips, Holland even has Rembrandts. But everyone you know is busy coming and going from Italy, and they're all bragging about what a wonderful time they had there. And for the rest of your life, you will say "Yes, that's where I was supposed to go. That's what I had planned." And the pain of that will never, ever go away, because the loss of that dream is a very significant loss. But if you spend your life mourning the fact that you didn't get to Italy, you may never be free to enjoy the very special, the very lovely things about Holland.[10]

And, after the initial adjustment, some parents turn their focus to advocacy. Most parent activism occurs when their offspring are children and relates to school, health, and other social structures and policies that affect their children. This is particularly true for parents of disabled children, although their advocacy is more likely to last beyond childhood into adulthood. Parents realize, as one mother said in the film *Refrigerator Mothers*, that to improve their own child's situation, the situation must be changed for all disabled children, and they become involved.[11] Sometimes their involvement grows, connecting them to existing mutual support groups and organizations, or they might even form new ones. Parents might become activists on local and even national and international levels.[12] Major foci often include advocacy for treatment options and for educational programming and accommodations.

Treatment Advocacy

One of the first realms that parents typically encounter is the medical establishment. Across many disability groups, parents advocate for medical treatments and interventions for their children, and their advocacy is often crucial to the developmental and dissemination of needed treatments. This may be in the form of medical expertise, medication, rehabilitation, and financial support needed to access these treatments. For example, parents of children with polio fought to gain access to treatment; parents of children with intellectual disabilities and autism fought to have better diagnosis and prognosis performed by skilled doctors rather than doctors who would just write them and their children off; parents of offspring with mental illness have fought to have a mental health care system equal in quality and availability to the physical health care system; and parents of children who use prosthetics have fought to change insurance rules to pay for more rapid replacement of medical technology to better meet the needs of growing children. Recently, parents attended rallies to protect Medicaid expansion for children and adults with disabilities. Children with complex medical conditions are living into adulthood in larger numbers than ever before, and more are living in community rather than hospital or institutional settings.[13] The prospective longevity of their child and the likelihood of community inclusion encourage some parents to form long-term relationships with organizations that support access to treatment via research, advocacy, and the provision of treatment. They serve on boards and present at conferences. Others focus on fundraising for research goals they support. Some become researchers themselves.

As we note in previous chapters, though, the relationship between treatment and disability is complicated, and debates continue on the degree to which treatment is appropriate and which treatments are useful. Some parents seem certain that the choices they made for treatment options were good ones, and, indeed, in some cases, parents of disabled children may feel that their parenting is inextricably linked to efforts to find a cure. For example, one Facebook mom, whose child is now a teenager, posts antivaccine essays, though this supposed cause for autism has been debunked for years. She is certain that her child's autism has been cured. Another mom is also antivaccine but for a completely different reason; she believes that medical experimentation programs have caused autism in African American children.[14]

Other parents seem less certain of the value of the medical model, or perhaps more open to new ideas and interpretations. Decisions about diet and vaccination recede, becoming less important than the excitement of watching their child develop new skills and pleasures. "Progress every day" is the mantra of a Facebook mom who reports on her child's new skills, behaviors, and abilities with pride and joy. Some move from a focus on medical interventions to seeking support or pursuing needed social and policy interventions. Others wrestle with broader social justice issues their children face.[15] For example, parents of disabled children of color have become very concerned that their children might be misunderstood as violent or dangerous by neighbors and police officers and put at risk of being hurt or killed. Others urge parents to listen to the perspectives of disabled children and adults. Kelly Green describes her Facebook group, Parenting Autistic Children with Love and Acceptance, as "a community for parents of Autistic children who choose to love and accept their Autistic children. A place to learn from the writing of Autistic adults. A place where parents can discuss supporting and accommodating Autistic children."[16] These parents do not necessarily eschew treatment, but they have decided to focus on raising their unique child and achieving the supports that they need without the relentless pursuit of cure or normalization.

Transition to and from School

For many parents, advocacy begins and is at its most intense during the school years and in the transition out of school into adult roles. Parents are faced with a mire of bureaucracy: there are different systems of support for children at the stages of early intervention and preschool, school age, and after; different laws and options for supports apply in different states; and there are clear disparities in access to services. But these systems also give parents a formal avenue for involvement. The laws and policies mandated a range of services and resources and provide parents with a basis for advocacy and appeal.

Because the receipt of services is heavily dependent on negotiations between parents and school systems, inequality is rampant and begins early, even with early intervention services. White, middle-class or privileged parents are more likely to be able to access information and supports, attain a useful diagnosis, and access desirable treatments and services much earlier than minorities and those living at low-income or poverty levels.[17] Districts themselves vary in economic resources and yield disparate success in identifying and addressing disability issues. Across all economic levels there are cases of children who are not diagnosed until they reach school age, when school professionals are available to evaluate and observe.

Disparities continue and broaden once the child reaches school age. Privileged parents are more likely to understand their rights, actively engage in the individualized educational plan (IEP) process, and turn to additional legal processes if necessary to ensure that resources they believe their child needs will be available to them.[18] Minority families who do fight often feel discounted in the process. Even for privileged families, success is not guaranteed and the process of advocating for needed services can be lengthy and exhausting. Parents experience the "team approach" to the IEP very differently, and many parents report feeling like school systems try to manage and subdue parents rather than working in true partnership with them.[19] Although the process is challenging, school-age children with disabilities have a right to an IEP and parents have a right to involvement and due process, which encourages their activism.

The transition from secondary educational to postsecondary educational or vocational prospects poses similar and new challenges. The preparation that parents and their children receive varies greatly by school system. Researchers have documented that parents and children are often relegated to passive roles in the processes that determine important future life choices. Some children and parents, though, are very actively involved in the transition planning process.[20] One example of successful parent advocacy in transition planning is the DREAM (Dreams Realized through Education Aspiration Model) Partnership in Pennsylvania,[21] as well as the work by other parent groups to encourage the establishment of postsecondary programs for students with intellectual and developmental disabilities on college campuses. Despite the successes of these initiatives, college programs for this population are still rare, geographically dispersed, and typically extremely expensive, often more expensive than college programs for nondisabled students at the same institutions.

Transition planning is a complicated process and constrained by funding systems that are very different than those for students in K–12 education. Federal law guarantees funding to support disabled children in educational attainment through the age of twenty-one. Funding and associated services and supports drop off sharply at the twenty-second birthday, a time referred to as the "disability cliff." States offer insufficient services to meet the need, and funding for vocational and residential programs is rationed, leading to long waiting lists and young adults relegated to segregated options or staying at home.[22] The formal role allocated to parents in the IEP may continue in some form in the delivery of adult services, particularly if guardianship is in place or if the adult offspring consents to parent participation, or it may disappear if the young adult has no services or receives local services unaffiliated with disability service systems, or if the young adult does not consent to parental involvement.

Those with complex medical conditions requiring twenty-four-hour nursing support have a particularly difficult transition because nurses are paid much more to support children going to primary and secondary school than adults residing in the community. Therefore, the quality of support and the pool of nurses willing to accept this type of position at the salary offered is joltingly different from what parents and children experience while the child is in public school. Not trusting the level of nursing support available in day programs, parents may believe that the only options for their previously engaged and active twenty-two-year-old child are to be trapped at home, in a nursing home, or in the community with a lower quality of nursing support.[23] Again, the economic status of the parents can make a crucial difference. Parents with resources (including financial resources, access to information, and networks of social support) can chart a very different life course for their graduating children as compared with parents who rely on the meager services granted to them by the state.

Disabled youth continuing on to college face new challenges. Because supports do not always transfer across state lines, students are restricted in their search. Moreover, limited funding for personal assistance makes it hard for students with disabilities to live far from family. Recent headlines drew attention to these problems. When New Jersey's Medicaid program cut Anna Landre's funding for personal assistance, it threatened the former high school valedictorian's ability to attend Georgetown University. Without adequate hours of personal assistance, she would need to move home and receive supplemental assistance from her mother. She launched a legal battle and social media campaign, fighting for a year before winning her case. She notes, though, that her victory benefits her but that many other young adults with physical disabilities find themselves in similar situations.[24]

Services provided by the colleges are also organized very differently than services in elementary and secondary schools. In primary and secondary school, the school system is responsible for identifying needs and providing services. In college, students must apply for disability support services, request specific supports for each class, and manage their own services.[25] If living on campus, they must navigate access barriers in an often expansive campus. Access to medical supports and mental health counseling can be insufficient. Negotiating these complex issues, especially if one's parents are not nearby, can be incredibly challenging.

For parents, the most important change is the structural shift toward self-advocacy and Family Educational Rights and Privacy Act (FERPA) rules protecting a student's privacy. These rules create a totally different structural relationship between the educational institution and parent than in K–12 schools; colleges in effect shut down parent activism (or interference). This can be both good and bad. College students have the opportunity to chart their own path, which may be different from the one parents have in mind, or they may be left stranded without needed supports.[26] Students themselves may be unclear, indecisive, or simply in denial about what they need. Universities have dedicated accessibility services that are cross-disability, but not all students are aware that they must ask for services and formally document their need for them, and even services to which students are legally entitled may involve budgetary limits. Some students may not want to identify as disabled and choose not to ask for supports, even if sorely needed, with devastating consequences to educational goals. Others may develop new disability issues during their first period away from home and simply have no idea where to go for help. Some disabled people may live at home or near home while getting undergraduate and postgraduate degrees simply as a means to ensure daily life supports are available. Or, as was the case for Deej Savaresse, a nonverbal man with autism, his mother moved with him to ensure his transition and well-being.[27]

Unemployment statistics for disabled people, with or without a college degree, are unfortunately quite high and income quite low across all educational levels. In this era, when competition is fierce and hyperproductivity is expected, both higher education and the workplace become spaces that are extremely difficult for disabled people to navigate successfully.[28] Sheltered workshops and day programs may appeal to parents as noncompetitive settings that offer flexibility, accommodations, and security. Parent advocacy fostered the development of vocational and day recreational opportunities for their children such as sheltered workshops. When first established these provided opportunities for adult children and respite for parents. Yet over time disabled activists and some parents became critical of this model as a form of warehousing without beneficial or meaningful occupation and instead insisted on alternatives that better integrated people into the community and paid living wages. Wages in sheltered workshops are often so low that they have been investigated by the Department of Justice. In a decision handed down in Rhode Island in 2014,[29] the U.S. Department of Justice decreed that all disabled people should work in community settings and should not be warehoused in sheltered workshops. However, this mandate did not provide economic supports or infrastructure and did not take into account that the budgets provided to day programs are shrinking, which hinders the provision of the individualized vocational supports required to move away from the sheltered workshop model. In recent years there has been a move toward smaller, more community-based services, but these often are unable to provide meaningful vocational activity and instead focus more on recreation. Despite the disadvantages, many parents continue to vehemently defend sheltered workshops and day programs because the likelihood of successful competitive employment or other venues of social integration seems so low (see Chapter 1).

Other parents, faced with the disadvantages and reduced availability of sheltered workshops and day programs, strive to create employment-friendly policies, awareness campaigns geared toward employers, and even specific entrepreneurial opportunities for their offspring (which may be more or less inclusive). Michael and Jennifer Myers, for example, opened Sam's Canterbury Café in Maryland to employ their son who is on the autism spectrum and others with disabilities. Jimmy and Karen Bellas similarly opened Sorriso Kitchen in New Jersey to ensure their son and others have a productive and respectful work setting.[30] While the extraordinary commitment of these families to create work opportunities is admirable, the continued need for families to create employment opportunities, almost seventy years after the founding of the Arc, speaks to the real challenges of social integration.

Transition also may or may not include moving out of one's family home. As with education and employment, residential options for disabled people are very limited in scope. In the era of deinstitutionalization in the 1970s and 1980s, parents under the developmental disability umbrella advocated for increased residential options, and community-based vocational and residential alternatives proliferated in the 1990s. Institutions were dismantled and community-based residential alternatives developed including intermediate care facilities, group homes, and supported apartment programs. There were even grant programs that allowed disabled adults to buy their own homes, created largely from parent activism. These new options often relied on extensive parent intervention, as parents ensured that local nonprofits offered quality care, trained staff on their offsprings' needs, and at times even hired and managed staff. Emina's story, featured at the start of Chapter 1, illustrates the intense parental involvement that often sustains individualized residential programs.

However, even at the best of times there have not been sufficient community options for everyone. Some people lived in institutions for long stretches because it was their parents' preference or simply because no other option existed. Housing options began to shrink even further with the budget crises of the late twentieth and early twenty-first centuries.[31] In the cases of those with significant physical disabilities, such as those on ventilators, there were rarely any good options other than shut-in home care or institutional care. People who fought hard to get out and stay out of institutions are still just a few unfortunate choices or bad-luck incidents away from being institutionalized again. With so few options, many of which are unstable and of poor quality, we see a growing wistful yearning of professionals and parents, wondering if institutional and segregated care would be a better alternative than community-based living for some autistic and disabled people. As parents have created work sites specifically for people with disabilities, they have also created residential sites, some of which are more or less integrated with the community. Some parents have moved forward with the development of new "intentional housing" communities that try to promise the stability and sense of community that integrated communities too often lack.[32] Given America's poor record with congregate care for people with developmental and mental disabilities, these musings and projects favoring institutional life built around disability seem ominous.

In this transition to the community, parent activism also changes. Parents have pressing concerns and needs, but the path for effective social change is much less clear. Public school systems and even social service agencies provide clearer legal avenues for involvement, whereas the legal and political avenues to reshape the range of private businesses, apartment complexes, and community organizations needed to ensure meaningful social integration is far more limited. When private entities in the community prove recalcitrant and unreliable, parents often turn to public social services and organizations run by parents, which may be less inclusive but feel far more amenable to parent input.

And while some parents have built social networks and advocacy skills throughout their child's youth that can be used to take on challenges throughout their offspring's adult years, other parents enter into the world of disability only when their child acquires a disability later in life. At that point, they need to confront treatment options, housing instability, and lack of accommodated work settings, but it is much harder at that later point to build strong connections to peers, to offer support to offspring who are legal adults and perhaps geographically distanced, and to advocate within systems that do not respect or that even legally bar parent involvement.

Communication

How does the ability to communicate and interact with the world influence parents' perceptions and visions of their children's potential futures? Communication access is one of the most important factors influencing children's relationship with their parents and service systems throughout their lives.[33] Children (and adults) who are able to communicate effectively have the potential to make their desires and dislikes known. Inability to communicate, or inability of the people in your environment to recognize what you are trying to communicate, is a serious barrier to a satisfying quality of life.[34]

Communication is not merely verbal and language based; it also may include facial expressions, body language, pointing, and sign language (which may vary by person or region). Communication may be enabled by human mediators (interpreters, revoicers, and facilitators) and technologies that include hearing aids or alternative and augmentative communication (AAC) devices such as letter boards, iPads, and other devices that provide symbol systems or text-based communication strategies.[35] Internet technologies make possible online discussion groups, social media networks, and even virtual communities where people create their own online identities. Some disabled individuals with mobility issues need to access communication technology via technological bridges that allow devices to be controlled by breath, eyes, tongue, or other specific body part. Achieving communication access may also be reliant on human supports, such as professionals who can help identify the most efficient strategies and nonprofessionals in one's daily life (e.g., family members, friends, teachers) who are supportive in the development of these strategies.

Some communication decisions and related activism take place very early in a child's life, some at school age, and some continue throughout life. Access to sign language and cochlear implants is an explosive topic in parent activism, in part because parents typically make this decision early in a child's life, well before the deaf child can provide input. The decision is usually made by hearing people including hearing parents and audiologists, and it affects a host of other life choices like educational integration versus Deaf schools, social assimilation versus Deaf culture, and parental activism that is either in favor of medical research, access to speech therapy, and funding for equipment and therapy *or* in favor of the provision of Deaf education and the availability of accommodations and interpreters for Deaf children and adults. Thus, a decision made very early in a child's life has a tremendous impact on the child and the family.[36] Most deaf children are born to hearing parents who desire that their children hear as well as possible and thereby attain the greatest access to the culture and relationships shared with the parents. Others, especially many Deaf adults, argue that oralism and a reliance on cochlear implants often fall far short of the promises and that sign language is crucial for full language development, self-expression, and connection to the disability community. The American Society for Deaf Children embraces "full access to language-rich environments" inclusive of *both* English and American Sign Language (ASL) and argues that access to ASL is an essential part of one's human right to communication.[37] In contrast, Hands and Voices states that it is "non-biased about communication methodologies and believes that families can make the best choices for their child if they have access to good information and support."[38] Politically speaking, this means that Hands and Voices is accepting of families who choose cochlear implants and non-ASL approaches and that it refutes the idea of an essential right of deaf children to learn ASL and participate in Deaf culture. It prioritizes family decision-making over mandating ASL access.

Other controversies exist regarding access to communication technology, some of which are more likely to emerge as children age and enter the school system. While some accommodations do not cost school districts much money, the provision of high-quality AAC devices can be costly (although new tablet technology is offering lower-cost options). Parents often have to fight for provision of the technology, adequate training, integration of the technology into the school, and full access to the technology in the home and community environments. As with other special education services, racial and class disparities exist in the receipt of services for communication access.[39] In addition to advocating for AAC devices in the schools, parents have partnered with technology firms such as Apple to test and advance accessible products and to push insurers to fund tablet-based AAC equipment usable at home, and opportunities for these alliances may also vary by socioeconomic status, class, and region.[40]

For communication, the skills and attitudes of people in the disabled person's daily life can be equally impeding. If family or staff do not believe that the disabled person is capable of communication, do not have the educational background or access to training to support AAC use, or fear the financial repercussions of potentially breaking a device, then AAC use, as well as parent activism for communication access, becomes more difficult or impossible.[41] The presumption of communication competence itself varies by gender, race, and disability. Kliewer, Biklen, and Kasa-Hendrickson provide historical case examples across disability, gender, and racial lines to show how the erroneous presumptions of communication incompetence have damaged disabled individuals and groups.[42] When Phyllis Wheatley started writing poetry, it was presumed that the words were not hers because she was of African descent. When Helen Keller wrote a short story as a child of eleven, she was accused of plagiarism because it was presumed she could not have been capable of such writing, and indeed she was so frightened by the experience she never wrote fiction again. As a final example, an entire classroom of special education students was denied literacy training because it was presumed that it was beyond the students' abilities. Only when one of the students learned to read outside the classroom did this presumption break down. In contrast, parents may adopt the strategy of Biklen and his colleagues in presuming competence as a way to advocate for communication access.[43] Parents may become aware of and advocate for new advances that local experts may not even know about, and in that way push technological innovation in service of their children.

Human support in communication may also be very direct, as in facilitated communication (FC). In FC, human touch and even holding of the arm, elbow, wrist, or shoulder of the person typing is an essential factor in the communication process. This touch theoretically circumvents neurological barriers to motor initiation and allows communication to take place. This is a controversial strategy with scientific evidence published both supporting and detracting from the validity of the style of communication.[44] Detractors, including some parents, claim that it is actually the facilitator who is communicating, not the individual, and many published studies support this claim, though some question whether the research designs and analysis strategies of studies truly support the conclusions reached. The American Psychological Association (APA), as well as several other professional associations, renounced the use of FC, citing a lack of supporting evidence. The APA website notes, "Perhaps the saddest part of this story is that the most vocal advocates of this technique continue to use it and insist that it is effective—despite the disconfirming evidence. As one parent said, even if the technique is merely an illusion, it is an illusion that they wish to continue."[45] Defenders, including some parents, many self-advocates, and users, note that there are cases where the person typing has communicated information that the facilitator did not know.[46] Doug Biklen and others have collected extensive qualitative evidence of people who began to communicate with FC but later were able to communicate without the need for direct human support.[47] Parents have often been central in encouraging and supporting the use of this technology, not only through advocacy but through directly supporting their child's typing. For those who use FC, the invalidation of one's access to communication is seen as having devastating consequences.[48] Eventually direct brain-computer interface technologies may be able to put this debate to rest, but in the meantime parents have been both major supporters and central figures in combating the use of this technique.

The use of FC has played out in several high-profile court cases, in particular where parents were accused of sexual abuse by their child communicating via FC. The Stubblefield case is an example of high-profile court cases where evidence of individuals using FC was discounted or not even presented in the first case.[49] DJ, an African American man with cerebral palsy in his thirties, who apparently was given no communication access as a child or young adult, was suddenly finding success communicating using FC. The family at first felt thrilled but later was suspicious. At the same time, Anna Stubblefield, the woman who had introduced DJ to FC, found herself falling in love with him. In a series of communications with DJ that she herself facilitated, DJ expressed that the feelings were mutual. A physical relationship, or sexual abuse depending on your views, ensued. Eventually, Stubblefield was charged with and convicted of aggravated sexual assault, as defined by New Jersey state laws, and served time in prison, though the conviction was subsequently overturned on grounds of the judge's decision to exclude FC from the trial.[50]

This example is fraught with illustrations of the importance of communication access, the problems that can happen when communication access is not available, and the complex pivotal role of parents in either supporting or preventing communication access. DJ went through the school system and apparently not even the simplest of communication strategies (even yes/ no or pointing) was ever established. This points to disparities in the educational system that failed DJ. The family were, at different times, comfortable in presuming communication incompetence, thrilled by the possibility that complex communication might be possible, and then reconfirmed in their original beliefs that DJ was unable to communicate in any way. One of the most troubling moments of the trial was when DJ was brought into the room holding the hands of his mother (he was not given a wheelchair or walker to use) to be paraded in front of the jury as an exhibit of his own supposed incompetence. At least one juror went on the record as receiving that message loud and clear.[51] The jury was told to presume incompetence, and it did. Incompetence was the prerequisite to a guilty conviction under New Jersey state law, which defined any sexual activity between a "mentally defective" and "normal" person as assault.[52]

People are drawn to passionate extremes in the debate about FC. Lives and reputations have been ruined by the controversy. Stubblefield contends that DJ is more imprisoned in his home than she was in prison, as he has been denied communication access and the ability to make life choices. DJ's family contends that he was the victim of a self-serving and abusive professional. Despite these high-profile cases, hundreds of children learn to use the technique, may or may not move on to independent typing, and may or may not find their communication access improved without any particular controversy. In the case of FC, as with so many controversies, parents must wade through scientific debates and weigh their personal experiences and values to determine the best course of action. Either way they risk criticism, for relying on unproven communication methods or for denying their child an opportunity for communication.

Sexuality and Adult Roles

The Stubblefield trial provides an example of another issue of significance between disabled children and their families—physical and sexual maturity. In their memoirs, parents at times express not just fear of sexuality but also fear of physical growth and maturation itself.[53] As kids grow larger, parents fear that it will become harder to provide care, handle menstruation and sexual urges, and cope with challenging behavior. Violent behavior becomes especially frightening as children grow bigger and more powerful than their parents. Among concerns related to maturation, though, sexuality receives both the most attention and the most silence. DJ's family, for example, was comfortable with him using FC until what was being communicated was an apparent desire for sexual freedom and a desire to move away from his family. The jurors and countless commentators on social media expressed horror at the thought of a nondisabled woman expressing sexual desire for a significantly disabled man—a man whom the media repeatedly portrayed as "diaper-wearing."[54] It is a common presumption that intellectually disabled people are perpetual children and have no sexual desires. This competes with another presumption that intellectually disabled people are hypersexual and that their sexuality is dangerous and must be controlled. Both these extremes, in their own way, actually render disabled people, especially those with communication impairments, as unfit to engage in sexuality and, simultaneously, increase their vulnerability to sexual abuse.[55] These culturally inspired fantasies and fears—extremes of believing disabled people are asexual to believing they are sexual predators and everything in between—rarely reflect the actual sexuality of disabled people. Respectful and accurate media representations of the experiences of disabled people living adult lives are unfortunately rare.[56]

In terms of parent activism, sexuality is an area that few parents tread, except to protect their offspring from sexual abuse. There is little push to raise awareness of the abilities of people with disabilities to be parents, to establish supports for parenting by people with disabilities, and to defend people with disabilities from the heightened likelihood that their children will be removed from their custody. Indeed, sexuality seems to be an area that parents, with the support of the social service system, often "manage" in order to avoid the perceived negative consequences of it.[57] The A&E reality show *Born This Way* offers a vivid example of the informal ways in which sexuality and parenthood are discouraged and denied. When one of the young women with Down syndrome discusses with her mother the desire to have a child, the mother respectfully tries to discourage this, as she feels that the responsibility of raising that child would fall largely on her. A tension exists between the young woman's desires for motherhood and her mother's desires, which include avoiding a situation in which her daughter has additional responsibilities she cannot handle, saving her daughter pain should the child be taken away, and avoiding the likely responsibilities placed on her for raising a grandchild. Many parents are not as honest about their fears and tell offspring that they are not ready to date or deny access to dating.[58] Some parents even turn to the ethically questionable use of reproductive technologies or sterilization to prevent such a thing from happening.[59]

Despite significant barriers, many disabled people engage in intimate sexual relationships. Some of these relationships are transient, some long term.[60] Some involve cohabitation and some do not. Some have children or wish to. If sexuality is unspeakable, parenthood by people with disabilities is perhaps even more so, and yet thousands of disabled people become parents every year. Disabled parents, no matter what the disability, often face a degree of surveillance of their parenting and are held to standards beyond what most nondisabled people face.[61] There are many cases of disabled people being reported, evaluated by social services, and losing parental rights. This is a justice issue addressed in both practical and policy levels by the organization Through the Looking Glass, which assists families where a parent, grandparent, or child is disabled. This organization provides everything from adaptive or assistive devices that aid with parenting tasks to legal advice. With the goal of moving beyond stereotypes that limit the lives of disabled people, the mission of Through the Looking Glass is "to provide and encourage respectful and empowering services—guided by personal disability experience and disability culture—for families that have children, parents, or grandparents with disability or medical issues."[62] Thus, sexuality and parenting are clear priorities of activists with disabilities, but rarely of parents (although some parents are certainly supportive, and some cultural traditions emphasize the importance of family continuity).

Aging, Independence, and Interdependency

Eventually some offspring become fully independent of their parents, but many others remain interdependent. Parents may manage their offspring's support systems and treatment; provide key supports like housing, transportation, and care; offer financial support; assist with self-advocacy; and serve as a primary social and friendship network. The long-standing intertwining of lives confers on parents a great deal of informal power and makes it challenging to pull apart the interests of particular family members. Even when parents and children live and work separately, parents may feel it is their right to make important life choices on their adult offspring's behalf, with or without guardianship. It may seem simply appropriate that disabled family members sacrifice some of their interests for the good of the family unit. The idea of rights may get deprioritized as managing the ongoing needs of multiple family members takes precedence.

A complex interdependency often emerges as parents age. This may include emotional interdependence, interdependencies of care, and financial interdependence as the financial benefits of a disabled person become a part of the family income. Care roles may somewhat reverse as disabled children begin to care for aging parents. Aging parents may seek to relocate for reasons including to retire, to adjust their financial commitments, to seek their own health care, or for other reasons, but the service system makes this challenging because services for their child do not easily cross state or even county lines. Thus, parents may feel trapped in the choice between their own mobility versus the need to preserve the status quo for their children. If parents move, they may leave the children behind to ensure the continuation of appropriate services or they may take their children with them despite an abrupt shift or even termination in services and the disruption of the offspring's relationships. Either way, the quality of life for the adult child is at risk. The complex lives of parents complicate their activism, as they must consider factors in their own lives—work, marriage, retirement, and so forth—and they may pursue choices deemed best for themselves or their families but not necessarily the preferred choices of the family member with a disability.

What happens when parents can no longer intervene? Parents continue to worry about what will happen to their adult children as the parents age and face mortality. The death of a parent may lead to a dramatic reduction of quality of life for the offspring. As parents age, parent advocacy turns to long-term planning for their absence, which may include creating financial trusts, establishing guardianship, building self-advocacy skills, or passing the torch to their other children to assist their siblings. Parents may choose or even create residential options, including possibly institutional settings, for their children, which they hope will be long-term, safe places of shelter. Siblings or other relatives might come to the fore. Of course there are cases of adults with disabilities who lived isolated and restricted lives with their parents and who, on the parent's passing, realized opportunities to engage in community life (day programs, employment, friendships, and romantic relationships) that were never before available to them.

At the other extreme are the parents who hope their children die before them because the fear of what might happen is too great for parents to bear, or even parents who choose to kill their children, and sometimes themselves, rather than continue to parent disabled children.[63] Often such parents receive sympathetic reactions in the media (that they are under so much pressure and not receiving any support, and so forth). This is in stark comparison to media representations of parents who kill their nondisabled children and are inevitably demonized. The Autistic Self Advocacy Network has organized annual days of mourning and defines this behavior as a hate crime.[64]

Conclusion

At each stage of the life course, parents face very different structures and triggers for activism, as well as points of connection and conflict between parent advocacy and disability rights perspectives. There is much contention over the biomedicalization of the diagnosis process, of the decisions parents make, and the skirmishes they engage in around treatment and education, communication access, sexuality, and adult roles. Yet at each stage is a potential for allegiance, connection, and shared engagement in struggles for social and policy change. In these transitioning life moments there is the potential for great injustice and for justice to be done. Change can bring bad things and good, and most often both. Choices made in these moments determine the course of lives.

Conclusion

I n this book we seek to identify the various roles played by and political positions advocated by parents in the lives of their disabled children. Where much of the existing literature on parental activism in disability approaches the topic from a social psychological perspective, or with studies of single organizations or single issues, we explore it within a macrosocial framework of social movements and a broadly comparative perspective, which allows us to address questions of how parent activism is positioned within the field of disability activism. We consider the various ways that organizations representing parents have worked in their communities and the larger society based on their understanding of the needs of their children, and how these organizations are viewed by disabled activists and organizations run by disabled activists. We are particularly interested in the convergences and tensions between parent activists and disabled activists.

Parent activists and organizations run by them have a complicated relationship with activists with disabilities and organizations run by them. We have sought to find themes, commonalities, and systematic patterns of variation within the complex history of parent activism in four disability movement fields—intellectual disability, mental illness, autism, and physical disability—while also appreciating the historical complexity and uniqueness of each of the fields and the impact that key individuals often have.

Among the most complicated discussions we have had as authors have been those about the importance of not replicating false or simplistic binaries. Must parents be either allies or obstacles? Must every individual be either parent or disabled person? Those categories are neither mutually exclusive nor monotonically uniform: there is ambiguity and situationality in the extent to which people self-identify as either. Similarly, must we discuss the medical model or the social model, disability rights or disability justice? Of course not! Yet finding ways to have discussions that move beyond such binaries has been a continuing challenge that we have sought to address throughout the book. If anything is clear beyond all doubt, it is that parents play varied and complex roles that change through history and over the course of the life span, according to their intersectional and relational positioning.

To these ends, we have employed a cross-disability and cross-movement analysis that treats social movements in each of four disability fields—intellectual disability, mental illness, autism, and physical disability—as historical case studies. Each case study (Chapters 1 through 4) explores the specific ways in which activism developed among parents and among self-advocates, points of alliance among them, and key points of contestation. We then use the case studies as a basis to analyze themes and patterns, as well as variations and tensions, in parent activism across disability groups and across time.

Allies, Obstacles, or Something in Between?

Insofar as we speak of parents' movements, we must keep in mind that parents' activism, on a macro level, is politically and organizationally fragmented and that, on a micro level, parents tend to be pragmatic, exhibiting variation and fluidity in their rhetoric and affiliations. Parents are rarely simplistically bound to particular ideologies or identities; overwhelmingly they frame their activism in terms of the needs of their offspring as a starting point and broaden their interests and commitments from that starting point. It is also unclear how well parent organizations actually represent parents. Many of these organizations have become professionalized, and thus, in addition to parents, they contain a population of professionals whose interests may differ from those of parents. A small number of parents sit on the board of directors, and "grassroots" parent activism within the organization is largely channeled by the organization into fundraising or specific political campaigns. Much parent activism is outside of an organizational context as parents fight with school systems, raise awareness online, and otherwise work to remake the world.

These things said, three patterns are common: First, parent activists generally present themselves and their actions in terms of their relation to a child with a disability, the impact of that disability, and their perceived responsibility to their child. Second, parent activists perceive disability as more than an individual or family issue; they demand that society engage. The disability experience is shaped by society, and parents impose obligations on society to respond to disability. Third, although parents demand action by the state and fellow citizens, parents typically assert parental expertise and authority in making choices regarding their child's best interests. Thus, they seek communal support, but not communal mandates.

Across the activism documented in this book, parents clearly intend to improve the lives of their offspring with a disability and others in similar situations, and thus, they see themselves as allies to disabled people. Yet there is much disagreement in the disability community about priorities and needs. The disability rights mantra of "Nothing about us without us" is certainly relevant, but who sits within the category of "us"? Parents often see themselves as insiders, but that is not always how they are perceived by individuals with disabilities. To a large extent, this hinges on the parental assertion of expertise and authority, which undermines the autonomy and self-determination of their child or the disability community collectively by presuming to make decisions for them without input or consent.

Of central relevance, both at the interpersonal level and organizationally, are the realities of power—that is, the distribution of various forms of resources and opportunity structures. Who has the power to decide or to make things happen? Who is constrained or compelled and how? The parent-child relationship is overwhelmingly unequal as parents have greater legal, economic, and political capital (resources) than children and children are dependent on their parents for their very survival. This is even more true for children with disabilities. This imbalance may resolve as the child grows into adulthood, but it may not. Interpersonally, inaccessible housing, employment discrimination, medical and social support needs, and other factors may sustain dependence on parents into and through adulthood. On a macro political level, parents who organize collectively tend to have a tremendous capital advantage—more money, greater political connections, public sympathy, cultural acceptance of parental authority—as compared with activists with disabilities. Disability status may confer particular forms of social and symbolic capital, in particular a communal belief in self-determination, but in political battles, parent organizations carry tremendous weight. Disabled activists have struggled to have their own voices heard and respected. That said, in disability politics the interests of other players such as medical professionals, service providers, and fiscal conservatives often take center stage, displacing the voices of people with disabilities and family members.

Insofar as parents exercising power is intrinsic to the concept of parental activism, tension between parent activists and disabled activists is perhaps unavoidable. In that way it may be impossible for parents to simply be allies, and the extent to which they tend more toward or away from being allies may hinge largely on their disposition toward using their power. There are both individual parents and parent groups who, at times, willingly cede control or decision-making power to disabled adults and groups led by disabled adults. There are other parents and parent groups who wish to retain power for themselves on behalf of their children or to cede decision-making power to clinicians rather than to disabled activists. Especially when parents are advocating for their young children, the experiences or priorities of disabled adults may seem distant or in direct conflict with what parents think is best. Some parents cede control when their children reach adulthood. Other parents—especially those whose juvenile or adult children are perceived as not having the ability to communicate or decide for themselves—perceive a need for lifelong control.

Organizational Frames

At the organizational level, the disposition to use power is closely bound to the organization's conceptual frame—that is, its understandings of disability and proposed solutions. Organizations with frames similar to each other are more likely to operate in a similar fashion and to ally with one another, whereas conflicting frames reduce likely alliance and may even position organizations on opposites sides of an issue, although there are circumstances under which organizations with divergent frames may nevertheless find it expedient to ally or coordinate efforts with each other.

Parents are more likely to ally with organizations led by disabled activists when they share the following features of a frame: (1) prioritization of a social model over a medical model of disability, (2) a goal of integration and access across work, education, and other community institutions instead of exclusion and segregation, and (3) empowerment of people with disabilities. Overall, their distribution on these features is useful in explaining the patterns of relations we observe between the two sets of organizations in our case studies. It also helps us understand where various organizations stand, for or against, on pieces of proposed disability legislation. Parent-led organizations run nearly the full gamut of possible configurations on these three elements, but the very fact that they are parent-led organizations tends to lead them to subvert in some ways the ideal of empowerment and self-determination for people with disabilities, which positions them in at least a degree of tension with disability activist organizations. As a "new social movement," it is imperative that people with disabilities own and lead their own movement. The political process is an end unto itself for their movement, which the power of parents potentially undermines.

These organizational frames are useful for understanding organizational behaviors, but far less useful for understanding the behavior of individuals. For example, it is unclear to what extent parents "on the ground" pay attention to or even understand the different frames among parent organizations or consider the broad political agenda of these organizations. The typical parent is far more likely to be pragmatic, joining a group based on diagnosis, network ties, or a single issue of interest, than to be motivated by the organizational frame.

The Timing of Parent Activism

The variation in parental activism across the life span depends on the timing with which the disability manifests in the life course, the shifting needs of people with disabilities and their parents, and when parents interact with various systems related to disability. Historically, the timing of the rise of parent activist organizations depends to a degree on the cultural construction and historical timing of emerging diagnoses, as the instances of autism and mental illness illustrate. As research shows for many other social movements, activism also depends on access to resources. Disability groups prior to World War II were less common, and each group tended to have a variety of local organizations. The Arc, United Cerebral Palsy (UCP), and the Muscular Dystrophy Association (MDA) all emerged circa 1950. The historical case studies we present suggest this was no coincidence but instead resulted from a combination of changing resources and political opportunity structure, including dissatisfaction with state institutions, changing social norms, a new middle-class image of what middle-class life was supposed to be, greater capital resources among middle-class families, and greater political opportunities. Cultural pioneers demanded and created improving disability infrastructure, and that infrastructure in turn provided greater and new opportunities for the families who followed them.

A key element of this process was a transition from isolated disability identities grounded in having similar patterns of social relations around disability to realizing collective identities around each disability, by deliberately and actively building connections to other people, other families, in the same situation. This communication and the founding of first informal and then formal organizations that it enabled also opened a spectrum of potential strategies. Isolated families had little choice but to either handle their concerns themselves or hand them off to some other person or a state agency. Organizing enabled them to engage in strategies of collective action and mobilized far greater resources for lobbying legislators, pursuing redress through courts, and getting help from schools and government agencies.

However, the rise of parent activism groups for intellectual disability and cerebral palsy was not paralleled in mental illness, autism, or many forms of physical disability. Intellectual disability and cerebral palsy were historically diagnosed in childhood, whereas mental illness was thought to be a condition of adults, a belief that has dramatically changed over the past twenty years. The prevalence and cultural understanding of the autism diagnosis has changed greatly in recent decades. Likewise many physical disabilities come later in life, and those that do manifest early, such as congenital deafness or blindness, already had existing groups of adult disabled activists, whose movements largely subsumed the interests and movements of youth with those disabilities. Parent-led national organizations did not emerge in the postwar era for diagnoses that were not primarily understood as childhood diagnoses or for which there was already activism led by adults with disabilities (e.g., blindness and deafness). The success of the Arc and UCP in getting legislation enacted, building disability infrastructure, and altering cultural models of disability led to the emergence of national parent activist organizations for some other disabilities decades later.

Strategies for Social Change

Many strategies exist for effecting social change. One can try to achieve results on one's own, or band together with others to produce a collective result. Individually or collectively, efforts can be made to educate people about a social problem. Where people are supportive and do not have vested interest to the contrary, education alone can be effective, but in other situations something more significant may be needed.

Groups can lobby the legislative branch of state or federal government to enact new laws and the executive branch to enforce existing laws. They can sue, using the judicial branch of government to achieve results, a strategy most effectively used by groups or by people with wealth. They can engage in civil disobedience to try to disrupt existing structures and cause change. In all these strategies groups can mobilize their members and seek alliances with other groups if they share goals or organizational frames. Various disability groups have had success with each of these strategies, and each of these strategies is used by organizations led by disability activists and those led by parents. The frequencies with which various groups use each strategy varies somewhat, and depends on goals, resources, and context.

In relation to organizations led by disabled activists, the strategies of parent-led groups often matter less than the content or goal. For example, many parent organizations lobby; alliance or conflict depends on the goal of lobbying rather than the act of lobbying itself. That said, groups of disability activists are far more likely to engage in civil disobedience and other protests than are parent organizations. This may be in part because parent organizations have easier access to, and may more easily get results from, legitimate mechanisms of social change, or because parents may eschew the risks inherent in civil disobedience. This disparity again places alliances on shaky grounds as people with disabilities tend to have fewer resources yet bear the brunt of risk in activism.

The State

The state can be an oppressive force, as in the case of institutionalization, from which relief and liberation are sought. It also represents a source of power to shape laws and impose obligations on other people via lobbying, lawsuits, and rights claims. The history of disability activism often involves action directed at or involving the various branches of government at the federal, state, or local level.

The state (keeping in mind that "the state" is not a monolithic entity but really many actors with various roles, interests, and claims to authority) is deeply entwined in people's lives and creates a relational paradox. Parents demand autonomy for themselves from state control, even when receiving services and supports from the state. On the one hand, parent activism encourages intervention by, and often expansion of, the state. On the other hand, the scope and power of the state are the greatest threat to the autonomy parents desire, the greatest likely interference in the family. When wielded effectively by others, like activists with disabilities, state mandates often increase the relational power of people with disabilities and limit parent choice and autonomy. Thus, the work of disabled activists often feels to parents like it too is constraining them.

Similarly, for disability activists the state offers both a power to produce opportunities but also state control, surveillance, and limits, a risk of swapping one dependency for another. Public education and educational supports for disability are almost wholly in the hands of the state, and often and ultimately it is the authority of the state that stands behind and maintains the institutions of the medical model of disability. Parents and people with disabilities are not the only players enacting the power of the state.

The Narrative of Rights and Ideas of Disability Justice

As the history of disability is bound with the state, it is also a history of disability rights and other pathways to justice. In the liberal tradition the concept of state and rights are wed. The state is the prime codifier and enforcer of rights. It was also the interests of the state in cutting costs that greased the door of deinstitutionalization, opening opportunities for many people to become full members in their communities but also making a public disinvestment in and privatizing the supports and services needed by people with disabilities while raising the illusion of rights. After decades of rights legislation, we still see too many people without the basics needed for survival and participation.

The concept of a right is perhaps still considered the basic building block for making claims to fulfill the perceived needs and supports for persons with disabilities. It appears commonly in the narratives of individuals and the frames and rhetoric of organizations. As we see in the narratives of parents, the rights frame offers several key benefits: among other things, it focuses attention on issues of equity, access, and discrimination; recognizes people with disabilities as valued members of society; and provides legal mechanisms for creating and implementing change.

However, the concept of rights is fraught with challenges. Rights are frequently contested. There can be competing claims; parents claim a right to act on behalf of their child while the child claims a right to self-determination. Since the concept of a right is often used as a loose, narrative claim to enhance the likelihood of achieving a desired outcome (a symbolic claim more than a legal one), the claim is often weak and situations may wind up being resolved on a case-by-case basis. The rhetoric of rights creates a door to empowerment that others may not wish to open, such as for parents who demanded rights for their children with intellectual disabilities but then balk when those (adult) children exercise a right to intimacy, sexuality, and a right to family.

Because they are often negotiated on a situational basis, rights tend to favor those who have resources to sustain them, such as middle-class families with the social and cultural capital to be familiar with their legal rights and hold their own when challenged by school, governmental, or medical authorities, and the time and financial capital to support a court fight, if necessary. This is one of the reasons that parent activism blossomed with the rise of the middle class in the postwar era. Families that lack those resources are at a disadvantage in demanding and defending their rights. Organizing into groups can reduce this inequality, but organizational membership too tends to reflect privilege. Unfortunately this means that the applicability of rights is uneven, arbitrarily or systematically biased against marginalized populations, including persons with disabilities. Rights can even be used by politicians to mask disinvestment and privatization, promising "freedom" while removing essential services and investment in a public infrastructure necessary for people with disabilities to thrive.

Disability justice scholars and activists are critical of a neoliberal, rights-based approach and instead advocate for social justice policies. Disability justice activists fight for a range of social justice policies. These may include broad social transformations attentive to how various inequalities such as racism and poverty intertwine with disability oppression, universal economic and social rights that involve restructuring public institutions (e.g., education, criminal justice) to minimize inequality, and the provision of human rights (e.g., basic income supports, universal health care). Disability justice approaches seek solutions that are not dependent on an individual or household having, and expending, a certain amount of capital just to satisfy basic needs, and that reduce competition among marginalized populations for scarce resources and instead promote the uplift of the most marginalized. Justice-based goals move beyond individual rights to consider the needs of groups, and especially groups with intersectional identities who experience multiple forms of oppression.

It has been a point of tension in writing this book to determine the best ways to bring in rights versus justice approaches and to consider how, if at all, parents draw on a disability justice approach. The focus on parent advocacy and variation among parents made it challenging to deal effectively with variation among disabled activists (masking divisions like rights versus justice), and the focus on established, national parent organizations overlooked much disability justice activism that happens in smaller, often local organizations and in minority communities. Justice approaches are increasingly informing disability activism and even parent activism. In justice approaches, full justice depends on inclusion of all, in contrast to the rights approach that includes some and excludes others via the results of legislative manipulation and policy making. Justice considers the needs of both those receiving and those giving care. Justice recognizes that these roles are not absolute but may shift back and forth—that the cared-for in one context may be the caregiver in another. As parents care for young children, so do adult children care for their parents as they age—and this also is true for those with disability experience. However, the interdependence so central to a justice-based narrative must center, not mask, relations of power, as it is possible to have interdependence that reinforces inequality and disparity in terms of gender, disability, or other statuses. Thus, it is important to trace pathways of power and control, and who may be directing and who may be manipulated, in any relationship between individuals or groups.

Temporal and Spatial Shifts

During different historical periods and throughout life spans, the roles parents play in their children's lives change over time. Looking across historical eras, institutionalization as a means for caring for people with disabilities waxed and waned over the twentieth and twenty-first centuries. In some periods, and for certain social groups, good parenting meant the creation and maintaining of these institutions and putting children in them. In other periods parents were expected to care for their children at home—no matter how complex the physical or emotional needs or the scarcity of resources to help them. Understandings of diagnoses have changed over time as feared conditions became treatable and treatable conditions became "curable"—at least in some parents' understandings.

In the United States and many other parts of the world, parents created structures and supports for their children where none yet existed. They generated and managed resources where structural support from governments was absent and worked to change laws and create policies to ensure needed structural supports would come into being and remain available. In the matters of generating resources and programs and ensuring eligibility for benefits, parent groups and those led by disabled people were able to work together effectively. However, in matters that involved control—the right to choose or refuse services or treatment, control finances, and live independently or in least restrictive environments—parent groups and groups led by disabled people often conflicted. The outcomes of this activism then shaped future opportunities, activism, and relationships.

Over the course of life, parents and their offspring age and transition across various life stages and through many social systems, a process dominated by fluidity. Parents of young children often are just building their networks with other parents and are enmeshed in medical and educational systems. Once their child graduates from high school, families hit the "disability cliff." Services disappear, clear avenues for parent involvement also disappear, and parents must navigate a complex landscape of public and private systems that may or may not offer jobs, housing, recreation, and other opportunities for their loved ones. If disability is acquired later in life, parents may find that they have almost no legitimate pathways to advocate for their adult son or daughter. Parents themselves also undergo life transitions, as they retire, age, divorce, or experience health changes. The service system fails miserably at adapting to the fluidity of life. Benefits do not easily transfer across state or even county lines, long waiting lists preclude easily changing services or providers, and the focus on bureaucratic efficiency at times brutally minimizes unpredictable variations, some of which are the wonders that make life fulfilling, such as the unexpected decision to stay out late or the chance encounter with a person that leads to romance. As parents themselves age, they worry. Most parent activists have invested significant energy into ensuring a high quality of life for their child, and sadly they have little faith that the community, politicians, or service providers will prioritize the best interests of their offspring. A lifetime of fights with systems and services, massive changes, and fluctuations with each new political administration have done little to reassure parents.

Disabled Parents

Often obscured or erased from the narrative is the reality of disabled parents. While we include some parents with disabilities in the interviews, stories and analysis, they did not receive sufficient attention as a distinct category of analysis. Again, our focus on large, established national parent organizations yielded few examples of parents who identified as disabled advocating for their disabled children. These parents may be primarily in organizations led by people with disabilities, yet another example of where simple binaries (e.g., nondisabled parents versus disabled children) do not represent the lived experience of many. When organizations led by people with disabilities focus on parenting, the focus tends to be on the rights of people with disabilities as parents (e.g., to engage in sexuality, to be free from sterilization, to maintain custody of their children, to have supports in parenting); they rarely frame their activism in terms of the rights of the children with disabilities.

There are many fascinating questions related to parent identification with disability: Does having the same diagnosis as your child or related disability experience provide insight and an increased tendency toward alliance? Are the disabled children of disabled parents more likely to be brought up in disability culture, disability pride, and with a greater exposure and commitment to activism? How do parents with disabilities situate their activism and how do they navigate the often distinct worlds of disability activism and parent activism? These questions are beyond the scope of this book, and offer a rich area for future research.

Building Alliances

One of the central goals of this book is to explore points of alliance between parents and disabled activists. We engage in this project not to criticize either group or further polarize, but to promote meaningful dialogue. In many ways it is a deeply personal project for us. For example, Pamela's mother, Barbara Kilcup, was a special education teacher and at first a strident parent advocate when her children were young. Over time, Barbara and her daughter Hope worked together and became strongly aligned with disabled activists. Barbara ended up withdrawing and even criticizing parent-led organizations such as the ARC and Autism Speaks, though she remained active in professional and activist organizations such as PAL, a Rhode Island parent information and advocacy organization,[1] and TASH,[2] in which parents worked in alliance with professionals and activists. For Pamela this served as a prime example of how parents can be powerful allies. Deeply impressed by this activist approach, Pamela asked Hope and Barbara to collaborate in writing articles and presenting at the Society for Disability Studies in 2007.[3] Barbara and Hope offer a potent example of a mother's activist choices.

In the process of researching this book we also learned about the powerful alliance work that sibling activist Gini Laurie engaged in throughout most of the twentieth century.[4] Virginia Grace Wilson "Gini" Laurie (June 10, 1913–June 28, 1989) is known as one of the "grandmothers" of the U.S. Independent Living Movement (the other "grandmother" being Mary Switzer). She was born after two of her older siblings died of polio and a third was disabled by polio and died when Gini was young. Her mother was an artist and her father a medical doctor, and they named her Virginia Grace after her two sisters who had died. Both parents were clearly dedicated to the cause of fighting polio, commemorating those who perished and supporting those who survived. Gini was profoundly affected by her family history and the death of her brother, who had survived polio but been disabled. Her parents and siblings influenced Gini's life course to support and advocate for disabled people. In the 1950s she founded Post-Polio Health International and International Ventilator Users Network, and later she supported cross-disability activism and the foundation of the Independent Living Movement in the 1970s.[5] There does not seem to have been a strong parent-advocacy component to polio activism. Polio activism involved a unified approach of disabled people, families, and professionals. Could this have been influenced by Gini Laurie's collaborative and alliance-based leadership?

As displayed by Pam's mother and Gini Laurie, crucial steps to alliance include working alongside disabled activists, nurturing and supporting one's family members in their own activism, and being humbly appreciative of and open to the perspectives of disabled activists. Disability activism tends to be strongest when organizations and even families work together. That said, alliance can be powerful but not if significant and noteworthy differences are erased in the process. There are distinct perspectives and forms of knowledge to be gained from social and life experiences of both parents and disabled people. It is also important to attend to particular experiences of these categories, as parenting and the disability experience can vary profoundly along lines of economic, race, ethnicity, and region. The realities of power, whether between parents and children or across these other fault lines, must always be acknowledged.

Politicians gain by pitting parents against each other, parents against disabled activists, and different disability groups against each other. When different groups are scratching for scarce resources, messaging and action get obscured and the political response can be minimal.

Together we can demand the rights and supports that we need to live fulfilled, active, and meaningful lives. This does not mean that we are all going to agree, but we need to engage in the conversation and look earnestly for ways to provide uplift for people across disabilities, races, sexualities, and socioeconomic classes. Parents discovered long ago that they could accomplish far more by working to benefit all children with disabilities rather than just their own child. This is a valuable lesson as we move forward and consider ways to continue to empower and support all people with disabilities.

Appendix

A Note on Methods

I n conducting our analysis, we rely on a broad range of data, including organizational documents, archived documents, news reports, and online primary sources such as blogs and chat rooms. Interviews were also used to supplement organizational and online sources. These interviews focused on established activists, older activists who had less online presence, and self-advocates with intellectual disabilities who also are less visible online than autistic and physically disabled activists. While interviews are an established and valuable data source, many activists today have accessible virtual presence, and there are also online repositories of interviews with parent activists and disabled activists. Therefore, taking the time of parents and activists to capture their public positions and ideas regarding disability activism seemed unwarranted except when there was not an alternative source. Moreover, our goal is to showcase the range of ideas and tensions across organizations, not gather representative, generalizable views across categories of parents. Interview data and online sources are used alongside each other as data.

Twenty-seven interviews were conducted. These included sixteen with parent or family-member activists, nine with self-advocates (two of whom were also parents, one of a child with a disability), and four with professionals in activist organizations. Interviews followed an interview guide with broad, open-ended questions focused on the content, strategies, and meaning of activism. The interviews focused on the interviewees' understandings of rights, their organizational affiliations, their perceptions of various disability-related organizations, and their knowledge of alliance or conflicts among organizations. Most interviews were conducted by phone, although a few were conducted in person; they were all audio-recorded, transcribed, and analyzed using techniques of grounded theory.[1] Interviews were approved by the Institutional Review Board at Shippensburg University. Table A.1 offers a summary of the interviewees.

TABLE A.1. INTERVIEWEE INFORMATION

Name (assigned)	Status	Age	Race	Disability category
Yvonne	Parent	67	White	Intellectual disability (ID)
Erica	Parent	76	African American	ID, autism, physical
Donna	Parent	65	White	ID, epilepsy
Harold	Parent	84	White	ID
Jack	Parent	88	White	ID
Sara	Parent	69	White	Autism, ID, physical
Liz	Parent	89	White	ID, medically complex
Christopher	Parent	71	White	Autism, ID, behavioral
Veronica	Parent	56	Asian	ID
Miriam	Parent	45	White	Physical, medically complex
Gail	Parent	39	White	ID
Emina	Parent	65	White immigrant	ID, cerebral palsy (CP), brain damage
Latasha	Parent, self-advocate	35	Mixed	Autism
Izzie	Parent, self-advocate	45	African American	ID, CP
Cindy	Sibling	58	White	ID
Destinee	Daughter	21	White	Mental illness
Jenny	Self-advocate	30	White	ID
Frank	Self-advocate	48	African American	ID
Jawon	Self-advocate	46	African American	ID
Mark	Self-advocate	52	White	ID
Sam	Self-advocate	54	White	ID
Tiffany	Self-advocate	46	African American	ID
Susan	Self-advocate	34	White	ID
Doug	Professional		White	Nondisabled
Naomi	Professional		White	Nondisabled
Becky	Professional		White	Nondisabled
Julie	Professional		White	Nondisabled

Notes

INTRODUCTION

1. Sophia Grant, *"One of Those": The Progress of a Mongoloid Child* (New York: Pageant, 1957), 17.

2. Ibid., 14.

3. Quoted in Kathleen W. Jones, "Education for Children with Mental Retardation: Parent Activism, Public Policy, and Family Ideology in the 1950s," in *Mental Retardation in America*, ed. Steven Noll and James W. Trent Jr. (New York: New York University Press, 2004), 339.

4. Boggs Center on Developmental Disabilities, "About Elizabeth M. Boggs, PhD," available at http://rwjms.rutgers.edu/boggscenter/about/about_elizabeth.html (accessed June 5, 2015).

5. "Supreme Court Says 'Congress Intended to Open the Door to All Qualified Children,'" *Wrightslaw*, available at http://www.wrightslaw.com/info/relsvcs.garretf.htm (accessed September 2, 2016); Cedar Rapids Community School District v. Garret F., 536 U.S. 66 (1999).

6. Steven E. Brown, "Zona and Ed Roberts: Twentieth Century Pioneers," *Disability Studies Quarterly* 20, no. 1 (2000): 26–42; Corbett Joan OToole, *Fading Scars: My Queer Disability History* (Fort Worth, TX: Autonomous Press, 2015).

7. Lisa Morguess, "Why I Fight for Inclusion for My Kids (And Your Kid Too)," April 29, 2014, available at http://www.lisamorguess.com/2014/04/29/fight-inclusion-kid-kid/.

8. For information on the development of disability rights movements, see Doris Zames Fleischer and Frieda Zames, *The Disability Rights Movement: From Charity to Confrontation* (Philadelphia: Temple University Press, 2011); Kim E. Nielsen, *A Disability History of the United States* (Boston: Beacon Press, 2012); Fred Pelka, *What We Have Done: An Oral History of the Disability Rights Movement* (Amherst: University of

Massachusetts Press, 2012); and Joseph P. Shapiro, *No Pity: People with Disabilities Forging a New Civil Rights Movement* (New York: Broadway Books, 1994).

9. Angela Frederick and Dara Shifrer, "Race and Disability: From Analogy to Intersectionality," *Sociology of Race and Ethnicity* 5, no. 2 (2019): 2000–2014; Alondra Nelson, *Body and Soul: The Black Panther Party and the Fight against Medical Discrimination* (Minneapolis: University of Minnesota Press, 2011); OToole, *Fading Scars*.

10. Elizabeth M. Boggs, "Who's Putting Whose Head in the Sand . . . or in the Clouds as the Case May Be," in *Parents Speak Out*, ed. A. P. Turnbull and H. R. Turnbull (Columbus, OH: Charles E. Merrill, 1978), 63.

11. Johanna Li, "Girl, 14, with Spinal Muscular Atrophy Decides to End Her Life: 'This Is Enough Pain,'" *Inside Edition*, July 15, 2016, available at http://www.insideedition.com/headlines/17543-girl-14-with-spinal-muscular-atrophy-decides-to-end-her-life-this-is-enough-pain.

12. Meg Wagner, "Activists Fight to Stop Wisconsin Teen with Incurable Disease Who Has Decided to Die," *New York Daily News*, September 7, 2016, available at http://www.nydailynews.com/news/national/activists-fight-stop-wisconsin-teen-plan-life-article-1.2781497.

13. Some scholars have illuminated the intense danger to the lives of people with disabilities and the number of disabled people killed by their own parents. See S. E. Smith, "When Parents Kill Disabled Children, We Must Hold Society Responsible," *Rewire News*, May 18, 2015, available at https://rewire.news/article/2015/05/18/parents-kill-disabled-children-must-hold-society-responsible/.

14. Rachel Premack, "'I'm Going to Be Free': Terminally Ill Wisconsin Teen Schedules Her Death and One 'Last Dance,'" *Washington Post*, July 21, 2016, available at https://www.washingtonpost.com/news/morning-mix/wp/2016/07/21/one-last-dance-for-this-wisconsin-teen-who-has-scheduled-her-own-death.

15. Diane Coleman, "Statement on Mourning the Death of Jerika Bolen," *Not Dead Yet*, September 23, 2016, available at http://notdeadyet.org/2016/09/statement-on-mourning-the-death-of-jerika-bolen.html.

16. See James I. Charlton, *Nothing About Us Without Us: Disability Oppression and Empowerment* (Berkeley: University of California Press, 2000); Fleischer and Zames, *The Disability Rights Movement*; Nielsen, *Disability History of the United States*; and Pelka, *What We Have Done*.

17. Case studies often focus on a single person, event, or organization. In this work, each case is the activism related to a specific impairment group—intellectual disability, psychiatric disability, autism, and physical disability—as it develops over time, focusing specifically on the activism of people with disabilities and parents.

18. Sara Green, Rosalyn Benjamin Darling, and Loren Wilbers, "Struggles and Joys: A Review of Research on the Social Experience of Parenting Disabled Children," in *Research in Social Science and Disability*, vol. 9, *Sociology Looking at Disability: What Did We Know and When Did We Know It*, ed. Sara E. Green and Sharon Barnartt (Bingley, UK: Emerald Press, 2016), 261–285.

19. Samuel R. Bagenstos, "The Disability Cliff," *Democracy* 35 (Winter 2015): 55–67; Michael Bérubé, "Don't Let My Son Plunge off the 'Disability Cliff' When I'm Gone," *USA Today*, April 2, 2018, available at https://www.usatoday.com/story/opinion/2018/04/02/dont-let-my-son-plunge-off-disability-cliff-column/443138002/; Valerie Leiter, *Their Time Has Come: Youth with Disabilities on the Cusp of Adulthood* (New Brunswick, NJ: Rutgers University Press, 2012).

20. Leiter, *Their Time Has Come*; Colin Ong-Dean, *Distinguishing Disability: Parents, Privilege, and Special Education* (Chicago: University of Chicago Press, 2009).

21. Rosalyn Benjamin Darling, *Disability and Identity: Negotiating Self in a Changing Society* (Boulder, CO: Lynne Rienner, 2013); Dennis Hogan, *Family Consequences of Childhood Disabilities* (New York: Russell Sage Foundation, 2012). See also David E. Gray, "Gender and Coping: The Parents of Children with High Functioning Autism," *Social Science and Medicine* 56 (2003): 631–642; and Sara Green, Rosalyn Benjamin Darling, and Loren Wilbers, "Has the Parent Experience Changed over Time? A Meta-analysis of Qualitative Studies of Parents of Children with Disabilities from 1960–2012," in *Research and Social Science and Disability*, vol. 7, *Disability and Intersecting Statuses*, ed. Barbara Altman and Sharon Barnartt (Bingley, UK: Emerald Group, 2012), 97–168.

22. For scholarship on scientific motherhood, see Rima D. Apple, *Perfect Motherhood: Science and Childbearing in America* (New Brunswick, NJ: Rutgers University Press, 2006); Kathleen Jones, "'Mother Made Me Do It': Mother-Blaming and the Women of the Child Guidance Movement," in *Bad Mothers: The Politics of Blame in Twentieth-Century America*, ed. Molly Ladd-Taylor and Lauri Umanski (New York: New York University Press, 1998), 99–126; and Jennifer Burek Pierce, "Science, Advocacy, and 'The Sacred and Intimate Things of Life': Republican Motherhood as a Progressive Era Cause in Women's Magazines," *American Periodicals* 18, no. 1 (2008): 69–95.

23. Linda M. Blum, "Mother-Blame in the Prozac Nation: Raising Kids with Invisible Disabilities," *Gender and Society* 21, no. 2 (2007): 2020–2026; Molly Ladd-Taylor and Lauri Umanski, eds., *Bad Mothers: The Politics of Blame in Twentieth-Century America* (New York: New York University Press, 1998).

24. Susan L. Neeley-Barnes, Heather Hall, Ruth J. Roberts, and J. Carolyn Graff, "Parenting a Child with an Autism Spectrum Disorder: Public Perceptions and Parental Conceptualizations," *Journal of Family Social Work* 14, no. 3 (2011): 208–225; Amy C. Sousa, "From Refrigerator Mothers to Warrior-Heroes: The Cultural Identity Transformation of Mothers Raising Children with Intellectual Disabilities," *Symbolic Interaction* 34, no. 2 (2011): 220–243.

25. Ladd-Taylor and Umanski, *Bad Mothers*.

26. Jones, "'Mother Made Me Do It'"; Gail Landsman, *Reconstructing Motherhood and Disability in an Age of "Perfect" Babies* (New York: Routledge, 2009).

27. Linda M. Blum, *Raising Generation Rx: Mothering Kids with Invisible Disabilities in an Age of Inequality* (New York: New York University Press, 2015); Laura Mauldin, *Made to Hear: Cochlear Implants and Raising Deaf Children* (Minneapolis: University of Minnesota Press, 2016); Joan Wolf, *Is Breast Best? Taking on the Breastfeeding Experts and the New High Stakes of Motherhood* (New York: New York University Press, 2011).

28. Victoria Pitts-Taylor, "The Plastic Brain: Neoliberalism and the Neuronal Self," *Health* 14, no. 6 (2010): 635–652; Ilina Singh, "Brain Talk: Power and Negotiation in Children's Discourse about Self, Brain, and Behavior," *Sociology of Health and Illness* 35, no. 6 (2013): 813–827; Maria Timberlake, Walter Lautz, Marji Warfield, and Guiseppina Chiri, "'In the Driver's Seat': Parent Perceptions of Choice in a Participant-Directed Medicaid Waiver Program for Young Children with Autism," *Journal of Autism and Developmental Disabilities* 44, no. 4 (2014): 903–914; Glenda Wall, "Mothers' Experiences with Intensive Parenting and Brain Development Discourse," *Women's Studies International Forum* 33, no. 3 (2010): 253–263.

29. Allan V. Horowitz, *Creating Mental Illness* (Chicago: University of Chicago, 2002); Ronald C. Kessler, Olga Demler, Richard G. Frank, Mark Olson, Harold Alan

Pincus, Ellen E. Walters, Philip Wang, Kenneth B. Wells, and Alan M. Zaslavsky, "Prevalence and Treatment of Mental Disorders," *New England Journal of Medicine* 352 (2005): 2515–2523.

30. Katie Caldwell, Sarah Parker Harris, and M. Renko, "The Potential of Social Entrepreneurship: Conceptual Tools for Applying Theory to Policy and Practice," *Intellectual and Developmental Disabilities* 50, no. 6 (2012): 505–518; Kelly Fritsch, "Contesting the Neoliberal Affects of Disabled Parenting: Towards a Relational Emergence of Disability," in *Disabling Domesticity*, ed. Michael Rembis (New York: Palgrave Macmillan, 2016), 243–267.

31. Sharon Hays, *The Cultural Contradictions of Motherhood* (New Haven, CT: Yale University Press, 1996).

32. Hogan, *Family Consequences of Childhood Disabilities*, 13.

33. Sylvia Ann Hewlett and Cornel West, *The War against Parents: What We Can Do for America's Beleaguered Moms and Dads* (New York: Houghton Mifflin, 1998).

34. Kelly Mullen-McWilliams, "What #ActuallyAustistic People Want You to Know about 'Autism Mommies' on the Internet," *Romper*, January 23, 2018, available at https://www.romper.com/p/what-actuallyautistic-people-want-you-to-know-about-autism-mommies-on-the-internet-7863758.

35. Annette Lareau, *Unequal Childhoods: Class, Race, and Family Life* (Berkeley: University of California Press, 2003); Ong-Dean, *Distinguishing Disability*.

36. Catherine Kramarczuk, "Parental 'Power' and Racial Inequality in Special Education," presentation at the Annual Meeting of the American Sociological Association, Philadelphia, August 11–14, 2018.

37. Thomas Knestrict and Debora Kuchey, "Welcome to Holland: Characteristics of Resilient Families Raising Children with Severe Disabilities," *Journal of Family Studies* 15, no. 3 (2009): 227–244.

38. Amber M. Angell and Olga Solomon, "'If I Was a Different Ethnicity, Would She Treat Me the Same?' Latino Parents' Experiences Obtaining Autism Services," *Disability and Society* 32, no. 8 (2017): 1142–1164.

39. Susan J. Martorell and Gabriela A. Martorell, "Bridging Uncharted Waters in Georgia: Down Syndrome Association of Atlanta Outreach to Latino/a Families," *American Journal of Community Psychology* 37, no. 3–4 (2006): 219–225; Summer L. G. Stanley, "The Advocacy Efforts of African American Mothers of Children with Disabilities in Rural Special Education: Considerations for School Professionals," *Rural Special Education Quarterly* 34, no. 4 (2015): 3–17.

40. Lanita Jacobs, Mary Lawlor, and Cheryl Mattingly, "I/We Narratives among African-American Families Raising Children with Special Needs," *Culture, Medicine, and Psychiatry* 35 (2011): 3–25.

41. Mauldin, *Made to Hear*; see also Erica Prussing, Elisa J. Sobo, Elizabeth Walker, and Paul S. Kurtin, "Between 'Desperation' and Disability Rights: A Narrative Analysis of Complimentary/Alternative Medicine Use by Parents for Children with Down Syndrome," *Social Science and Medicine* 60, no. 3 (2005): 587–598.

42. Jennifer A. Reich, *Calling the Shots: Why Parents Reject Vaccines* (New York: New York University Press, 2016).

43. Gail (pseudonym), phone interview by the author, September 2018. See the Appendix for more about our interview methods.

44. Larry A. Jones, *Doing Disability Justice: 75 Years of Family Advocacy* (n.p.: Lulu, 2010).

45. Allison C. Carey, *On the Margins of Citizenship: Intellectual Disability and Civil Rights in Twentieth-Century America* (Philadelphia: Temple University Press, 2009); Al Condeluci, *The Essence of Interdependence* (Pittsburgh: Lash Associates, 2009); Eva Kittay, "When Caring Is Justice and Justice Is Caring," in *Public Cultures*, ed. Carol A. Breckenridge and Candace Volger, (Durham: University of North Carolina Press, 2001), 557–580; Galvin Rose, "Challenging the Need for Gratitude," *Journal of Sociology* 40, no. 2 (2004): 137–155.

46. Allison C. Carey, "Citizenship and the Family: Parents of Children with Disabilities, the Pursuit of Rights, and Paternalism," in *Civil Disabilities: Citizenship, Membership, and Belonging*, ed. Nancy J. Hirschmann and Beth Linker (Philadelphia: University of Pennsylvania, 2015), 165–185.

47. Simi Linton, *Claiming Disability: Knowledge and Identity* (New York: New York University Press, 1998); Michael Oliver, *Understanding Disability: From Theory to Practice*, 2nd ed. (Cambridge, UK: Red Globe Press, 2009).

48. Nancy Fraser and Linda Gordon, "Contract versus Charity," *Socialist Review* 22, no. 3 (1992): 45–67; Nancy Fraser, "Genealogy of Dependency: Tracing a Keyword of the US Welfare State," *Signs* 19, no. 2 (1994): 309–336; Judith Levine, *Ain't No Trust* (Berkeley: University of California Press, 2013).

49. Angela Frederick, "Mothering while Disabled," *Contexts* 13, no. 4 (2014): 30–35.

50. Molly Ladd-Taylor, *Fixing the Poor: Eugenic Sterilization and Child Welfare in the Twentieth Century* (Baltimore: Johns Hopkins University Press, 2017).

51. For works on the liberal criteria for rights, see Licia Carlson, *The Faces of Intellectual Disability* (Bloomington: University of Indiana Press, 2009); Eva Feder Kittay and Licia Carlson, eds., *Cognitive Disability and Its Challenges to Moral Philosophy* (Malden, MA: Wiley-Blackwell, 2010); and Carey, *On the Margins of Citizenship*.

52. OToole, *Fading Scars*, 241, 244.

53. Sara (pseudonym), phone interview by the author, July 2014.

54. Bérubé, "Don't Let My Son Plunge off the 'Disability Cliff.'"

55. Andrew Solomon, *Far from the Tree: Parents, Children, and the Search for Identity* (New York: Scribner, 2013).

56. Harmony D. Newman and Laura M. Carpenter, "Embodiment without Bodies? Analysis of Embodiment in US-Based Pro-Breastfeeding and Anti-male Circumcision Movements," *Sociology of Health and Illness* 36, no. 5 (2014): 639–654.

57. OToole, *Fading Scars*, 235.

58. Ibid., 244.

59. Jeffrey J. Iovannone, "The Mad Woman in the Garden: Decolonizing Domesticity in Shani Mootoo's *Cereus Blooms at Night*," in Rembis, *Disabling Domesticity* (New York: Palgrave Macmillan, 2017), 270; see also Zachary A. Richter, "Melting Down the Family Unit: A Neuroqueer Critique of Table-Readiness," in Rembis, *Disabling Domesticity*, 335–348.

60. Susan Moller Okin, *Justice, Gender, and the Family* (New York: Basic Books, 1989).

61. Katalin Fábián and Elźbieta Korolczuk, *Rebellious Parents: Parental Movements in Central Eastern Europe and Russia* (Bloomington: Indiana University Press, 2017).

62. Mario Diani, "Organizational Fields and Social Movement Dynamics," in *The Future of Social Movement Research: Dynamics, Mechanisms, and Processes*, ed. Jacquelien van Stekelenburg, Conny Roggeband, and Bert Klandermans (Minneapolis: University of Minnesota Press, 2013), 141–168.

63. For scholarship on new social movements, see Steven E. Buechler, "New Social Movement Theories," *Sociological Quarterly* 36, no. 3 (1995): 441–464; and Steven E. Buechler, *Social Movements in Advanced Capitalism* (Oxford: Oxford University Press, 1999).

64. Brigitte Charmak, "Autism and Social Movements: French Parents' Associations and International Autistic Individuals' Organizations," *Sociology of Health and Illness* 30, no. 1 (2008): 76–96.

65. Hanna B. Rosqvist, Charlotte Brownlow, and Linsday O'Dell, "'An Association for All'—Notions of the Meaning of Autistic Self-Advocacy Politics within a Parent-Dominated Movement," *Journal of Community and Applied Psychology* 25, no. 3 (2015): 219–231.

66. Alison Kafer, *Feminist Queer Crip* (Bloomington: Indiana University Press, 2013), 28.

67. Ibid., 46.

68. Madeline C. Burghardt, *Broken: Institutions, Families, and the Construction of Intellectual Disability* (Montreal: McGill-Queen's University Press, 2018), 66.

69. Naomi (pseudonym), phone interview by the author, June 2014.

70. Melissa Stoltz, "Voice," *Garden of My Heart* (blog), January 8, 2016, available at http://gardenofmyheart.com/2016/01/08/voice/.

71. Nancy Mairs, *Waist High in the World* (Boston: Beacon Press, 1996).

CHAPTER 1

1. Emina (pseudonym), interview by the author, May 2019.

2. For the history of parent activism related to intellectual disability, see Barbara Blair, "The Parents Council for Retarded Children and Social Change in Rhode Island, 1951–1970," *Rhode Island History* 40 (1981): 145–159; Allison C. Carey, *On the Margins of Citizenship: Intellectual Disability and Civil Rights in Twentieth-Century America* (Philadelphia: Temple University Press, 2009); David Goode, *And Now Let's Build a Better World: The Story of the Association for the Help of Retarded Children, New York City, 1948–1998* (Ph.D. diss., City University of New York, 1998); Larry A. Jones, *Doing Disability Justice: 75 Years of Family Advocacy* (n.p.: Lulu, 2010); and Susan Schwarzenberger, *Becoming Citizens: Family Life and the Politics of Disability* (Seattle: University of Washington Press, 2005).

3. Robert Bogdan and Steven Taylor, "The Judged, Not the Judges: An Insider's View of Mental Retardation," *American Psychologist* 31 (1976): 47–52.

4. Robert L. Schalock et al., *Intellectual Disability: Definition, Classifications and Systems of Support*, 11th ed. (Washington, DC: American Association on Intellectual and Developmental Disabilities, 2010).

5. Note that "developmental disability" is sometimes used to mean "intellectual disability," but by law "developmental disability" is an umbrella term that encompasses all disabilities originating before the age of twenty-two. Similarly, "cognitive disability" is an umbrella term for all disabilities that affect cognitive processing, including, but not limited to, intellectual disability.

6. Kim Nielsen, *A Disability History of the United States* (Boston: Beacon Press, 2012); Parnel Wickham, "Idiocy and the Laws in Colonial England," *Mental Retardation* 39, no. 2 (2001): 104–113.

7. James W. Trent Jr., *Inventing the Feeble Mind: A History of Mental Retardation in the United States* (Berkeley: University of California Press, 1994); Carey, *On the Mar-*

gins of Citizenship; Steven Noll, *Feeble-Minded in Our Midst* (Chapel Hill: University of North Carolina Press, 1995); Nicole H. Rafter, "The Criminalization of Mental Retardation," in *Mental Retardation in America*, ed. James W. Trent Jr. and Steven Noll (New York: New York University Press, 2004), 232–257.

8. John H. Blume, Sheri Lynn Johnson, Paul Marcus, and Emily Paavola, "A Tale of Two (and Possibly Three) *Atkins*: Intellectual Disability and Capital Punishment Twelve Years after the Supreme Court's Creation of a Categorical Bar," *William and Mary Bill of Rights* 23 (2014): 393–414. In response to the *Atkins* decision, Florida created a strict IQ cutoff of 70, and Texas made it increasingly difficult to prove deficits in adaptive functioning.

9. Nielsen, *A Disability History*.

10. James W. Trent Jr., *The Manliest Man: Samuel G. Howe and the Contours of Nineteenth-Century Reform* (Amherst: University of Massachusetts, 2012).

11. Philip M. Ferguson, *Abandoned to Their Fate: Social Policy and Practice toward Severely Retarded People in America, 1820–1920* (Philadelphia: Temple University Press, 1994); Liat Ben-Moshe, Chris Chapman, and Allison Carey, eds., *Disability Incarcerated: Disability and Imprisonment in the United States and Canada* (New York: Palgrave Macmillan, 2014).

12. Kathleen W. Jones, "Education for Children with Mental Retardation: Parent Activism, Public Policy, and Family Ideology in the 1950s," in Trent and Noll, *Mental Retardation in America*, 332–350; David Wright, *Downs: A History of a Disability* (Oxford: Oxford University Press, 2011).

13. Trent, *Inventing the Feeble Mind*.

14. George Howard Earle III, "Remarks of Governor George H. Earle, Governor of Pennsylvania, at Ground-Breaking Ceremonies, Laurelton State Village," September 23, 1937, box 15, Speeches, 1937–1938, Governor George Howard Earle III Papers, Pennsylvania State Archives, Harrisburg, PA.

15. Allison C. Carey and Lucy Gu, "Walking the Line between the Past and the Future: Parents' Resistance and Commitment to Institutionalization," in Ben-Moshe, Chapman, and Carey, *Disability Incarcerated*, 101–119.

16. Minnesota Council on Developmental Disabilities, "Willowbrook Leads to New Protections of Rights," *Moments in Disability History* 9 (2013), available at http://mn.gov/web/prod/static/mnddc/live/ada-legacy/ada-legacy-moment9.html.

17. Burton Blatt and Fred Kaplan, *Christmas in Purgatory: A Photographic Essay on Mental Retardation* (Boston: Allyn and Bacon, 1966); Geoffrey Reaume, *Remembrance of Patients Past* (Toronto: University of Toronto Press, 2009); Steven J. Taylor, *Acts of Conscience: World War II, Mental Institutions, and Religious Objectors* (Syracuse, NY: Syracuse University Press, 2009).

18. Letter from Mrs. J. V. Fackiner to Governor James Duff, March 29, 1948, box 25, Mental Health, James H. Duff Official Papers, Pennsylvania State Archives.

19. *Unforgotten: Twenty-Five Years after Willowbrook*, dir. Jack Fisher (Studio Lights Pictures, 1996), available at https://www.youtube.com/watch?v=FcjRIZFQcUY.

20. Nielsen, *A Disability History*; Trent, *The Manliest Man*.

21. Phil Brown et al., "Embodied Health Movements: New Approaches to Social Movements in Health," *Sociology of Health and Illness* 26, no. 1 (2004): 50–80.

22. Ibid., 62.

23. Jones, *Doing Disability Justice*.

24. John D. McCarthy and Mayer N. Zald, "Resource Mobilization and Social Movements: A Partial Theory," *American Journal of Sociology* 82, no. 6 (1977): 1212–1241.

Resource mobilization theory focuses on the role of resources in social movement activity and suggests that social movement activity increases as access to resources increases.

25. In 1890 fourteen states had institutions for people with intellectual disabilities, but by 1923 forty states had at least one institution, and several states had multiple state-run institutions. James W. Trent Jr. documented that "between 1950 and 1970, state authorities built, refurbished, and added to more public facilities than in any other period of American history." Trent, *Inventing the Feeble Mind*, 237.

26. Margret A. Winzer, *The History of Special Education: From Isolation to Integration* (Washington, DC: Gallaudet University Press, 1993).

27. On relative deprivation theory, see Denton E. Morrison, "Some Notes toward Theory on Relative Deprivation, Social Movements, and Social Change," *American Behavioral Scientist* 14, no. 5 (1971): 675–690.

28. Anonymous letter to Governor Duff, May 30, 1949, box 25, Mental Health, James H. Duff Official Papers, Pennsylvania State Archives.

29. Doug McAdam, *Political Process and the Development of Black Insurgency, 1930–1970* (Chicago: University of Chicago Press, 1982); Doug McAdam, "Political Opportunities: Conceptual Origins, Current Problems, Future Directions," in *Comparative Perspectives on Social Movements*, ed. Doug McAdam, John D. McCarthy, and Mayer N. Zald (Cambridge: Cambridge University Press, 1996), 20–40.

30. Edward Shorter, *The Kennedy Family and the Story of Mental Retardation* (Philadelphia: Temple University Press, 2000).

31. Robert D. Benford and David A. Snow, "Framing Processes and Social Movements: An Overview and Assessment," *Annual Review of Sociology* 26 (2000): 611–639; David A. Snow and Robert D. Benford, "Master Frames and Cycles of Protest," in *Frontiers in Social Movement Theory*, ed. Aldon D. Morris and C. M. Mueller (New Haven, CT: Yale University Press, 1992), 133–155.

32. Katherine Castles, "'Nice, Average Americans': Postwar Parents, Groups and the Defense of the Normal Family," in Trent and Noll, *Mental Retardation in America*, 351–370; Rosemary F. Dybwad, *Perspectives on a Parent Movement: The Revolt of Parents of Children with Intellectual Limitations* (Brookline, MA: Brookline Books, 1990); Jones, "Education for Children with Mental Retardation."

33. The Arc has gone through several name changes: In 1950 it was established as the National Association of Parents and Friends of Mentally Retarded Children, in 1952 the name was changed to the National Association for Retarded Children (NARC), in 1973 the name was changed to the National Association for Retarded Citizens (NARC), and in 1992 it became the Arc. Because of the brevity of this history and for simplicity's sake, we refer to it as the Arc regardless of the time period.

34. Eleanor Elkin, interview by Visionary Voices, available at https://disabilities.temple.edu/voices/detailVideo.html?media=005-04 (accessed November 29, 2019).

35. Kate and David Fialkowski, interview by Visionary Voices, available at https://disabilities.temple.edu/voices/detailVideo.html?media=019-03 (accessed November 29, 2019).

36. Alfred H. Katz, *Parents of the Handicapped: Self-Organized Parents' and Relatives' Groups for Treatment of Ill and Handicapped Children* (Springfield, IL: Charles C. Thomas, 1961); Robert M. Segal, *Mental Retardation and Social Action* (Springfield, IL: Charles C. Thomas, 1970).

37. "Not Like Other Children," *Parents Magazine* 18 (October 1943): 34.

38. Richard H. Hungerford, "A Bill of Rights for the Retarded," *American Journal of Mental Deficiency* 63 (April 1959): 937. The organization was known at the time as NARC.

39. Allison C. Carey, "Parents and Professionals: Parents' Reflections on Professionals, Support Systems, and the Family in the Twentieth-Century United States," in *Disability Histories*, ed. Susan Burch and Michael Rembis (Champaign: University of Illinois Press, 2014), 58–76; Simon Olshansky, Gertrude C. Johnson, and Leon Sternfeld, "Attitudes of Some GP's towards Institutionalizing Mentally Retarded Children," *Mental Retardation* 1 (1963): 18–20, 57–59.

40. Douglas Hunt, preface to *The World of Nigel Hunt: The Diary of a Mongoloid Youth*, by Nigel Hunt (New York: Garrett, 1967), 22.

41. Ibid.

42. Sophia Grant, *"One of Those": The Progress of a Mongoloid Child* (New York: Pageant, 1957).

43. Ibid., 11.

44. For the social model of disability, see Michael Oliver, *The Politics of Disablement* (New York: St. Martin's Press, 1990); and Simi Linton, *Claiming Disability: Knowledge and Identity* (New York: New York University Press, 1998).

45. Eugene Gramm, "Just One Voice to Speak for All of America's Retarded," *Children Limited* 1, no. 1 (1952): 1.

46. Children with IQs between 50 and 70 were more likely to be served by public schools, whereas children with IQs below 50 were widely considered "uneducable" and denied a public education.

47. Segal, *Mental Retardation and Social Action*.

48. Goode, *And Now Let's Build a Better World*.

49. Jones, *Doing Disability Justice*, 117.

50. "Bill of Rights for Pennsylvania's Retarded Citizens," *Pennsylvania Message* 5, no. 2 (1969): 8.

51. Pennsylvania Association for Retarded Children (PARC) v. Commonwealth of Pennsylvania, 334 F. Supp. 1260 (1971).

52. Winzer, *The History of Special Education*.

53. Jones, *Doing Disability Justice*.

54. For more information, see Carey and Gu, "Walking the Line between the Past and the Future." See also Steven J. Taylor, "Caught in the Continuum: A Critical Analysis of the Principle of the Least Restrictive Environment," *Journal of the Association for the Severely Handicapped* 13, no. 1 (1998): 41–53.

55. Letter from Ruth S. Hayes to John S. Fine, September 25, 1952, folder 20, box 29, Subject File, 1951–1955, John S. Fine Papers, Pennsylvania State Archives.

56. "What Prompts PARC's Action toward Institutions," *Pennsylvania Message* 9, no. 2 (1973): 1.

57. Halderman v. Pennhurst, 446 F. Supp. 1319 (1977).

58. New York State Association for Retarded Children, Inc., v. Rockefeller, 357 F. Supp. 752 (1973).

59. Paul A. Offit, *Vaccinated: One Man's Quest to Defeat the World's Deadliest Diseases* (New York: Smithsonian Books/Collins, 2007).

60. Linda H. Drummond, ed., *Arc Pennsylvania Historical Overview, 1949–1990* (Harrisburg, PA: ARC, n.d.), app. D.

61. Polly Spare, phone interview by the author, July 2014.

62. Much of this brief history of self-advocacy is also found in Carey's *On the Margins of Citizenship*.

63. Valerie Schaaf with Hank Bersani Jr., "People First of Oregon: An Organizational History and Personal Perspective," in *New Voices: Self-Advocacy by People with Disabilities*, ed. Gunnar Dybwad and Hank Bersani Jr. (Cambridge, MA: Brookline Books, 1996), 171.

64. Paul Williams and Bonnie Shultz, *We Can Speak for Ourselves* (Bloomington: Indiana University Press, 1982), 19.

65. Ibid, 23.

66. Speaking for Ourselves, "History: 1982–2002," in the author's possession.

67. Roland Johnson, *Lost in a Desert World* (Plymouth Meeting, PA: Speaking for Ourselves, 1999), 67.

68. Self Advocates Becoming Empowered, "Our Mission," available at http://www.sabeusa.org (accessed November 25, 2019).

69. Mark Friedman and Ruthie-Marie Beckwith, "Self-Advocacy: The Emancipation Movement Led by People with Intellectual and Developmental Disability," in Ben-Moshe, Chapman, and Carey, *Disability Incarcerated*, 237–254.

70. U.S. Department of Health and Human Services, *Closing the Gap: A National Blueprint to Improve the Health of Persons with Mental Retardation* (Washington, DC: U.S. Department of Health and Human Services, 2002).

71. Liz Obermayer, "Choices," in *"Community for All" Tool Kit: Resources for Supporting Community Living* (Syracuse, NY: Human Policy Press, 2004), 131, available at http://thechp.syr.edu/wp-content/uploads/2013/02/Community_for_All_Toolkit_Version1.1 .pdf.

72. The Arc, "Joint Letter from the Arc for Legislators, Governor, and the Media," in *"Community for All" Tool Kit*.

73. Ronald J. Berger, *Introducing Disability Studies* (Boulder, CO: Lynne Rienner, 2013).

74. Frank Stephens, testimony to U.S. House of Representatives Subcommittee on Labor, Health and Human Services, and Education, October 25, 2017, available at https://docs.house.gov/meetings/AP/AP07/20171025/106526/HHRG-115-AP07 -Wstate-StephensF-20171025.pdf.

75. Quoted in Friedman and Beckwith, "Self-Advocacy," 245.

76. Ibid., 246.

77. Carey and Gu, "Walking the Line between the Past and the Future."

78. Jawon (pseudonym), phone interview by the author, May 2015.

79. Steven J. Taylor, "On Choice," *Tash Connections* 27, no. 2 (2001): 8–10.

80. Sheryl Larson, Charlie Lakin, and Shannon Hill, "Behavioral Outcomes of Moving from Institutional to Community Living for People with Intellectual and Developmental Disabilities: U.S. Studies from 1977 to 2010," *Research and Practice for People with Severe Disabilities* 37, no. 4 (2012): 235–246.

81. Sara (pseudonym), phone interview by the author, July 2014.

82. Erin Evans, "Voices: A Thoughtful Debate over Inclusion," *WNYC*, November 16, 2011, available at http://www.wnyc.org/story/301701-voices-a-thoughtful -debate-over-inclusion/.

83. Gail (pseudonym), phone interview by the author, September 2018.

84. Ibid.

85. Valerie Leiter, *Their Time Has Come: Youth with Disabilities on the Cusp of Adulthood* (New Brunswick, NJ: Rutgers University Press, 2012).

86. Ruthie-Marie Beckwith, *Disability Servitude: From Peonage to Poverty* (New York City: Palgrave Macmillan, 2016).

87. Sam (pseudonym), phone interview by the author, June 2015.

88. Theresa Vargas, "Virginia Woman Seeks Power to Live the Way She Wants," *Washington Post*, July 20, 2013, available at https://www.washingtonpost.com/local/virginia-woman-with-down-syndrome-seeks-power-to-live-the-way-she-wants/2013/07/20/76102a82-d789-11e2-a9f2-42ee3912ae0e_story.html.

89. Michael Bérubé, "Equality, Freedom, and/or Justice for All," in *Cognitive Disability and Its Challenge to Moral Philosophy*, ed. Eva Feder Kittay and Licia Carlson (Malden, MA: Wiley-Blackwell, 2010), 105.

90. Doug (pseudonym), phone interview by the author, June 2014.

91. Ibid.

92. Debbie Robinson, interview by Visionary Voices, available at https://disabilities.temple.edu/voices/detailVideo.html?media=010-01 (accessed November 29, 2019).

93. Jones, *Doing Disability Justice*.

94. Melanie Panitch, *Disability, Mothers, and Organization: Accidental Activists* (New York: Routledge, 2008).

95. Jones, *Doing Disability Justice*, 224.

CHAPTER 2

1. This brief account summarizes the narrative provided in Pete Earley, *Crazy: A Father's Search through America's Mental Health Madness* (New York: Berkley Books, 2006).

2. Allan V. Horowitz, *Creating Mental Illness* (Chicago: University of Chicago, 2002); Michael MacDonald, *Mystical Bedlam: Madness, Anxiety, and Healing in Seventeenth-Century England* (Cambridge: Cambridge University Press, 1981); Andrew Scull, *Madness in Civilization* (London: Thames and Hudson, 2015).

3. Horowitz, *Creating Mental Illness*.

4. Stephan P. Hinshaw, *The Mark of Shame: Stigma of Mental Illness and an Agenda for Change* (Oxford: Oxford University Press, 2007).

5. Elina A. Stafanovics et al., "Witchcraft and Biosocial Causes of Mental Illness: Attitudes and Beliefs about Mental Illness among Health Professionals in Five Countries," *Journal of Nervous and Mental Disease* 204, no. 3 (2016): 169–174.

6. For a history of mental illness, see Scull, *Madness in Civilization*; and Andrew Scull, *Social Order/Mental Disorder: Anglo-American Psychiatry in Historical Perspective* (Berkeley: University of California Press, 1989).

7. For studies of institutionalization, see Gerald N. Grob, *From Asylum to Community: Mental Health Policy in Modern America* (Princeton, NJ: Princeton University Press, 1991); Gerald N. Grob, *The Mad among Us: A History of the Care of America's Mentally Ill* (New York: Free Press, 1994); James E. Moran, *Committed to the State Asylum* (Montreal: McGill-Queen's University Press, 2000); and Geoffrey Reaume, *Remembrance of Patients Past* (Toronto: University of Toronto Press, 2009).

8. Scull, *Social Order/Mental Disorder*.

9. Kerry Michael Dobransky, *Managing Madness in the Community* (New Brunswick, NJ: Rutgers University Press, 2014).

10. Liat Ben-Moshe, "Why Prisons Are Not the New Asylums," *Punishment and Society* 19, no. 3 (2017): 72–289. Homelessness was also exacerbated by the shrinking stock of low-cost housing, especially the single room occupancy facilities such as boarding houses and inexpensive residential hotels that vanished as a result of urban renewal and gentrification.

11. Valerie Leiter, *Their Time Has Come: Youth with Disabilities on the Cusp of Adulthood* (New Brunswick, NJ: Rutgers University Press, 2012).

12. Andrew Scull, *Madness: A Very Short Introduction* (Oxford: Oxford University Press, 2011), 114, 115.

13. Michael Rembis, "The New Asylums: Madness and Mass Incarceration in the Neoliberal Era," in *Disability Incarcerated: Imprisonment and Disability in the United States and Canada*, ed. Liat Ben-Moshe, Chris Chapman, and Allison C. Carey (New York: Palgrave-Macmillan, 2014), 139–159.

14. Dobransky, *Managing Madness in the Community*.

15. Bernard E. Harcourt, "Reducing Mass Incarceration: Lessons from the Deinstitutionalization of Mental Hospitals in the 1960s," *Ohio State Journal of Criminal Law* 9 (2011): 53–88; Bernard E. Harcourt, "From the Asylum to the Prison: Rethinking the Incarceration Revolution," *Texas Law Review* 84 (2006): 1751–1786.

16. Jonathon Metzl, *The Protest Psychosis* (Boston: Beacon Press, 2010).

17. Anne E. Parsons, *From Asylum to Prison: Deinstitutionalization and the Rise of Mass Incarceration after 1945* (Chapel Hill: University of North Carolina Press, 2018); Rembis, "The New Asylums."

18. Quoted in Liz Szabo, "Mental Illness: Families Cut Out of Care," *USA Today*, February 26, 2016, available at https://www.usatoday.com/story/news/2016/02/26/privacy-law-harms-care-mentally-ill-families-say/80880880/.

19. National Alliance for Caregiving, *On Pins and Needles: Caregivers of Adults with Mental Illness* (Bethesda, MD: National Alliance for Caregiving, 2016).

20. Ronald C. Kessler et al., "Prevalence and Treatment of Mental Disorders," *New England Journal of Medicine* 352 (2005): 2515–2523.

21. Horowitz, *Creating Mental Illness*, 4.

22. U.S. Department of Commerce, Bureau of Census, *Insane and Feeble-Minded in Institutions, 1910* (Washington, DC: Government Printing Office, 1914); Kids Mental Health, "How Is Mental Illness in Children Diagnosed," available at http://www.kidsmentalhealth.org/how-is-mental-illness-in-children-diagnosed (accessed November 26, 2019).

23. Steven J. Taylor, *Acts of Conscience: World War II, Mental Institutions, and Religious Objectors* (Syracuse, NY: Syracuse University Press, 2009).

24. Ibid.

25. Athena McLean, "The Mental Health Consumer Survivors Movement in the United States," in *A Handbook for the Study of Mental Health: Social Contexts, Theories, and Systems*, 2nd ed., ed. Teresa L. Scheid and Tony N. Brown (New York: Cambridge University Press, 2009), 461–477.

26. Quoted in Fred Pelka, *What We Have Done: An Oral History of the Disability Rights Movement* (Amherst: University of Massachusetts Press, 2012), 285.

27. Ibid., 283.

28. McLean, "Mental Health Consumer Survivors Movement"; Nancy Tomes, "The Patient as a Policy Factor: A Historical Case Study of the Consumer/Survivor Movement in Mental Health," *Health Affairs* 25, no. 3 (2006): 720–729.

29. McLean, "Mental Health Consumer Survivors Movement," 464.

30. Ibid.

31. Tomes, "The Patient as a Policy Factor."

32. McLean, "Mental Health Consumer Survivors Movement," 466.

33. Ibid., 465.

34. U.S. Department of Health and Human Services, *Mental Health: A Report of the Surgeon General* (Rockville, MD: U.S. Department of Health and Human Services, Substance Abuse and Mental Health Services Administration, Center for Mental Health Services, National Institutes of Health, National Institute of Mental Health, 1999), 95.

35. McLean, "Mental Health Consumer Survivors Movement," 468.

36. Ibid., 467.

37. John D. McCarthy and Mayer N. Zald, "Resource Mobilization and Social Movements: A Partial Theory," *American Journal of Sociology* 82, no. 6 (1977): 1212–1241.

38. Richard K. Scotch, *From Good Will to Civil Rights: Transforming Federal Disability Policy* (Philadelphia: Temple University Press, 1984).

39. Allison C. Carey, *On the Margins of Citizenship: Intellectual Disability and Civil Rights in Twentieth-Century America* (Philadelphia: Temple University Press, 2009).

40. Mark Tausig, Janet Michelle, and Sree Subedi, *A Sociology of Mental Illness*, 2nd ed. (Upper Saddle River, NJ: Pearson Press, 2013).

41. Nana Kusi Appiah, "A Study of Factors Influencing Public Officials and City Planners to Engage Citizens in Governmental Land-Use Decisions" (Ph.D. diss., University of Texas at Dallas, 2014).

42. U.S. Department of Health and Human Services, *Mental Health*, 92.

43. Douglas Martin, "Harriet Shetler, Who Helped to Found Mental Illness Group, Dies at 92," *New York Times*, April 3, 2010, p. A22.

44. Agnes B. Hatfield, "Self-Help Groups for Families of the Mentally Ill," *Social Work* 26 (1981): 408–413.

45. Agnes B. Hatfield, "Families as Advocates for the Mentally Ill: A Growing Movement," *Hospital and Community Psychiatry* 32, no. 9 (1981): 641–642; James W. Howe, "Families as Advocates," *Hospital and Community Psychiatry* 27, no. 10 (1986): 1051–1052.

46. Hatfield, "Families as Advocates for the Mentally Ill."

47. U.S. Department of Health and Human Services, *Mental Health*, 96.

48. Tomes, "The Patient as a Policy Factor."

49. National Alliance on Mental Illness, "Learning to Help Your Child and Your Family," available at https://www.nami.org/find-support/family-members-and-caregivers/learning-to-help-your-child-and-your-family (accessed November 26, 2019).

50. Hatfield, "Families as Advocates for the Mentally Ill," 642.

51. Ibid.

52. Szabo, "Mental Illness."

53. Ibid.

54. Daniel Goleman, "States Move to Ease Laws Committing Mentally Ill," *New York Times*, December 9, 1986, available at http://www.nytimes.com/1986/12/09/science/states-move-to-ease-law-committing-mentally-ill.html?pagewanted=all.

55. Association for Young People's Health, *Supporting Young People with Mental Health Problems: Results of a Survey of Parents* (London: AYPH, 2016).

56. Ibid., 2.

57. Erving Goffman, *Stigma: Notes on the Management of a Spoiled Identity* (New York: Simon and Schuster, 1963); Douglas Engelman, "Endings and Beginnings: A Father's Journey through His Son's Madness, Loss, and a Quest for Meaning" (unpublished paper, 2018).

58. Edward Cohen et al., "Parents' Perspectives on Access to Child and Mental Health Services," *Social Work in Mental Health* 10, no. 4 (2012): 300.

59. Lisa Lambert, "Why Parents Are Silent about Mental Illness," Child Mind Institute, available at https://childmind.org/article/why-parents-are-silent-about-mental-illness (accessed June 18, 2019).

60. Michael Schofield, *January First: A Child's Descent into Madness and Her Father's Struggle to Save Her* (New York: Broadway Books, 2013), viii.

61. Tomes, "The Patient as a Policy Factor."

62. Judith Gruber and Edison J. Trickett, "Can We Empower Others? The Paradox of Empowerment in the Governing of an Alternative High School," *American Journal of Community Psychology* 15, no. 3 (1987): 370.

63. Agnes B. Hatfield, "National Alliance for the Mentally Ill: The Meaning of a Movement," *International Journal of Mental Health* 15, no. 4 (1986): 89–90.

64. McLean, "Mental Health Consumer Survivors Movement," 475.

65. Benedict Carey, "Mental Health Groups Split on Bill to Overhaul Care," *New York Times*, April 2, 2014, available at https://www.nytimes.com/2014/04/03/health/mental-health-groups-split-on-bill-to-revamp-care.html.

66. Jeanett, April 27, 2014, comments to Angela McClanahan, "Admitting a Child to Inpatient Psychiatric Treatment: A Parent's Perspective," *Healthy Place*, January 17, 2012, available at https://www.healthyplace.com/blogs/parentingchildwithmentalillness/2012/01/admitting-a-child-to-inpatient-psychiatric-treatment-a-parents-perspective.

67. Ross, September 12, 2014, comment to McClanahan, "Admitting a Child."

68. McLean, "Mental Health Consumer Survivors Movement," 475.

69. Ibid., 476–477.

70. Quoted in Pelka, *What We Have Done*, 291.

71. McLean, "Mental Health Consumer Survivors Movement," 469.

72. Ibid.

73. Ken Silverstein, "Prozac.org," *Mother Jones*, November–December 1999, available at https://www.motherjones.com/politics/1999/11/outfront-0/.

74. Gardiner Harris, "Drug Makers Are Advocacy Group's Biggest Donors," *New York Times*, October 21, 2009, available at https://www.nytimes.com/2009/10/22/health/22nami.html.

75. Ibid.

76. Susannah L. Rose et al., "Patient Advocacy Organizations, Industry Funding, and Conflicts of Interest," *JAMA Internal Medicine* 177, no. 3 (2017): 344–350.

77. Schofield, *January First*, vii.

CHAPTER 3

1. Pamela Block, Hope Block, and Barbara Kilcup, "Autism, Communication, Family and Community," paper presented at the American Anthropological Association Meetings, San Francisco, CA, November 21, 2008, available at http://pamelablock.blogspot.com/2015/10; Elizabeth Grace, "Are You Neuroqueer?" *NeuroQueer* (blog), September

18, 2013, available at http://neuroqueer.blogspot.ca/2013/09/are-you-neuroqueer.html; Anne McGuire, *War on Autism: On the Cultural Logic of Normative Violence* (Ann Arbor: University of Michigan Press, 2016); Nick Walker, "Neurodiversity: Some Basic Terms and Definitions," *Neurocosmopolitanism* (blog), September 27, 2014, available at https://neurocosmopolitanism.com/neurodiversity-some-basic-terms-definitions; Melanie Yergeau, *Authoring Autism: On Rhetoric and Neurological Queerness* (Durham, NC: Duke University Press, 2018).

2. Bonnie Evans, "How Autism Became Autism," *History of the Human Sciences* 26, no. 3 (2013): 3–31.

3. Douglas Biklen et al., *Autism and the Myth of the Person Alone* (New York: New York University Press, 2005), 31; Pamela Block and Fatima Cavalcante, "Historical Perceptions of Autism in Brazil: Professional Treatment, Family Advocacy, and Autistic Pride, 1943–2010," in *Disability Histories*, ed. Susan Burch and Michael Rembis, (Champaign: University of Illinois Press, 2014), 77–97; Leo Kanner, "Autistic Disturbances of Affective Contact," *Nervous Child* 2 (1943): 217–250; Steve Silberman, *Neurotribes: The Legacy of Autism and the Future of Neurodiversity* (New York: Penguin Random House, 2015).

4. Block and Cavalcante, "Historical Perceptions of Autism in Brazil."

5. Silberman, *Neurotribes*.

6. Edith Sheffer, *Asperger's Children: The Origins of Autism in Nazi Vienna* (New York: W. W. Norton, 2018).

7. Ariel M. Cascio, "Cross-Cultural Autism Studies, Neurodiversity, and Conceptualizations of Autism," *Culture, Medicine and Psychiatry* 39, no. 2 (2015): 207–212.

8. Block and Cavalcante, "Historical Perceptions of Autism in Brazil"; Elizabeth Fein and Clarice Rios, *Autism in Translation: An Intercultural Conversation on Autism Spectrum Conditions* (New York: Palgrave, 2018); Rachel S. Brezis, Thomas S. Weisner, and Tamara C. Daley, "Parenting a Child with Autism in India: Narratives before and after a Parent-Child Intervention Program," *Culture, Medicine and Psychiatry* 39, no. 2 (2015): 277–298; Jennifer C. Sarrett, "Custodial Homes, Therapeutic Homes, and Parental Acceptance: Parental Experiences of Autism in Kerala, India and Atlanta, GA USA," *Culture, Medicine and Psychiatry* 39, no. 2 (2015): 254–276.

9. Elizabeth Fein, "Making Meaningful Worlds: Role-Playing Subcultures and the Autism Spectrum," *Culture, Medicine and Psychiatry* 39, no. 2 (2015): 299–321; Olga Solomon, "'But—He'll Fall!' Children with Autism, Interspecies Intersubjectivity, and the Problem of 'Being Social,'" *Culture, Medicine and Psychiatry* 39, no. 2 (2015): 323–344.

10. Kanner, "Autistic Disturbances of Affective Contact." See also Bruno Bettelheim, *The Empty Fortress: Infantile Autism and the Birth of the Self* (New York: Free Press, 1967).

11. Sue Gerrard, "Refrigerator Mothers," *What Is Autism Anyway?* (blog), May 11, 2012, available at https://whatisautismanyway.wordpress.com/2012/05/11/refrigerator-mothers.

12. *Refrigerator Mothers*, dir. David E. Simpson (Chicago: Kartemquin Educational Films, 2002).

13. Ibid.

14. Quoted in Mary Langan, "Parental Voices and Controversies in Autism," *Disability and Society* 26, no. 2 (2011): 196.

15. Block and Cavalcante, "Historical Perceptions of Autism in Brazil."

16. Quoted in Langan, "Parental Voices and Controversies in Autism."

17. Ibid., 196.

18. Bernard Rimland, *Infantile Autism: The Syndrome and Its Implications for a Neural Theory of Behaviour* (Upper Saddle River, NJ: Prentice Hall, 1964).

19. Andrew J. Wakefield et al., "Ileal-Lymphoid-Nodular Hyperplasia, Non-specific Colitis, and Pervasive Developmental Disorder in Children," *The Lancet* 351, no. 9103 (1998): 637–641 (retracted).

20. Richard R. Grinker, *Unstrange Minds: Remapping the World of Autism* (Cambridge, MA: Basic Books, 2007).

21. R. Wiegerink and J. W. Pelosi, eds., *Developmental Disabilities: The Developmental Disabilities Movement* (Baltimore: Paul H. Brookes, 1979).

22. Grinker, *Unstrange Minds*.

23. Block and Cavalcante, "Historical Perceptions of Autism in Brazil"; E. M. Ornitz and Edward Ritvo, "The Syndrome of Autism: A Critical Review," *American Journal of Psychiatry* 133 (1976): 609–621; Michael Rutter, "Diagnosis and Definitions of Childhood Autism," *Journal of Autism and Childhood Schizophrenia* 8, no. 2 (1978): 130–161; Lorna Wing and Judith Gould, "Severe Impairments of Social Interactions and Associated Abnormalities in Children: Epidemiology and Classification," *Journal of Autism and Developmental Disorders* 9, no. 1 (1979): 11–29.

24. Simon Baron-Cohen, Alan Leslie, and Uta Frith, "Does the Autistic Child Have a 'Theory of Mind'?" *Cognition* 21, no. 1 (1985): 37–46.

25. McGuire, *War on Autism*; Yergeau, *Authoring Autism*; Yergeau, "Clinically Significant Disturbance: On Theorists Who Theorize Theory of Mind," *Disability Studies Quarterly* 33, no. 4 (2013), available at http://dsq-sds.org/article/view/3876/3405; Melanie Yergeau, "Circle Wars: Reshaping the Typical Autism Essay," *Disability Studies Quarterly* 30, no. 1 (2010), available at http://dsq-sds.org/article/view/1063/1222.

26. Clara Claiborne Park, quoted in Langan, "Parental Voices and Controversies in Autism."

27. Lorna Wing and D. Potter, "The Epidemiology of Autistic Spectrum Disorders: Is the Prevalence Rising?" *Mental Retardation and Developmental Research Reviews* 8, no. 3 (2002): 151–161.

28. Ole Ivar Lovaas, "Behavioral Treatment and Normal Educational and Intellectual Functioning in Young Children with Autism," *Journal of Consulting and Clinical Psychology* 55, no. 1 (1987): 3–9.

29. Stanley Greenspan, *Engaging Autism* (Philadelphia: Da Capo Press, 2006).

30. A. Jean Ayres, *Sensory Integration and Learning Disorders* (Los Angeles: Western Psychological Services, 1973).

31. Gary B. Mesibov, Victoria Shea, and Eric Schopler, *The TEACCH Approach to Autism Spectrum Disorders* (New York: Springer, 2004).

32. Lovaas, "Behavioral Treatment."

33. Ariel M. Cascio, "Neurodiversity: Autism Pride among Mothers of Children with Autism Spectrum Disorders," *Intellectual and Developmental Disabilities* 50, no. 3, (2012): 273–283.

34. Parent of child with autism, personal communication with Pamela Block, May 2011.

35. Morton A. Gernsbacher, "Is One Style of Early Behavioral Intervention 'Scientifically Proven'?" *Journal of Developmental and Learning Disorders* 7 (2003): 19–25; Julia F. Gruson-Wood, "Autism, Expert Discourses, and Subjectification: A Critical Examina-

tion of Applied Behavioural Therapies," *Studies in Social Justice* 10, no. 1 (2016): 38–58; Max Sparrow, "ABA," *Unstrange Mind* (blog), October 20, 2016, available at http://unstrangemind.com/aba/; Tracy Dee Whitt, "My Thoughts on Applied Behavior Analysis (ABA)—Autism," *Lovin' Adoptin' and Autism* (blog), March 26, 2014, available at http://lovinadoptin.com/2014/03/26/my-thoughts-on-applied-behavior-analysis-aba-autism/; Yergeau, *Authoring Autism*.

36. Olga Bogdashina, *Theory of Mind and the Triad of Perspectives on Autism and Asperger Syndrome: A View from the Bridge* (London: Jessica Kingsley, 2005); Gruson-Wood, "Autism, Expert Discourses, and Subjectification."

37. Tracy Dee Whitt, "More Perspectives on Applied Behavior Analysis (ABA)—Autism," *Lovin' Adoptin' and Autism* (blog), April 9, 2014, available at http://lovinadoptin.com/2014/04/09/more-perspectives-on-applied-behavior-analysis-aba-autism/.

38. Autism Speaks, "About Us," available at https://www.autismspeaks.org/about-us (accessed November 26, 2019).

39. "Bob Wright," *Wikipedia*, October 19, 2019, available at https://en.wikipedia.org/wiki/Bob_Wright.

40. Autism Speaks, "About Us."

41. "Bob Wright."

42. Mark Hyman, "Can Autism Be Cured?" *Children's Health Defense*, 2016, available at https://childrenshealthdefense.org/wp-content/uploads/2016/10/Can_Autism_be_Cured-Dr.MarkHyman.pdf.

43. Ibid.

44. Ashley Steinbrinck, "How Dr. Hyman Helped an Autistic Boy with a Functional Medicine Approach," *Natural Health Concepts* (blog), June 18, 2013, available at http://blog.naturalhealthyconcepts.com/2013/06/18/how-to-treat-or-possibly-cure-autism-naturally-with-a-functional-medicine-approach/.

45. McGuire, *War on Autism*; Amy C. Sousa, "From Refrigerator Mothers to Warrior-Heroes: The Cultural Identity Transformation of Mothers Raising Children with Intellectual Disabilities," *Symbolic Interaction* 34, no. 2 (2011): 220–243; Emily C. Yochim and Vesta T. Silva, "Everyday Expertise, Autism, and 'Good' Mothering in the Media Discourse of Jenny McCarthy," *Communication and Critical/Cultural Studies* 10, no. 4 (2013): 406–426.

46. Cascio, "Neurodiversity."

47. Yochim and Silva, "Everyday Expertise, Autism, and 'Good' Mothering."

48. Sousa, "From Refrigerator Mothers to Warrior-Heroes."

49. Kerima Çevik, "#AutisticWhileBlack: Diezel Braxton and Becoming Indistinguishable from One's Peers," *Autism Wars* (blog), July 24, 2018, available at http://theautismwars.blogspot.com/2018/07/autisticwhileblack-diezel-braxton-and_24.html.

50. Sousa, "From Refrigerator Mothers to Warrior-Heroes."

51. The website is available at https://tacanow.org/category/family-stories/recovered-from-autism/.

52. Grinker, *Unstrange Minds*; Cloe Silverman, *Understanding Autism* (Princeton, NJ: Princeton University Press, 2011).

53. Grinker, *Unstrange Minds*; Silverman, *Understanding Autism*.

54. Mel Baggs, "Aspie Supremacy Can Kill," *Ballastexistenz* (blog), March 7, 2010, available at https://ballastexistenz.wordpress.com/2010/03/07/aspie-supremacy-can-kill/.

55. Silverman, *Understanding Autism*, 143.

56. Ibid., 90.

57. Silverman, *Understanding Autism*.

58. Sousa, "From Refrigerator Mothers to Warrior-Heroes."

59. Joseph F. Kras, "The 'Ransom Notes' Affair: When the Neurodiversity Movement Came of Age," *Disability Studies Quarterly* 30, no. 1 (2010), available at http://dsq-sds.org/article/view/1065/1254; Ronnie Thibault, "Can Autistics Redefine Autism? The Cultural Politics of Autistic Activism," *Transcripts* 4 (2014): 57–88.

60. McGuire, *War on Autism*.

61. Yochim and Silva, "Everyday Expertise, Autism, and 'Good' Mothering."

62. Barney Calman, "The Great Autism Rip-Off . . . How a Huge Industry Feeds on Parents Desperate to Cure Their Children," *Daily Mail*, June 4, 2008, available at http://www.dailymail.co.uk/health/article-1023351/The-great-autism-rip---How-huge-industry-feeds-parents-desperate-cure-children.html.

63. Bernice M. Olivas, "What I Mean When I Say Autism: Rethinking the Roles of Language and Literacy in Autism Discourse" (master's thesis, University of Nebraska, Lincoln, 2012).

64. Yochim and Silva, "Everyday Expertise, Autism, and 'Good' Mothering," 409.

65. Silverman, *Understanding Autism*, 136.

66. Kras, "The 'Ransom Notes' Affair"; Joanne Kaufman, "Ransom-Note Ads about Children's Health Are Canceled," *New York Times*, December 20, 2007, available at http://www.nytimes.com/2007/12/20/business/media/20child.html?_r=0; Ari Ne'eman, "An Urgent Call to Action: Tell NYU Child Study Center to Abandon Stereotypes against People with Disabilities," Autistic Self Advocacy Network, December 8, 2007, available at http://autisticadvocacy.org/2007/12/tell-nyu-child-study-center-to-abandon-stereotypes/.

67. Autism Women's Network, "Why Boycott Autism Speaks," *Boycott Autism Speaks*, March 16, 2016, available at https://boycottautismspeaks.wordpress.com/2016/03/16/why-boycott-autism-speaks/.

68. Autistic Self Advocacy Network, "ASAN Calls for Federal Hate Crime Prosecution for the Murder of Alex Spourdalakis," June 18, 2013, available at http://autisticadvocacy.org/2013/06/asan-calls-for-federal-hate-crime-prosecution-for-the-murder-of-alex-spourdalakis/.

69. ADAPT, "ADAPT Responds to FDA Announcement of Their Intent to Ban Electric Shock Devices," available at https://adapt.org/adapt-responds-to-fda-announcement-of-their-intent-to-ban-electric-shock-devices/ (accessed January 4, 2019).

70. Autistic Self Advocacy Network, "ASAN Calls for Federal Hate Crime Prosecution."

71. The information presented here on online autistic communities is part of Pamela Block's larger ethnographic research project on discourses on occupations and experiences of autistic adults as presented in online forums, blogs, individual interviews, and observations of meetings and conferences.

72. Grace, "Are You Neuroqueer?"; Walker, "Neurodiversity"; Yergeau, *Authoring Autism*.

73. Steve Silberman, "Our Neurodiverse World," *Slate*, September 23, 2015, available at https://slate.com/technology/2015/09/the-neurodiversity-movement-autism-is-a-minority-group-neurotribes-excerpt.html.

74. Sparrow, "ABA."

75. Ibid.

76. Amy S. F. Lutz, "Who Decides Where Autistic Adults Live?" *The Atlantic*, May 26, 2015, available at http://www.theatlantic.com/health/archive/2015/05/who-decides-where-autistic-adults-live/393455/.

77. Grace, "Are You Neuroqueer?"; Yergeau, *Authoring Autism*.

78. J. Queen, "Neurodiversity and Autism: Where Do We Draw the Line?" *Neuroethics Blog*, December 4, 2012, available at http://www.theneuroethicsblog.com/2012/12/neurodiversity-and-autism-where-do-we.html.

79. Michele Friedner and Pamela Block, "Deaf Studies Meets Autistic Studies," *Senses and Society* 12, no. 3 (2017): 282–300.

80. Rachel Robertson, "Sharing Stories: Motherhood, Autism and Culture," in *Disability and Mothering: Liminal Spaces of Embodied Knowledge*, ed. Cynthia Lewiecki-Wilson and Jen Cellio (New York: Syracuse University Press, 2011), 140–155.

81. Solomon, "'But—He'll Fall!'"; Douglas Biklen and Jamie Burke, "Presuming Competence," *Equity and Excellence in Education* 39, no. 2 (2006): 166–175; Christopher Kliewer, Douglas Biklen, and C. Kasa-Hendrickson, "Who May Be Literate? Disability and Resistance to the Cultural Denial of Competence," *American Educational Research Journal* 43, no. 2 (2006): 163–192.

82. Cascio, "Neurodiversity."

83. Julie Bascom, ed., *Loud Hands: Autistic People Speaking* (Washington, DC: Autistic Self-Advocacy Network, 2012).

84. Amy Sequenzia and Elizabeth Grace, *Typed Words, Loud Voices* (Fort Worth, TX: Autonomous Press, 2015).

85. Melanie Yergeau, "I Stim, Therefore I Am," *YouTube*, January 26, 2012, available at http://www.youtube.com/watch?v=s2QSvPIDXwA.

86. Pamela Block, "Conversations in Autism and Sign Language," presentation at Stony Brook University, New York, December 16, 2014.

87. Fein, "Making Meaningful Worlds."

88. Clarice Rios and Barbara Costa Andrade, "The Changing Face of Autism in Brazil," *Culture, Medicine and Psychiatry* 39 (2015): 213–234.

89. Pamela Block and Fatima Cavalcante, "Autism in Brazil from Advocacy and Self-Advocacy Perspectives: A Preliminary Research Report," *Autism around the Globe*, 2012, available at http://www.autismaroundtheglobe.org/countries/Brazil.asp; Block and Cavalcante, "Historical Perceptions of Autism in Brazil."

90. Bogdashina, *Theory of Mind and the Triad of Perspectives on Autism and Asperger Syndrome*; Gruson-Wood, "Autism, Expert Discourses, and Subjectification"; Yergeau, *Authoring Autism*.

91. Olivas, "What I Mean When I Say Autism," 11.

92. *Refrigerator Mothers*.

93. Ibid.

94. Cascio, "Neurodiversity."

95. Eugen Bleuler, *Dementia Praecox or the Group of Schizophrenias* (1911; repr., New York: International Universities, 1950); Bernard Bettelheim, *The Empty Fortress: Infantile Autism and the Birth of the Self* (Glencoe, IL: Free Press, 1967); Kanner, "Autistic Disturbances of Affective Contact."

96. Olivas, "What I Mean When I Say Autism."

97. Kerima Çevik, "Autistic while Black: The Erasure of Blacks from Histories of Autism," *InterSected* (blog), January 22, 2016, available at http://intersecteddisability.blogspot.com/2016/01/autistic-while-black-erasure-of-blacks.html.

98. *Refrigerator Mothers.*

99. Çevik, "Autistic while Black."

100. Ibid.

101. Autism in Black, "Resources," available at http://www.autisminblack.com/re sources.html (accessed November 26, 2019).

CHAPTER 4

1. This account is largely drawn from Steven E. Brown, "Zona and Ed Roberts: Twentieth Century Pioneers," *Disability Studies Quarterly* 20, no. 1 (Winter 2000): 26–42.

2. Judith Sealander, *The Failed Century of the Child: Governing America's Young in the Twentieth Century* (New York: Cambridge University Press, 2003).

3. Ibid., 273.

4. See, for example, Susan Burch, *Signs of Resistance: American Deaf Cultural History, 1900 to World War II* (New York: New York University Press, 2002); and Floyd Matson, *Walking Together and Marching Together: A History of the Organized Blind Movement in the United States, 1940–1990* (Baltimore: National Federation of the Blind, 1990).

5. Richard K. Scotch, *From Good Will to Civil Rights: Transforming Federal Disability Policy* (Philadelphia: Temple University Press, 1984).

6. Elaine Tyler May, *Homeward Bound: American Families in the Cold War Era* (New York: Basic Books, 2008).

7. Ibid.

8. Hugh G. Gallagher, *FDR's Splendid Deception: The Moving Story of Roosevelt's Massive Disability—and the Intense Efforts to Conceal It from the Public* (New York: Dodd, Mead, 1985).

9. Laurie Block and Jay Allison, "World War II Rehabilitation," *National Public Radio*, 1998, available at https://www.npr.org/programs/disability/ba_shows.dir/work .dir/highlights/ww2.html.

10. Audra Jennings, *Out of the Horrors of War: Disability Politics in World War II America* (Philadelphia: University of Pennsylvania, 2016).

11. Alondra Nelson, *Body and Soul: The Black Panther Party and the Fight against Medical Discrimination* (Minneapolis: University of Minnesota Press, 2011); Susan Schweik, "Lomax's Matrix: Disability, Solidarity, and the Black Power of 504," *Disability Studies Quarterly* 31, no. 1 (2011), available at http://dsq-sds.org/article/view/1371/1539.

12. Linda R. Shaw, "Judy Heumann," in *Enabling Lives: Biographies of Six Prominent Americans with Disabilities*, ed. Brian T. McMahon and Linda R. Shaw (Boca Raton, FL: CRC Press, 2000), 87–106.

13. Brown, "Zona and Ed Roberts."

14. Alfred H. Katz, *Parents of the Handicapped: Self-Organized Parents and Relatives Groups for Treatment of Ill and Handicapped Children* (Springfield, IL: Charles C. Thomas, 1961), 59–60.

15. Theda Skocpol and Jillian Dickert, "Speaking for Families and Children in a Changing Civic America," in *Who Speaks for America's Children? The Role of Child Advocates in Public Policy*, ed. Carol J. DeVita and Rachel Mosher-Williams (Washington, DC: Urban Institute, 2001), 137–164.

16. John Gliedman and William Roth, *The Unexpected Minority: Handicapped Children in America* (New York: Harcourt Brace Jovanovich, 1980).

17. Ibid., 167–168.

18. Ibid., 170.

19. Mayo Clinic, "Cerebral Palsy," available at https://www.mayoclinic.org/diseases-conditions/cerebral-palsy/symptoms-causes/syc-20353999 (accessed November 26, 2019).

20. Ibid.

21. Natalie N. Jean, "United Cerebral Palsy Association," in *Encyclopedia of American Disability History*, ed. Susan Burch (New York: Facts on File, 2009), 3:915–916.

22. Leonard H. Goldenson, with Marvin J. Wolf, *Beating the Odds: The Untold Story behind the Rise of ABC; The Stars, Struggles, and Egos That Transformed Network Television by the Man Who Made It Happen* (New York: Charles Scribner's Sons, 1991).

23. United Cerebral Palsy, "Our History," available at https://ucp.org/our-history (accessed November 26, 2019).

24. Fred Pelka, "United Cerebral Palsy Associations Inc. (UCPA)," in *The ABC-CLIO Companion to the Disability Rights Movement* (Santa Barbara, CA: ABC-CLIO, 1997), 309–310.

25. Jean, "United Cerebral Palsy Association."

26. Katz, *Parents of the Handicapped*, 25.

27. Ibid., 29.

28. Lewis P. Rowland, *NINDS at 50: An Incomplete History Celebrating the Fiftieth Anniversary of the National Institute of Neurological Disorders and Stroke* (New York: Demos Medical, 2003), 15–16.

29. Ingrid G. Ferreras, Caroline Hannaway, and Victoria A. Hardin, eds., *Mind, Brain, Body, and Behavior: Foundations of Neuroscience and Behavioral Research at the National Institutes of Health* (Washington, DC: IOS Press, 2004), 20–24.

30. Paul K. Longmore, *Telethons: Spectacle, Disability, and the Business of Charity* (New York: Oxford University Press, 2016), 93.

31. Marie Killilea, *Karen* (New York: Prentice-Hall, 1952).

32. Ibid., 23.

33. Ibid., 34.

34. Ibid., 120.

35. Ibid., 137.

36. Marie Killilea, *With Love from Karen* (New York: Prentice-Hall, 1963).

37. Pelka, "United Cerebral Palsy Associations Inc. (UCPA)."

38. United Cerebral Palsy, "Our Mission," available at https://ucp.org/our-mission/ (accessed January 4, 2019); Jean, "United Cerebral Palsy Association," 916.

39. For a discussion of the DD Act, see Allison Carey, *On the Margins of Citizenship: Intellectual Disability and Civil Rights in Twentieth-Century America* (Philadelphia: Temple University Press, 2009), 138–140.

40. Pelka, "United Cerebral Palsy Associations Inc. (UCPA)."

41. Jean, "United Cerebral Palsy Association," 916.

42. Mayo Clinic, "Muscular Dystrophy," available at https://www.mayoclinic.org/diseases-conditions/muscular-dystrophy/symptoms-causes/syc-20375388 (accessed November 26, 2019).

43. Katz, *Parents of the Handicapped*, 40.

44. Muscular Dystrophy Association, "About Us," available at https://www.mda.org/about-mda/history (accessed November 26, 2019).

45. Katz, *Parents of the Handicapped*, 42.

46. Ibid., 43.

47. Ibid., 42.

48. Muscular Dystrophy Association, "About Us."

49. Marsha M. Olsen-Wiley, "Easter Seals," in Burch, *Encyclopedia of American Disability History*, 1:305–306.

50. Paul H. King, "Edgar F. 'Daddy' Allen," November 1940, Joseph A. Caulder Collection, available at http://www.nlis.net/~freedomi/rotary/caulder/DaddyAllenPage.htm.

51. Pat Boone, *The Human Touch* (New York: Weisser and Weiser, 1991).

52. Ibid., 37.

53. Ibid., 182.

54. Easterseals, "Legislative Landmarks," available at http://www.easterseals.com/get-involved/advocacy/legislative-landmarks.html (accessed January 2, 2019).

55. Lester M. Salamon and Alan J. Abramson, "The Nonprofit Sector," in *The Reagan Experiment*, ed. John L. Palmer and Isabel V. Sawhill (Washington, DC: Urban Institute Press, 1982), 219–243.

56. Longmore, *Telethons*.

57. Ibid., 172.

58. Ibid., 176.

59. Ibid., 187–195.

60. Ibid., 195–197.

61. Fred Pelka, "Telethons," in *The ABC-CLIO Companion to the Disability Rights Movement*, 301–302.

62. Longmore, *Telethons*, 104–105.

63. *Vital Signs: Crip Culture Talks Back*, dir. David Mitchell and Sharon Snyder (Brooklyn, NY: Fanlight Productions, 1995).

CHAPTER 5

1. Rosalyn B. Darling, "Parental Entrepreneurship: A Consumerist Response to Professional Dominance," *Journal of Social Issues* 44, no. 1 (1988): 141–158.

2. Scholars and activists often differentiate between capital "D" in "Deaf," which signifies an affiliation with Deaf culture and a Deaf political identity, and lowercase "d," which signifies the belief that one's deafness or hearing impairment is a disability to be treated by medical professionals and hearing audiologists. When speaking of deafness as an impairment or in reference to a broad population, we use "d." Nondeaf parents tend to see deafness as an impairment or to move among interpretations, so we also use "d" when discussing most parent activism. We use "D" to discuss Deaf activists and organizations that promote Deaf culture and political identity.

3. For work on the role of embodiment in social movements, see Pamela Block et al., "Building Pediatric Multiple Sclerosis Community Using a Disability Studies Framework of Empowerment," in *Research in Social Science and Disability*, vol. 6, *Disability and Community*, ed. Allison C. Carey and Richard Scotch, (Bingley, UK: Emerald Group, 2011), 85–112; and Phil Brown et al., "Embodied Health Movements: New Approaches to Social Movements in Health," *Sociology of Health and Illness* 26, no. 1 (2004): 50–58.

4. For the classic work on resource mobilization theory, see John D. McCarthy and Mayer N. Zald, "Resource Mobilization and Social Movements: A Partial Theory," *American Journal of Sociology* 82, no. 6 (1977): 1212–1241.

5. James W. Trent, *Inventing the Feeble Mind: A History of Mental Retardation in the United States* (Berkeley: University of California Press, 1994).

6. R. Rudy Higgins-Evenson, *The Price of Progress: Public Service, Taxation, and the American Corporate State, 1877 to 1929* (Baltimore: Johns Hopkins University Press, 2003), 75.

7. Margret Winzer, *The History of Special Education: From Isolation to Integration* (Washington, DC: Gallaudet University Press, 1993).

8. For work on relative deprivation and social movements, see Denton E. Morrison, "Some Notes toward a Theory on Relative Deprivation, Social Movements, and Social Change," *American Behavioral Scientist* 14, no. 5 (1971): 675–690.

9. For classic work on political opportunity theory, see Doug McAdam, *Political Process and the Development of Black Insurgency, 1930–1970* (Chicago: University of Chicago Press, 1982); and Doug McAdam, "Political Opportunity: Conceptual Origins, Current Problems, Future Directions," in *Comparative Perspectives on Social Movements*, ed. Doug McAdam, John D. McCarthy, and Mayer N. Zald (Cambridge: Cambridge University Press, 1996), 20–40.

10. U.S. Department of Commerce, Bureau of the Census, *Insane and Feeble-Minded in Institutions, 1910* (Washington, DC: Government Printing Office, 1914), 187.

11. Cerebral Palsy Alliance, "How Does Cerebral Palsy Affect People?" available at https://www.cerebralpalsy.org.au/what-is-cerebral-palsy/how-cerebral-palsy -affects-people/ (accessed November 26, 2019).

12. U.S. Department of Commerce, Bureau of the Census, *Feeble-Minded and Epileptics in Institutions in 1923* (Washington, DC: Government Printing Office, 1926); U.S. Department of Commerce, Bureau of the Census, *Insane and Feeble-Minded in Institutions, 1910*. Further breakdowns were not provided.

13. Kids Mental Health, "How Is Mental Illness in Children Diagnosed," available at http://www.kidsmentalhealth.org/how-is-mental-illness-in-children-diagnosed (accessed November 26, 2019).

14. Kathleen Reis Merikangas et al., "Prevalence and Treatment of Mental Disorders among US Children in the 2001–2004 NHANES," *Pediatrics* 125 (2010): 75–81.

15. Wanda J. Blanchett, "'Telling It Like It Is': The Role of Race, Class, and Culture in the Perpetuation of Learning Disability as a Privileged Category for the White Middle Class," *Disability Studies Quarterly* 30, no. 3 (2010), available at http://dsq -sds.org/article/view/1233/1280; Linda M. Blum, *Raising Generation Rx: Mothering Kids with Invisible Disabilities in an Age of Inequality* (New York: New York University Press, 2015); Victoria Pitts-Taylor, "The Plastic Brain: Neoliberalism and the Neuronal Self," *Health* 14, no. 6 (2010): 635–652.

16. National Federation of the Blind, "Blindness Statistics," January 2019, available at https://nfb.org/blindness-statistics.

17. James W. Trent, *The Manliest Man: Samuel G. Howe and the Contours of Nineteenth-Century American Reform* (Amherst: University of Massachusetts Press, 2012).

18. National Federation of the Blind, "About NOPBC," available at http://www .nopbc.org/about (accessed November 26, 2019).

19. National Black Disability Coalition, "About Us," available at http://www .blackdisability.org/content/about-us (accessed November 26, 2019).

20. Jane Dunhamn, "From the Director's Desk," National Black Disability Coalition, available at http://www.blackdisability.org/content/directors-desk-0 (accessed November 26, 2019).

21. Kerima Çevik, phone interview by the author, September 5, 2018.

22. Autism Speaks, "About Us," available at https://www.autismspeaks.org/about-us (accessed November 26, 2019).

23. Hands and Voices, "Information about Hands and Voices," available at http://www.handsandvoices.org/about/index.htm (accessed November 27, 2019).

24. Hands and Voices, "Mission," available at http://www.handsandvoices.org/about/mission.htm (accessed November 27, 2019).

CHAPTER 6

A version of this chapter was previously published as Allison C. Carey, Pamela Block, and Richard K. Scotch, "Sometimes Allies: Parent-Led Disability Organizations and Social Movements," *Disability Studies Quarterly* 39, no. 1 (2019), available at http://dsq-sds.org/article/view/6281/5183.

1. James I. Charlton, *Nothing About Us Without Us: Disability Oppression and Empowerment* (Berkeley: University of California Press, 2000); Sharon Barnartt and Richard K. Scotch, *Disability Protests: Contentious Politics, 1970–1999* (Washington, DC: Gallaudet University Press, 2001); Nella Van Dyke and Holly J. McCammon, "Introduction," in *Strategic Alliances: Coalition Building and Social Movements*, ed. Nella Van Dyke and Holly J. McCammon (Minneapolis: University of Minnesota Press, 2010), xi–xxviii; Mayer N. Zald and John D. McCarthy, eds., *Social Movements in an Organizational Society: Collected Essays* (New York: Routledge, 1997).

2. Jurgen Gerhards and Diechter Rucht, "Mesomobilization: Organizing and Framing in Two Protest Campaigns in West Germany," *American Journal of Sociology* 98 (1992): 555–595; Holly J. McCammon and Nella Van Dyke, "Applying Qualitative Comparative Analysis to Empirical Studies of Social Movement Coalition Formation," in Van Dyke and McCammon, *Strategic Alliances*, 292–325; Suzanne Staggenborg, "Conclusion: Research on Social Movement Coalitions," in Van Dyke and McCammon, *Strategic Alliances*, 316–330.

3. David A. Snow et al., "Frame Alignment Processes, Micromobilization, and Movement Participation," *American Sociological Review* 51, no. 4 (1986): 464–481.

4. Staggenborg, "Conclusion: Research on Social Movement Coalitions."

5. Stafanija Giric, "Strange Bedfellows: Antiabortion and Disability Rights Advocacy," *Journal of Law and the Biosciences* 3, no. 3 (2016): 736–742.

6. Nelson A. Pichardo, "New Social Movements: A Critical Review," *Annual Review of Sociology* 23 (1997): 411–430.

7. Thomas D. Beamish and Amy J. Luebbers, "Alliance Building across Social Movements," *Social Problems* 56, no. 4 (2009): 647–676.

8. Charlton, *Nothing About Us Without Us*.

9. Paul K. Longmore, *Why I Burned My Book and Other Essays on Disability* (Philadelphia: Temple University Press, 2003).

10. National Disability Leadership Alliance, "About NDLA," available at http://www.disabilityleadership.org/about (accessed November 27, 2019).

11. Hannah B. Rosqvist, Charlotte Brownlow, and Linsday O'Dell, "'An Association for All'—Notions of the Meaning of Autistic Self-Advocacy Politics within a Parent-Dominated Movement," *Journal of Community and Applied Psychology* 25, no. 3 (2015): 219–231.

12. Simi Linton, *Claiming Disability: Knowledge and Identity* (New York: New York University Press, 1998); Michael Oliver and Colin Barnes, *The New Politics of Disablement* (New York: Palgrave Macmillan, 2012).

13. Scholarship has also increasingly examined how these models intertwine and interact. See Tobin Siebers, *Disability Theory* (Ann Arbor: University of Michigan Press, 2008); and Carol Thomas, "The Disabled Body," in *Real Bodies*, ed. Mary Evans and Ellie Lee (London: Palgrave, 2002), 64–78.

14. National Federation of the Blind, "About NOPBC," available at http://www.nopbc.org/about (accessed November 26, 2019).

15. See the home page of the National Federation of the Blind, at http://www.nfb.org.

16. Anita Silvers and Leslie Francis, eds., *Americans with Disabilities: Exploring Implications of the Law for Individuals and Institutions* (New York: Routledge, 2000).

17. Richard K. Scotch, *From Good Will to Civil Rights: Transforming Federal Disability Policy* (Philadelphia: Temple University Press, 1984).

18. See the United Cerebral Palsy home page, at https://ucp.org; and United Cerebral Palsy, "Our Mission," available at https://ucp.org/our-mission (accessed January 4, 2020).

19. United Cerebral Palsy, "Our History," available at https://ucp.org/our-history (accessed November 26, 2019).

20. Brian R. Grossman, "Same Mandate, Changing Concept of Community: An Analysis of Bills to Mandate Medicaid Coverage of Community-Based Attendant Services and Supports (1997–2010)," in *Research in Social Science and Disability*, vol. 6, *Disability and Community*, ed. Allison C. Carey and Richard Scotch (Bingley, UK: Emerald Group, 2011), 215–240.

21. David A. Ervin et al., "Healthcare for People with Intellectual and Developmental Disabilities in the Community," *Frontiers in Public Health* 2, no. 83 (2014): 1–8; Gloria L. Krahn, Deborah Klein Walker, and Rosalyn Correa Araujo, "Persons with Disabilities as an Unrecognized Health Disparity Population," supplement, *American Journal of Public Health* 105, no. S2 (2015): S198–S206.

22. Arc, "Health," 2017, available at https://thearc.org/position-statements/health/.

23. National Alliance on Mental Illness, "Parity for Mental Health Coverage," available at https://www.nami.org/Learn-More/Public-Policy/Parity-for-Mental-Health-Coverage (accessed November 27, 2019).

24. Eric Parens and Adrienne Asche, eds., *Prenatal Testing and Disability Rights* (Washington, DC: Georgetown University Press, 2000); Gareth M. Thomas, *Down's Syndrome Screening and Reproductive Politics* (London: Routledge, 2017).

25. Capital "D" in Deaf signifies an affiliation with Deaf culture and a Deaf political identity; lowercase "d" signifies the belief that one's deafness or hearing impairment is a disability to be treated via medical professionals and hearing audiologists. Little "d" deaf people typically do not embrace Deaf culture or ASL.

26. Michael Bérubé, *Life as Jamie Knows It: An Exceptional Child Grows Up* (Boston: Beacon Press, 2016).

27. National Alliance on Mental Illness, "Policy Platform," available at https://www.nami.org/About-NAMI/Policy-Platform (accessed November 27, 2019).

28. National Alliance on Mental Illness, "Personal Stories: How Invalidating My Bipolar Disorder Invalidates Me," available at https://www.nami.org/Personal-Stories/How-Invalidating-My-Bipolar-Disorder-Invalidates-M# (accessed November 27, 2019).

29. Autism Speaks, "About Us," available at https://www.autismspeaks.org/about-us (accessed November 26, 2019).

30. Ibid.

31. Eli Clare, *Brilliant Imperfection: Grappling with Cure* (Durham, NC: Duke University Press, 2017).

32. Cassandra Evans, *Asylum to Community and In-Between: Examining the Post-deinstitutionalization Experiences of Individuals with Mental Disabilities in Suffolk County, New York* (Ph.D. diss., Stony Brook University, Stony Brook, NY, 2017).

33. American Childhood Cancer Organization, "About ACCO," available at https://www.acco.org/about (accessed February 2, 2020).

34. See the American Childhood Cancer Organization home page, at http://acco.org.

35. American Childhood Cancer Organization, "Childhood Cancer Statistics," available at https://www.acco.org/childhood-cancer-statistics (accessed February 2, 2020).

36. Anne McGuire, *War on Autism: On the Cultural Logic of Normative Violence* (Ann Arbor: University of Michigan Press, 2016).

37. Autism NOW Center and Autistic Self Advocacy Network, "Welcome to the Autistic Community!" 2014, available at http://autisticadvocacy.org/wp-content/uploads/2014/02/WTTAC-Adult-FINAL-2.pdf; Julia Bascom, ed., *Loud Hands: Autistic People Speaking* (Washington, DC: Autistic Self Advocacy Network, 2012).

38. McGuire, *War on Autism*.

39. National Down Syndrome Society, "Research and Down Syndrome," available at https://www.ndss.org/resources/research-down-syndrome (accessed November 27, 2019).

40. Clare, *Brilliant Imperfection*; Eunjung Kim, *Curative Violence: Rehabilitating Disability, Gender, and Sexuality in Modern Korea* (Durham, NC: Duke University Press, 2017).

41. Nirmala Erevelles further illuminates this debate, arguing that for people of color and in poverty, disability is often caused by war and intersecting oppressions. The uncritical demand to celebrate the value of disability may further oppression by ignoring the material realities leading to their disability. Still, solutions cannot remain solely with the medical model. Rather, power redistribution and disability justice are essential. Nirmala Erevelles, *Disability and Difference in Global Contexts: Enabling a Transformative Body Politic* (New York: Palgrave Macmillan, 2011).

42. Sara Maria Acevedo, "Enabling Geographies: Neurodivergence, Self-Authorship, and the Politics of Social Space" (Ph.D. diss., California Institute of Integral Studies, San Francisco, 2018); Brent White, "Banging My Head on the Neurotypical Wall," ACAT: Ala Costa Adult Transition Program, January 22, 2016, available at https://alacosta-acat.org/2016/01/22/banging-my-head-on-the-neurotypical-wall/.

43. National Federation of the Blind, "About the NOPBC," available at http://www.nopbc.org/about (accessed January 9, 2020).

44. National Federation of the Blind, "Resolution 2019-02: Regarding the Continued Exploitation of Workers with Disabilities under Section 14(c) of the Fair Labor Standards Act," 2019, available at https://www.nfb.org/resources/speeches-and-reports/resolutions/2019-resolutions#02.

45. Carlton Anne Cook Walker, "Blind Students and the IEP Process," *Future Reflections* 36, no. 2 (2017), available at https://www.nfb.org/images/nfb/publications/fr/fr36/2/fr360202.htm.

46. National Federation of the Blind, "Resolution 2019-02."

47. Arc, "Inclusion," 2015, available at https://www.thearc.org/who-we-are/position-statements/rights/inclusion.

48. Steven J. Taylor, "Caught in the Continuum: A Critical Analysis of the Principle of the Least Restrictive Environment," *Journal of the Association for the Severely Handicapped* 13, no. 1 (1998): 41–53; Evans, *Asylum to Community and In-Between*.

49. Quoted in Cara Matthews, "Sheltered Workshops for Disabled to Be Phased Out," *USA Today*, July 28, 2014, available at https://www.usatoday.com/story/news/nation/2014/07/28/sheltered-workshops-disabled-phased-out/13302139.

50. Quoted in Rick Karlin, "Sheltered Workshops Are in Midst of a Storm," *Times Union* (Albany, NY), July 20, 2013, available at https://www.timesunion.com/local/article/Sheltered-workshops-are-in-midst-of-a-storm-4677272.php.

51. Harlan Lane, "Constructions of Deafness," in *Disability Studies Reader*, ed. Lennard Davis (New York City: Routledge, 2006), 79–92.

52. National Association of the Deaf, "Position Statement on Inclusion," January 26, 2002, available at https://www.nad.org/about-us/position-statements/position-statement-on-inclusion.

53. The totalizing nature of these systems is akin to Erving Goffman's concept of "total institutions" as developed in Erving Goffman, *Asylums: Essays on the Social Situation of Mental Patients and Other Inmates* (New York: Anchor Books, 1961).

54. See the VOR website, at https://www.vor.net.

55. Quoted in Daniel Goleman, "States Move to Ease Laws Committing Mentally Ill," *New York Times*, December 6, 1986, available at http://www.nytimes.com/1986/12/09/science/states-move-to-ease-law-committing-mentally-ill.html?pagewanted=all.

56. National Alliance on Mental Illness, "Legal Issues: Right to Treatment," available at https://www.nami.org/About-NAMI/Policy-Platform/9-Legal-Issues (accessed November 27, 2019).

57. Kerima Çevik, "About Mrs. Ç," *Autism Wars* (blog), available at http://theautismwars.blogspot.com/p/blog-page.html (accessed November 27, 2019).

58. Steven E. Brown, "Zona and Ed Roberts: Twentieth Century Pioneers," *Disability Studies Quarterly* 20, no. 1 (2000): 26–42.

59. One person was both a parent and self-identified and is counted in both percentages.

60. Two self-advocates identified experience in self-advocacy organizations and one self-identified as a person with a relevant diagnosis who is also a parent of a person diagnosed. The latter person is counted both as a parent and as a self-advocate.

61. Arc, "What We Do," previously available at http://www.thearc.org/what-we-do (accessed June 2017). By January 2020, the Arc website had modified this claim to a more modest one—that the organization is "the largest national community-based organization advocating for people with intellectual and developmental disabilities." See Arc, "About Us," available at http://www.thearc.org/about-us (accessed February 2, 2020).

62. National Federation of the Blind, "About NOPBC," available at http://www.nopbc.org/about (accessed January 9, 2020).

63. Mary Giliberti, letter to Representatives Tim Murphy and Eddie Johnson, June 12, 2015, available at https://www.nami.org/getattachment/Blogs/From-the-Executive-Director/June-2015/An-Opportunity-for-Comprehensive-Mental-Health-Ref/Murphy-Johnson-letter-6-12-2015.pdf.

64. National Disability Leadership Alliance, letter to Representatives Fred Upton and Frank Pallone, July 26, 2015, available at http://www.ncmhr.org/downloads/ndla-letter-re-HR2646.pdf.

65. "H.R. 2646 (114th): Helping Families in Mental Health Crisis Act of 2016," *Gov-Track*, June 20, 2016, available at https://www.govtrack.us/congress/bills/114/hr2646/summary.

66. Michelle Diament, "Advocates, Big Pharma Make Push for Autism Drugs," *Disability Scoop*, March 20, 2012, available at https://www.disabilityscoop.com/2012/03/20/advocates-big-pharma-drugs/15213/.

67. Autistic Self Advocacy Network, "ASAN Resources on Coverage for Autism-Related Services," available at https://autisticadvocacy.org/policy/toolkits/healthcoverage (accessed November 27, 2019).

68. For more information on the criticisms of Autism Speaks, see Autistic Self Advocacy Network, "Before You Donate to Autism Speaks, Consider the Facts," March 2019, available at https://autisticadvocacy.org/wp-content/uploads/2019/03/AutismSpeaksFlyer2019.pdf.

69. Voice of Reason, "About VOR," available at https://www.vor.net/about-vor (accessed November 27, 2019).

70. See Voice of Reason, "Ohio—Update on the Ball v. Kasich Class Action," available at https://www.vor.net/legislative-voice/legislation/item/ohio-updates-on-the-ball-v-kasich-class-action (accessed February 3, 2020).

71. Voice of Reason, "Please Oppose the Disability Integration Act," available at https://vor.net/legislative-voice/action-alerts/item/please-oppose-the-disability-integration-act (accessed June 19, 2019).

72. "The Gag," *Ragged Edge*, November–December 1998, available at http://www.raggededgemagazine.com/1199/polly.html.

73. Pichardo, "New Social Movements."

74. Eva Feder Kittay, "Forever Small: The Strange Case of Ashley X," *Hypatia* 26, no. 3 (2011): 610–631; Kelly Underman, Paige L. Sweet, and Claire Laurier, "Custodial Citizenship in the Omnibus Autism Proceeding," *Sociological Forum* 32, no. 3 (2017): 544–565.

75. Linda M. Blum, *Raising Generation Rx: Mothering Kids with Invisible Disabilities in an Age of Inequality* (New York: New York University Press, 2015); Victoria Pitts-Taylor, "The Plastic Brain: Neoliberalism and the Neuronal Self," *Health* 14, no. 6 (2010): 635–652; Kittay, "Forever Small"; Michael Rembis, ed., *Disabling Domesticity* (New York: Palgrave Macmillan, 2016).

76. McGuire, *War on Autism*; Zachary A. Richter, "Melting Down the Family Unit: A Neuroqueer Critique of Table-Readiness," in Rembis, *Disabling Domesticity*, 335–348.

77. Dan Goodley, "Becoming Rhizomatic Parents: Deleuze, Guattari, and Disabled Babies," *Disability and Society* 22, no. 2 (2007): 145–160.

78. Beamish and Luebbers, "Alliance Building across Social Movements."

79. Jennifer L. Erkulwater, "How the Nation's Largest Minority Became White: Race Politics and the Disability Rights Movement, 1970–1980," *Journal of Policy History* 30, no. 3 (2018): 367–399; Angela Frederick and Dara Shifrer, "Race and Disability: From Analogy to Intersectionality," *Sociology of Race and Ethnicity* 5, no. 2 (2019): 2000–2014; Corbette Joan OToole, *Fading Scars: My Queer Disability History* (Fort Worth: Autonomous Press, 2015).

CHAPTER 7

1. Richard K. Scotch, "Disability as the Basis for a Social Movement," *Journal of Social Issues* 44, no. 1 (1988): 159–172.

2. Michael Schofield, *January First: A Child's Descent into Madness and Her Father's Struggle to Save Her* (New York: Broadway Books, 2013).

3. Sharon Barnartt and Richard Scotch, *Disability Protests: Contentious Politics, 1970–1999* (Washington, DC: Gallaudet University Press, 2001), 17.

4. Ibid., 16.

5. Allison C. Carey, *On the Margins of Citizenship: Intellectual Disability and Civil Rights in Twentieth-Century America* (Philadelphia: Temple University Press, 2009), 109–113.

6. Ibid., 125–126.

7. Sharon Barnartt, Kay Shriner, and Richard K. Scotch, "Advocacy and Political Action," in *Handbook of Disability Studies*, ed. Gary L. Albrecht, Katherine D. Seelman, and Michael Bury (Thousand Oaks, CA: Sage, 2001), 430–449.

8. Richard K. Scotch, *From Good Will to Civil Rights: Transforming Federal Disability Policy* (Philadelphia: Temple University Press, 1984).

9. Muscular Dystrophy Association, "Innovations in Care," available at https://www.mda.org/care/mda-care-centers (accessed November 27, 2019).

10. Barnartt and Scotch, *Disability Protests*.

11. Carey, *On the Margins of Citizenship*, 105–106.

12. Ibid., 120–121.

13. Ibid., 125.

14. Public Law 94-142.

15. James G. McCullagh, "Challenging the Proposed Deregulation of P.L. 94-142: A Case Study of Citizen Advocacy," *Journal of Sociology and Social Welfare* 15, no. 3 (1988): 65–81.

16. Susan Heller Anderson, "The Reagan Effect: Goals on Handicapped Meet Wide Resistance," *New York Times*, November 14, 1982, available at https://www.nytimes.com /1982/11/14/education/the-reagan-effect-goals-on-handicapped-meet-wide-resistance .html.

17. McCullagh, "Challenging the Proposed Deregulation of P.L. 94-142."

18. Ibid., 73.

19. Little Lobbyists, "Our Story," available at https://littlelobbyists.org/new-folder (accessed November 27, 2019).

20. Pennsylvania Association for Retarded Children (PARC) v. Commonwealth of Pennsylvania, 343 F. Supp. 279 (1972).

21. Fred Pelka, *What We Have Done: An Oral History of the Disability Rights Movement* (Amherst: University of Massachusetts Press, 2012).

22. Ibid., 136–137.

23. Ibid., 139.

24. Scotch, *From Good Will to Civil Rights*, 37–38.

25. Halderman v. Pennhurst State School and Hospital, 446 F. Supp. 1319 (1979).

26. Fred Pelka, *The ABC-CLIO Companion to the Disability Rights Movement* (Santa Barbara, CA: ABC-CLIO, 1997), 146.

27. Lennard J. Davis, *Enabling Acts: The Hidden Story of How the Americans with Disabilities Act Gave the Largest US Minority Its Rights* (Boston: Beacon Press, 2015).

28. Ibid., 165.

29. Indigenous Action, "Accomplices Not Allies: Abolishing the Ally Industrial Complex," May 4, 2014, available at http://www.indigenousaction.org/accomplices-not -allies-abolishing-the-ally-industrial-complex/.

30. See the UCP website, at https://ucp.org.

31. See the Autism Speaks website, at https://www.autismspeaks.org.

32. NAMI's website is available at https://www.nami.org.

33. See the Arc's website, at https://thearc.org.

CHAPTER 8

1. Arc, "Community-Based Long Term Supports and Services," available at https://www.thearc.org/what-we-do/public-policy/policy-issues/long-term (accessed November 27, 2019).

2. Mental Health America, "2017 State of Mental Health in America—Access to Care Data," available at https://www.mhanational.org/issues/2017-state-mental-health-america-access-care-data (accessed January 9, 2020).

3. National Alliance on Mental Illness, *Engagement: A New Standard for Mental Health Care* (Arlington, VA: NAMI, 2016), 14.

4. Ibid., 2.

5. Family of Liam Huff, "Fully Include Liam in First Grade and Treat Him with Dignity," *Change.org*, 2015, available at https://www.change.org/p/fully-include-liam-in-first-grade-and-treat-him-with-dignity.

6. Family of Liam Huff, "Important Update: MVSD Ramps Up Abuse of Liam's Rights," *Change.org*, September 10, 2015, available at https://www.change.org/p/fully-include-liam-in-first-grade-and-treat-him-with-dignity/u/13317336.

7. Yvonne (pseudonym), phone interview by the author, July 2014.

8. Erica (pseudonym), phone interview by the author, May 2015.

9. Donna (pseudonym), phone interview by the author, July 2014.

10. Liz Szabo, "Cost of Not Caring: Stigma Set in Stone," *USA Today*, June 25, 2014, available at https://www.usatoday.com/story/news/nation/2014/06/25/stigma-of-mental-illness/9875351.

11. Eugene Gramm, "New Hope for a Different Child," *Parents Magazine* 26, no. 48 (1951): 154.

12. Jill Critchfield, "ADHD, Autism and Discrimination at School," *Parenting ADHD and Autism*, February 15, 2016, available at http://parentingadhdandautism.com/2016/02/15/adhd-autism-discrimination-school.

13. Elise Young, "Clinton Plan to End Subminimum Wage Stirs Debate," *Disability Scoop*, June 6, 2016, available at https://www.disabilityscoop.com/2016/06/06/clinton-submininum-debate/22372.

14. Jaclyn Okin Barney, "PIE's Testimony to City Council Regarding: Oversight: Special Education Instruction and Student Achievement," October 28, 2014, available at http://www.parentsforinclusiveeducation.com/wp-content/uploads/2014/10/2014.10.28-PIE-Testimony-for-City-Council-Hearing1.pdf.

15. Nikki, April 10, 2011, comment to Alexa Posney, "Inclusive Schools," *Homeroom* (blog), March 17, 2011, available at https://blog.ed.gov/2011/03/inclusive-schools.

16. Cindy (pseudonym), phone interview by the author, May 2015.

17. David M. Perry, "Four Disabled People Dead in Another Week of Police Brutality," *The Nation*, September 22, 2017, available at https://www.thenation.com/article/four-disabled-dead-in-another-week-of-police-brutality.

18. See also Leroy F. Moore Jr., Talila A. Lewis, and Lydia X. Z. Brown, "Accountable Reporting on Disability, Race, and Police Violence: A Community Response to the 'Ruderman White Paper on the Media Coverage of Use of Force and Disability,'" Harriet Tubman Collective, May 2016, available at https://docs.google.com/document/d/117eoVeJVP594L6-1bgL8zpZrzgojfsveJwcWuHpkNcs/edit.

19. National Resource Center for Supported Decision-Making, "Ryan King—Updated," available at http://supporteddecisionmaking.org/impact-stories/ryan-king (accessed November 27, 2019).

20. Mark (pseudonym), focus group interview by the author, September 2014.

21. Nicte M., quoted in Ellen Stumbo, "Should Kids Be Present at Their Own IEPs?" *The Mighty*, January 24, 2018, available at https://themighty.com/2018/01/iep-should-i-bring-my-child/.

22. Donna, phone interview by the author.

23. Yvonne, phone interview by the author.

24. Joe F., quoted in Ann Schimke, "Inside One Colorado Family's Long Legal Journey to Affirm Their Son's Right to a Meaningful Education," *Chalkbeat*, November 15, 2017, available at https://www.chalkbeat.org/posts/co/2017/11/15/inside-one-colorado-familys-long-legal-journey-to-affirm-their-sons-right-to-a-meaningful-education/.

25. Quoted in Laura McKenna, "How a New Supreme Court Ruling Could Affect Special Education," *The Atlantic*, March 23, 2017, available at https://www.theatlantic.com/education/archive/2017/03/how-a-new-supreme-court-ruling-could-affect-special-education/520662.

26. Harold (pseudonym), phone interview by the author, September 2018.

27. Joseph T. Weingold and Rudolf P. Hormuth, "Group Guidance of Parents of Mentally Retarded Children," *Journal of Clinical Psychology* 9, no. 2 (1953): 118.

28. American Psychiatric Association, "Family Caregivers Face Many Challenges," *APA Blogs*, March 8, 2016, available at https://www.psychiatry.org/news-room/apa-blogs/apa-blog/2016/03/family-caregivers-face-many-challenges.

29. Destinee (pseudonym), phone interview by the author, November 2016.

30. L. Anderson et al., "Family and Individual Needs for Disability Supports: Community Report, 2017," 2018, available at https://thearc.org/wp-content/uploads/forchapters/FINDS_report-2017-FINAL-VERSION.pdf.

31. Erica, phone interview by the author.

32. Quoted in "UN Experts Examine Disability Issues, Family Support," *UN News*, May 15, 2007, available at https://news.un.org/en/story/2007/05/218862-un-experts-examine-disability-issues-family-support. See also Family Caregiver Alliance, "A Caregiver's Bill of Rights," available at https://www.caregiver.org/caregiver%E2%80%99s-bill-rights (accessed November 27, 2019).

33. Yvonne, phone interview by the author.

34. Jack (pseudonym), phone interview by the author, November 2014.

35. Allison C. Carey, "Citizenship and the Family: Parents of Children with Disabilities, the Pursuit of Rights, and Paternalism," in *Civil Disabilities: Citizenship, Membership, and Belonging*, ed. Nancy J. Hirschmann and Beth Linker (Philadelphia: University of Pennsylvania Press, 2015), 165–185.

36. Sara (pseudonym), phone interview by the author, July 2014.

37. Yvonne, phone interview by the author.

38. Liz Szabo, "Mental Illness: Families Cut Out of Care," *USA Today*, February 26, 2016, available at https://www.usatoday.com/story/news/2016/02/26/privacy-law -harms-care-mentally-ill-families-say/80880880/.

39. Laura Mauldin, *Made to Hear: Cochlear Implants and Raising Deaf Children* (Minneapolis: University of Minnesota Press, 2016).

40. Heather Kirnlanier, "On Radical Acceptance (and Not Fixing Your Kid)," *Star in Her Eye* (blog), July 5, 2016, available at https://starinhereye.wordpress.com/ 2016/07/05/on-radical-acceptance-not-fixing-your-kid/?fbclid=IwAR0ptpVeSc BaVc3Q4mONgfV53jUbbCIieV1LiGDNQaY4gbmXwWUFI1P15nw (emphasis in original).

41. Ibid.

42. Sara, phone interview by the author.

43. Cindy, phone interview by the author.

44. Yvonne, phone interview by the author.

45. Liz (pseudonym), phone interview by the author, July 2014.

46. Yvonne, phone interview by the author.

47. Sara, phone interview by the author.

48. Cindy, phone interview by the author.

49. Handspeak, "Cochlear Implants: Not Our Choice," available at https:// www.handspeak.com/culture/index.php?id=126 (accessed November 27, 2019).

50. Wendy Fournier, "Kevin and Avonte's Law Has Passed," National Autism Association, March 23, 2018, available at http://nationalautismassociation.org/ kevin-avontes-law-has-passed.

51. Szabo, "Mental Illness."

52. Fern Kupfer, *Before and After Zachariah* (Chicago: Chicago Review Press, 1998), 179.

53. Theresa Vargas, "Virginia Woman Seeks Power to Live the Way She Wants," *Washington Post*, July 20, 2013, available at https://www.washingtonpost.com/local/ virginia-woman-with-down-syndrome-seeks-power-to-live-the-way-she-wants/2013/ 07/20/76102a82-d789-11e2-a9f2-42ee3912ae0e_story.html.

54. Doug Stanglin, "2-Year-Old Whose Yemeni Mother Was Initially Denied a Visa under Trump's Travel Ban Dies in California Hospital," *USA Today*, December 29, 2018, available at https://www.usatoday.com/story/news/world/2018/12/29/ terminally-ill-boy-whose-yemeni-mom-initially-denied-visa-dies/2439574002/.

55. Michael Waters, "Our Immigration System Is Especially Cruel to Disabled Children," *The Outline*, June 26, 2018, available at https://theoutline.com/post/5074/ immigration-disability-children-ice-detention?zd=1&zi=5s4zzygg.

56. Dolores Gaspar Garcia, "Don't Let This DACA-Eligible Youth with Mental Developmental Delays Get Deported," *¡Somos! Presente*, 2018, available at https://somos.presente.org/petitions/don-t-let-this-daca-eligible-youth-with-downs -syndrome-get-deported.

57. Sylvia Ann Hewlett and Cornel West, *The War against Parents* (New York: Houghton Mifflin, 1998).

58. Aimi Hamraie, *Building Access: Universal Design and the Politics of Disability* (Minneapolis: University of Minnesota Press, 2017).

59. Marta Russell, *Beyond Ramps: Disability at the End of the Social Contract* (Monroe, ME: Common Courage Press, 1998), 113.

60. Barbara Altman, "Caring for a Son with Microcephaly," *Washington Post*, November 29, 2016, available at http://www.windsorstar.com/caring+with+micro cephaly/12451721/story.html.

61. Sara Maria Acevedo, "Enabling Geographies: Neurodivergence, Self-Authorship, and the Politics of Social Space" (Ph.D. diss., California Institute of Integral Studies, San Francisco, 2018); Brent White, "Banging My Head on the Neurotypical Wall," ACAT: Ala Costa Adult Transition Program, January 22, 2016, available at https://ala costa-acat.org/2016/01/22/banging-my-head-on-the-neurotypical-wall/.

62. Allison C. Carey and Lucy Gu, "Walking the Line between the Past and the Future: Parents' Resistance and Commitment to Institutionalization," in *Disability Incarcerated*, ed. Liat Ben-Moshe, Chris Chapman, and Allison C. Carey (New York: Palgrave Macmillan, 2014), 101–119.

63. Christopher (pseudonym), phone interview by the author, November 2014.

64. Erica, phone interview by the author.

65. See Anne M. Kincaid, "News Summary," Disability and Abuse Project, August 5, 2013, available at http://disability-abuse.com/newsfeed/2013-08-05.htm.

66. Cindy, phone interview by the author.

67. Harold, phone interview by the author.

68. Justin Jouvenal, "Man Accused of Stealing $5 in Snacks Died in Jail as He Waited for Space at Mental Hospital," *Washington Post*, September 29, 2017, available at https://www.washingtonpost.com/local/crime/man-accused-of-stealing-5 -in-snacks-died-in-jail-as-he-waited-for-space-at-mental-hospital/2015/09/29/7ceac8a2 -5aff-11e5-9757-e49273f05f65_story.html; David M. Perry, "Four Disabled People Dead in Another Week of Police Brutality," *The Nation*, September 22, 2017, available at https://www.thenation.com/article/four-disabled-dead-in-another-week-of-police -brutality.

69. Sara, phone interview by the author.

70. Destinee, phone interview by the author.

71. Rebecca Koller, "Sexuality and Adolescents with Autism," *Sexuality and Disability* 18, no. 2 (2000): 125–135; Alan Santinele Martino, "Power Struggles over the Sexualities of Individuals with Disabilities," in *Dis/Consent: Perspectives on Sexual Consent and Sexual Violence*, ed. KelleyAnne Malinen (Halifax, NS: Fernwood, 2019), 98–197.

72. Miriam (pseudonym), phone interview by the author, September 2018.

73. For discussions of disability justice, see Patty Berne, "Disability Justice—a Working Draft," *Sins Invalid*, June 9, 2015, available at https://sinsinvalid.org/blog/disability -justice-a-working-draft-by-patty-berne; Mia Mingus, "Reflection toward Practice: Some Questions on Disability Justice," in *Criptiques*, ed. Caitlin Wood (self-published, 2014), 107–114, available at https://criptiques.files.wordpress.com/2014/05/crip-final-2.pdf; and Leah Lakshmi Piepzna-Samarasinha, *Care Work: Dreaming Disability Justice* (Vancouver, BC: Arsenal Pulp Press, 2018).

74. Michael Bérubé, "Don't Let My Son Plunge off the 'Disability Cliff' When I'm Gone," *USA Today*, April 2, 2018, available at https://www.usatoday.com/story/opinion/2018/ 04/02/dont-let-my-son-plunge-off-disability-cliff-column/443138002. See also Beth Miller, "New Rule Highlights Disability Housing Debate," *Delaware Online*, November 30, 2014, available at https://www.delawareonline.com/story/news/local/2014/11/30/ two-sides-disability-housing-debate/19721065/.

75. Cal Montgomery, "Developmental Disability Community Faces a Housing Crisis," *NOS Magazine*, April 5, 2018, available at http://nosmag.org/disability-community-faces -a-housing-crisis-modern-asylums-not-a-solution-hcbs.

76. Jack, phone interview by the author.

77. Cindy, phone interview by the author.

78. Jack, phone interview by the author.

79. Quoted in Alan Zarembo, "Warrior Parents Fare Best in Securing Autism Services," *Los Angeles Times*, December 12, 2011, available at https://www.latimes.com/local/ autism/la-me-autism-day-two-html-htmlstory.html.

80. Yvonne, phone interview by the author.

81. Erica, phone interview by the author.

82. Sara, phone interview by the author.

83. It is important to note that these activists were all involved in organizations dominated by white activists, which may reflect their belief in cross-race alliance. Interviews with minority activists in primarily minority organizations would likely yield a more critical stance regarding the need to address race specifically.

84. Erica, phone interview by the author.

85. Becky (pseudonym), phone interview by the author, May 2015.

86. Amber Angell and Olga Solomon, "'If I Was a Different Ethnicity, Would She Treat Me the Same?': Latino Parents' Experiences Obtaining Autism Services," *Disability and Society* 32, no. 8 (2017): 1153.

87. Emina (pseudonym), interview by the author, May 2019.

88. John Zogby, foreword to *The Values Divide: American Politics and Culture in Transition*, ed. John Kenneth White (Washington, DC: CQ Press, 2003), ix–xiv.

89. For a discussion of parental rejection of mandates based on the public good in favor of individual autonomy, see Jennifer A. Reich, *Calling the Shots: Why Parents Reject Vaccines* (New York: New York University Press, 2016).

CHAPTER 9

1. Sharon N. Barnartt, "Disability as a Fluid State: Introduction," in *Research in Social Science and Disability*, vol. 5, *Disability as a Fluid State*, ed. Sharon N. Barnartt (Bingley, UK: Emerald Group, 2010), 1–23.

2. Brian R. Grossman, "Barriers to Cross-State Movement for Disabled People and Their Families: A Social Problem," *Disability Studies Quarterly* 38, no. 2 (2018), available at http://dsq-sds.org/article/view/6097/4913.

3. Ronald J. Berger, *Introducing Disability Studies* (Boulder, CO: Lynne Rienner, 2013).

4. Priya Lalvani and Lauren Polvere, "Historical Perspectives on Studying Families of Children with Disabilities: A Case for Critical Research," *Disability Studies Quarterly* 33, no. 3 (2013), available at http://dsq-sds.org/article/view/3209/3291.

5. Douglas Engelman, "Endings and Beginnings: A Father's Journey through His Son's Madness, Loss, and a Quest for Meaning," unpublished paper, 2018; Sara E. Green, "'They Are Beautiful and They Are Ours': Swapping Tales of Mothering Children with Disabilities through Interactive Interviews," *Journal of Loss and Trauma* 8 (2003): 1–13.

6. Carolyn M. Fowle, "The Effect of the Severely Mentally Retarded Child on His Family," *American Journal of Mental Deficiency* 73 (1968): 468–473; Simon Olshansky,

"Chronic Sorrow: A Response to Having a Mentally Defective Child," *Social Casework* 43 (1962): 190–193; Albert J. Solnit and Mary H. Stark, "Mourning and the Birth of a Defective Child," *Psychoanalytic Study of the Child* 16 (1961): 523–537; Lalvani and Polvere, "Historical Perspectives on Studying Families of Children with Disabilities."

7. John P. Frank, *My Son's Story* (New York: Alfred A. Knopf, 1952); Fern Kupfer, *Before and After Zachariah* (Chicago: Chicago Review Press, 1998); Michael Schofield, *January First: A Child's Descent into Madness and Her Father's Struggle to Save Her* (New York: Broadway Books, 2013).

8. Angela McClanahan, "Admitting a Child to Inpatient Psychiatric Treatment: A Parent's Perspective," *Healthy Place*, January 17, 2012, available at https://www.healthyplace.com/blogs/parentingchildwithmentalillness/2012/01/admitting-a-child-to-inpatient-psychiatric-treatment-a-parents-perspective; Schofield, *January First*; Kim Stagliano, *All I Can Handle: I'm No Mother Teresa* (New York: Skyhorse, 2010); Kim Stagliano, "The AutismLand That Neurodiversity Forgot," *Age of Autism*, January 25, 2016, available at https://www.ageofautism.com/2016/01/the-autismland-that-neurodiversity-forgot.html.

9. Kelly Mullen-McWilliams, "What #ActuallyAutistic People Want You to Know about 'Autism Mommies' on the Internet," *Romper*, January 23, 2018, available at https://www.romper.com/p/what-actuallyautistic-people-want-you-to-know-about-autism-mommies-on-the-internet-7863758.

10. Emily P. Kingsley, "Welcome to Holland," 1987, available at https://archives.library.illinois.edu/erec/University%20Archives/1008015/CD/Disability%20Information/Welcome%20to%20Holland.pdf.

11. *Refrigerator Mothers*, dir. David E. Simpson (Chicago: Kartemquin Educational Films, 2002).

12. Pamela Block and Fatima Cavalcante, "Historical Perceptions of Autism in Brazil: Professional Treatment, Family Advocacy, and Autistic Pride, 1943–2010," in *Disability Histories*, ed. Susan Burch and Michael Rembis (Champaign: University of Illinois Press, 2014), 77–97; Allison C. Carey, "Parents and Professionals: Parents' Reflections on Professionals, the Support System, and the Family in the Twentieth-Century United States," in Burch and Rembis, *Disability Histories*, 58–76.

13. Pamela Block, with Sini Diallo, "Activism, Anthropology, and Disability Studies in Times of Austerity," *Current Anthropology*, November 19, 2019, available at https://www.journals.uchicago.edu/doi/abs/10.1086/705762; Pamela Block, Brooke Ellison, and Mary Squillace, "VENTure Think Tank: The Politics, Technologies, and Occupations of Disability and Mechanical Ventilation," in *Occupational Therapies without Borders: Integrating Justice with Practice*, ed. Dikaios Sakellariou and Nick Pollard (Cambridge, UK: Elsevier, 2016), 541–548. See also the website of Little Lobbyists, at https://www.littlelobbyists.org/.

14. D. Amari Jackson, "African–Americans, Vaccines and a History of Suspicion," *Vaccine Reaction*, May 8, 2017, available at https://thevaccinereaction.org/2017/05/african-americans-vaccines-and-a-history-of-suspicion/.

15. Kerima Çevik, "Understanding the Disability Rights Movement: On the Washington Post's Neurodiversity Article," *Autism Wars* (blog), July 21, 2015, available at http://theautismwars.blogspot.com/2015/07/understanding-of-disability-rights.html; Kerima Çevik, "Autistic while Black: The Erasure of Blacks from Histories of Autism," *InterSected* (blog), January 22, 2016, available at http://intersecteddisability.blogspot.com/2016/01/autistic-while-black-erasure-of-blacks.html.

16. Kelly Green, "About," Parenting Autistic Children with Love and Acceptance, available at https://www.facebook.com/ParentingAutisticChildrenWith LoveAcceptance/info?tab=page_info (accessed November 19, 2018).

17. Katherine E. Zuckerman et al., "Racial, Ethnic, and Language Disparities in Early Childhood Developmental/Behavioral Evaluations: A Narrative Review," *Clinical Pediatrics* 53, no. 7 (2013): 619–631.

18. Amber M. Angell and Olga Solomon, "'If I Was a Different Ethnicity, Would She Treat Me the Same?': Latino Parents' Experiences of Obtaining Autism Services," *Disability and Society* 32, no. 8 (2017): 1142–1164; Catherine Kramarczuk, "Parental 'Power' and Racial Inequality in Special Education," paper presented at the Annual Meeting of the American Sociological Association, Philadelphia, August 11–14, 2018; Colin Ong-Dean, *Distinguishing Disability: Parents, Privilege, and Special Education* (Chicago: University of Chicago Press, 2009).

19. Pamela Pruitt Garriott, Donna Wandry, and Lynne Snyder, "Teachers as Parents, Parents as Children: What's Wrong with This Picture," *Preventing School Failure: Alternative Education for Children and Youth* 45, no. 1 (2001): 37–43; Ann P. Turnbull and H. Rutherford Turnbull, *Families, Professionals, and Exceptionality: A Special Partnership* (Upper Saddle River, NJ: Prentice Hall, 1997).

20. Valerie Leiter, *Their Time Has Come: Youth with Disabilities on the Cusp of Adulthood* (New Brunswick, NJ: Rutgers University Press, 2012); Eva Rodriguez, "Self Advocacy and Self Determination for Youth with Disability and Their Parents during School Transition Planning," in *Occupying Disability: Critical Approaches to Community, Justice and Decolonizing Disability*, ed. Pamela Block et al. (New York: Springer, 2016), 247–256.

21. See the DREAM Partnership website, at http://dreampartnership.org/.

22. Leiter, *Their Time Has Come.*

23. Block with Diallo, "Activism, Anthropology, and Disability Studies in Times of Austerity"; Block, Ellison, and Squillace, "VENTure Think Tank."

24. Philip Moeller, "A 20-Year-Old Fights Back against Her Health Insurer," *PBS News Hour*, June 14, 2019, available at https://www.pbs.org/newshour/nation/column -a-20-year-old-fights-back-against-her-health-insurer.

25. Leiter, *Their Time Has Come.*

26. Ibid.

27. *Deej*, dir. Robert Rooy (Frederick, MD: Roy Media, 2017).

28. Akemi Nishida, "Neoliberal Academia and a Critique from Disability Studies," in Block et al., *Occupying Disability*, 145–157.

29. U.S. Department of Justice, "Department of Justice Reaches Landmark Americans with Disabilities Act Settlement Agreement with Rhode Island," April 8, 2014, available at https://www.justice.gov/opa/pr/department-justice-reaches -landmark-americans-disabilities-act-settlement-agreement-rhode.

30. Yvonne Wenger, "In Baltimore and Beyond, Parents Are Creating Employment Opportunities for Adult Children with Autism," *Baltimore Sun*, February 22, 2018, available at https://www.baltimoresun.com/news/maryland/balti more-city/bs-md-disabled-adults-working-20180105-story.html.

31. Liat Ben-Moshe, "Why Prisons Are Not the New Asylums," *Punishment and Society* 19, no. 3 (2017): 72–289.

32. Michael Bérubé, "Don't Let My Son Plunge off the 'Disability Cliff' When I'm Gone," *USA Today*, April 2, 2018, available at https://www.usatoday.com/story/opinion/ 2018/04/02/dont-let-my-son-plunge-off-disability-cliff-column/443138002.

33. Devva Kasnitz and Pamela Block, "Participation, Time, Effort, and Speech Disability Justice," in *Politics of Occupation-Centered Practice: Reflections on Occupational Engagement across Cultures*, ed. Nick Pollard and Dikaios Sakellariou (Oxford, UK: Elsevier Churchill Livingstone, 2012), 197–216; Pamela Block et al., "Disability, Sexuality and Intimacy," in Pollard and Sakellariou, *Politics of Occupation-Centered Practice*, 162–179.

34. Douglas Biklen and Jamie Burke, "Presuming Competence," *Equity and Excellence in Education* 39, no. 2 (2006): 166–175; Amy Sequenzia and Elizabeth Grace, *Typed Words, Loud Voices* (Fort Worth, TX: Autonomous Press, 2015).

35. Michele Friedner and Pamela Block, "Deaf Studies Meets Autistic Studies," *Senses and Society* 12, no. 3 (2017): 282–300.

36. Laura Mauldin, *Made to Hear: Cochlear Implants and Raising Deaf Children* (Minneapolis: University of Minnesota Press, 2016).

37. American Society for Deaf Children, "Core Beliefs," available at https://www.deafchildren.org/about/core-values (accessed November 27, 2019).

38. Hands and Voices, "Information about Hands and Voices," available at http://www.handsandvoices.org/about/index.htm (accessed November 27, 2019).

39. Ibid.; see also Ovetta Harris, "A Cultural Bases to Develop Strong Advocates for Client and Family Involvement in the Speech-Generated Device Evaluation and Funding Process," *Perspectives on Augmentative and Alternative Communication* 24 (2015): 142–146.

40. Meryl Alper, *Giving Voice: Mobile Communication, Disability and Inequality* (Cambridge, MA: MIT University Press, 2017).

41. Ibid.; Daniel Engber, "The Strange Case of Anna Stubblefield Revisited," *New York Times Magazine*, April 18, 2018, available at https://www.nytimes.com/2018/04/05/magazine/the-strange-case-of-anna-stubblefield-revisited.html.

42. Christopher Kliewer, Douglas Biklen, and C. Kasa-Hendrickson, "Who May Be Literate? Disability and Resistance to the Cultural Denial of Competence," *American Educational Research Journal* 43, no. 2 (2006): 163–192.

43. Biklen and Burke, "Presuming Competence."

44. Douglas Biklen et al., *Autism and the Myth of the Person Alone* (New York: New York University Press, 2005), 31; Kasnitz and Block, "Participation, Time, Effort, and Speech Disability Justice"; Kliewer, Biklen, and Kasa-Hendrickson, "Who May Be Literate?"

45. American Psychological Association, "Facilitated Communication: Sifting the Psychological Wheat from the Chaff," November 20, 2003, available at https://www.apa.org/research/action/facilitated.

46. Biklen et al., *Autism and the Myth of the Person Alone*; Biklen and Burke, "Presuming Competence"; Kasnitz and Block, "Participation, Time, Effort, and Speech Disability Justice."

47. Biklen et al., *Autism and the Myth of the Person Alone*, 31.

48. Sequenzia and Grace, *Typed Words, Loud Voices*.

49. Engber, "Strange Case of Anna Stubblefield Revisited"; Mark Sherry, "Facilitated Communication, Anna Stubblefield, and Disability Studies," *Disability and Society* 31, no. 7 (2016): 974–982.

50. Engber, "Strange Case of Anna Stubblefield Revisited."

51. Kevin Mintz, "Ableism, Ambiguity and the Anna Stubblefield Case," *Disability and Society* 32, no. 10 (2017): 1666–1670.

52. Pamela Block, "Disability, Sexuality, and Defect in New Jersey," *Pamela Block Disability Studies* (blog), October 16, 2015, available at http://pamelablock.blogspot .com/2015/10/disability-sexuality-and-defect-in-new.html.

53. Carey, "Parents and Professionals."

54. See, for example, Louise Boyle, "Rutgers Professor Accused of Raping Disabled, Nonverbal, Diaper-Wearing Man with Cerebral Palsy Says He Wanted Sex and They Were in Love," *Daily Mail*, September 25, 2015, available at https://www.dailymail.co .uk/news/article-3249484/Professor-takes-stand-against-claims-raped-disabled-non verbal-diaper-wearing-man-cerebral-palsy-says-love.html.

55. Pamela Block, "Sexuality, Fertility and Danger: Twentieth Century Images of Women with Cognitive Disabilities," *Sexuality and Disability* 18, no. 4 (2000): 239–254; Diane Nelson Bryen, Allison C. Carey, and Beverly Franz, "Ending the Silence: Adults Who Use Augmentative Communication and Their Experiences as Victims of Crime," *Augmentative and Alternative Communication* 19, no. 2 (2003): 125–134.

56. Beth Haller, *Representing Disability in an Ableist World: Essays on Mass Media* (Rockville Center, NY: Avocado Press, 2010).

57. David S. Evans et al., "Sexuality and Personal Relationships for People with Intellectual Disability, Part II: Staff and Family Carer Perspectives," *Journal of Intellectual Disability Research* 53, no. 11 (2009): 913–921.

58. Alan Santinele Martino, "Microaggressions in the Erotic Sphere: The Experiences of Adults with Intellectual Disabilities in Ontario, Canada," presentation at the American Sociological Association Annual Meeting, Philadelphia, August 11–14, 2018.

59. M. Bambrick and G. E. Roberts, "The Sterilization of People with Mental Handicap: The Views of Parents," *Journal of Intellectual Disability Research* 34, no. 4 (1991): 353–363.

60. Block et al., "Disability, Sexuality and Intimacy"; Michael Gill, *Already Doing It: Intellectual Disability and Sexual Agency* (Minneapolis: University of Minnesota Press, 2015).

61. Angela Frederick, "Mothering while Disabled," *Contexts* 13, no. 4 (2014): 30–35.

62. Through the Looking Glass, "Mission," available at https://www.lookingglass.org/ who-we-are/mission (accessed November 19, 2018).

63. Autistic Self Advocacy Network, "ASAN Calls for Federal Hate Crime Prosecution for the Murder of Alex Spourdalakis," June 18, 2013, available at http:// autisticadvocacy.org/2013/06/asan-calls-for-federal-hate-crime-prosecution-for-the -murder-of-alex-spourdalakis/.

64. Ibid.; Autistic Self Advocacy Network, "Disability Community Day of Mourning," available at https://autisticadvocacy.org/projects/community/mourning/ (accessed November 30, 2019).

CONCLUSION

1. For more information, see PAL Quality of Life Initiative, "Moving from Awareness to Action: A Five-Year Report," December 2004, available at https://www.hsri .org/files/uploads/publications/NCIstate.RI.QLI_2005_Year_Report.pdf.

2. For more information, see the TASH website, at https://tash.org.

3. Pamela Block et al., "Disability, Sexuality and Intimacy," in *Politics of Occupation-Centered Practice: Reflections on Occupational Engagement across Cultures*, ed. Nick

Pollard and Dikaios Sakellariou (Oxford, UK: Elsevier Churchill Livingstone, 2012), 162–179; Devva Kasnitz and Pamela Block, "Participation, Time, Effort, and Speech Disability Justice," in Pollard and Sakellariou, *Politics of Occupation-Centered Practice*, 197–216.

4. See Joan L. Headley, "Independent Living: The Role of Gini Laurie," *Post-Polio Health*, October 1997, available at http://www.post-polio.org/about/ginilaurie1.html.

5. See the website of Post-Polio Health International, at http://www.post-polio .org, and the website of International Ventilator Users Network, at http://www.ventusers .org.

APPENDIX

1. Barney Glaser and Anselm Strauss, *The Discovery of Grounded Theory: Strategies for Qualitative Research* (New York: Aldine, 1999).

Bibliography

Acevedo, Sara Maria. "Enabling Geographies: Neurodivergence, Self-Authorship, and the Politics of Social Space." Ph.D. diss., California Institute of Integral Studies, San Francisco, 2018.

ADAPT. "ADAPT Responds to FDA Announcement of Their Intent to Ban Electric Shock Devices." Available at https://adapt.org/adapt-responds-to-fda-announcement -of-their-intent-to-ban-electric-shock-devices/ (accessed January 4, 2019).

Alper, Meryl. *Giving Voice: Mobile Communication, Disability and Inequality*. Cambridge, MA: MIT University Press, 2017.

Altman. Barbara. "Caring for a Son with Microcephaly." *Washington Post*, November 29, 2016. Available at http://www.windsorstar.com/caring+with+microcephaly/1245 1721/story.html.

American Childhood Cancer Organization. "About ACCO." Available at https://www .acco.org/about (accessed February 2, 2020).

———. "Childhood Cancer Statistics." Available at https://www.acco.org/childhood -cancer-statistics (accessed February 2, 2020).

American Psychiatric Association. "Family Caregivers Face Many Challenges." *APA Blogs*, March 8, 2016. Available at https://www.psychiatry.org/news-room/apa-blogs/ apa-blog/2016/03/family-caregivers-face-many-challenges.

American Psychological Association. "Facilitated Communication: Sifting the Psychological Wheat from the Chaff." November 20, 2003. Available at https://www.apa .org/research/action/facilitated.

American Society for Deaf Children. "Core Beliefs." Available at https://www.deaf children.org/about/core-values (accessed November 27, 2019).

Anderson, L., A. Hewitt, S. Pettingell, A. Lulinski, M. Taylor, and J. Reagan. "Family and Individual Needs for Disability Supports: Community Report, 2017." 2018.

Available at https://thearc.org/wp-content/uploads/forchapters/FINDS_report-2017
-FINAL-VERSION.pdf.

Anderson, Susan Heller. "The Reagan Effect: Goals on Handicapped Meet Wide Resistance." *New York Times,* November 14, 1982. Available at https://www.nytimes
.com/1982/11/14/education/the-reagan-effect-goals-on-handicapped-meet-wide
-resistance.html.

Angell, Amber M., and Olga Solomon. "'If I Was a Different Ethnicity, Would She Treat
Me the Same?': Latino Parents' Experiences Obtaining Autism Services." *Disability
and Society* 32, no. 8 (2017): 1142–1164.

Appiah, Nana Kusi. "A Study of Factors Influencing Public Officials and City Planners
to Engage Citizens in Governmental Land-Use Decisions." Ph.D. diss., University of
Texas at Dallas, 2014.

Apple, Rima D. *Perfect Motherhood: Science and Childbearing in America.* New Brunswick, NJ: Rutgers University Press, 2006.

Arc. "About Us." Available at http://www.thearc.org/about-us (accessed February 2,
2020).

———. "Community-Based Long Term Supports and Services." Available at https://
www.thearc.org/what-we-do/public-policy/policy-issues/long-term (accessed November 27, 2019).

———. "Health." 2017. Available at https://thearc.org/position-statements/health/.

———. "Inclusion." 2015. Available at https://www.thearc.org/who-we-are/position
-statements/rights/inclusion.

———. "Joint Letter from the Arc for Legislators, Governor and Media." In *"Community
for All" Tool Kit: Resources for Supporting Community Living.* Syracuse, NY: Human
Policy Press, 2004. Available at http://thechp.syr.edu/wp-content/uploads/2013/02/
Community_for_All_Toolkit_Version1.1.pdf.

Association for Young People's Health. *Supporting Young People with Mental Health
Problems: Results of a Survey of Parents.* London: AYPH, 2016.

Autism in Black. "Resources." Available at http://www.autisminblack.com/resources
.html (accessed November 26, 2019).

Autism NOW Center and Autistic Self Advocacy Network. "Welcome to the Autistic
Community!" 2014. Available at http://autisticadvocacy.org/wp-content/uploads/
2014/02/WTTAC-Adult-FINAL-2.pdf.

Autism Speaks. "About Us." Available at https://www.autismspeaks.org/about-us (accessed November 26, 2019).

Autism Women's Network. "Why Boycott Autism Speaks." *Boycott Autism Speaks,*
March 16, 2016. Available at https://boycottautismspeaks.wordpress.com/2016/03/16/
why-boycott-autism-speaks/.

Autistic Self Advocacy Network. "ASAN Calls for Federal Hate Crime Prosecution for
the Murder of Alex Spourdalakis." June 18, 2013. Available at http://autisticadvocacy
.org/2013/06/asan-calls-for-federal-hate-crime-prosecution-for-the-murder-of-alex
-spourdalakis/.

———. "ASAN Resources on Coverage for Autism-Related Services." Available at
https://autisticadvocacy.org/policy/toolkits/healthcoverage (accessed November 27,
2019).

———. "Before You Donate to Autism Speaks, Consider the Facts." March 2019.
Available at https://https://autisticadvocacy.org/wp-content/uploads/2019/03/Autism
SpeaksFlyer2019.pdf.

———. "Disability Community Day of Mourning." Available at https://autisticadvocacy .org/projects/community/mourning/ (accessed November 30, 2019).

Ayres, A. Jean. *Sensory Integration and Learning Disorders*. Los Angeles: Western Psychological Services, 1973.

Bagenstos, Samuel R. "The Disability Cliff." *Democracy* 35 (Winter 2015): 55–67.

Baggs, Mel. "Aspie Supremacy Can Kill." *Ballastexistenz* (blog), March 7, 2010. Available at https://ballastexistenz.wordpress.com/2010/03/07/aspie-supremacy-can-kill/.

Bambrick, M., and G. E. Roberts. "The Sterilization of People with Mental Handicap: The Views of Parents." *Journal of Intellectual Disability Research* 34, no. 4 (1991): 353–363.

Barnartt, Sharon N. "Disability as a Fluid State: Introduction." In *Research in Social Science and Disability*, vol. 5, *Disability as a Fluid State*, edited by Sharon N. Barnartt, 1–23. Bingley, UK: Emerald Group, 2010.

Barnartt, Sharon, and Richard K. Scotch. *Disability Protests: Contentious Politics, 1970–1999*. Washington, DC: Gallaudet University Press, 2001.

Barnartt, Sharon, Kay Shriner, and Richard K. Scotch. "Advocacy and Political Action." In *Handbook of Disability Studies*, edited by Gary L. Albrecht, Katherine D. Seelman, and Michael Bury, 430–449. Thousand Oaks, CA: Sage, 2001.

Barney, Jaclyn Okin. "PIE's Testimony to City Council Regarding: Oversight: Special Education Instruction and Student Achievement." October 28, 2014. Available at http://www.parentsforinclusiveeducation.com/wp-content/uploads/2014/10/2014 .10.28-PIE-Testimony-for-City-Council-Hearing1.pdf.

Baron-Cohen, Simon, Alan Leslie, and Uta Frith. "Does the Autistic Child Have a 'Theory of Mind'?" *Cognition* 21, no. 1 (1985): 37–46.

Bascom, Julia, ed. *Loud Hands: Autistic People Speaking*. Washington, DC: Autistic Self Advocacy Network, 2012.

Beamish, Thomas D., and Amy J. Luebbers. "Alliance Building across Social Movements." *Social Problems* 56, no. 4 (2009): 647–676.

Beckwith, Ruthie-Marie. *Disability Servitude: From Peonage to Poverty*. New York: Palgrave Macmillan, 2016.

Benford, Robert D., and David A. Snow. "Framing Processes and Social Movements: An Overview and Assessment." *Annual Review of Sociology* 26 (2000): 611–639.

Ben-Moshe, Liat. "Why Prisons Are Not the New Asylums." *Punishment and Society* 19, no. 3 (2017): 72–289.

Ben-Moshe, Liat, Chris Chapman, and Allison Carey, eds. *Disability Incarcerated: Disability and Imprisonment in the United States and Canada*. New York: Palgrave Macmillan, 2014.

Berger, Ronald J. *Introducing Disability Studies*. Boulder, CO: Lynne Rienner, 2013.

Berne, Patty. "Disability Justice—a Working Draft." *Sins Invalid*, June 9, 2015. Available at https://sinsinvalid.org/blog/disability-justice-a-working-draft-by-patty-berne.

Bérubé, Michael. "Don't Let My Son Plunge off the 'Disability Cliff' When I'm Gone." *USA Today*, April 2, 2018. Available at https://www.usatoday.com/story/opinion/ 2018/04/02/dont-let-my-son-plunge-off-disability-cliff-column/443138002.

———. "Equality, Freedom, and/or Justice for All." In *Cognitive Disability and Its Challenge to Moral Philosophy*, edited by Eva F. Kittay and Licia Carlson, 97–109. Malden, MA: Wiley-Blackwell, 2010.

———. *Life as Jamie Knows It: An Exceptional Child Grows Up*. Boston: Beacon Press, 2016.

Bettelheim, Bruno. *The Empty Fortress: Infantile Autism and the Birth of the Self.* New York: Free Press, 1967.

Biklen, Douglas, with Richard Attfield, Larry Bissonette, and Lucy Blackman. *Autism and the Myth of the Person Alone.* New York: New York University Press, 2005.

Biklen, Douglas, and Jamie Burke. "Presuming Competence." *Equity and Excellence in Education* 39, no. 2 (2006): 166–175.

"Bill of Rights for Pennsylvania's Retarded Citizens." *Pennsylvania Message* 5, no. 2 (1969): 8.

Blair, Barbara. "The Parents Council for Retarded Children and Social Change in Rhode Island, 1951–1970." *Rhode Island History* 40 (1981): 145–159.

Blanchett, Wanda J. "'Telling It Like It Is': The Role of Race, Class, and Culture in the Perpetuation of Learning Disability as a Privileged Category for the White Middle Class." *Disability Studies Quarterly* 30, no. 3 (2010). Available at http://dsq-sds.org/article/view/1233/1280.

Blatt, Burton, and Fred Kaplan. *Christmas in Purgatory: A Photographic Essay on Mental Retardation.* Boston: Allyn and Bacon, 1966.

Bleuler, Eugen. *Dementia Praecox or the Group of Schizophrenias.* 1911. Reprint, New York: International Universities, 1950.

Block, Laurie, and Jay Allison. "World War II Rehabilitation." *National Public Radio,* 1998. Available at https://www.npr.org/programs/disability/ba_shows.dir/work.dir/highlights/ww2.html.

Block, Pamela. "Conversations in Autism and Sign Language." Presentation at Stony Brook University, New York, December 16, 2014.

———. "Disability, Sexuality, and Defect in New Jersey." *Pamela Block Disability Studies* (blog), October 16, 2015. Available at http://pamelablock.blogspot.com/2015/10/disability-sexuality-and-defect-in-new.html.

———. "Sexuality, Fertility and Danger: Twentieth Century Images of Women with Cognitive Disabilities." *Sexuality and Disability* 18, no. 4 (2000): 239–254.

Block, Pamela, Hope Block, and Barbara Kilcup. "Autism, Communication, Family and Community." Paper presented at the American Anthropological Association Meetings, San Francisco, CA, November 21, 2008. Available at http://pamelablock.blogspot.com/2015/10.

Block, Pamela, and Fatima Cavalcante. "Autism in Brazil from Advocacy and Self-Advocacy Perspectives: A Preliminary Research Report." *Autism around the Globe,* 2012. Available at http://www.autismaroundtheglobe.org/countries/Brazil.asp.

———. "Historical Perceptions of Autism in Brazil: Professional Treatment, Family Advocacy, and Autistic Pride, 1943–2010." In *Disability Histories,* edited by Susan Burch and Michael Rembis, 77–97. Champaign: University of Illinois Press, 2014.

Block, Pamela, with Sini Diallo. "Activism, Anthropology, and Disability Studies in Times of Austerity." *Current Anthropology,* November 19, 2019. Available at https://www.journals.uchicago.edu/doi/abs/10.1086/705762.

Block, Pamela, Brooke Ellison, and Mary Squillace. "VENTure Think Tank: The Politics, Technologies, and Occupations of Disability and Mechanical Ventilation." In *Occupational Therapies without Borders: Integrating Justice with Practice,* edited by Dikaios Sakellariou and Nick Pollard, 541–548. Cambridge, UK: Elsevier, 2016.

Block, Pamela, Devva Kasnitz, Akemi Nichida, and Nick Pollard, eds. *Occupying Disability: Critical Approaches to Community, Justice, and Decolonizing Disability.* New York: Springer, 2016.

Block, Pamela, Eva L. Rodriguez, Maria C. Milazzo, William S. MacAllister, Lauren B. Krupp, Akemi Nishida, Nina Slota, Alyssa M. Broughton, and Christopher B. Keys. "Building Pediatric Multiple Sclerosis Community Using a Disability Studies Framework of Empowerment." In *Research in Social Science and Disability*, vol. 6, *Disability and Community*, edited by Allison C. Carey and Richard Scotch, 85–112. Bingley, UK: Emerald Group, 2011.

Block, Pamela, Russell Shuttleworth, Jacob Pratt, Hope Block, and Linda Rammier. "Disability, Sexuality and Intimacy." In *Politics of Occupation-Centered Practice: Reflections on Occupational Engagement across Cultures*, edited by Nick Pollard and Dikaios Sakellariou, 162–179. Oxford, UK: Elsevier Churchill Livingstone, 2012.

Blum, Linda M. "Mother-Blame in the Prozac Nation: Raising Kids with Invisible Disabilities." *Gender and Society* 21, no. 2 (2007): 2020–2026.

——. *Raising Generation Rx: Mothering Kids with Invisible Disabilities in an Age of Inequality*. New York: New York University Press, 2015.

Blume, John H., Sheri Lynn Johnson, Paul Marcus, and Emily Paavola. "A Tale of Two (and Possibly Three) *Atkins*: Intellectual Disability and Capital Punishment Twelve Years after the Supreme Court's Creation of a Categorical Bar." *William and Mary Bill of Rights* 23 (2014): 393–414.

"Bob Wright." *Wikipedia*, October 19, 2019. Available at https://en.wikipedia.org/wiki/Bob_Wright.

Bogdan, Robert, and Steven Taylor. "The Judged, Not the Judges: An Insider's View of Mental Retardation." *American Psychologist* 31 (1976): 47–52.

Bogdashina, Olga. *Theory of Mind and the Triad of Perspectives on Autism and Asperger Syndrome: A View from the Bridge*. London: Jessica Kingsley, 2005.

Boggs, Elizabeth M. "Who's Putting Whose Head in the Sand . . . or in the Clouds as the Case May Be?" In *Parents Speak Out*, edited by A. P. Turnbull and H. R. Turnbull, 50–68. Columbus, OH: Charles E. Merrill, 1978.

Boggs Center on Developmental Disabilities. "About Elizabeth M. Boggs, PhD." Available at http://rwjms.rutgers.edu/boggscenter/about/about_elizabeth.html (accessed June 5, 2015).

Boone, Pat. *The Human Touch*. New York: Weisser and Weiser, 1991.

Boyle, Louise. "Rutgers Professor Accused of Raping Disabled, Nonverbal, Diaper-Wearing Man with Cerebral Palsy Says He Wanted Sex and They were in Love." *Daily Mail*, September 25, 2015. Available at https://www.dailymail.co.uk/news/article-3249484/Professor-takes-stand-against-claims-raped-disabled-nonverbal-diaper-wearing-man-cerebral-palsy-says-love.html.

Brezis, Rachel S., Thomas S. Weisner, and Tamara C. Daley. "Parenting a Child with Autism in India: Narratives before and after a Parent-Child Intervention Program." *Culture, Medicine and Psychiatry* 39, no. 2 (2015): 277–298.

Brown, Phil, Stephen Zavestoski, Sabrina McCormick, Brian Mayer, Rachel Morello-Frosch, and Rebecca Gasior Altman. "Embodied Health Movements: New Approaches to Social Movements in Health." *Sociology of Health and Illness* 26, no. 1 (2004): 50–80.

Brown, Steven E. "Zona and Ed Roberts: Twentieth Century Pioneers." *Disability Studies Quarterly* 20, no. 1 (2000): 26–42.

Bryen, Diane Nelson, Allison C. Carey, and Beverly Franz. "Ending the Silence: Adults Who Use Augmentative Communication and Their Experiences as Victims of Crime." *Augmentative and Alternative Communication* 19, no. 2 (2003): 125–134.

Buechler, Steven E. "New Social Movement Theories." *Sociological Quarterly* 36, no. 3 (1995): 441–464.

———. *Social Movements in Advanced Capitalism*. Oxford: Oxford University Press, 1999.

Burch, Susan. *Signs of Resistance: American Deaf Cultural History, 1900 to World War II*. New York: New York University Press, 2002.

Burghardt, Madeline C. *Broken: Institutions, Families, and the Construction of Intellectual Disability*. Montreal: McGill-Queen's University Press, 2018.

Caldwell, Katie, Sarah Parker Harris, and M. Renko. "The Potential of Social Entrepreneurship: Conceptual Tools for Applying Theory to Policy and Practice." *Intellectual and Developmental Disabilities* 50, no. 6 (2012): 505–518.

Calman, Barney. "The Great Autism Rip-Off . . . How a Huge Industry Feeds on Parents Desperate to Cure Their Children." *Daily Mail*, June 4, 2008. Available at http://www.dailymail.co.uk/health/article-1023351/The-great-autism-rip---How-huge-industry-feeds-parents-desperate-cure-children.html.

Carey, Allison C. "Citizenship and the Family: Parents of Children with Disabilities, the Pursuit of Rights, and Paternalism." In *Civil Disabilities: Citizenship, Membership, and Belonging*, edited by Nancy J. Hirschmann and Beth Linker, 165–185. Philadelphia: University of Pennsylvania, 2015.

———. *On the Margins of Citizenship: Intellectual Disability and Civil Rights in Twentieth-Century America*. Philadelphia: Temple University Press, 2009.

———. "Parents and Professionals: Parents' Reflections on Professionals, the Support System, and the Family in the Twentieth-Century United States." In *Disability Histories*, edited by Susan Burch and Michael Rembis, 58–76. Champaign: University of Illinois Press, 2014.

Carey, Allison C., and Lucy Gu. "Walking the Line between the Past and the Future: Parents' Resistance and Commitment to Institutionalization." In *Disability Incarcerated*, edited by Liat Ben-Moshe, Chris Chapman, and Allison C. Carey, 101–119. New York: Palgrave Macmillan, 2014.

Carey, Benedict. "Mental Health Groups Split on Bill to Overhaul Care." *New York Times*, April 2, 2014. Available at https://www.nytimes.com/2014/04/03/health/mental-health-groups-split-on-bill-to-revamp-care.html.

Carlson, Licia. *The Faces of Intellectual Disability*. Bloomington: University of Indiana Press, 2009.

Cascio, Ariel M. "Cross-Cultural Autism Studies, Neurodiversity, and Conceptualizations of Autism." *Culture, Medicine and Psychiatry* 39, no. 2 (2015): 207–212.

———. "Neurodiversity: Autism Pride among Mothers of Children with Autism Spectrum Disorders." *Intellectual and Developmental Disabilities* 50, no. 3 (2012): 273–283.

Castles, Katherine. "'Nice, Average Americans': Postwar Parents, Groups and the Defense of the Normal Family." In *Mental Retardation in America*, edited by James W. Trent and Steven Noll, 351–370. New York: New York University Press, 2004.

Cedar Rapids Community School District v. Garret F. 536 U.S. 66 (1999).

Cerebral Palsy Alliance. "How Does Cerebral Palsy Affect People?" Available at https://www.cerebralpalsy.org.au/what-is-cerebral-palsy/how-cerebral-palsy-affects-people/ (accessed November 26, 2019).

Çevik, Kerima. "About Mrs. Ç." *Autism Wars* (blog). Available at http://theautismwars.blogspot.com/p/blog-page.html (accessed November 27, 2019).

———. "#AutisticWhileBlack: Diezel Braxton and Becoming Indistinguishable from One's Peers." *Autism Wars* (blog), July 24, 2018. Available at http://theautismwars .blogspot.com/2018/07/autisticwhileblack-diezel-braxton-and_24.html.

———. "Autistic while Black: The Erasure of Blacks from Histories of Autism." *Inter-Sected* (blog), January 22, 2016. Available at http://intersecteddisability.blogspot .com/2016/01/autistic-while-black-erasure-of-blacks.html.

———. "Understanding the Disability Rights Movement: On the Washington Post's Neurodiversity Article." *Autism Wars* (blog), July 21, 2015. Available at http://the autismwars.blogspot.com/2015/07/understanding-of-disability-rights.html.

Charlton, James I. *Nothing About Us Without Us: Disability Oppression and Empowerment.* Berkeley: University of California Press, 2000.

Charmak, Brigitte. "Autism and Social Movements: French Parents' Associations and International Autistic Individuals' Organizations." *Sociology of Health and Illness* 30, no. 1 (2008): 76–96.

Clare, Eli. *Brilliant Imperfection: Grappling with Cure.* Durham, NC: Duke University Press, 2017.

Cohen, Edward, Esperanza Calderon, Gerard Salinas, Saumitra SenGupta, and Michael Reiter. "Parents' Perspectives on Access to Child and Mental Health Services." *Social Work in Mental Health* 10, no. 4 (2012): 294–310.

Coleman, Diane. "Statement on Mourning the Death of Jerika Bolen." *Not Dead Yet*, September 23, 2016. Available at http://notdeadyet.org/2016/09/statement-on-mourning -the-death-of-jerika-bolen.html.

Condeluci, Al. *The Essence of Interdependence.* Pittsburgh, PA: Lash, 2009.

Critchfield, Jill. "ADHD, Autism and Discrimination at School." *Parenting ADHD and Autism*, February 15, 2016. Available at http://parentingadhdandautism.com/2016/ 02/15/adhd-autism-discrimination-school.

Darling, Rosalyn Benjamin. *Disability and Identity: Negotiating Self in a Changing Society.* Boulder, CO: Lynne Rienner, 2013.

———. "Parental Entrepreneurship: A Consumerist Response to Professional Dominance." *Journal of Social Issues* 44, no. 1 (1988): 141–158.

Davis, Lennard J. *Enabling Acts: The Hidden Story of How the Americans with Disabilities Act Gave the Largest US Minority Its Rights.* Boston: Beacon Press, 2015.

Deej. Directed by Robert Rooy. Frederick, MD: Roy Media, 2017.

Diament, Michelle. "Advocates, Big Pharma Make Push for Autism Drugs." *Disability Scoop*, March 20, 2012. Available at https://www.disabilityscoop.com/2012/03/20/ advocates-big-pharma-drugs/15213/.

Diani, Mario. "Organizational Fields and Social Movement Dynamics." In *The Future of Social Movement Research: Dynamics, Mechanisms, and Processes*, edited by Jacquelien van Stekelenburg, Conny Roggeband, and Bert Klandermans, 141–168. Minneapolis: University of Minnesota Press, 2013.

Dobransky. Kerry Michael. *Managing Madness in the Community.* New Brunswick, NJ: Rutgers University Press, 2014.

Drummond, Linda H., ed. *Arc Pennsylvania Historical Overview, 1949–1990.* Harrisburg, PA: ARC, n.d.

Dunhamn, Jane. "From the Director's Desk." National Black Disability Coalition. Available at http://www.blackdisability.org/content/directors-desk-0 (accessed November 26, 2019).

Dybwad, Rosemary F. *Perspectives on a Parent Movement: The Revolt of Parents of Children with Intellectual Limitations.* Brookline, MA: Brookline Books, 1990.

Earley, Pete. *Crazy: A Father's Search through America's Mental Health Madness.* New York: Berkley Books, 2006.

Easterseals. "Legislative Landmarks." Available at http://www.easterseals.com/get-involved/advocacy/legislative-landmarks.html (accessed January 2, 2019).

Elkin, Eleanor. Interview by Visionary Voices. Available at https://disabilities.temple.edu/voices/detailVideo.html?media=005-04 (accessed November 29, 2019).

Engber, Daniel. "The Strange Case of Anna Stubblefield Revisited." *New York Times Magazine,* April 18, 2018. Available at https://www.nytimes.com/2018/04/05/magazine/the-strange-case-of-anna-stubblefield-revisited.html.

Engelman, Douglas. "Endings and Beginnings: A Father's Journey through His Son's Madness, Loss, and a Quest for Meaning." Unpublished paper, 2018.

Erevelles, Nirmala. *Disability and Difference in Global Contexts: Enabling a Transformative Body Politic.* New York: Palgrave Macmillan, 2011.

Erkulwater, Jennifer L. "How the Nation's Largest Minority Became White: Race Politics and the Disability Rights Movement, 1970–1980." *Journal of Policy History* 30, no. 3 (2018): 367–399.

Ervin, David A., Brian Hennen, Joav Merrick, and Mohammed Morad. "Healthcare for People with Intellectual and Developmental Disabilities in the Community." *Frontiers in Public Health* 2, no. 83 (2014): 1–8.

Evans, Bonnie. "How Autism Became Autism." *History of the Human Sciences* 26, no. 3 (2013): 3–31.

Evans, Cassandra. *Asylum to Community and In-Between: Examining the Post-deinstitutionalization Experiences of Individuals with Mental Disabilities in Suffolk County, New York.* Ph.D. diss., Stony Brook University, Stony Brook, NY, 2017.

Evans, David S., Brian E. McGuire, E. Healy, and S. L. Carley. "Sexuality and Personal Relationships for People with Intellectual Disability, Part II: Staff and Family Carer Perspectives." *Journal of Intellectual Disability Research* 53, no. 11 (2009): 913–921.

Evans, Erin. "Voices: A Thoughtful Debate over Inclusion." *WNYC,* November 16, 2011. Available at http://www.wnyc.org/story/301701-voices-a-thoughtful-debate-over-inclusion.

Fábián, Katalin, and Elżbieta Korolczuk. *Rebellious Parents: Parental Movements in Central Eastern Europe and Russia.* Bloomington: Indiana University Press, 2017.

Family Caregiver Alliance. "A Caregiver's Bill of Rights." Available at https://www.caregiver.org/caregiver%E2%80%99s-bill-rights (accessed November 27, 2019).

Family of Liam Huff. "Fully Include Liam in First Grade and Treat Him with Dignity." *Change.org,* 2015. Available at https://www.change.org/p/fully-include-liam-in-first-grade-and-treat-him-with-dignity.

———. "Important Update: MVSD Ramps Up Abuse of Liam's Rights." *Change.org,* September 10, 2015. Available at https://www.change.org/p/fully-include-liam-in-first-grade-and-treat-him-with-dignity/u/13317336.

Fein, Elizabeth. "Making Meaningful Worlds: Role-Playing Subcultures and the Autism Spectrum." *Culture, Medicine and Psychiatry* 39, no. 2 (2015): 299–321.

Fein, Elizabeth, and Clarice Rios. *Autism in Translation: An Intercultural Conversation on Autism Spectrum Conditions.* New York: Palgrave, 2018.

Ferguson, Philip M. *Abandoned to Their Fate: Social Policy and Practice toward Severely Retarded People in America, 1820–1920.* Philadelphia: Temple University Press, 1994.

Ferreras, Ingrid G., Caroline Hannaway, and Victoria A. Hardin, eds. *Mind, Brain, Body, and Behavior: Foundations of Neuroscience and Behavioral Research at the National Institutes of Health.* Washington, DC: IOS Press, 2004.

Fialkowski, Kate, and David Fialkowski. Interview by Visionary Voices. Available at https://disabilities.temple.edu/voices/detailVideo.html?media=019-03 (accessed November 29, 2019).

Fleischer, Doris Zames, and Frieda Zames. *The Disability Rights Movement: From Charity to Confrontation.* Philadelphia: Temple University Press, 2011.

Fournier, Wendy. "Kevin and Avonte's Law Has Passed." National Autism Association, March 23, 2018. Available at http://nationalautismassociation.org/kevin-avontes-law-has-passed.

Fowle, Carolyn M. "The Effect of the Severely Mentally Retarded Child on His Family." *American Journal of Mental Deficiency* 73 (1968): 468–473.

Frank, John P. *My Son's Story.* New York: Alfred A. Knopf, 1952.

Fraser, Nancy. "Genealogy of Dependency: Tracing a Keyword of the US Welfare State." *Signs* 19, no. 2 (1994): 309–336.

Fraser, Nancy, and Linda Gordon. "Contract versus Charity." *Socialist Review* 22, no. 3 (1992): 45–67.

Frederick, Angela. "Mothering while Disabled." *Contexts* 13, no. 4 (2014): 30–35.

Frederick, Angela, and Dara Shifrer. "Race and Disability: From Analogy to Intersectionality." *Sociology of Race and Ethnicity* 5, no. 2 (2019): 2000–2014.

Friedman, Mark, and Ruthie-Marie Beckwith. "Self-Advocacy: The Emancipation Movement Led by People with Intellectual and Developmental Disability." In *Disability Incarcerated*, edited by Liat Ben-Moshe, Chris Chapman, and Allison Carey, 237–254. New York: Palgrave Macmillan.

Friedner, Michele, and Pamela Block. "Deaf Studies Meets Autistic Studies." *Senses and Society* 12, no. 3 (2017): 282–300.

Fritsch, Kelly. "Contesting the Neoliberal Affects of Disabled Parenting: Towards a Relational Emergence of Disability." In *Disabling Domesticity*, edited by Michael Rembis, 243–267. New York: Palgrave Macmillan, 2016.

"The Gag." *Ragged Edge*, November–December 1998. Available at http://www.raggededgemagazine.com/1199/polly.html.

Gallagher, Hugh G. *FDR's Splendid Deception: The Moving Story of Roosevelt's Massive Disability—and the Intense Efforts to Conceal It from the Public.* New York: Dodd, Mead, 1985.

Garcia, Dolores Gaspar. "Don't Let this DACA-Eligible Youth with Mental Developmental Delays Get Deported." *¡Somos! Presente*, 2018. Available at https://somos.presente.org/petitions/don-t-let-this-daca-eligible-youth-with-downs-syndrome-get-deported.

Gerhards, Jurgen, and Diechter Rucht. "Mesomobilization: Organizing and Framing in Two Protest Campaigns in West Germany." *American Journal of Sociology* 98 (1992): 555–595.

Gernsbacher, Morton A. "Is One Style of Early Behavioral Intervention 'Scientifically Proven'?" *Journal of Developmental and Learning Disorders* 7 (2003): 19–25.

Gerrard, Sue. "Refrigerator Mothers." *What Is Autism Anyway?* (blog), May 11, 2012. Available at https://whatisautismanyway.wordpress.com/2012/05/11/refrigerator-mothers.

Giliberti, Mary. Letter to Representatives Tim Murphy and Eddie Johnson. June 12, 2015. Available at https://www.nami.org/getattachment/Blogs/From-the-Executive

-Director/June-2015/An-Opportunity-for-Comprehensive-Mental-Health-Ref/
Murphy-Johnson-letter-6-12-2015.pdf.

Gill, Michael. *Already Doing It: Intellectual Disability and Sexual Agency.* Minneapolis: University of Minnesota Press, 2015.

Giric, Stafanija. "Strange Bedfellows: Antiabortion and Disability Rights Advocacy." *Journal of Law and the Biosciences* 3, no. 3 (2016): 736–742.

Glaser, Barney, and Anselm Strauss. *The Discovery of Grounded Theory: Strategies for Qualitative Research.* New York: Aldine, 1999.

Gliedman, John, and William Roth. *The Unexpected Minority: Handicapped Children in America.* New York: Harcourt Brace Jovanovich, 1980.

Goffman, Erving. *Asylums: Essays on the Social Situation of Mental Patients and Other Inmates.* New York: Anchor Books, 1961.

———. *Stigma: Notes on the Management of a Spoiled Identity.* New York: Simon and Schuster, 1963.

Goldenson, Leonard H., with Marvin J. Wolf. *Beating the Odds: The Untold Story behind the Rise of ABC: The Stars, Struggles, and Egos That Transformed Network Television by the Man Who Made It Happen.* New York: Charles Scribner's Sons, 1991.

Goleman, Daniel. "States Move to Ease Laws Committing Mentally Ill." *New York Times,* December 6, 1986. Available at http://www.nytimes.com/1986/12/09/science/states -move-to-ease-law-committing-mentally-ill.html?pagewanted=all.

Goode, David. *And Now Let's Build a Better World: The Story of the Association for the Help of Retarded Children, New York City, 1948–1998.* Ph.D. diss., City University of New York, 1998.

Goodley, Dan. "Becoming Rhizomatic Parents: Deleuze, Guattari, and Disabled Babies." *Disability and Society* 22, no. 2 (2007): 145–160.

Grace, Elizabeth. "Are You Neuroqueer?" *NeuroQueer* (blog), September 18, 2013. Available at http://neuroqueer.blogspot.ca/2013/09/are-you-neuroqueer.html.

Gramm, Eugene. "Just One Voice to Speak for All of America's Retarded." *Children Limited* 1, no. 1 (1952): 1.

———. "New Hope for a Different Child." *Parents Magazine* 26, no. 48 (1951): 152–156.

Grant, Sophia. *"One of Those": The Progress of a Mongoloid Child.* New York: Pageant, 1957.

Gray, David E. "Gender and Coping: The Parents of Children with High Functioning Autism." *Social Science and Medicine* 56 (2003): 631–642.

Green, Kelly. "About." Parenting Autistic Children with Love and Acceptance. Available at https://www.facebook.com/ParentingAutisticChildrenWithLoveAcceptance/info ?tab=page_info (accessed November 19, 2018).

Green, Sara E. "'They Are Beautiful and They Are Ours': Swapping Tales of Mothering Children with Disabilities through Interactive Interviews." *Journal of Loss and Trauma* 8 (2003): 1–13.

Green, Sara E., Rosalyn Benjamin Darling, and Loren Wilbers. "Has the Parent Experience Changed over Time? A Meta-analysis of Qualitative Studies of Parents of Children with Disabilities from 1960 to 2012." In *Research in Social Science and Disability,* vol. 7, *Disability and Intersecting Statuses,* edited by Barbara Altman and Sharon Barnartt, 97–168. Bingley, UK: Emerald Group, 2012.

———. "Struggles and Joys: A Review of Research on the Social Experience of Parenting Disabled Children." In *Research in Social Science and Disability,* vol. 9, *Sociology*

Looking at Disability: What Did We Know and When Did We Know It?, edited by Sara E. Green and Sharon Barnartt, 261–285. Bingley, UK: Emerald Press, 2016.

Greenspan, Stanley. *Engaging Autism.* Philadelphia: Da Capo Press, 2006.

Grinker, Richard R. *Unstrange Minds: Remapping the World of Autism.* Cambridge, MA: Basic Books, 2007.

Grob, Gerald N. *From Asylum to Community: Mental Health Policy in Modern America.* Princeton, NJ: Princeton University Press, 1991.

———. *The Mad among Us: A History of the Care of America's Mentally Ill.* New York: Free Press, 1994.

Grossman, Brian R. "Barriers to Cross-State Movement for Disabled People and Their Families: A Social Problem." *Disability Studies Quarterly* 38, no. 2 (2018). Available at http://dsq-sds.org/article/view/6097/4913.

———. "Same Mandate, Changing Concept of Community: An Analysis of Bills to Mandate Medicaid Coverage of Community-Based Attendant Services and Supports (1997–2010)." In *Research in Social Science and Disability*, vol. 6, *Disability and Community*, edited by Allison C. Carey and Richard Scotch, 215–240. Bingley, UK: Emerald Group, 2011.

Gruber, Judith, and Edison J. Trickett. "Can We Empower Others? The Paradox of Empowerment in the Governing of an Alternative High School." *American Journal of Community Psychology* 15, no. 3 (1987): 353–371.

Gruson-Wood, Julia F. "Autism, Expert Discourses, and Subjectification: A Critical Examination of Applied Behavioural Therapies." *Studies in Social Justice* 10, no. 1 (2016): 38–58.

Halderman v. Pennhurst State School and Hospital. 446 F. Supp. 1295 (1977).

Haller, Beth. *Representing Disability in an Ableist World: Essays on Mass Media.* Rockville Center, NY: Avocado Press, 2010.

Hamraie, Aimi. *Building Access: Universal Design and the Politics of Disability.* Minneapolis: University of Minnesota Press, 2017.

Hands and Voices. "Information about Hands and Voices." Available at http://www.handsandvoices.org/about/index.htm (accessed November 27, 2019).

———. "Mission." Available at http://www.handsandvoices.org/about/mission.htm (accessed November 27, 2019).

Handspeak. "Cochlear Implants: Not Our Choice." Available at https://www.handspeak.com/culture/index.php?id=126 (accessed November 27, 2019).

Harcourt, Bernard E. "From the Asylum to the Prison: Rethinking the Incarceration Revolution." *Texas Law Review* 84 (2006): 1751–1786.

———. "Reducing Mass Incarceration: Lessons from the Deinstitutionalization of Mental Hospitals in the 1960s." *Ohio State Journal of Criminal Law* 9 (2011): 53–88.

Harris, Gardiner. "Drug Makers Are Advocacy Group's Biggest Donors." *New York Times*, October 21, 2009. Available at https://www.nytimes.com/2009/10/22/health/22nami.html.

Harris, Ovetta. "A Cultural Bases to Develop Strong Advocates for Client and Family Involvement in the Speech-Generated Device Evaluation and Funding Process." *Perspectives on Augmentative and Alternative Communication* 24 (2015): 142–146.

Hatfield, Agnes B. "Families as Advocates for the Mentally Ill: A Growing Movement." *Hospital and Community Psychiatry* 32, no. 9 (1981): 641–642.

———. "National Alliance for the Mentally Ill: The Meaning of a Movement." *International Journal of Mental Health* 15, no. 4 (1986): 79–93.

———. "Self-Help Groups for Families of the Mentally Ill." *Social Work* 26 (1981): 408–413.

Hays, Sharon. *The Cultural Contradictions of Motherhood.* New Haven, CT: Yale University Press, 1996.

Headley, Joan L. "Independent Living: The Role of Gini Laurie." *Post-Polio Health*, October 1997. Available at http://www.post-polio.org/about/ginilaurie1.html.

Hewlett, Sylvia Ann, and Cornel West. *The War against Parents.* New York: Houghton Mifflin, 1998.

Higgins-Evenson, R. Rudy. *The Price of Progress: Public Service, Taxation, and the American Corporate State, 1877 to 1929.* Baltimore: Johns Hopkins University Press, 2003.

Hinshaw, Stephan P. *The Mark of Shame: Stigma of Mental Illness and an Agenda for Change.* Oxford: Oxford University Press, 2007.

Hirschmann, Nancy J., and Beth Linker, eds. *Civil Disabilities: Citizenship, Membership, and Belonging.* Philadelphia: University of Pennsylvania Press, 2015.

Hogan, Dennis. *Family Consequences of Childhood Disabilities.* New York: Russell Sage Foundation, 2012.

Horowitz, Allan V. *Creating Mental Illness.* Chicago: University of Chicago, 2002.

Howe, James W. "Families as Advocates." *Hospital and Community Psychiatry* 27, no. 10 (1986): 1051–1052.

"H.R. 2646 (114th): Helping Families in Mental Health Crisis Act of 2016." *GovTrack*, June 20, 2016. Available at https://www.govtrack.us/congress/bills/114/hr2646/summary.

Hungerford, Richard H. "A Bill of Rights for the Retarded." *American Journal of Mental Deficiency* 63 (April 1959): 937–938.

Hunt, Douglas. Preface to *The World of Nigel Hunt: The Diary of a Mongoloid Youth*, by Nigel Hunt, 15–42. New York: Garrett, 1967.

Hyman, Mark. "Can Autism Be Cured?" *Children's Health Defense*, 2016. Available at https://childrenshealthdefense.org/wp-content/uploads/2016/10/Can_Autism_be_Cured-Dr.MarkHyman.pdf.

Indigenous Action. "Accomplices Not Allies: Abolishing the Ally Industrial Complex." May 4, 2014. Available at http://www.indigenousaction.org/accomplices-not-allies-abolishing-the-ally-industrial-complex/.

Iovannone, Jeffrey J. "The Mad Woman in the Garden: Decolonizing Domesticity in Shani Mootoo's *Cereus Blooms at Night*." In *Disabling Domesticity*, edited by Michael Rembis, 269–285. New York: Palgrave Macmillan, 2017.

Jackson, D. Amari. "African–Americans, Vaccines and a History of Suspicion." *Vaccine Reaction*, May 8, 2017. Available at https://thevaccinereaction.org/2017/05/african-americans-vaccines-and-a-history-of-suspicion/.

Jacobs, Lanita, Mary Lawlor, and Cheryl Mattingly. "I/We Narratives among African-American Families Raising Children with Special Needs." *Culture, Medicine, and Psychiatry* 35 (2011): 3–25.

Jean, Natalie N. "United Cerebral Palsy Association." In *Encyclopedia of American Disability History*, vol. 3, edited by Susan Burch, 915–916. New York: Facts on File, 2009.

Jennings, Audra. *Out of the Horrors of War: Disability Politics in World War II America.* Philadelphia: University of Pennsylvania, 2016.

Johnson, Roland. *Lost in a Desert World.* Plymouth Meeting, PA: Speaking for Ourselves, 1999.

Jones, Kathleen. "Education for Children with Mental Retardation: Parent Activism, Public Policy, and Family Ideology in the 1950s." In *Mental Retardation in America*, edited by James W. Trent and Steven Noll, 322–350. New York: New York University Press, 2004.

———. "'Mother Made Me Do It': Mother-Blaming and the Women of the Child Guidance Movement." In *Bad Mothers: The Politics of Blame in Twentieth-Century America*, edited by Molly Ladd-Taylor and Lauri Umansky, 99–126. New York: New York University Press, 1998.

Jones, Larry A. *Doing Disability Justice: 75 Years of Family Advocacy*. n.p.: Lulu, 2010.

Jouvenal, Justin. "Man Accused of Stealing $5 in Snacks Died in Jail as He Waited for Space at Mental Hospital." *Washington Post*, September 29, 2017. Available at https://www.washingtonpost.com/local/crime/man-accused-of-stealing-5-in-snacks-died-in-jail-as-he-waited-for-space-at-mental-hospital/2015/09/29/7ceac8a2-5aff-11e5-9757-e49273f05f65_story.html.

Kafer, Alison. *Feminist Queer Crip*. Bloomington: Indiana University Press, 2013.

Kanner, Leo. "Autistic Disturbances of Affective Contact." *Nervous Child* 2 (1943): 217–250.

Karlin, Rick. "Sheltered Workshops Are in Midst of a Storm." *Times Union* (Albany, NY), July 20, 2013. Available at https://www.timesunion.com/local/article/Sheltered-workshops-are-in-midst-of-a-storm-4677272.php.

Kasnitz, Devva, and Pamela Block. "Participation, Time, Effort, and Speech Disability Justice." In *Politics of Occupation-Centered Practice: Reflections on Occupational Engagement across Cultures*, edited by Nick Pollard and Dikaios Sakellariou, 197–216. Oxford, UK: Elsevier Churchill Livingstone, 2012.

Katz, Alfred H. *Parents of the Handicapped: Self-Organized Parents' and Relatives' Groups for Treatment of Ill and Handicapped Children*. Springfield, IL: Charles C. Thomas, 1961.

Kaufman, Joanne. "Ransom-Note Ads about Children's Health Are Canceled." *New York Times*, December 20, 2007. Available at http://www.nytimes.com/2007/12/20/business/media/20child.html?_r=0.

Kessler, Ronald C., Olga Demler, Richard G. Frank, Mark Olfson, Harold Alan Pincus, Ellen E. Walters, Philip Wang, Kenneth B. Wells, and Alan M. Zaslavsky. "Prevalence and Treatment of Mental Disorders." *New England Journal of Medicine* 352 (2005): 2515–2523.

Kids Mental Health. "How Is Mental Illness in Children Diagnosed," Available at http://www.kidsmentalhealth.org/how-is-mental-illness-in-children-diagnosed (accessed November 26, 2019).

Killilea, Marie. *From Karen with Love*. New York: Prentice-Hall, 1963.

———. *Karen*. New York: Prentice-Hall, 1952.

Kim, Eunjung. *Curative Violence: Rehabilitating Disability, Gender, and Sexuality in Modern Korea*. Durham, NC: Duke University Press, 2017.

Kincaid, Anne M. "News Summary." Disability and Abuse Project, August 5, 2013. Available at http://disability-abuse.com/newsfeed/2013-08-05.htm.

King, Paul H. "Edgar F. 'Daddy' Allen." November 1940. Joseph A. Caulder Collection. Available at http://www.nlis.net/~freedomi/rotary/caulder/DaddyAllenPage.htm.

Kingsley, Emily P. "Welcome to Holland." 1987. Available at https://archives.library.illinois.edu/erec/University%20Archives/1008015/CD/Disability%20Information/Welcome%20to%20Holland.pdf.

Kirnlanier, Heather. "On Radical Acceptance (and Not Fixing Your Kid)." *Star in Her Eye* (blog), July 5, 2016. Available at https://starinhereye.wordpress.com/2016/07/05/on-radical-acceptance-not-fixing-your-kid/?fbclid=IwAR0ptpVeScBaVc3Q4mONgf V53jUbbCIieV1LiGDNQaY4gbmXwWUFI1P15nw.

Kittay, Eva Feder. "Forever Small: The Strange Case of Ashley X." *Hypatia* 26, no. 2 (2011): 610–631.

———. "When Caring Is Justice and Justice Is Caring." In *Public Cultures*, edited by Carol A. Breckenridge and Candace Volger, 557–580. Durham: University of North Carolina Press, 2001.

Kittay, Eva Feder, and Licia Carlson, eds. *Cognitive Disability and Its Challenges to Moral Philosophy*. Malden, MA: Wiley-Blackwell, 2010.

Kliewer, Christopher, Douglas Biklen, and C. Kasa-Hendrickson. "Who May Be Literate? Disability and Resistance to the Cultural Denial of Competence." *American Educational Research Journal* 43, no. 2 (2006): 163–192.

Knestrict, Thomas, and Debora Kuchey. "Welcome to Holland: Characteristics of Resilient Families Raising Children with Severe Disabilities." *Journal of Family Studies* 15, no. 3 (2009): 227–244.

Koller, Rebecca. "Sexuality and Adolescents with Autism." *Sexuality and Disability* 18, no. 2 (2000): 125–135.

Krahn, Gloria L., Deborah Klein Walker, and Rosalyn Correa Araujo. "Persons with Disabilities as an Unrecognized Health Disparity Population." Supplement, *American Journal of Public Health* 105, no. S2 (2015): S198–S206.

Kramarczuk, Catherine. "Parental 'Power' and Racial Inequality in Special Education." Paper presented at the Annual Meeting of the American Sociological Association, Philadelphia, August 11–14, 2018.

Kras, Joseph F. "The 'Ransom Notes' Affair: When the Neurodiversity Movement Came of Age." *Disability Studies Quarterly* 30, no. 1 (2010). Available at http://dsq-sds.org/article/view/1065/1254.

Kupfer, Fern. *Before and After Zachariah*. Chicago: Chicago Review Press, 1998.

Ladd-Taylor, Molly. *Fixing the Poor: Eugenic Sterilization and Child Welfare in the Twentieth Century*. Baltimore: Johns Hopkins University Press, 2017.

Ladd-Taylor, Molly, and Lauri Umanski, eds. *Bad Mothers: The Politics of Blame in Twentieth-Century America*. New York: New York University Press, 1998.

Lalvani, Priya, and Lauren Polvere. "Historical Perspectives on Studying Families of Children with Disabilities: A Case for Critical Research." *Disability Studies Quarterly* 33, no. 3 (2013). Available at http://dsq-sds.org/article/view/3209/3291.

Lambert, Lisa. "Why Parents Are Silent about Mental Illness." Child Mind Institute Available at https://childmind.org/article/why-parents-are-silent-about-mental-illness (accessed June 18, 2019).

Landsman, Gail. *Reconstructing Motherhood and Disability in an Age of "Perfect" Babies*. New York: Routledge, 2009.

Lane, Harlan. "Constructions of Deafness." In *Disability Studies Reader*, edited by Lennard Davis, 79–92. New York: Routledge, 2006.

Langan, Mary. "Parental Voices and Controversies in Autism." *Disability and Society* 26, no. 2 (2011): 193–203.

Lareau, Annette. *Unequal Childhoods: Class, Race, and Family Life*. Berkeley: University of California Press, 2003.

Larson, Sheryl, Charlie Lakin, and Shannon Hill. "Behavioral Outcomes of Moving from Institutional to Community Living for People with Intellectual and Developmental Disabilities: U.S. Studies from 1977 to 2010." *Research and Practice for People with Severe Disabilities* 37, no. 4 (2012): 235–246.

Leiter, Valerie. *Their Time Has Come: Youth with Disabilities on the Cusp of Adulthood.* New Brunswick, NJ: Rutgers University Press, 2012.

Levine, Judith. *Ain't No Trust.* Berkeley: University of California Press, 2013.

Li, Johanna. "Girl, 14, with Spinal Muscular Atrophy Decides to End Her Life: 'This Is Enough Pain.'" *Inside Edition,* July 15, 2016. Available at http://www.insideedition.com/ headlines/17543-girl-14-with-spinal-muscular-atrophy-decides-to-end-her-life-this -is-enough-pain.

Linton, Simi. *Claiming Disability: Knowledge and Identity.* New York: New York University Press, 1998.

Little Lobbyists. "Our Story." Available at https://littlelobbyists.org/new-folder (accessed November 27, 2019).

Longmore, Paul K. *Telethons: Spectacle, Disability, and the Business of Charity.* New York: Oxford University Press, 2016.

———. *Why I Burned My Book and Other Essays on Disability.* Philadelphia: Temple University Press, 2003.

Lovaas, Ole Ivar. "Behavioral Treatment and Normal Educational and Intellectual Functioning in Young Children with Autism." *Journal of Consulting and Clinical Psychology* 55, no. 1 (1987): 3–9.

Lutz, Amy S. F. "Who Decides Where Autistic Adults Live?" *The Atlantic,* May 26, 2015. Available at http://www.theatlantic.com/health/archive/2015/05/who-decides-where -autistic-adults-live/393455/.

MacDonald, Michael. *Mystical Bedlam: Madness, Anxiety, and Healing in Seventeenth-Century England.* Cambridge: Cambridge University Press, 1981.

Mairs, Nancy. *Waist High in the World.* Boston: Beacon Press, 1996.

Martin, Douglas. "Harriet Shetler, Who Helped to Found Mental Illness Group, Dies at 92." *New York Times,* April 3, 2010, p. A22.

Martino, Alan Santinele. "Microaggressions in the Erotic Sphere: The Experiences of Adults with Intellectual Disabilities in Ontario, Canada." Presentation at the American Sociological Association Annual Meeting, Philadelphia, August 11–14, 2018.

———. "Power Struggles over the Sexualities of Individuals with Disabilities." In *Dis/Consent: Perspectives on Sexual Consent and Sexual Violence,* edited by KelleyAnne Malinen, 98–197. Halifax, NS: Fernwood, 2019.

Martorell, Susan J., and Gabriela A. Martorell. "Bridging Uncharted Waters in Georgia: Down Syndrome Association of Atlanta Outreach to Latino/a Families." *American Journal of Community Psychology* 37, no. 3–4 (2006): 219–225.

Matson, Floyd. *Walking Together and Marching Together: A History of the Organized Blind Movement in the United States, 1940–1990.* Baltimore: National Federation of the Blind, 1990.

Matthews, Cara. "Sheltered Workshops for Disabled to Be Phased Out." *USA Today,* July 28, 2014. Available at https://www.usatoday.com/story/news/nation/2014/07/28/ sheltered-workshops-disabled-phased-out/13302139.

Mauldin, Laura. *Made to Hear: Cochlear Implants and Raising Deaf Children.* Minneapolis: University of Minnesota Press, 2016.

May, Elaine Tyler. *Homeward Bound: American Families in the Cold War Era*. New York: Basic Books, 2008.

Mayo Clinic. "Cerebral Palsy." Available at https://www.mayoclinic.org/diseases-condi tions/cerebral-palsy/symptoms-causes/syc-20353999 (accessed November 26, 2019).

———. "Muscular Dystrophy." Available at https://www.mayoclinic.org/diseases-con ditions/muscular-dystrophy/symptoms-causes/syc-20375388 (accessed November 26, 2019).

McAdam, Doug. "Political Opportunities: Conceptual Origins, Current Problems, Future Directions." In *Comparative Perspectives on Social Movements*, edited by Doug McAdam, John D. McCarthy, and Mayer N. Zald, 20–40. Cambridge: Cambridge University Press, 1996.

———. *Political Process and the Development of Black Insurgency, 1930–1970*. Chicago: University of Chicago Press, 1982.

McCammon, Holly J., and Nella Van Dyke. "Applying Qualitative Comparative Analysis to Empirical Studies of Social Movement Coalition Formation." In *Strategic Alliances: Coalition Building and Social Movements*, edited by Nella Van Dyke and Holly J. McCammon, 292–325. Minneapolis: University of Minnesota Press, 2010.

McCarthy, John D., and Mayer N. Zald. "Resource Mobilization and Social Movements: A Partial Theory." *American Journal of Sociology* 82, no. 6 (1977): 1212–1241.

McClanahan, Angela. "Admitting a Child to Inpatient Psychiatric Treatment: A Parent's Perspective." *Healthy Place*, January 17, 2012. Available at https://www.healthy place.com/blogs/parentingchildwithmentalillness/2012/01/admitting-a-child -to-inpatient-psychiatric-treatment-a-parents-perspective.

McCullagh, James G. "Challenging the Proposed Deregulation of P.L. 94-142: A Case Study of Citizen Advocacy." *Journal of Sociology and Social Welfare* 15, no. 3 (1988): 65–81.

McGuire, Anne. *War on Autism: On the Cultural Logic of Normative Violence*. Ann Arbor: University of Michigan Press, 2016.

McKenna, Laura. "How a New Supreme Court Ruling Could Affect Special Education." *The Atlantic*, March 23, 2017. Available at https://www.theatlantic.com/education/ archive/2017/03/how-a-new-supreme-court-ruling-could-affect-special-education/ 520662.

McLean, Athena. "The Mental Health Consumer Survivors Movement in the United States." In *A Handbook for the Study of Mental Health: Social Contexts, Theories, and Systems*, 2nd ed., edited by Teresa L. Scheid and Tony N. Brown, 461–477. New York: Cambridge University Press, 2009.

Mental Health America. "2017 State of Mental Health in America—Access to Care Data." Available at https://www.mhanational.org/issues/2017-state-mental-health -america-access-care-data (accessed January 9, 2020).

Merikangas, Kathleen Reis, Jian-Ping He, Debra Brody, Prudence W. Risher, Karen Bourdon, and Doreen S. Korentz. "Prevalence and Treatment of Mental Disorders among US Children in the 2001–2004 NHANES." *Pediatrics* 125 (2010): 75–81.

Mesibov, Gary B., Victoria Shea, and Eric Schopler. *The TEACCH Approach to Autism Spectrum Disorders*. New York: Springer, 2004.

Metzl, Jonathon. *The Protest Psychosis*. Boston: Beacon Press, 2010.

Miller, Beth. "New Rule Highlights Disability Housing Debate." *Delaware Online*, November 30, 2014. Available at https://www.delawareonline.com/story/news/local/ 2014/11/30/two-sides-disability-housing-debate/19721065/.

Mingus, Mia. "Reflection toward Practice: Some Questions on Disability Justice." In *Criptiques*, edited by Caitlin Wood, 107–114. Self-published, 2014. Available at https://criptiques.files.wordpress.com/2014/05/crip-final-2.pdf.

Minnesota Council on Developmental Disabilities. "Willowbrook Leads to New Protections of Rights." *Moments in Disability History* 9 (2013). Available at http://mn.gov/web/prod/static/mnddc/live/ada-legacy/ada-legacy-moment9.html.

Mintz, Kevin. "Ableism, Ambiguity and the Anna Stubblefield Case." *Disability and Society* 32, no. 10 (2017): 1666–1670.

Moeller, Philip. "A 20-Year-Old Fights Back against Her Health Insurer." *PBS News Hour*, June 14, 2019. Available at https://www.pbs.org/newshour/nation/column-a-20-year-old-fights-back-against-her-health-insurer.

Montgomery, Cal. "Developmental Disability Community Faces a Housing Crisis." *NOS Magazine*, April 5, 2018. Available at http://nosmag.org/disability-community-faces-a-housing-crisis-modern-asylums-not-a-solution-hcbs.

Moore, Leroy F., Jr., Talila A. Lewis, and Lydia X. Z. Brown. "Accountable Reporting on Disability, Race, and Police Violence: A Community Response to the 'Ruderman White Paper on the Media Coverage of Use of Force and Disability.'" May 2016. Available at https://docs.google.com/document/d/117eoVeJVP594L6-1bgL8zpZrzgojfsveJwcWuHpkNcs/edit.

Moran, James E. *Committed to the State Asylum*. Montreal: McGill-Queen's University Press, 2000.

Morguess, Lisa. "Why I Fight for Inclusion for My Kids (and Your Kid Too)." April 29, 2014. Available at http://www.lisamorguess.com/2014/04/29/fight-inclusion-kid-kid/.

Morrison, Denton E. "Some Notes toward Theory on Relative Deprivation, Social Movements, and Social Change." *American Behavioral Scientist* 14, no. 5 (1971): 675–690.

Mullen-McWilliams, Kelly. "What #ActuallyAutistic People Want You to Know about 'Autism Mommies' on the Internet." *Romper*, January 23, 2018. Available at https://www.romper.com/p/what-actuallyautistic-people-want-you-to-know-about-autism-mommies-on-the-internet-7863758.

Muscular Dystrophy Association. "About Us." Available at https://www.mda.org/about-mda/history (accessed November 26, 2019).

———. "Innovations in Care." Available at https://www.mda.org/care/mda-care-centers (accessed November 27, 2019).

National Alliance for Caregiving. *On Pins and Needles: Caregivers of Adults with Mental Illness*. Bethesda, MD: NAC, 2016.

National Alliance on Mental Illness. *Engagement: A New Standard for Mental Health Care*. Arlington, VA: NAMI, 2016.

———. "Learning to Help Your Child and Your Family." Available at https://www.nami.org/find-support/family-members-and-caregivers/learning-to-help-your-child-and-your-family (accessed November 26, 2019).

———. "Legal Issues: Right to Treatment." Available at https://www.nami.org/About-NAMI/Policy-Platform/9-Legal-Issues (accessed November 27, 2017).

———. "Parity for Mental Health Coverage." Available at https://www.nami.org/Learn-More/Public-Policy/Parity-for-Mental-Health-Coverage (accessed November 27, 2019).

———. "Personal Stories: How Invalidating My Bipolar Disorder Invalidates Me." Available at https://www.nami.org/Personal-Stories/How-Invalidating-My-Bipolar-Disorder-Invalidates-M# (accessed November 27, 2019).

———. "Policy Platform." Available at https://www.nami.org/About-NAMI/Policy -Platform (accessed November 27, 2019).

National Association of the Deaf. "Position Statement on Inclusion." January 26, 2002. Available at https://www.nad.org/about-us/position-statements/position-statement -on-inclusion.

National Black Disability Coalition. "About Us." Available at http://www.blackdisability .org/content/about-us (accessed November 26, 2019).

National Disability Leadership Alliance. "About NDLA." Available at http://www .disabilityleadership.org/about (accessed November 27, 2019).

———. Letter to Representatives Fred Upton and Frank Pallone. July 26, 2015. Available at http://www.ncmhr.org/downloads/ndla-letter-re-HR2646.pdf.

National Down Syndrome Society. "Research and Down Syndrome." Available at https:// www.ndss.org/resources/research-down-syndrome (accessed November 27, 2019).

National Federation of the Blind. "About the NOPBC." Available at http://www.nopbc .org/about (accessed January 9, 2020).

———. "Blindness Statistics." January 2019. Available at https://nfb.org/blindness -statistics.

———. "Resolution 2019-02: Regarding the Continued Exploitation of Workers with Disabilities under Section 14(c) of the Fair Labor Standards Act." 2019. Available at https://www.nfb.org/resources/speeches-and-reports/resolutions/2019-resolutions #02.

National Resource Center for Supported Decision-Making. "Ryan King—Updated." Available at http://supporteddecisionmaking.org/impact-stories/ryan-king (accessed November 27, 2019).

Neeley-Barnes, Susan L., Heather Hall, Ruth J. Roberts, and J. Carolyn Graff. "Parenting a Child with an Autism Spectrum Disorder: Public Perceptions and Parental Conceptualizations." *Journal of Family Social Work* 14, no. 3 (2011): 208–225.

Ne'eman, Ari. "An Urgent Call to Action: Tell NYU Child Study Center to Abandon Stereotypes against People with Disabilities." Autistic Self Advocacy Network, December 8, 2007. Available at http://autisticadvocacy.org/2007/12/tell-nyu-child-study -center-to-abandon-stereotypes/.

Nelson, Alondra. *Body and Soul: The Black Panther Party and the Fight against Medical Discrimination*. Minneapolis: University of Minnesota Press, 2011.

Newman, Harmony D., and Laura M. Carpenter. "Embodiment without Bodies? Analysis of Embodiment in US-Based Pro-Breastfeeding and Anti-male Circumcision Movements." *Sociology of Health and Illness* 36, no. 5 (2014): 639–654.

New York State Association for Retarded Children, Inc. v. Rockefeller. 357 F. Supp. 752 (1973).

Nielsen, Kim E. *A Disability History of the United States*. Boston: Beacon Press, 2012.

Nishida, Akemi. "Neoliberal Academia and a Critique from Disability Studies." In *Occupying Disability: Critical Approaches to Community, Justice and Decolonizing Disability*, edited by Pamela Block, Devva Kasnitz, Akemi Nishida, and Nick Pollard, 145–157. New York: Springer, 2016.

Noll, Steven. *Feeble-Minded in Our Midst*. Chapel Hill: University of North Carolina Press, 1995.

"Not Like Other Children." *Parents Magazine*, October 18, 1943, pp. 34, 98–102.

Obermayer, Liz. "Choices." In *"Community for All" Tool Kit: Resources for Supporting Community Living*, 131. Syracuse, NY: Human Policy Press, 2004. Available at http://

thechp.syr.edu/wp-content/uploads/2013/02/Community_for_All_Toolkit_Version1
.1.pdf.

Offit, Paul A. *Vaccinated: One Man's Quest to Defeat the World's Deadliest Diseases*. New York: Smithsonian Books/Collins, 2007.

Okin, Susan Moller. *Justice, Gender, and the Family*. New York: Basic Books, 1989.

Olivas, Bernice M. "What I Mean When I Say Autism: Rethinking the Roles of Language and Literacy in Autism Discourse." Master's thesis, University of Nebraska, Lincoln, 2012.

Oliver, Michael. *The Politics of Disablement*. New York: St. Martin's Press, 1990.

———. *Understanding Disability: From Theory to Practice*, 2nd ed. Cambridge, UK: Red Globe Press, 2009.

Oliver, Michael, and Colin Barnes. *The New Politics of Disablement*. New York: Palgrave Macmillan, 2012.

Olsen-Wiley, Marsha M. "Easter Seals." In *Encyclopedia of American Disability History*, vol. 1, edited by Susan Burch, 305–306. New York: Facts on File, 2009.

Olshansky, Simon. "Chronic Sorrow: A Response to Having a Mentally Defective Child." *Social Casework* 43 (1962): 190–193.

Olshansky, Simon, Gertrude C. Johnson, and Leon Sternfeld. "Attitudes of Some GP's towards Institutionalizing Mentally Retarded Children." *Mental Retardation* 1 (1963): 18–20, 57–59.

Ong-Dean, Colin. *Distinguishing Disability: Parents, Privilege and Special Education*. Chicago: University of Chicago Press, 2009.

Ornitz, E. M., and Edward Ritvo. "The Syndrome of Autism: A Critical Review." *American Journal of Psychiatry* 133 (1976): 609–621.

OToole, Corbett Joan. *Fading Scars: My Queer Disability History*. Fort Worth, TX: Autonomous Press, 2015.

PAL Quality of Life Initiative. "Moving from Awareness to Action: A Five-Year Report." December 2004. Available at https://www.hsri.org/files/uploads/publications/ NCIstate.RI.QLI_2005_Year_Report.pdf.

Panitch, Melanie. *Disability, Mothers, and Organization: Accidental Activists*. New York: Routledge, 2008.

Parens, Eric, and Adrienne Asche, eds. *Prenatal Testing and Disability Rights*. Washington, DC: Georgetown University Press, 2000.

Parsons, Anne E. *From Asylum to Prison: Deinstitutionalization and the Rise of Mass Incarceration after 1945*. Chapel Hill: University of North Carolina Press, 2018.

Pelka, Fred. *The ABC-CLIO Companion to the Disability Rights Movement*. Santa Barbara, CA: ABC-CLIO, 1997.

———. *What We Have Done: An Oral History of the Disability Rights Movement*. Amherst: University of Massachusetts Press, 2012.

Pennsylvania Association for Retarded Children (PARC) v. Commonwealth of Pennsylvania. 334 F. Supp. 1257 (1971).

Pennsylvania Association for Retarded Children (PARC) v. Commonwealth of Pennsylvania. 343 F. Supp. 279 (1972).

Perry, David M. "Four Disabled People Dead in Another Week of Police Brutality." *The Nation*, September 22, 2017. Available at https://www.thenation.com/article/four -disabled-dead-in-another-week-of-police-brutality.

Pichardo, Nelson A. "New Social Movements: A Critical Review." *Annual Review of Sociology* 23 (1997): 411–430.

Piepzna-Samarasinha, Leah Lakshmi. *Care Work: Dreaming Disability Justice*. Vancouver, BC: Arsenal Pulp Press, 2018.

Pierce, Jennifer Burek. "Science, Advocacy, and 'The Sacred and Intimate Things of Life': Republican Motherhood as a Progressive Era Cause in Women's Magazines." *American Periodicals* 18, no. 1 (2008): 69–95.

Pitts-Taylor, Victoria. "The Plastic Brain: Neoliberalism and the Neuronal Self." *Health* 14, no. 6 (2010): 635–652.

Posney, Alexa. "Inclusive Schools." *Homeroom* (blog), March 17, 2011. Available at https://blog.ed.gov/2011/03/inclusive-schools.

Premack, Rachel. "'I'm Going to Be Free': Terminally Ill Wisconsin Teen Schedules Her Death and One 'Last Dance.'" *Washington Post*, July 21, 2016. Available at https://www.washingtonpost.com/news/morning-mix/wp/2016/07/21/one-last-dance-for-this-wisconsin-teen-who-has-scheduled-her-own-death.

Pruitt, Pamela Garriott, Donna Wandry, and Lynne Snyder. "Teachers as Parents, Parents as Children: What's Wrong with This Picture?" *Preventing School Failure: Alternative Education for Children and Youth* 45, no. 1 (2001): 37–43.

Prussing, Erica, Elisa J. Sobo, Elizabeth Walker, and Paul S. Kurtin. "Between 'Desperation' and Disability Rights: A Narrative Analysis of Complimentary/Alternative Medicine Use by Parents for Children with Down Syndrome." *Social Science and Medicine* 60, no. 3 (2005): 587–598.

Queen, J. "Neurodiversity and Autism: Where Do We Draw the Line?" *Neuroethics Blog*, December 4, 2012. Available at http://www.theneuroethicsblog.com/2012/12/neurodiversity-and-autism-where-do-we.html.

Rafter, Nicole H. "The Criminalization of Mental Retardation." In *Mental Retardation in America*, edited by James W. Trent Jr. and Steven Noll, 232–257. New York: New York University Press, 2004.

Reaume, Geoffrey. *Remembrance of Patients Past*. Toronto: University of Toronto Press, 2009.

Refrigerator Mothers. Directed by David E. Simpson. Chicago: Kartemquin Educational Films, 2002.

Reich, Jennifer A. *Calling the Shots: Why Parents Reject Vaccines*. New York: New York University Press, 2016.

Rembis, Michael, ed. *Disabling Domesticity*. New York: Palgrave Macmillan, 2016.

———. "The New Asylums: Madness and Mass Incarceration in the Neoliberal Era." In *Disability Incarcerated: Imprisonment and Disability in the United States and Canada*, edited by Liat Ben-Moshe, Chris Chapman, and Allison C. Carey, 139–159. New York: Palgrave Macmillan, 2014.

Richter, Zachary A. "Melting Down the Family Unit: A Neuroqueer Critique of Table-Readiness." In *Disabling Domesticity*, edited by Michael Rembis, 335–348. New York: Palgrave Macmillan, 2016.

Rimland, Bernard. *Infantile Autism: The Syndrome and Its Implications for a Neural Theory of Behaviour*. Upper Saddle River, NJ: Prentice Hall, 1964.

Rios, Clarice, and Barbara Costa Andrade. "The Changing Face of Autism in Brazil." *Culture, Medicine and Psychiatry* 39 (2015): 213–234.

Robertson, Rachel. "Sharing Stories: Motherhood, Autism and Culture." In *Disability and Mothering: Liminal Spaces of Embodied Knowledge*, edited by Cynthia Lewiecki-Wilson and Jen Cellio, 140–155. New York: Syracuse University Press, 2011.

Robinson, Debbie. Interview by Visionary Voices. Available at https://disabilities.temple
.edu/voices/detailVideo.html?media=010-01 (accessed November 29, 2019).

Rodriguez, Eva. "Self Advocacy and Self Determination for Youth with Disability and Their Parents during School Transition Planning." In *Occupying Disability: Critical Approaches to Community, Justice and Decolonizing Disability*, edited by Pamela Block, Devva Kasnitz, Akemi Nishida, and Nick Pollard, 247–256. New York: Springer, 2016.

Rose, Galvin. "Challenging the Need for Gratitude." *Journal of Sociology* 40, no. 2 (2004): 137–155.

Rose, Susannah L., Janelle Highland, Matthew T. Karafa, and Steven Joffe. "Patient Advocacy Organizations, Industry Funding, and Conflicts of Interest." *JAMA Internal Medicine* 177, no. 3 (2017): 344–350.

Rosqvist, Hanna B., Charlotte Brownlow, and Linsday O'Dell. "'An Association for All'—Notions of the Meaning of Autistic Self-Advocacy Politics within a Parent-Dominated Movement." *Journal of Community and Applied Psychology* 25, no. 3 (2015): 219–231.

Rowland, Lewis P. *NINDS at 50: An Incomplete History Celebrating the Fiftieth Anniversary of the National Institute of Neurological Disorders and Stroke*. New York: Demos Medical, 2003.

Russell, Marta. *Beyond Ramps: Disability at the End of the Social Contract*. Monroe, ME: Common Courage Press, 1998.

Rutter, Michael. "Diagnosis and Definitions of Childhood Autism." *Journal of Autism and Childhood Schizophrenia* 8, no. 2 (1978): 130–161.

Salamon, Lester M., and Alan J. Abramson. "The Nonprofit Sector." In *The Reagan Experiment*, edited by John L. Palmer and Isabel V. Sawhill, 219–243. Washington, DC: Urban Institute Press, 1982.

Sarrett, Jennifer C. "Custodial Homes, Therapeutic Homes, and Parental Acceptance: Parental Experiences of Autism in Kerala, India and Atlanta, GA USA." *Culture, Medicine and Psychiatry* 39, no. 2 (2015): 254–276.

Schaaf, Valerie, with Hank Bersani Jr. "People First of Oregon: An Organizational History and Personal Perspective." In *New Voices: Self-Advocacy by People with Disabilities*, edited by Gunnar Dybwad and Hank Bersani Jr., 171–179. Cambridge, MA: Brookline Books, 1996.

Schalock, Robert L., Sharon A. Borthwick-Duffy, Valerie J. Bradley, Wil H. E. Buntinx, David L. Coulter, Ellis M. (Pat) Craig, Sharon C. Gomez, et al. *Intellectual Disability: Definition, Classifications and Systems of Support*. 11th ed. Washington, DC: American Association on Intellectual and Developmental Disabilities, 2010.

Schimke, Ann. "Inside One Colorado Family's Long Legal Journey to Affirm Their Son's Right to a Meaningful Education." *Chalkbeat*, November 15, 2017. Available at https://www.chalkbeat.org/posts/co/2017/11/15/inside-one-colorado-familys-long
-legal-journey-to-affirm-their-sons-right-to-a-meaningful-education/.

Schofield, Michael. *January First: A Child's Descent into Madness and Her Father's Struggle to Save Her*. New York: Broadway Books, 2013.

Schwarzenberger, Susan. *Becoming Citizens: Family Life and the Politics of Disability*. Seattle: University of Washington Press, 2005.

Schweik, Susan. "Lomax's Matrix: Disability, Solidarity, and the Black Power of 504." *Disability Studies Quarterly* 31, no. 1 (2011). Available at http://dsq-sds.org/article/
view/1371/1539.

Scotch, Richard K. "Disability as the Basis for a Social Movement." *Journal of Social Issues* 44, no. 1 (1988): 159–172.

———. *From Good Will to Civil Rights: Transforming Federal Disability Policy.* Philadelphia: Temple University Press, 1984.

Scull, Andrew. *Madness: A Very Short Introduction.* Oxford: Oxford University Press, 2011.

———. *Madness in Civilization.* London: Thames and Hudson, 2015.

———. *Social Order/Mental Disorder: Anglo-American Psychiatry in Historical Perspective.* Berkeley: University of California Press, 1989.

Sealander, Judith. *The Failed Century of the Child: Governing America's Young in the Twentieth Century.* New York: Cambridge University Press, 2003.

Segal, Robert M. *Mental Retardation and Social Action.* Springfield, IL: Charles C. Thomas, 1970.

Self Advocates Becoming Empowered. "Our Mission." Available at http://www.sabeusa .org (accessed November 25, 2019).

Sequenzia, Amy, and Elizabeth Grace. *Typed Words, Loud Voices.* Fort Worth, TX: Autonomous Press, 2015.

Shapiro, Joseph P. *No Pity: People with Disabilities Forging a New Civil Rights Movement.* New York: Broadway Books, 1994.

Shaw, Linda R. "Judy Heumann." In *Enabling Lives: Biographies of Six Prominent Americans with Disabilities,* edited by Brian T. McMahon and Linda R. Shaw, 87–106. Boca Raton, FL: CRC Press, 2000.

Sheffer, Edith. *Asperger's Children: The Origins of Autism in Nazi Vienna.* New York: W. W. Norton, 2018.

Sherry, Mark. "Facilitated Communication, Anna Stubblefield, and Disability Studies." *Disability and Society* 31, no. 7 (2016): 974–982.

Shorter, Edward. *The Kennedy Family and the Story of Mental Retardation.* Philadelphia: Temple University Press, 2000.

Siebers, Tobin. *Disability Theory.* Ann Arbor: University of Michigan Press, 2008.

Silberman, Steve. *Neurotribes: The Legacy of Autism and the Future of Neurodiversity.* New York: Penguin Random House, 2015.

———. "Our Neurodiverse World." *Slate,* September 23, 2015. Available at https://slate .com/technology/2015/09/the-neurodiversity-movement-autism-is-a-minority -group-neurotribes-excerpt.html.

Silverman, Cloe. *Understanding Autism.* Princeton, NJ: Princeton University Press, 2011.

Silvers, Anita, and Leslie Francis, eds. *Americans with Disabilities: Exploring Implications of the Law for Individuals and Institutions.* New York: Routledge, 2000.

Silverstein, Ken. "Prozac.org." *Mother Jones,* November–December 1999. Available at https://www.motherjones.com/politics/1999/11/outfront-0/.

Singh, Ilina. "Brain Talk: Power and Negotiation in Children's Discourse about Self, Brain, and Behavior." *Sociology of Health and Illness* 35, no. 6 (2013): 813–827.

Skocpol, Theda, and Jillian Dickert. "Speaking for Families and Children in a Changing Civic America." In *Who Speaks for America's Children? The Role of Child Advocates in Public Policy,* edited by Carol J. DeVita and Rachel Mosher-Williams, 137–164. Washington, DC: Urban Institute, 2001.

Smith, S. E. "When Parents Kill Disabled Children, We Must Hold Society Responsible." *Rewire News,* May 18, 2015. Available at https://rewire.news/article/2015/05/18/ parents-kill-disabled-children-must-hold-society-responsible/.

Snow, David A., and Robert D. Benford. "Master Frames and Cycles of Protest." In *Frontiers in Social Movement Theory*, edited by Aldon D. Morris and C. M. Mueller, 133–155. New Haven, CT: Yale University Press, 1992.

Snow, David A., E. Burke Rochford Jr., Steven K. Worden, and Robert D. Benford. "Frame Alignment Processes, Micromobilization, and Movement Participation." *American Sociological Review* 51, no. 4 (1986): 464–481.

Solnit, Albert J., and Mary H. Stark. "Mourning and the Birth of a Defective Child." *Psychoanalytic Study of the Child* 16 (1961): 523–537.

Solomon, Andrew. *Far from the Tree: Parents, Children, and the Search for Identity*. New York: Scribner, 2013.

Solomon, Olga. "'But—He'll Fall!': Children with Autism, Interspecies Intersubjectivity, and the Problem of 'Being Social.'" *Culture, Medicine and Psychiatry* 39, no. 2 (2015): 323–344.

Sousa, Amy. "From Refrigerator Mothers to Warrior-Heroes: The Cultural Identity Transformation of Mothers Raising Children with Intellectual Disabilities." *Symbolic Interaction* 34, no. 2 (2011): 220–243.

Sparrow, Max. "ABA." *Unstrange Mind* (blog), October 20, 2016. Available at http://unstrangemind.com/aba/.

Speaking for Ourselves. "History: 1982–2002." In the author's possession.

Stafanovics, Elina A., Hongbo He, Maria Cavalcanti, Helio Neto, Angello Ofori-Atta, Meaghan Leddy, Adesuwa Ighodaro, and Robert Rosenheck. "Witchcraft and Bio-social Causes of Mental Illness: Attitudes and Beliefs about Mental Illness among Health Professionals in Five Countries." *Journal of Nervous and Mental Disease* 204, no. 3 (2016): 169–174.

Staggenborg, Suzanne. "Conclusion: Research on Social Movement Coalitions." In *Strategic Alliances: Coalition Building and Social Movements*, edited by Nella Van Dyke and Holly J. McCammon, 316–330. Minneapolis: University of Minnesota Press, 2010.

Stagliano, Kim. *All I Can Handle: I'm No Mother Teresa*. New York: Skyhorse, 2010.

———. "The AutismLand That Neurodiversity Forgot." *Age of Autism*, January 25, 2016. Available at https://www.ageofautism.com/2016/01/the-autismland-that-neurodiversity-forgot.html.

Stanglin, Doug. "2-Year-Old Whose Yemeni Mother Was Initially Denied a Visa under Trump's Travel Ban Dies in California Hospital." *USA Today*, December 29, 2018. Available at https://www.usatoday.com/story/news/world/2018/12/29/terminally-ill-boy-whose-yemeni-mom-initially-denied-visa-dies/2439574002/.

Stanley, Summer L. G. "The Advocacy Efforts of African American Mothers of Children with Disabilities in Rural Special Education: Considerations for School Professionals." *Rural Special Education Quarterly* 34, no. 4 (2015): 3–17.

Steinbrinck, Ashley. "How Dr. Hyman Helped an Autistic Boy with a Functional Medicine Approach." *Natural Health Concepts* (blog), June 18, 2013. Available at http://blog.naturalhealthyconcepts.com/2013/06/18/how-to-treat-or-possibly-cure-autism-naturally-with-a-functional-medicine-approach/.

Stephens, Frank. Testimony to U.S. House of Representatives Subcommittee on Labor, Health and Human Services, and Education, October 25, 2017. Available at https://docs.house.gov/meetings/AP/AP07/20171025/106526/HHRG-115-AP07-Wstate-StephensF-20171025.pdf.

Stoltz, Melissa. "Voice." *Garden of My Heart* (blog), January 8, 2016. Available at http://gardenofmyheart.com/2016/01/08/voice/.

Stumbo, Ellen. "Should Kids Be Present at Their Own IEPs?" *The Mighty*, January 24, 2018. Available at https://themighty.com/2018/01/iep-should-i-bring-my-child/.

"Supreme Court Says 'Congress Intended to Open the Door to All Qualified Children.'" *Wrightslaw*. Available at http://www.wrightslaw.com/info/relsvcs.garretf.htm (accessed September 2, 2016).

Szabo, Liz. "Cost of Not Caring: Stigma Set in Stone." *USA Today*, June 25, 2014. Available at https://www.usatoday.com/story/news/nation/2014/06/25/stigma-of-mental-illness/9875351.

———. "Mental Illness: Families Cut Out of Care." *USA Today*, February 26, 2016. Available at https://www.usatoday.com/story/news/2016/02/26/privacy-law-harms-care-mentally-ill-families-say/80880880/.

Tausig, Mark, Janet Michelle, and Sree Subedi. *A Sociology of Mental Illness*. 2nd ed. Upper Saddle River, NJ: Pearson Press, 2003.

Taylor, Steven J. *Acts of Conscience: World War II, Mental Institutions, and Religious Objectors*. Syracuse, NY: Syracuse University Press, 2009.

———. "Caught in the Continuum: A Critical Analysis of the Principle of the Least Restrictive Environment." *Journal of the Association for the Severely Handicapped* 13, no. 1 (1998): 41–53.

———. "On Choice." *Tash Connections* 27, no. 2 (2001): 8–10.

Thibault, Ronnie. "Can Autistics Redefine Autism? The Cultural Politics of Autistic Activism." *Transcripts* 4 (2014): 57–88.

Thomas, Carol. "The Disabled Body." In *Real Bodies*, edited by Mary Evans and Ellie Lee, 64–78. London: Palgrave, 2002.

Thomas, Gareth M. *Down's Syndrome Screening and Reproductive Politics*. London: Routledge, 2017.

Through the Looking Glass. "Mission." Available at https://www.lookingglass.org/who-we-are/mission (accessed November 19, 2018).

Timberlake, Maria, Walter Lautz, Marji Warfield, and Guiseppina Chiri. "'In the Driver's Seat': Parent Perceptions of Choice in a Participant-Directed Medicaid Waiver Program for Young Children with Autism." *Journal of Autism and Developmental Disabilities* 44, no. 4 (2014): 903–914.

Tomes, Nancy. "The Patient as a Policy Factor: A Historical Case Study of the Consumer/Survivor Movement in Mental Health." *Health Affairs* 25, no. 3 (2006): 720–729.

Trent, James W., Jr. *Inventing the Feeble Mind: A History of Mental Retardation in the United States*. Berkeley: University of California Press, 1994.

———. *The Manliest Man: Samuel G. Howe and the Contours of Nineteenth-Century Reform*. Amherst: University of Massachusetts, 2012.

Turnbull, Ann P., and H. Rutherford Turnbull. *Families, Professionals, and Exceptionality: A Special Partnership*. Upper Saddle River, NJ: Prentice Hall, 1997.

Underman, Kelly, Paige L. Sweet, and Claire Laurier. "Custodial Citizenship in the Omnibus Autism Proceeding." *Sociological Forum* 32, no. 3 (2017): 544–565.

"UN Experts Examine Disability Issues, Family Support." *UN News*, May 15, 2007. Available at https://news.un.org/en/story/2007/05/218862-un-experts-examine-disability-issues-family-support.

Unforgotten: Twenty-Five Years after Willowbrook. Directed by Jack Fisher. Studio Lights Pictures, 1996. Available at https://www.youtube.com/watch?v=FcjRIZFQcUY.

United Cerebral Palsy. "Our History." Available at https://ucp.org/our-history (accessed November 26, 2019).

———. "Our Mission." Available at https://ucp.org/our-mission/ (accessed January 4, 2020).

U.S. Department of Commerce, Bureau of the Census. *Feeble-Minded and Epileptics in Institutions in 1923*. Washington, DC: Government Printing Office, 1926.

———. *Insane and Feeble-Minded in Institutions, 1910*. Washington, DC: Government Printing Office, 1914.

U.S. Department of Health and Human Services. *Closing the Gap: A National Blueprint to Improve the Health of Persons with Mental Retardation*. Washington, DC: U.S. Department of Health and Human Services, 2002.

———. *Mental Health: A Report of the Surgeon General*. Rockville, MD: U.S. Department of Health and Human Services, Substance Abuse and Mental Health Services Administration, Center for Mental Health Services, National Institutes of Health, National Institute of Mental Health, 1999.

U.S. Department of Justice. "Department of Justice Reaches Landmark Americans with Disabilities Act Settlement Agreement with Rhode Island." April 8, 2014. Available at https://www.justice.gov/opa/pr/department-justice-reaches-landmark-americans-disabilities-act-settlement-agreement-rhode.

Van Dyke, Nella, and Holly J. McCammon. Introduction to *Strategic Alliances: Coalition Building and Social Movements*, edited by Nella Van Dyke and Holly J. McCammon, xi–xxviii. Minneapolis: University of Minnesota Press, 2010.

Vargas, Theresa. "Virginia Woman Seeks Power to Live the Way She Wants." *Washington Post*, July 20, 2013. Available at https://www.washingtonpost.com/local/virginia-woman-with-down-syndrome-seeks-power-to-live-the-way-she-wants/2013/07/20/76102a82-d789-11e2-a9f2-42ee3912ae0e_story.html.

Vital Signs: Crip Culture Talks Back. Directed by David Mitchell and Sharon Snyder. Brooklyn, NY: Fanlight Productions, 1995.

Voice of Reason. "About VOR." Available at https://www.vor.net/about-vor (accessed November 27, 2019).

———. "Ohio—Update on the Ball v. Kasich Class Action." Available at https://www.vor.net/legislative-voice/legislation/item/ohio-updates-on-the-ball-v-kasich-class-action (accessed February 3, 2020).

———. "Please Oppose the Disability Integration Act." Available at https://vor.net/legislative-voice/action-alerts/item/please-oppose-the-disability-integration-act (accessed June 19, 2019).

Wagner, Meg. "Activists Fight to Stop Wisconsin Teen with Incurable Disease Who Has Decided to Die." *New York Daily News*, September 7, 2016. Available at http://www.nydailynews.com/news/national/activists-fight-stop-wisconsin-teen-plan-life-article-1.2781497.

Wakefield, Andrew J., Simon H. Murch, Andi Anthony, Jeff Linnell, D. D. Casson, Mohsin Malik, M. Berelowitz, et al. "Ileal-Lymphoid-Nodular Hyperplasia, Non-specific Colitis, and Pervasive Developmental Disorder in Children." *The Lancet* 351, no. 9103 (1998): 637–641 (retracted).

Walker, Carlton Anne Cook. "Blind Students and the IEP Process." *Future Reflections* 36, no. 2 (2017). Available at https://www.nfb.org/images/nfb/publications/fr/fr36/2/fr360202.htm.

Walker, Nick. "Neurodiversity: Some Basic Terms and Definitions." *Neurocosmopolitanism* (blog), September 27, 2014. Available at https://neurocosmopolitanism.com/neurodiversity-some-basic-terms-definitions.

Wall, Glenda. "Mothers' Experiences with Intensive Parenting and Brain Development Discourse." *Women's Studies International Forum* 33, no. 3 (2010): 253–263.

Waters, Michael. "Our Immigration System Is Especially Cruel to Disabled Children." *The Outline*, June 26, 2018. Available at https://theoutline.com/post/5074/immigration-disability-children-ice-detention?zd=1&zi=5s4zzygg.

Weingold, Joseph T., and Rudolf P. Hormuth. "Group Guidance of Parents of Mentally Retarded Children." *Journal of Clinical Psychology* 9, no. 2 (1953): 118–124.

Wenger, Yvonne. "In Baltimore and Beyond, Parents Are Creating Employment Opportunities for Adult Children with Autism." *Baltimore Sun*, February 22, 2018. Available at https://www.baltimoresun.com/news/maryland/baltimore-city/bs-md -disabled-adults-working-20180105-story.html.

"What Prompts PARC's Action toward Institutions." *Pennsylvania Message* 9, no. 2 (1973): 1.

White, Brent. "Banging My Head on the Neurotypical Wall." ACAT: Ala Costa Adult Transition Program, January 22, 2016. Available at https://alacosta-acat.org/ 2016/01/22/banging-my-head-on-the-neurotypical-wall/.

Whitt, Tracy Dee. "More Perspectives on Applied Behavior Analysis (ABA)—Autism." *Lovin' Adoptin' and Autism* (blog), April 9, 2014. Available at http://lovinadoptin .com/2014/04/09/more-perspectives-on-applied-behavior-analysis-aba-autism/.

———. "My Thoughts on Applied Behavior Analysis (ABA)—Autism." *Lovin' Adoptin' and Autism* (blog), March 26, 2014. Available at http://lovinadoptin.com/2014/03/26/ my-thoughts-on-applied-behavior-analysis-aba-autism/.

Wickham, Parnel. "Idiocy and the Laws in Colonial England." *Mental Retardation* 39, no. 2 (2001): 104–113.

Wiegerink, R., and J. W. Pelosi, eds. *Developmental Disabilities: The Developmental Disabilities Movement*. Baltimore: Paul H. Brookes, 1979.

Williams, Paul, and Bonnie Shultz. *We Can Speak for Ourselves*. Bloomington: Indiana University Press, 1982.

Wing, Lorna, and Judith Gould. "Severe Impairments of Social Interactions and Associated Abnormalities in Children: Epidemiology and Classification." *Journal of Autism and Developmental Disorders* 9, no. 1 (1979): 11–29.

Wing, Lorna, and D. Potter. "The Epidemiology of Autistic Spectrum Disorders: Is the Prevalence Rising?" *Mental Retardation and Developmental Disabilities Research Reviews* 8, no. 3 (2002): 151–161.

Winzer, Margret A. *The History of Special Education: From Isolation to Integration*. Washington, DC: Gallaudet University Press, 1993.

Wolf, Joan. *Is Breast Best? Taking on the Breastfeeding Experts and the New High Stakes of Motherhood*. New York: New York University Press, 2011.

Wright, David. *Downs: A History of a Disability*. Oxford: Oxford University Press, 2011.

Yergeau, Melanie. *Authoring Autism: On Rhetoric and Neurological Queerness*. Durham, NC: Duke University Press, 2018.

———. "Circle Wars: Reshaping the Typical Autism Essay." *Disability Studies Quarterly* 30, no. 1 (2010). Available at http://dsq-sds.org/article/view/1063/1222.

———. "Clinically Significant Disturbance: On Theorists Who Theorize Theory of Mind." *Disability Studies Quarterly* 33, no. 4 (2013). Available at http://dsq-sds.org/ article/view/3876/3405.

———. "I Stim, Therefore I Am." *YouTube*, January 26, 2012. Available at http://www .youtube.com/watch?v=s2QSvPIDXwA.

Yochim, Emily C., and Vesta T. Silva. "Everyday Expertise, Autism, and 'Good' Mothering in the Media Discourse of Jenny McCarthy." *Communication and Critical/Cultural Studies* 10, no. 4 (2013): 406–426.

Young, Elise. "Clinton Plan to End Subminimum Wage Stirs Debate." *Disability Scoop*, June 6, 2016. Available at https://www.disabilityscoop.com/2016/06/06/clinton-sub mininum-debate/22372.

Zald, Mayer N., and John D. McCarthy, eds. *Social Movements in an Organizational Society: Collected Essays.* New York: Routledge, 1997.

Zarembo, Alan. "Warrior Parents Fare Best in Securing Autism Services." *Los Angeles Times*, December 12, 2011. Available at https://www.latimes.com/local/autism/ la-me-autism-day-two-html-htmlstory.html.

Zogby, John. Foreword to *The Values Divide: American Politics and Culture in Transition*, by John Kenneth White, ix–xiv. Washington, DC: CQ Press, 2003.

Zuckerman, Katherine E., Kimber M. Mattox, Brianna K. Sinche, Gregory S. Blansche, and Christina Bethell. "Racial, Ethnic, and Language Disparities in Early Childhood Developmental/Behavioral Evaluations: A Narrative Review." *Clinical Pediatrics* 53, no. 7 (2013): 619–631.

Index

Allison C. Carey is a Professor in the Department of Sociology and Anthropology at Shippensburg University. She is the author of *On the Margins of Citizenship: Intellectual Disability and Civil Rights in Twentieth-Century America* (Temple) and coeditor of *Disability Incarcerated: Disability and Imprisonment in the United States and Canada* and *Disability and Community.*

Pamela Block is a Professor of Anthropology at Western University. She is coeditor of *Occupying Disability: Critical Approaches to Community, Justice, and Decolonizing Disability.*

Richard K. Scotch is Professor of Sociology and Public Policy at the University of Texas, Dallas. He is the author of *From Good Will to Civil Rights: Transforming Federal Disability Policy* (Temple), coauthor of *Disability Protests: Contentious Politics, 1970–1999*, and coeditor of *Disability and Community.*